S0-BBN-453

Theory of the Firm

Springer
Berlin
Heidelberg
New York
Barcelona
Hong Kong
London
Milan
Paris
Singapore
Tokyo

H. Albach · K. Brockhoff · E. Eymann
P. Jungen · M. Steven · A. Luhmer

Theory of the Firm

Erich Gutenberg's Foundations and Further Developments

With 39 Figures
and 5 Tables

Prof. Dr. Dr. h.c. Horst Albach
WHU Koblenz
Otto Beisheim Graduate School
of Management
Burgplatz 2
D-56179 Vallendar

Prof. Dr. Klaus K.L. Brockhoff
WHU Koblenz
Otto Beisheim Graduate School
of Management
Burgplatz 2
D-56179 Vallendar

Dr. Egbert Eymann
VWH Vorrichtungs-
und Werkzeugbau GmbH
Bahnhofstraße 104
D-56414 Herschbach

Peter Jungen
Peter Jungen Management Holding
GmbH
Gustav-Heinemann-Ufer 54
D-50968 Köln

Prof. Dr. Marion Steven
Ruhr-Universität Bochum
Fakultät für Wirtschaftswissenschaft
Lehrstuhl für Angewandte BWL I
D-44780 Bochum

Prof. Dr. Alfred Luhmer
University of Magdeburg
Fakultät für Wirtschaftslehre/
Controlling
Universitätsplatz 2
D-39106 Magdeburg

ISBN 3-540-66318-5 Springer-Verlag Berlin Heidelberg New York

Library of Congress Cataloging-in-Publication Data
Die Deutsche Bibliothek – CIP-Einheitsaufnahme
Theory of the firm: Erich Gutenberg's foundations and further developments; with 5 tables / H. Albach et al. – Berlin; Heidelberg; New York; Barcelona; Hong Kong; London; Milan; Paris; Singapore; Tokyo: Springer, 2000
ISBN 3-540-66318-5

Hardcover-Design: Erich Kirchner, Heidelberg

SPIN 10724591 42/2202-5 4 3 2 1 0 – Printed on acid-free paper

Preface

This book has an objective and a focus. It provides the reader with:

- an in-depth acquaintance with the theory of the firm developed by Erich Gutenberg
- an insight into a coherent body of current German research in the theory of the firm.

The book is divided into two parts. The first part lays the foundations. It presents Gutenberg's theory of the firm to the English speaking reader. Considering the great importance that Erich Gutenberg has had in Germany and taking into consideration the impact that the translations of his path-breaking three volumes "Principles of Management" have had in France, the Spanish speaking countries, and in Japan, it was felt that it was necessary, on the occasion of his 100th anniversary, to present a concise summary of his contributions to the theory of the firm to an English speaking scientific community.

Six papers present Gutenberg's theory in the light of the theoretical advances that he stimulated as well as in the framework of other theoretical developments like capital market theory, transaction cost theory, principal agent theory, and contract theory. The papers show that Gutenberg's theory is highly relevant for theory and highly influential in the practice of management.

The second part deals with theoretical developments in managerial functions and reviews these developments in the light of the foundations laid by Erich Gutenberg. Jan Pieter Krahnen studies the financing function in the firm and works contributions to optimizing it in the light of modern capital market theory. Harald Hruschka presents results of empirical tests of Gutenberg's doubly-kinked demand curve and confronts them with estimates of other functional forms of the firm's demand function. Söhnke Albers takes up the question of sales persons versus independent dealers and Gutenberg's answers to it and develops a model which answers this question by simultaneously optimizing sales regents. Joachim Reese contributes a paper on the most controversial factor of production in Gutenberg's theory of the firm: management. Gutenberg avoided any attempt to incorporate management in the production function quantitatively. He felt that management with its creativity, its setting of objectives for the firm and providing leadership for its employees could not be captured in a production function. Reese shows how management can be integrated quantitatively into a system of inventory control production. Alfred Luhmer, building on Gutenberg's production model, constructs dynamic production models which allow for change of the production function. This is a problem also that Klaus Brockhoff deals with in his contribution on the dynamics of technological competence. Hermann Jahnke introduces uncertainty into Gutenberg's production model, and Robert F. Göx contributes to our understanding of capacity planning under uncertainty. Günter Fandel extends Gutenberg's production theory to encompass more complex production systems like network and process models. Horst Glaser and Marlies Rogalski give proof of the importance of Gutenberg's production theory for modern cost accounting and control systems.

The volume contains a selection of the papers that were contributed to a conference held by the Erich Gutenberg Society in Cologne on September 12 and 13, 1997 in memory of Erich Gutenberg's birthday on December 13, 1897. The volume of proceedings of that scientific conference has been published by Springer-Verlag also under the title "Die Theorie der Unternehmung in Forschung und Praxis" under the editorship of Horst Albach and others.

The editors wish to thank Deutsche Forschungsgemeinschaft for financial support of publishing this volume. Dr. Werner Müller was responsible for making this project come true at Springer publishers. His commitment to the project is greatly appreciated. Dr. Martina Bihn gave unwavering support during the process of translating and printing. I am grateful to her for making collaboration with the publisher a pleasure.

Professor Gerry Lawson has shouldered the burden of checking the translations submitted by the authors and bringing the text into good English. I greatly appreciate his tremendous efforts and his admirable skill in bringing the translations into better form. All of us that have ever been involved in the task of correcting a text as a native speaker appreciate the effort and the skills required. Sometimes it seems easier to translate directly than to correct an author's translation. So it is with the greatest admiration that we express our gratitude to Professor Lawson for his devotion to the task and his personal friendship.

Last but not least I would like to thank my assistant, Dipl.-Volkswirt Patrik Berend, for supervising all the organizational tasks involved in getting the scripts into the prescribed form, communicating with the publisher and with the printing house and clarifying problems and answering questions with the authors. The amount of time going into such a project is hardly ever correctly appreciated. Of course, the greatest reward is a favorable reception of the volume, and I do sincerely hope that the reception of the book in the English speaking world of business economics will greatly exceed Patrik's opportunity cost in time and effort.

Horst Albach

Contents

Part I: Foundations

Part I: Foundations

Erich Gutenberg and the Theory of the Firm[1]

R. H. Schmidt[2]

Overview

When Professor Gutenberg wrote his *Grundlagen der Betriebswirtschaftslehre* in the 1950s, his work was firmly rooted in the theory of the firm as it stood at the time. In the 1970s and 80s, this close relationship largely disappeared as a consequence of the profound changes which the microeconomic theory of the firm underwent under the influence of the new institutional economics. However, in the last few years, the pendulum has swung back. This is mainly due to the introduction of the new concept of complementarity into the theory of the firm.

The introduction of this concept not only shows that Erich Gutenberg's view of the firm is still relevant. It also permits business economists to take an economic approach to issues such as internal organisation and strategy which in the past were largely discussed using non-economic concepts. Finally and perhaps most importantly, the concept of complementarity can be used to define a new role for "general management" - in German: *Allgemeine Betriebswirtschaftslehre* - as a field of academic research and teaching, and at the same time constitute its central element. If the role and content of *Allgemeine Betriebswirtschaftslehre* are seen in this light, general management can again become the core of business administration, as it was in Erich Gutenberg's conception of the discipline.

Keywords: Theory of the firm, organisation, corporate strategy, complementarity

---

1 Slightly revised version of the paper presented at the conference of the Gutenberg Arbeitsgemeinschaft on the occasion of the centenary of Erich Gutenberg in Cologne, Dec. 12./13. 1997. Some additions have been made in order to facilitate the understanding of readers who are not familiar with the German context. I am grateful to Stephanie Grohs, Bernd Schauenberg and in particular Jens Maßmann for valuable suggestions and support, and to Paul Keast for improving my English.

2 Prof. Dr. Reinhard H. Schmidt, Wilhelm Merton-Professor for International Banking and Finance, Johann Wolfgang Goethe-Universität Frankfurt/Main, Sophienstraße 44, D-60487 Frankfurt/Main,
e-mail: rschmidt@wiwi.uni-frankfurt.de

1 Can Gutenberg's theory of the firm still be relevant today?

Professor Gutenberg was without any doubt the most influential and the most theoretically inclined researcher and teacher in the field of business administration (Betriebswirtschaftslehre) in the German-speaking countries after World War II. His theory of the firm, the conceptual foundations of which were already contained in his 1929 Habilitationsschrift, the thesis he presented in order to qualify as a university professor, is fully developed in his seminal three-volume work Grundlagen der Betriebswirtschaftslehre.[3] The present paper discusses the relationship between Gutenberg's theory and recent developments in the theory of the firm. Although the occasion for this lecture, the centenary of Erich Gutenberg's birth, would in itself suffice to justify my choice of topic, one might ask whether such a paper can perhaps do more than merely pay tribute to past achievements. Is it at all possible that Gutenberg's theory still has scientific relevance for current discussions on the theory of the firm?

There are certainly some strong arguments to support the view that his theory is simply outdated. His terminology reflects times gone by;[4] and although the discussions in his *Grundlagen* are highly abstract, beneath them lie impressions which Gutenberg gained while working for a small Silesian factory in the early 1920s and as a public accountant in the 1930s (Gutenberg 1989, pp 11, 104). Despite the fact that the multinational enterprise, outsourcing and market strategies had been around for quite some time, Gutenberg never took note of these phenomena, and therefore could not discuss them in his writing. Thus, his undeniable merits should not prevent us from accepting the *possibility* that the entire approach behind Gutenberg's theory of the firm might be outdated in both method and substance.

Indeed, ten years ago it would have been quite difficult to find any meaningful relationship between his work and the theory of the firm. However, this may have been due to the state of the theory of the firm ten years ago. It is the main objective of the present paper to show why this was indeed the case ten years ago and why recent developments in the theory of the firm call for a different assessment. Moreover, I intend to show that comparing them with Gutenberg's main work can lead to a deeper understanding of these recent theoretical developments, and can help us to appreciate *their* relevance.

---

3 Vol. 1, Die Produktion [Production], 1st ed. 1951, last ed. 1983; Vol. 2, Der Absatz [Sales/distribution], 1955/1984; Vol. 3, Die Finanzen [Finance], 1969/1980. (All translations are mine, RHS)

4 Even in the 1958 edition, managers are referred to as "Führungsgehilfen" [approximately: "leadership-assistants"].

The section which follows provides an overview of the main issues addressed by the theory of the firm, and of the main lines of research in these areas. Then, in section III, Gutenberg's theory is characterised from a present-day perspective. Section IV explains why, in my view, there would indeed seem to be hardly any common ground between the work of Erich Gutenberg and the theory of the firm of the 1970s and 80s. Section V, which is the core section of the paper, first presents what I perceive as the most important recent developments in the theory of the firm. It then demonstrates why, and in what respect, Gutenberg's theory of the firm is significant in the light of these developments. This leads to the conclusion that his theory is indeed relevant for developing an up-to-date concept of *Allgemeine Betriebswirtschaftslehre*, which can, with some reservations, be regarded as a German analogue to a theory of general management or a general theory of the business enterprise.

2 The nature and the content of theories of the firm

For the purpose of this paper, it would be useful to have an unambiguous definition of what the nature, the functions and the content of a theory of the firm are or should be. Unfortunately, there is no single concept of a theory of the firm. Even the use of the term "theory of the firm" among economists and researchers in the field of business administration provides no clear and simple answer to the question of what the role and the content of a theory of the firm is or should be. In fact, it is possible to identify three distinct strands of literature which employ the same term, yet differ as regards their underlying concept of theory and the issues they address.

(1) The *traditional theory of the firm* is part of the economic theory of markets, and as such is a clearly established concept among experts. Its *only* role is to explain market prices. This function determines its substance and method. In essence, it describes the enterprise ("the firm") as a production function, defining how inputs acquired in markets can be transformed into outputs sold in markets. The "firm" is modelled as a profit-maximising or, in multi-period models, a market value-maximising entity which reacts promptly and in an optimal manner to any exogenous change in the market prices of inputs and outputs.

Paradoxical as it may seem, because of this one-sided focus on market price formation, the enterprise as such does not appear at all in the traditional (or neoclassical) theory of the firm.[5] Its function provides the rationale for abstracting from the complexity of real enterprises and from all those aspects which would

---

5 See Machlup (1967), who offers the same assessment and a vigorous defence against critics who regarded this feature as a weakness.

make them genuinely interesting subjects for research. As a consequence, the traditional theory of the firm has no particular motive to even ask what "the nature" of the firm is, what constitutes its boundaries, and why firms exist in the first place, as the theory's implicit answers to these questions are trivial: Only production appears to be "essential", because "firms" can only make a profit through production at low costs; and this possibility is the only reason why the "firms" modelled in neoclassical theory exist at all. The traditional theory of the firm also provides no conceptual framework for analysing why all enterprises share certain institutional features and why the precise nature of these features varies according to factors such as industry, firm size and legal form. Finally, markets and firms are typically modelled in such a way that there is no need to discuss, and indeed no possible way of discussing strategy and internal organisation in a fruitful way.

If this well-known criticism is repeated here, it should not be taken to imply that the traditional theory does not deal with decision problems at the level of the individual firm. The traditional theory does pose the question of how a firm can and should react in an optimal manner to given - and possibly changing - market conditions, and it provides detailed and non-trivial answers. However, even these issues are dealt with in such a way that deriving implications about market prices takes precedence over providing a more differentiated or "realistic" view of the problems encountered at the enterprise level, or over suggesting solutions which might also be useful for managers. Thus it is hardly surprising that the traditional theory of the firm is not generally perceived as the basis of an agenda for research into, and teaching about, firms and the problems they face from a managerial perspective, i.e. from a perspective that is not constrained by an overriding interest in market price formation.[6]

(2) Theories of the firm have also been a central element of the standard literature in the field of *business administration* and in particular within the German discipline known as *Betriebswirtschaftslehre*.[7] However, although they form a distinct group, these theories are quite heterogeneous, and the concept of a theory of the firm, or rather of the enterprise, does not have a very precise meaning in this strand of the literature. If one analyses all those positions which claim to be "theories of the firm or enterprise", i.e. if one adopts an extremely liberal attitude and

---

6 Even though the traditional theory of the firm does not seem to lend itself to serving as a general conceptual basis for a theory of business policy, many of its concepts and results are clearly valuable elements of such a theory.

7 *Betriebswirtschaftslehre* in the German-speaking countries has a different tradition from business administration in the Anglo-Saxon world. In particular, *Betriebswirtschaftslehre* has, since its origins at the beginning of this century, regarded itself as an academic field with an identity of its own. English-speaking readers are referred to the relevant articles in the "Handbook of German Business Management (1990), ed. by E. Grochla. A lucid and highly critical account of this search for identity can be found in Schneider (1993, p. 219)

accepts this claim at face value, one can typically find one or more of the following characteristics:

- They refer explicitly or implicitly to the question of what the object of the theory and the field of study defined by this theory is, or should be, in the view of the respective author.
- They are general in the sense that they refer to the entire enterprise and to all enterprises and do not confine themselves to specific functions or parts of enterprises or to firms from certain industries.
- They are theoretical in the colloquial sense of being formal and/or systematic.

The fact that many theories in business administration which claim to be about "the theory of the firm or enterprise" address the "deep" question of what constitutes "the nature of the firm" does not, however, lead to a substantial clarification, as it is equally unclear what the sought-after "nature" of the firm could be. Is it

- the totality of those aspects and features which are considered to be important, relevant or "essential" for firms or enterprises, or
- those aspects and features which distinguish firms, or enterprises, from entities which are not firms or enterprises, or
- those aspects and features which all firms/enterprises have in common?

All too often, so-called theories of the firm and the alleged search for the essence of a firm or enterprise within business administration are no more than thinly disguised programmatic statements: they are simply an expression of what the authors would like their peers and followers to study.[8]

These theories of the firm or the enterprise do not, of course, restrict themselves to speculating about the "essence" of the firm or enterprise. They also investigate the concrete thing called a firm or an enterprise, and several of its aspects and features. When this is done in a scientific manner, the object of the investigation is always a mental product or concept, shaped both by real-life experience and by the specific way of looking at reality advocated by a given approach or theory.[9] Natu-

---

8 To me as a German author, it appears that the literature on *Betriebswirtschaftslehre* is particularly well-endowed with "approaches" which almost invariably claim to be based on a novel and pathbreaking notion of what the "nature" or "essence" of the firm might be. As a student, I was expected to learn about "the firm as a social system" (Nicklisch, 1928), as a "productive system" (Gutenberg 1951/1983), as a "decision system" (Heinen, 1962, 1976) and even as an "action centre" (Kosiol, 1966). Careful and mainly critical assessments of this proliferation of "approaches" to the theory of the firm can be found in Albach (1991), Schauenberg (1993), Schneider (1997) and, last but not least, Gutenberg (1989, pp 29–43).

9 Gutenberg emphasised this as long ago as 1929 (p. 42); for a more recent source, see Schneider (1997, p. 2).

rally the notion of what constitutes the "essence" of a firm or enterprise according to the theory in question determines to a great extent which aspects or features of firms rank highest as research topics.

The *modern theory of the firm* which was mainly developed in the 1970s and 80s by Anglo-Saxon economists with a certain inclination towards business administration, addresses questions like the following: Why do firms exist at all, how are they structured, and what constitutes the specific differences between different types of firms or enterprises? It studies the boundaries of the firm and their determinants, the objectives of firms and the persons who shape those objectives, and the governance systems of enterprises. This strand of the literature may appear less "essentialistic" (to use Popper's term) than the theories of the firm in traditional German *Betriebswirtschaftslehre*, but as the title of the now well-known, but long overlooked article by Ronald Coase (1937) indicates, not only German authors try to uncover "the nature of the firm" and gain insights into the "essence" that lies behind the appearance. The modern theory of the firm is discussed at greater length in section IV below.

3 Gutenberg's theory of the firm

3.1 Is Gutenberg's main work really a theory of the firm at all?

Gutenberg regarded himself as a theoretician, and his *Grundlagen* was generally acknowledged as an important contribution to the theory of business administration. In the light of my earlier remarks concerning the content, function and attributes of a theory of the firm in the domain of German *Betriebswirtschaftslehre*, this assessment is certainly justified. Four main arguments can be put forward to support it:

1. Gutenberg's theory is a comprehensive and thoroughly systematic intellectual edifice, centred around the firm and in particular the capitalistic firm for which he reserves the term "enterprise".[10]

2. Gutenberg's pre-eminent aspiration was a profound understanding of what constitutes the "essence" or the "nature" of a firm in general and of an enterprise in particular.

10 In German: *Betrieb* and *Unternehmung*. Note that other German authors make other terminological distinctions between *Betrieb* and *Unternehmung* or use both terms interchangeably.

3. Compared with what was common in the German literature at the time he wrote his *Habilitationsschrift* and his *Grundlagen*, Gutenberg's writings demonstrate an unusual familiarity with, and proximity to, the current microeconomic theory of his time, and an unusual degree of formalism and rigour.

4. Despite its extensive use of microeconomic tools and concepts, Gutenberg's system does not fall into the domain of the traditional economic theory of the firm, but rather is genuine *Betriebswirtschaftslehre* because he discusses production, sales/distribution and financing problems not in order to study the formation of market prices but as important problems in their own right.

3.2 Issues explicitly addressed by Gutenberg's theory

Gutenberg's explicit theory of the firm and the enterprise can be summarised in a few words: The common feature of firms in all types of economic systems is to produce, sell and distribute some kind of output. A firm is a system of human and non-human factors of production which produces goods or services and makes them available to other economic units. Production and sales/distribution are made possible by combining the factors of production under the leadership ("*Führung*") of what Gutenberg calls the "dispositive factor", i.e. the people who perform important management functions. Production and sales/distribution, the system of productive factors, the process of combining the productive factors and the role of management are, in Gutenberg's words, "facts which are independent of the economic system"[11] in which a firm operates. But there are, in his view, two additional "system-independent facts", namely two "principles" which all firms have to follow and, as he seems to assume, do indeed follow. They are the "principle of efficiency" and the "principle of financial equilibrium". Not only capitalistic enterprises, but also firms in centrally planned economies, workers' co-operatives and non-profit firms have to obey these two principles, as they too try to avoid wasting resources and to protect their operations from disturbances which might result from liquidity problems.

Enterprises are the predominant type of firms in a capitalist market economy. They are characterised by two additional principles, the "principle of autonomy" and the "principle of profitability",[12] which he also calls "system-dependent facts". For Gutenberg the second of these "principles", i.e. the profit-orientation of enterprises, is based on, in his words, the "assumption ... that on an economy-wide level the optimal provision of goods and services is achieved when each individual enterprise strives for maximum long-term return on the invested capital" (1983, p.

11 The German term used by Gutenberg is *systemindifferente Tatbestände*, in contrast to the *systembedingten Tatbeständen* (system-dependent facts) to be discussed below.

12 In German *Autonomieprinzip* and *erwerbswirtschaftliches Prinzip*.

464). The meaning of the principle of autonomy is that no authority external to the firm can determine what decisions have to be made within the firm.

Evidently, Gutenberg's view of what constitutes an enterprise is closely related to the common view of the firm in microeconomic theory. An enterprise is regarded as an element of a market system. Nevertheless, there is a clear distinction between Gutenberg's theory and the traditional theory insofar as his is not designed as a building block for a theory of market price formation. For it to perform that function, his description of the production process and of the relationship between a given enterprise and the markets is much too differentiated[13] and, perhaps even more importantly, the markets in which the enterprises operate are treated as being too imperfect.

So what is the central idea of Gutenberg's theory of the firm or, to put it another way, what is "the nature of the firm" for Gutenberg? A perfectly legitimate answer to this question would be that the firm is seen essentially as a "productivity relationship". Such an interpretation would certainly do justice to Erich Gutenberg and in particular to those like Horst Albach (1981) who have a strong claim to knowing what Gutenberg really wanted to say.[14] A firm or an enterprise is a productive system; and it owes its productivity not only to the potential productivity inherent in each individual factor of production, but even more so to the way in which they are combined and the fact that they can therefore complement each other.[15]

Nevertheless, I have my doubts as to whether this interpretation really grasps what may have appeared most important to Gutenberg himself and what may be the most interesting theoretical concept of his work. My doubts result from re-reading his *Habilitationsschrift*. In this early book, Gutenberg's concept of a theoretical system is not yet overshadowed as much as in his later *Grundlagen* by his innovative contributions to the theory of production and the theory of markets, the "type B production function" and the "double-kinked demand curve".[16]

The central point of his system is to understand how the three elements of a firm/enterprise – namely production, sales/distribution and financing – are interrelated. In 1929, he writes:

---

13 This applies in particular to the later editions of his *Grundlagen*.

14 See in particular Albach (1981). Albach is not only Gutenberg's most prominent disciple and an eminent scholar in his own right, but also Gutenberg's son-in-law.

15 In recent publications, both Alchian (1993) and Demsetz (1991) cite this fact, which was already established by Adam Smith, as being the most important explanation of the existence of enterprises.

16 Gutenberg's "type B production function" which is discussed in Vol. 1 of his *Grundlagen* (1983, pp. 326-337) has certain similarities to engineering production functions; see Shephard, R.W. (1953). His theory of the double-kinked demand curve which is discussed in Vol. 2 (1984, pp. 233-265) has certain similarities to ideas presented by Sweezy (1939).

"Viewed thus, one can describe the enterprise as a complex of quantities whose relationship to one another is that of interdependence (they are linked by virtue of their reciprocal functionality) ..." (1929, S. 42);

and later in the same treatise:

"The proper subject matter of a theory of the firm from the standpoint of business administration, the subject matter that lies closest to the economic reality of a firm, is that sequence of reactions precipitated by changes of data which the enterprise undergoes, which transform one situation into another, which shoot through not only the internal sector (i.e. production, R.H.S.) but also, to the same degree, the procurement and sales sectors." (1929, p. 96, emphasised in the original)

For Gutenberg the "essence of the object of theoretical business administration" is that "the specific phenomena in the three sectors influence each other and are conditional on one another" (1929, p. 105). As he emphasises, this interdependence not only determines how enterprises react to changes of external parameters, but also raises the question of how a reaction at the level of the entire enterprise, which takes all three sectors and their interdependence into account, is brought about, and this leads him to take a closer look at the role of management[17] which consists, in his view, of assuring the required co-ordination between the sectors.

While the theoretical concept of productivity, which undeniably plays an important role in Gutenberg's theory, has been widely accepted in the discipline and elaborated in several respects in a fruitful manner, I am not aware that the same has yet happened to any appreciable degree with the, even more important, theoretical concept of the complementarity between the various parts of an enterprise. As complementarity is an important concept in the recent literature on the theory of the firm, there should be an unexpected, but possibly important, parallel between Gutenberg's theory and the most recent developments in the theory of the firm.

3.3 Issues not covered sufficiently in Gutenberg's theory

Despite the breadth of ideas, problems and topics covered in Erich Gutenberg's main work and the important role they play in the analytical structure of his theory, obviously no book can encompass everything. It is also important to consider what he did not address, or what he merely hinted at, as omissions quite often provide a clue to understanding a theoretical approach. That is why I would like to comment briefly on three topics which are missing from, or not sufficiently integrated into, his work.

---

17 In 1929, Gutenberg used a very idiosyncratic, simply untranslatable term, *psycho-physisches Subjekt*, to denote what we would now call the management.

(1) The first example is the imperfection of the factor and product markets in which enterprises are embedded. Of course, market imperfections are not ignored in Gutenberg's work. They play a certain role in the first volume of his *Grundlagen* and are covered extensively in the second volume. Nevertheless, they do not seem to have shaped the structure, i.e. the architecture, of his theory, and if he had paid more attention to them, it might have improved his understanding of what constitutes the "nature" of the firm or enterprise. In fact, market imperfections could be regarded as the centrepiece of what one might call Gutenberg's implicit theory of the firm: If productivity required the joint use of several factors of production and if this were, for technical reasons, only possible in firms, then this would provide a straightforward explanation, in a Coasian vein, of why firms and enterprises exist.[18]

(2) Despite his extensive use of microeconomic concepts, Gutenberg appears to be a true representative of the *Betriebswirtschaftslehre* of his day insofar as he consistently treats an enterprise as an entity unto itself rather than as an instrument of economic agents, i.e. people. Although enterprises are profit-oriented by definition, his theory does not attribute this orientation to the fact that it is in the interests of capitalists. Irrespective of whether they are run by owners or by employed managers, the enterprises of Gutenberg's theory are not "driven" by the interests of capitalists or other self-interested people, but rather by something non-human, namely the "principles" of efficiency, financial equilibrium and profitability. At first glance, this element of his theory appears to be simply odd, perhaps a remnant of the "German philosophy" to which he was exposed as a doctoral student. One could leave it at that and pass over a presumed mistake in his theory with either some words of criticism or benign neglect. But I believe this would not be an appropriate response. Rather, I tend to think of the strong, but nevertheless implicit, assumption in his *idealised* concept of the enterprise that the "dispositive factor", i.e. the management, is relatively independent in its decisions, as something deliberate and even as an important element of his theory.[19]

---

18 See also Alchian (1993) and the attempt to provide a modern interpretation of Gutenberg in Schauenberg/Schmidt (1983).

19 The strongest support for my argument that Gutenberg did not simply make a mistake when he treated the enterprise as being relatively independent of individual agents' interests comes from one of the opening statements - and the entire approach - of the third volume of his *Grundlagen*. In this volume, which deals with *Die Finanzen* and which is meant to provide the concluding element of his entire theoretical system, the financing of a corporation is treated as *merely* the *Voraussetzung für den gesamtbetrieblichen Leistungsvollzug* which is, in a not-too-literal translation, "the precondition for the entire firm to perform its function", and this function is only defined in terms of production and sales/distribution. In other words, finance is completely disconnected from corporate governance, and the way in which a firm or enterprise is financed has nothing to do with what it is supposed to do. (For a further discussion see Schmidt/Terberger (1997, pp 13-37)).

A central issue in today's theory of the firm is whether it is permissible from a theoretical perspective to assume a certain degree of management independence from the interests of individual agents, and how far this independence might go. The mere fact that many real-life enterprises are indeed quite independent does not justify this assumption in a theoretical treatise like Gutenberg's *Grundlagen*. Moreover, the idea of the enterprise as an entity which is quite independent of individual agents' interests has been attacked vigorously by the theory of finance of the 1970s and 80s. As is well known, this criticism is based on the premise that perfect capital markets make it both possible and desirable in welfare-economic terms for corporations to be run strictly and exclusively in the interests of their shareholders.

In addition, Gutenberg's implicit assumption that enterprises are relatively independent of the interests of individual economic agents seems to violate the principle of "methodological individualism", a doctrine in the philosophy of science which recommends that each and every fact be reduced to the interests and the actions of individual agents. However, we should not rule out the possibility that an overly strict and overly impatient adherence to this, undoubtedly sound, principle might prevent us from coming to grips with some of the central problems in the field of business administration. I have the impression that this has for a long time been the case with topics like corporate strategy, management and internal organisation. Possibly because they do not lend themselves easily to a straightforward application of the principle of methodological individualism, they have in the past been grossly neglected in German *Betriebswirtschaftslehre* and discussed in the American management literature without any substantive use of economic concepts. This consideration raises the question of whether there might be sound economic arguments behind Gutenberg's implicit and perhaps only intuitive assumption that enterprises enjoy a certain independence from the people who would want to use them for their own ends. This question is taken up in section V below.

(3) The absence of a discussion of the relationship between owners or shareholders and other stakeholders on the one hand, and the enterprise on the other, points to a more general class of omissions in Gutenberg's theory of the firm. In his work, organisational problems are discussed only in a disjointed manner and without any connection to the general structure of his theory. It appears as if organisation were nothing but a detail of the planning of production and sales/distribution. In this neglect of the economic aspects of organisation, Gutenberg exhibits a surprising similarity to the traditional economic theory of the firm. He does address problems of the governance of enterprises in the concluding chapter of *Die Produktion*, but fails to establish any connection to his detailed analysis of the functions of management in an early part of the same book. It therefore comes as no surprise that one finds in his work little discussion of the interrelationship between strategy, governance and management.

To avoid a possible misunderstanding I would like to repeat and stress that it would be absurd to criticise Gutenberg for not having written about phenomena and problems which had not been discussed in the academic discourse and which could not even be recognised as relevant and tractable at the time of his writing. My motive was, rather, to identify and highlight gaps in his system which might be closed by inserting insights that stem from the most recent developments in the theory of the firm.

4 Modern theories of the firm

4.1 Origins and affinities

This section offers a somewhat closer examination of the so-called modern theory of the firm. On the one hand, I intend to show what it is that its various strands have in common; on the other, I aim to lay the foundations for my assertion that hardly any substantial links exist between this theory and Gutenberg's system.

During the past 25 years or so, there has been an appreciable revival in the discussion on the basic questions and the foundations of the theory of the firm - on the "essence or the nature of the firm", so to speak. All of the variants of the modern theory of the firm that are still regarded as important today can be traced back to a common origin: the emergence of the new institutional economics as an important branch of microeconomics (Terberger, 1994). The modern theorists questioned the ostensibly self-evident truth of traditional notions, such as the following:

- The existence of firms is a fact, and therefore it is not important to ask why they exist.
- Firms are owned by the providers of equity or risk-capital and therefore must be profit-oriented.
- It is methodologically valid to treat firms as homogenous structures or "quasi individuals", and therefore their internal organisation, while of interest from a technical point of view, is not relevant to a theory of the firm.

The objections that began to be raised were directed not only against the standard notions contained in management literature (and, to a large extent, current in *Betriebswirtschaftslehre*) but also against the theoretically more refined picture of firms that had by that time been painted by Arrow, Debreu and other proponents of a theory of general equilibrium and its simplified variants within the theory of finance. This theory - and in this respect it has close affinities to the traditional theory of the firm - sees enterprises as being constrained by a very tight corset consisting of perfect (capital) markets, and enterprises' internal and external relationships as being strictly determined by complete contracts. And indeed, the combination of perfect markets and complete contracts not only renders superfluous questions of corporate strategy and corporate governance, but also reduces questions of internal organisation and corporate management to a trivial, or at least non-economic, level.

The revival of the discussion on the theory of the firm is generally associated with the insight that enterprises do not merely have an organisational structure that is, moreover, vital to their ability to function, but that they are - like real markets - themselves a form of organisation through which economic advantages can be gained. In other words, the enterprise is an institution which has the function of safeguarding the benefits of a lasting co-operation against the hazards of opportunism and short-sightedness (Schauenberg/Schmidt, 1983, pp. 257f).

4.2 Theoretical building blocks

Having emphasised their similarities, we should not lose sight of the fact that there are various trends within the modern theory of the firm which differ from one another substantially on key issues, as the following survey shows.[20]

(1) In his 1937 essay on "The Nature of the Firm", which did not receive attention from a wider audience until the 1970s, Ronald Coase raised the obvious question of why enterprises exist that are more complex than the "firm" of conventional pricing theory. His answer is simple: they exist because use of the market mechanism is not costless. However, his comments on what the "costs of using the market mechanism" might be certainly cannot be described as particularly informative, and still less enlightening are his ideas on how enterprises' internal co-ordination works. Coase developed a methodology which consisted of turning the make-or-buy-decision into a general rule for determining what is co-ordinated inside and outside enterprises, i.e. via the pricing mechanism or other internal mechanisms, but this was not, in my view, his decisive contribution to the debate. What *was* decisive was the very fact that he turned his attention to the task of explaining the existence of firms, defined as a problem of organisation within a market system, and in doing so inspired researchers to compare real forms of organisation.

Williamson (1975, 1985) expanded on Coase's ideas to develop the so-called transaction cost approach, which focuses on the definition of various organisational forms for "transactions", with the firm at one extreme and the near-ideal-typical (real) market at the other, and on what he calls "matching transactions with

---

20 A similar characterisation is given in Terberger (1994, pp. 110 - 117) and, with a rather different slant, in Picot et al. (1997, pp. 53 - 94) and Holmström/Tirole (1989).

governance structures".[21] Like Coase, Williamson is concerned to assess alternative forms of organisation in economic terms and to explain their existence by demonstrating their efficiency for organising transactions.[22] To be sure, Williamson goes much further than Coase in his characterisation of internal organisational structures and also of what makes it difficult to use the market under certain conditions; yet the underlying idea remains the same. The "nature of the firm" according to Coase and Williamson lies in that which distinguishes it from the market. Firms have boundaries which make it possible to distinguish between internal and external relationships and within which economic activities can be organised differently than in the market: specifically, they tend to be organised hierarchically and thus "somehow" more efficiently. Or, to put it succinctly, a firm is an instrument for reducing transaction costs.

(2) The theory of agency is the second building block in the modern theory of the firm. An agency relationship exists when one party, the agent, acts and takes decisions on behalf of another, the principal. An agency relationship becomes problematic, and therefore of interest from an economic point of view, when the principal cannot monitor precisely whether the agent's actions are always taken entirely for his - the principal's - benefit, and at best has only imperfect means of controlling the agent's self-interested actions. The agency theory is a general theory of economic structures; like the theory of exchange, it addresses a type of relationship. Relationships of this type are a common phenomenon in the real world, and many different institutional arrangements exist which can be construed as attempts to minimise the disadvantages - the so-called agency costs - arising from the fact that actions are unobservable and/or that contracts between principals and agents are incomplete.

The connection between the agency theory and the theory of the firm is most clearly drawn by Jensen/Meckling (1976).[23] Proceeding from the empirical finding by Berle and Means (1932) that in many large firms ownership is separated from control, they investigate why it may not be economically irrational for the role of owners, as holders of residual claims, to be separated from the role of managers, as decision-makers. These ideas were later generalised and applied to various types of firms (Fama/Jensen 1983a and 1983b). The point of interest in our present context is what can be concluded from all of this as far as the "nature of the firm" is concerned. The firm is - or in the authors' opinion could usefully be regarded as - "a legal fiction which is at the center of a nexus of contracts" (Jensen/Meckling, 1976, p. 310). Thus, contrary to Coase's assertion, it cannot be assumed that a firm has clear boundaries. Moreover, the position of the owners is also less explicit and less specific than, for example, in Alchian/Demsetz (1972), who can also be

---

21 See Williamson (1985, p. 72).

22 For a detailed account of Williamson's analysis, see Picot et al. (1997, pp. 53 - 94); for a more critical account, see Terberger (1994, pp. 110 - 116).

23 See also Fama (1980), Fama/Jensen (1983a and 1983b) and Jensen (1983).

classified as proponents of agency theory, yet whose goal was to explain a phenomenon which differs from than in which Jensen/Meckling were interested.[24]

Using arguments that are closely related to those of agency theory, Alchian and Demsetz (1972) introduced the issue of property rights into the theory of the firm. Their aim was to explain why the owner-managed firm is an efficient institutional arrangement.[25] The pivotal tenet of their argument was that there are benefits associated with production in a team, or more generally, with co-operation, the realisation of which is conditional upon the possibility of controlling the incentives to shirking by those involved in the co-operation. This is only possible, Alchian and Demsetz believe, if someone is observing and enforcing the work input of the people involved. Given the observability problems, it would seem to make sense to have a "central monitor". To counteract the natural tendency of the central monitor to shirk, it is suggested that he should receive the total marginal revenue of his effort. This is the residual return, i.e. that amount left over from the revenue of the firm after all contractual payments have been made. If one defines an owner as being the economic agent who has a claim on the residual return - or in short, as the residual claimant - then the unity of ownership and control is shown to be economically efficient, and the "classic", owner-managed firm is explained in economic terms. Thus Alchian and Demsetz focus their analysis on the advantages of internal organisation in terms of the observability of actions; yet they do not actually say very much about internal organisation, and what they do say is extremely undifferentiated.

(3) Alchian and Demsetz's basic idea was taken further by Grossman and Hart. Based on the theory of incomplete contracts,[26] the third building block in the modern theory of the firm, they analysed the economic factors which define the rights to take decisions on matters that are not governed by contracts, which specify whom these "residual control rights" should be assigned to, and which determine the extent of the assets to which these residual control rights should apply. For the advocates of the property rights approach, a firm is an entity that is held together economically through the joint ownership of "non-human assets".[27]

---

24 This assessment is also given by Holmström/Milgrom (1994), and is supported by remarks by Demsetz (1991).

25 At the same time, they wished to demonstrate that the categorical difference which Coase claimed to have found between internal relationships within a firm and external market relationships did not in fact exist. In retrospect, they can be said to have failed in this second objective, which is why no further mention need be made of it in the remainder of this paper.

26 See the initial paper by Grossman/Hart (1986), also the more detailed work by Hart (1995) and, in the context of financial relationships, C. Laux (1996).

27 It is interesting to note the very different routes by which Alchian/Demsetz on the one hand, and Gutenberg on the other, derive the right to manage. For Alchian/Demsetz it is the result of an efficient contract, whereas for Gutenberg it follows "from the law". See Gutenberg (1983, p. 246).

This theoretical approach is a synthesis of the two previously described approaches insofar as, through the construction of incomplete contracts, it takes on board Williamson's notions of transaction costs and "bounded rationality", and also incorporates, through the definition of the firm as a collection of non-human assets under common control, the property rights dimension introduced by Alchian and Demsetz. With their "incomplete contracts approach" Grossman and Hart obtain conclusive findings regarding the economically efficient limits of the firm and also analyse, for the first time within a self-contained theoretical framework, the conditions under which transactions within a firm are more or less expensive than those executed via the market. Yet they too remain remarkably vague when it comes to showing whether, and why, internal organisational structures are advantageous and in particular why the same problems that occur in external relationships do not arise at an internal level, albeit in a different guise.

4.3 Theory and the real world have moved on since Gutenberg's day

For all their differences of substance, methodology and, above all, terminology, the three approaches I have subsumed under the heading "modern theory of the firm" are closely related to one another. All three emphasise the importance of institutional aspects, and all three give answers - albeit different ones - to the question of what can be conceived of as the "nature of the firm". In recognising the importance of this question and seeking an answer to it, they are closer than the traditional theory of the firm to Gutenberg's theory and his aim of constructing a system.[28] Yet this is where the possible affinity to Gutenberg ends, for, unlike the themes of the traditional theory of the firm, the issues which the theory of the firm of the 1970s' and 80s' highlightd are not the same as those of Gutenberg's *Grundlagen*.

The theoretical building blocks on which the modern theory of the firm rests are not marginal phenomena within microeconomics. On the contrary, they are at the very centre of theoretical development, and accordingly the relative importance of the traditional theory of the firm is declining.[29] Thus, due on the one hand to immanent developments in microeconomic theory, Gutenberg's system appears less well founded when viewed from the perspective of 1980s economic theory than it looked in the 1950s. On the other hand, developments in the real world

---

28 And, insofar as they deal with institutional aspects, they offer many interesting starting points for lines of investigation within *Allgemeine Betriebswirtschaftslehre* and its numerous sub-disciplines. Cf. Ordelheide/Rudolph/Büsselmann (1991). Furthermore, they are not the topics covered by "management", as it is taught at American business schools.

29 This is reflected in all good modern textbooks, such as the one by Kreps (1990).

were taking place at approximately the same time which were to rob Gutenberg's system of its immediate persuasive power. There has been a change in the structures and the role of real-world firms. A typical large firm of today is a multinational group. It has very little in common with the Silesian agricultural machinery factory that Gutenberg knew. If firms were once organisations with pronounced hierarchies, clear boundaries, a narrow range of products and arm's length, market-based relationships with suppliers and purchasers, the large-scale enterprises of today have become complex structures with less clearly defined hierarchies, fuzzy boundaries and diversified ranges of products.[30] This is important not only because it calls into question the affinity between the model of the enterprise in Gutenberg's theory and the real thing. Most importantly it raises the question of whether, for today's enterprises, economically efficient production is, as in the 1950s (and going by the literature of *Betriebswirtschaftslehre*[31] also in Gutenberg's theory) still the central problem, whose solution is the main task of top management.

Yet despite the developments that have taken place in theory and in the real world, there are also reasons for doubting that these changes have rendered Gutenberg's theory of the firm obsolete. These reasons are examined in the next section. Recent developments in microeconomic theory, and specifically in the theory of the firm, that have occurred since roughly the start of the 1990s reveal the relevance and topicality of those elements of Gutenberg's theory of the firm that have not previously received as much scholarly attention as the productivity relationship.

5 Recent developments in the theory of the firm

5.1 Overview and a proposition

When it tries to explain why firms exist, the modern theory of the firm refers extensively to what it perceives as the weaknesses of markets, i.e. to market failure, whereas it does not have much to say about what firms or enterprises are particularly good at. Yet for a meaningful explanation of the existence of enterprises, the weaknesses of markets and the strengths of enterprises - and also vice-versa - are equally important. Moreover, for a theory of the firm which claimed to

---

30 For a fundamental assessment, see Dunning (1988) and, following on from there, Schmidt (1995).

31 See Wöhe (1959) and Köhler (1966) as relevant and representative sources on the methodological discussions within *Betriebswirtschaftslehre* and Wöhe (1996) as a still-influential textbook.

fall into the domain of business administration it would be particularly striking admission of inadequacy if all it had to say was that in firms orders are given and have to be obeyed. Alchian and Demsetz (1972, p. 777) simply miss the point when they state that an entrepreneur does not *need* to be able to do more than to "fire or sue" his employees if they do not do what he orders them to do.

Only recently has the theory of the firm started to compare firms and markets from the opposite angle by investigating in detail what firms are good at, and what they can do better than markets. With this more balanced approach, which employs all three building blocks of the modern - and by now well-established - theory of the firm presented in section IV, researchers are now able to address issues which have long been at the very heart of business administration. In a nutshell, the message of the most recent theory of the firm, and also its answer to the question of the "nature of the firm" can be put like this:

A firm or enterprise is a network of explicit and implicit contracts in an environment of imperfect markets. It has at its disposal ways and means to create incentives for employees and to control what they do, which the market does not have, and by using them it can earn economic rents on a lasting basis.

Over the past few decades, business administration has suffered from a tendency towards fragmentation and from a lack of a coherent economic basis. Only too often, the various corporate policy problems have been treated as if they were unconnected, and have largely been addressed without the use of economic concepts. This applies in particular to two areas of great practical importance, namely internal organisation and corporate strategy. My proposition is that - as I attempt to show in this section - the recent advances in the theory of the firm offer the prospect of integrating the various sub-fields which today make up the discipline of business administration within a comprehensive *economic* theory of the business enterprise. Since finding an economic approach to issues of internal organisation and strategy seems to be a particularly difficult task, these two areas are given special consideration in what follows.

The prospect of being able to elaborate a new, integrated economic theory of the business enterprise might bring back to life what was evidently Erich Gutenberg's academic dream: to gain a profound economic understanding of how the different parts and functions of an enterprise are interrelated, of what constitutes the main role of management (the "dispositive factor") and ultimately even of what can be regarded as "the nature of the firm".

The key to answering these questions lies in the concept of complementarity. Complementarity between the various elements which in their totality constitute the enterprise as a system is a precondition for the success of any enterprise and, ultimately, it is the main reason why complex enterprises exist in reality. This is precisely why I consider Gutenberg to be a forerunner of the contemporary theory of the firm. His theoretical approach to the theory of the firm is unique, at least in the German *Betriebswirtschaftslehre*, in emphasising and elaborating early on that an enterprise can only be understood - and managed - if it is regarded as a system in which the various elements have to be adjusted to each other, and not as an accidental collection of assets and functions.[32]

In the following sub-section, I first show how internal organisation and strategy can be integrated into an economic approach to the theory of the firm. This serves as a first demonstration of how - according to recent theory - firms are better able to perform certain functions. I then attempt to demonstrate that complementarity is the guiding principle for organisational design and choice of strategy.

5.2 Internal organisation and strategy in the recent theory of the firm

5.2.1 Internal organisation

Organisational design is about defining tasks, bundling together various tasks to form jobs, and assigning these bundles of tasks or jobs to a person, a group of persons, a department or some other organisational unit. The definition of tasks and jobs implies three things: certain decision rights and other property rights over assets which are needed to fulfil the tasks have to be transferred to the person or unit assigned to the job; methods have to be defined for measuring performance; and a system of rewarding performance has to be put in place.

For Gutenberg, an "organisation (is) *only* that apparatus which has the task of realising an order which has been determined *in advance* in the process of planning".[33] Even today, this is still acceptable as a definition of organisation. However, it might lead to the misunderstanding that the organisation is a perfect, more or less frictionless machine for putting into practice whatever management wants and, in addition, that management always has all the necessary information to design and implement the organisation it wants to have in place. However, contrary to this overly technical view, firms have to find economic - and not technical - solutions for two facts of life: that the people who are tied together by an organisation typically have divergent interests; and that information is distributed unevenly among economic agents. Therefore, management is typically unable and/or unwilling to find, and implement, the organisational design that would be optimal in an ideal world.

---

32 As Albach wrote in the editorial to the issue of *Zeitschrift für Betriebswirtschaft* commemorating the 90th anniversary of Gutenberg's birth, the common feature of members of the "Gutenbergian school" is that their understanding of the enterprise is based "on the *interdependence* of all the sub-components of the firm." (Translated from Albach, 1988, p. 9, emphasis in the original).

33 Translated from Gutenberg 1983, p. 232; emphasis added.

In real life, jobs often comprise more than one task. There is an important economic reason for bundling together various tasks into one job: information gained in performing one task might be useful or indeed necessary for the other tasks. But if a person[34] has to perform a multi-task job, what determines how much time, attention and effort is devoted to each of the various tasks? At least to a certain extent this decision is made by the person to whom the job has been assigned and cannot be observed by other people. Thus, the person can be assumed to follow her own interests and the incentives provided to her in the form of performance measurement and reward systems. Typically, performance measurement and reward systems are costly; therefore there are sound economic reasons why they are inevitably imperfect. Putting these two considerations together leads to an important implication, namely because of the reusability of information it can be economically efficient to combine in one job several tasks which differ in the degree to which their fulfilment can be measured and rewarded. Take the example of a central heating engineer whose job is to install radiators in a new building and at the same time to help his fellow workmen with whatever problems arise during the installation, and also to train an apprentice. From the point of view of the firm which employs the workmen, it is desirable for his time and attention to be divided among the three tasks in a "balanced" way.[35] However, only one of these tasks involves easily measurable results, i.e. the number of radiators installed. If the heating engineer's remuneration is a function of his performance in this one task, he will - simply because his time and attention are finite - neglect the not (easily) measurable tasks. In helping his colleagues, or explaining something to an apprentice, he would incur opportunity costs for which he would not be compensated.

In this example a (simple) performance-related payment scheme with performance measured in terms of the number of radiators installed has the desirable effect of making the engineer work hard at installing radiators, and the undesirable effect of inducing non-co-operative behaviour towards his colleagues and the apprentice. This incentive structure is almost exactly the one that a market solution would bring about if the individual central heating engineer were a firm operating as a subcontractor. If, in this example, the negative effects of a strictly performance-related payment were greater than the positive effects, then the market-like incentives would be *too strong*, and it would be desirable to find a way of weakening the incentives relative to those of a pure market solution. This is precisely what the employer of the heating engineer in the example would want to do, *and can do*. He could pay the engineer not (only) according to the easily measurable output of his work, and he would seek and find - inevitably imperfect,

---

34 The following applies equally to divisions or other organisational units of an enterprise.

35 See Holmström/Milgrom 1991.

but not completely ineffective - ways of providing incentives for the worker to perform *all* of the various tasks which are assigned to him.

The foregoing example contains an important general lesson. It is a specific strength of enterprises over markets that they are "low-powered incentive systems" (Holmström/Milgrom, 1994, p. 989) and *as such* can make better use of the instrument of job design to encourage co-operative behaviour as well as the multiple use of information. The greater the importance of combining several tasks in one job and the greater the importance of co-operation, the *weaker* should be the incentives for performing the particular task which is easy to measure. This has far-reaching implications for, among other things, deciding which tasks should be performed within a given firm, or enterprise, and which tasks can be "outsourced". Tasks whose impact on the value of other activities is great but hard to measure must be performed internally. These are the "strategic" or "core" activities of a firm.

5.2.2 Strategy

Strategic decisions are also an important issue for enterprises and a challenge for *Betriebswirtschaftslehre*. Academic interest in strategy-related issues developed late, and it quickly drifted off into a discussion about techniques and methods without any reference to the methods and results of economic theory. This did not change until the publication of Porter's studies (1980, 1985). Since then, the literature on strategy has had a firmer grounding in economics. Porter directs his attention mainly to sales markets, which he regards as temporarily imperfect. He shows how an enterprise can gain, exploit and maintain a competitive advantage in such markets.

The main application of Porter's ideas is in connection with strategies pursued by individual business units. However, most large firms today are active in several markets, which raises the question of corporate strategies: is an enterprise a "portfolio" of mainly unconnected "businesses", or do connections exist between the various business units? What should the composition of the portfolio be, and what are the advantages of having a conglomeration of units rather than allowing the same units to operate in isolation? Porter also developed a "framework" for dealing with these questions,[36] the essence of which is captured neatly in the definition offered by Collis/Montgomery (1997, p. 5): "Corporate strategy is the way a company creates value through the configuration and co-ordination of its multimarket activities."

A relatively new approach, which is also grounded in economics, is known as the "resource-based view of the firm". This view starts from the premise that input

---

36 See Porter (1994) on the difference between frameworks and theories and on the significance of the frameworks.

markets are also characterised by imperfections, and indeed may be even more imperfect than sales markets.[37] Successful enterprises have special "assets" or "resources" which cannot (easily) be transferred or imitated and which are therefore also not easily acquired by competitors. Such "resources" can be more or less concrete, and they can be used in a single business unit, or in several at once, or at a company-wide level. If they are not concrete and are at least similar to skills in certain respects, they are labelled "core competences" in the evocative jargon of strategy researchers and advisers. If firms are able to operate successfully in several markets at once, it is because they possess a wide variety of usable resources, or core competences, or a single resource that can be spread over several markets. Obviously, these multiple resources need careful co-ordination to ensure that they are deployed in the right place for the right activity at the right time.

The resource-based view of corporate strategy shows, even more clearly than Porter's view, that strategies serve the purpose of generating economic rents and creating the preconditions for rents to be earned in the future. This is not to deny the importance of the imperfections of output markets. But it does suggest that market imperfections in factor and intermediate-goods markets should be regarded as more important. In addition, the resource-based view points to an intertemporal dimension which the established literature tends to overlook, namely, the imperfection of the markets for specific resources makes it economically unattractive to sell these resources. Therefore they have to be used over more than one time period. Evidently, this is only possible if a given firm remains in existence. Thus the most recent contributions to the literature on corporate strategy lend unexpected support to central concepts in Gutenberg's theoretical approach which appear odd in the light of standard neo-classical theory, namely the overriding importance of the "principle of financial equilibrium" and the relative autonomy of corporate interests from the interests of individual economic agents which this principle and other elements of his theory imply.

There are indeed several links between the new, economics-inspired thinking about strategy and the most recent theory of the firm. Market imperfections and the incompleteness of contracts are central to both. In a world of perfect markets and complete and costless contracts there would no reason for the existence of firms, and there would not be much to say about strategy. Only now do both strands of the literature share the same view of the world.

How does this relate to Gutenberg's work? He hardly mentions strategies, let alone corporate-level strategies. The real-world firms which seem to have inspired his theory of the firm were not internationally operating concerns with a broad spectrum of activities and a need for subtle "configurations". Yet the need for co-

---

37 On this approach, see Wernerfelt (1984), Barney (1991), Peteraf (1993), Winter (1995) and the chapter 2 of the textbook by Collis/Montgomery (1997).

ordination was something he did emphasise strongly. Indeed, the enterprises of Gutenberg's theory gain a competitive advantage only by being particularly good at doing what was particularly important and also particularly difficult at the time he designed the theoretical structure of his *Grundlagen der Betriebswirtschafts-lehre*: producing at low costs, adjusting to changing circumstances, and protecting the enterprise from financial disequilibrium. Comparison with these basic, or strategic, needs, the attempt to exploit output market imperfections is of only secondary importance. The strategic imperatives always depend on the time and place. For his time, Gutenberg implicitly provided the appropriate strategic orientation and explicitly developed the instruments needed to implement the right strategy.

5.3 Theory of the firm and complementarity

5.3.1 The concept of complementarity

The idea of complementarity is a very simple one that is familiar to us from our everyday lives. Consider the example of an evening out at a restaurant. The experience comprises various elements, including the food, the drinks, the decor of the restaurant, the quality of the service and the price. Each person has her own idea of what a "successful evening out" means. It is immediately apparent that for an evening to be successful, the individual elements - food, wine, service, decor, etc. - must match or complement each other. No matter how good a wine is in itself, if it does not "go with" the food and the surroundings, its (enjoyment) value is lessened. Good restaurant managers offer complementary services at an appropriate price. This does not mean that, as a manager or a patron, one cannot or should not choose between different restaurants. However, the decision should not hinge solely on how good the food is at a particular restaurant. A harmonious relationship between food, wine, atmosphere and price is surely at least as important. One can assume that, of all the restaurants in Cologne, those at which everything fits together will be the most competitive. When a restaurant manager wants to upgrade his or her restaurant, he or she has to change many things at the same time, otherwise the customers may stop coming.

The attribute "complementary" can be applied to a system as a whole and to the elements of a given system. A system exhibits complementarity if its elements, or some of its elements, reinforce each other in terms of their respective effectiveness in better achieving the goal of that system, or, in other words, if its elements are themselves complementary. For the special case in which the system is a firm and the elements of the system are the productive activities performed in the firm, one can define the activities as complementary if "increases in the level of some activities raise the marginal productivity of the other activities" (Milgrom/Roberts, 1992, p. 118). In general, we call the elements of a system complementary if the value taken on by one of the elements determines which value of the other elements is optimal for the system *and* if a higher value of one (or some) element(s) has the effect that the optimal value for the other(s) is (are) also higher. However, the concept of complementarity can be applied to all kinds of systems, and its usefulness is not restricted to systems whose elements are measurable in numerical terms.

A system consisting of elements which are well (optimally) adjusted to each other can also be called a "regime". Competition - or some other process of selection - typically takes place between alternative regimes, as systems with well-adjusted elements, e.g. good restaurants of different styles, are the only relevant candidates for selection. Systems which have the property of complementarity, or regimes, adjust to changes in external parameters differently from those which do not have this property: regimes tend to be stable in the case of "small" changes of parameters, and to "break", i.e. to undergo far-reaching changes in the case of "large" parameter changes.[38]

Although complementarity may be no more than a difficult name for a common feature of everyday life, it may appear rather strange to an economist who is used to the standard assumption of convexity in economic models. Just imagine how a production system with complementarity would look in a three-dimensional graph relating two complementary inputs and one output. In contrast to the familiar shape of a hill whose gradient becomes flatter and flatter, the output surface resembles a mountain valley whose floor rises as we move further along it.

At the end of the first volume of Gutenberg's *Grundlagen*, we find a straightforward application of the concept of complementarity. The "principles" referred to above, which together define the various types of firms, must be consistent with one another; if they are not, only unproductive "frictions" occur (1983, pp. 507-510). The manner in which a similar idea seems to shape what Gutenberg has to say about planning and the role of the top management of a firm or enterprise, is discussed below.

5.3.2 Complementarity and organisation

The main elements of the organisation of an enterprise, which Brickley/Smith/Zimmerman (1997) aptly call "the organizational architecture" are the allocation of decision rights, the systems for measuring performance, and the reward system. All three of these main pillars of the architecture are composed of several building blocks. The allocation of decision rights includes organisational

---

38 See Milgrom/Roberts (1990, 1995) and, for the special case of financial systems, the empirical studies by Franks/Mayer (1995), Schmidt/Tyrell (1997) and Knobling (1999) and the game-theoretical model of regimes by Hackethal/Tyrell (1998). For the dynamic implications of complementarity in the case of national corporate governance systems, see Schmidt/Spindler (1998).

rules about who determines the use of certain assets; performance measurement system includes the stock market valuation of a firm as well as its internal accounting system; and rules for determining how higher-level positions are filled in a firm are a part of the reward system.

The concept of complementarity is extremely helpful to an understanding and assessing of a given organisational architecture. There is insufficient space to discuss details here.[39] Two simple examples of what constitutes a consistent architecture may suffice to demonstrate how important the consistency and the complementarity of a given system is. The following examples refer to the design of the job of an individual person working for a firm. Similar considerations could also be applied to a given department of a firm, a subsidiary of a multinational corporation or even to an entire large corporation. In the latter case, an analytically minded observer would try to demonstrate how the decision rights are allocated between the various organisational units, how the reward entitlements of the units are measured, how incentives are created for, and restrictions imposed on, people and organisational units; and whether all the elements are compatible with each other and well-adjusted to the technology and the market situation of the corporation and how they *therefore* contribute to its overall success.

As a first example, consider a job for which it is easy to measure performance by observing results. In this case it is possible to use strong financial incentives which depend only on the success which can be attributed to a given person; and it is not necessary to impose limitations on what that person can do or issue orders on what she should do. Given the financial incentives, her self-interest will make her do what is expected of her. At the same time it is possible, and also advisable, to locate this person outside the physical and legal boundaries of the firm, provided that, in fulfilling her tasks, she does not need, and does not use, important resources of the firm whose value depends on how carefully she handles them[40] The obvious example for such a job design is an independent sales agent working for an insurance company.[41]

However, performance-based pay is also possible for staff who work within the firm. An obvious case in point is that of the worker on an assembly line who has to perform very well-defined simple tasks. In this case, no high level of qualification is required, and there is thus also no need for either side, the worker or the firm, to undertake any major investment in firm-specific skills, i.e. in skills which

---

39 But see Brickley/Smith/Zimmerman (1997, chapters 8 - 14), Milgrom/Roberts (1992, esp. chapters 4 and 9) and Kreps (1997).

40 If her job could only be done well if she had resources at her disposal whose value to the firm depends on her handling of them, and if her care in using these resources could not be observed easily ex-post, her job would be more complex and her overall performance would be difficult to measure. In this case keeping her inside the firm would make economic sense.

41 See Holmström/Milgrom (1994).

the worker would not be able to use in another employment relationship. There is also no strong economic reason, from either point of view, why the employment relationship should be long-term; the firm could easily replace the worker, whilst he would unnecessarily give up his flexibility if he made a long-term commitment to one particular firm. On the contrary, as an assembly line typically requires a high level of physical capital investment and as the costs of physical capital cannot be adjusted in the short run, it is all the more important for a firm to be able to hire, fire and rehire workers as the situation demands without losing valuable investment in human capital, i.e. for it to remain flexible, at least as far as labour costs are concerned. This kind of employment policy is only acceptable for workers if, at any point in time, they have already received adequate compensation for all the work they have done for the firm.

As a second example, assume that the job of a given person is complex and comprises several tasks, requires close co-ordination with other people and therefore makes flexibility and firm-specific knowledge necessary. In this case the firm can typically not reward her on the basis of the performance of any given time span. Pay for performance requires that performance is easy to measure. It also undermines flexibility or, to put it another way, pay for performance is only appropriate if flexibility is not important in a job. The inflexibility results from the employee's fear of reduced pay if she were made to switch to some task which is, or appears to be, less well paid than her normal task on which the salary system is based. On the other hand, fixed, non-output-based salaries reduce work effort and provide an incentive for the staff to undertake activities which are not in the interests of the firm. Therefore in these cases the job design includes limiting the scope for the staff to exercise their discretion (Milgrom 1994), e.g. by designing open-plan offices, establishing precise office hours and requiring the presence of staff in the office even though, in the absence of "moral hazard", working in smaller offices, greater flexibility and even working at home would simply be more productive. Incentives to provide effort must be created through other devices such as internal promotion. But this will only have the intended effect of eliciting effort if the implicit promise that good work will be rewarded by a sequence of promotions is credible. Promotion is only a plausible "carrot" if the organisation has a hierarchy with many layers and provides an implicit employment guarantee. All of these organisational devices bond the firm and the employee together, as a consequence of which it is less risky and more rewarding for both sides to increase the qualification of the staff and to invest in firm-specific human capital, which in turn strengthens the mutual commitment - or increases the cost of discontinuing the employment relationship - and provides for greater flexibility of the firm.

As the examples of two vastly different job designs illustrate, *any* consistent organisational architecture relies on the complementary of its elements. This feature has implications for their development over time. It stabilises them, and at the same time makes it very difficult to change them even if a change is called for. It may be quite easy to change one or a few elements of an organisational architecture. However, such a change is likely to merely introduce inconsistencies into what had previously been a regime, a consistent system. Inconsistencies lead to visible problems, which call for fast solutions. The easiest way to solve such problems is to readjust the element that no longer fits in with the rest any more - which is why organisations revert to their old "architecture". A change of regime is only likely in the event of an acute crisis.[42] However, a simultaneous and comprehensive change in an enterprise is rarely limited to its organisation; it usually also includes its overall strategy.

5.3.3 Complementarity, organisation and strategy

Organisational architecture is not an end in itself. Its function is to create incentives and define people's, or units', scope for action such that it induces decisions and activities which improve the competitive position of the enterprise and thereby contribute to achieving its objectives. Organisational design is a part of the overall strategy and structure, and the combination of strategy and structure is again a complementary system. In addition to the organisational architecture, the elements of this system are the firm's resources, including its core competences, its products, its technology, its marketing strategy and even its governance system and its goals.

The inclusion of corporate governance and the firm's goals as endogenous elements of the overall system and strategy may appear strange, as these are typically regarded as given. It therefore needs to be explained. There is a reciprocal dependence between the financial structure and the governance of an enterprise, and these two variables jointly determine the goals which the management is likely to pursue. Thus financial structure, governance system and goals cannot be determined in isolation, and the combination of these elements should optimally be determined in the light of the enterprise's critical resources, because this combination determines the expectations, and therefore also the incentives, of employees, suppliers and customers. Their expectations and incentives are important determinants of the availability of resources, and partners, and of what a firm can gain from having those resources and from co-operating with those partners.[43]

The complementarity between the various elements of the system as a whole can best be illustrated by means of an example. The clearest real-world example is undoubtedly that of "Lincoln Electric", the subject of the most successful and, for many years, the best-selling Harvard Case Study (Lincoln Electric Company,

---

42 The example of a crisis-induced comprehensive change in the German car industry is discussed in Wiedeking (1995).

43 On theoretical and empirical aspects of the interdependence of financing and governance see Schmidt/Tyrell (1997). The nexus of finance/governance/goals and the expectations and incentives of resource providers is discussed in Schmidt/Spindler (1997) and Schmidt (1997).

1975). Every MBA student at a better American business school is exposed to this case for precisely the reason that it demonstrates so well what complementarity means and why it is important. At Lincoln, the organisation of production, the technology which is used, the sales and distribution system, the financing of the corporation and many more aspects harmonise so thoroughly that the entire system is extremely successful as a business enterprise.[44] Corporate governance and the company's goals are also part of the system at Lincoln Electric Company. It has implemented what amounts to de facto co-determination and its workers hold a large fraction of its shares. These features, which shape the governance system and the goals, are essential to the functioning and the stability of the overall system.[45]

Having an overall strategy and a comprehensive system is also not an end in itself. Consistency of the system is a necessary, but not a sufficient, condition for success. Precisely which internally consistent system would be best for a given enterprise *to have in place* depends on external factors such as its market, available technologies and the institutional, regulatory and political environment. (Brickley/Smith/Zimmerman, 1997, p. 147).

What system and strategy an enterprise can and should *adopt* at any given point in time also depends on its history and present situation. Given the requirement of complementarity between the elements of a system, it is extremely difficult to make piecemeal changes to the structure of the system. Moreover, consistent and stable expectations are required for the functioning of incentive systems and implicit contracts. And, last but not least, the functioning of system and strategy requires a great deal of non-transferable or "idiosyncratic" knowledge. The difficulty of arriving at a system and a strategy which are internally consistent and at the same time well-adapted to the environment has an interesting and important corollary. It is the reason why an enterprise which is consistent internally and well-adjusted to its environment is shielded from the forces of competition by an effective entry barrier. Complementarity thus turns out to be a "resource" which is hard for others to imitate even if they can easily see how valuable it is.[46]

What does this consideration imply with regard to the "essential" or strategic tasks of highest-level decision makers? Four tasks appear to be particularly important.

(1) Setting goals for the enterprise. Goals, in the sense of general principles to which an enterprise adheres, or strives to adhere, in its policy and operations are, *among other things*, a part both of the system of incentives and control which is so

---

44 See Milgrom/Roberts (1995).

45 The other well known example is Toyota's "modern manufacturing system". See Womack/Jones/Ross (1990) and Milgrom/Roberts (1990, 1992) on the systemic properties of Toyota.

46 See the account of failed attempts of competitors to imitate Lincoln's successful system in Milgrom/Roberts (1995, p. 203).

crucial for success, and of the implicit contracts between the corporation and its employees, suppliers, customers and other stakeholders. Even in a capitalist market economy in which the interests of owners or shareholders have a special weight, there are likely to be conflicts between the two roles of goals, namely, that of assuring that the enterprise is run in accordance with the interests of its owners, and that of providing incentives and orientation for those who enter into contracts with the enterprise. Therefore, the decisions involved in striking a balance between these two roles - defining the goals of the enterprise accordingly and communicating them effectively to all stakeholder groups - have to be taken at the highest level. Goals which might be considered acceptable insofar as they correspond closely enough to the different specific objectives of the various stakeholder groups might include the continued existence of an enterprise, a constant or increasing market share, and growth. However, entrusting the task of setting goals for the enterprise as a whole to its top management or its board of directors raises a problem of opportunism that should not be overlooked, since management itself and board members themselves are interested parties and will be tempted to use their mandate to pursue their own interests.[47]

(2) Determining strategy in the sense of "configuration and co-ordination" as defined by Collis and Montgomery (1997). Configuring resources and activities, co-ordinating departments and units, and ensuring that configuration and co-ordination are compatible with each other, are tasks reserved for top management because in a strictly complementary system decentralised, lower-level decision makers do not have sufficient information or incentives to generate the kind of co-ordination that would optimise the system as a whole. In many cases the internal relationships are structurally different from market relationships. Hence, attempts to use market-like mechanisms, such as internal transfer prices, to facilitate internal co-ordination processes may prove to be dysfunctional.[48]

(3) A firm's top management is responsible for creating a relationship of complementarity between the elements of the system as a whole, for consolidating and expanding this relationship and for ensuring that partial changes do not endanger the consistency of the system. This task should be conceived of, and implemented, in such a manner that not all impulses towards reform are smothered, and includes the idea that the management should define the boundaries of the firm. This is important because in most cases the properties of the system will be affected by whether certain activities are located within or outside the firm.

(4) A firm's top management must examine whether a system that is coherent is also still desirable, and, if not, must instigate a change of "regime" by introducing comprehensive reforms. Precisely because of its systemic implications, this task

---

47 See the sources in footnote 41 above.

48 See Neus (1997). In the recent theory of the firm, the main function of transfer prices is to control behaviour; see Baker/Gibbons/Murphy (1997).

cannot be carried out in a succession of individual steps but must rather be implemented in a single concerted and co-ordinated effort, which makes it probably the most difficult task of all.

The recent theory of the firm not only shows top management and board members what their important tasks are, but also makes it easier for them to accomplish these tasks. The insight that complementarity is a prerequisite for any successful strategy has reduced the set of alternatives which merit closer consideration. Strategies which are not based on complementarity will not work or could be imitated too easily, and therefore can be ruled out from the start.

It is almost unnecessary to point to the similarities between these considerations and what Gutenberg writes about the role of top management or, as he calls it, "the dispositive factor". Even though he does not refer to complementarity as the main reason why there are "genuine leadership decisions" which "can only be made from the point of view of the enterprise as a whole".[49] His description of these decisions is completely consistent with the most recent developments in the theory of the firm.

6 The theory of the firm as *Allgemeine Betriebswirtschaftslehre*

In contrast to the theory of the firm of the 1970s and 80s, which was almost exclusively concerned with issues of a theoretical and conceptual nature and thus removed from the main concerns of managers, the theory of the firm of the 1990s addresses problems of immediate practical relevance. It is particularly relevant for top management as it covers fundamental - or, as they are conventionally called, "strategic" - decisions with far-reaching and hard-to-reverse consequences for the entire enterprise which, almost by definition, fall into the domain of top management. In order to be able to make well-informed strategic decisions, top management needs to have a thorough understanding of

(1) how the complex system of production technology, marketing strategy, organisational design - including the relationship with suppliers and customers, financing and corporate governance - can be structured in a consistent and coherent manner;

(2) how the complementarities between the elements of this system can be turned into a competitive advantage; and

(3) how a lack of coherence can threaten the very existence of an enterprise.

---

49 Gutenberg (1983, p 134), defines "*echte Führungsentscheidungen*" as those which "*nur aus dem Ganzen des Unternehemens heraus getroffen werden können*".

In my view, the recent theory of the firm can claim, and has the potential, to become a *theory of general management.*[50] and at the same time a *general theory of business administration.*

I have already explained why I regard it as a theoretical basis for general management. It has much more to say about what top management should do and how they can do it than conventional approaches; and it also holds the promise of improving the quality and the reputation of management as an academic discipline.[51]

Given that its central topic is the interdependence of the various parts and functions of a firm, the recent theory of the firm is also a general theory of business administration or an *Allgemeine Betriebswirtschaftslehre* in the sense in which Gutenberg wanted his theory of the firm to form the basis for the academic discipline of business administration. Such an *Allgemeine Betriebswirtschaftslehre* would fit perfectly into his research programme of business administration as an economic discipline.[52] For many years, the question of whether we still need an *Allgemeine Betriebswirtschaftslehre* and what it should be about has been a contentious issue among professors of business administration in German-speaking countries. In recent, strongly worded, contributions, Professors Schneider (1990) and Elschen (1995) contended that *Allgemeine Betriebswirtschaftslehre* should be at the centre of business administration in a double sense namely, that it should investigate, on the basis of economics, what constitute the central aspects of an enterprise; and that this research should have a central place in the research agenda and in teaching. I concur with this view. The recent theory of the firm can perhaps help to make this wish become reality, and thus protect the *Allgemeine Betriebswirtschaftslehre* from being no more than a repository for all those academically unattractive bits and pieces which the various sub-disciplines like accounting, finance and marketing fail to cover, or a diluted version of what these

50 And indeed, this is precisely how it has recently come to be regarded at those American business schools which are actively conducting research into this field, e.g. Harvard (Jensen, Baker, Montgomery and others), MIT (Holmström), Stanford (Milgrom, Roberts, Kreps), Rochester (Brickley and others) and Northwestern University (Besanko and others).

51 According to the view of some critical observers (notably Schneider, 1997, p.441), at present management as an academic subject has little to offer apart from an incoherent mixture of bombastic rhetoric, the main function of which is to ease the minds of managers who fear that they might not be able to do what they are expected to do and that others might notice this *("Dompteursprache"* and *"Manatschment-Gequatschment")*, and management techniques with little economic substance.

52 Gutenberg was awarded several honorary doctoral degrees for maintaining close ties between business administration and economics and for resisting the drift of business administration into an eclectic discipline based mainly on the social sciences.

sub-disciplines teach anyway without paying due attention to how they are related.[53]

The position advanced by Schneider and Elschen and, by implication, also by Gutenberg, can be strengthened by drawing a parallel between discussions *within* the recent theory of the firm and discussions *about* the role and content of a theory of general management and of a general theory of business administration. In almost the same way that corporate strategy should consist in establishing and safeguarding complementarity in a corporation, thereby enabling that firm to gain a competitive advantage, so general management, as an academic discipline, should focus on complementarity in research and teaching, thereby offering leadership and orientation to business research in specialised fields such as accounting, marketing and finance, and thus strengthening the entire discipline. If the role and content of *Allgemeine Betriebswirtschaftslehre* are seen in this light, general management can again become the core of business administration, as it was in Erich Gutenberg's conception of the discipline - and that would certainly increase the attractiveness of business studies for scholars and students.

7 References

Albach, H. (1981): The Nature of the Firm - A Production-theoretical Viewpoint; in: Journal of Institutional and Theoretical Economics, Vol. 137, pp. 717 - 722

Albach, H. (1988): Editorial; in: Zeitschrift für Betriebswirtschaft, Vol. 58, pp. 3 - 10

Albach, H. (1991): Betriebswirtschaftslehre als Wissenschaft; in: Zeitschrift für Betriebswirtschaft, Supplement 3/93, pp. 7 - 26

Alchian, A. (1993): Thoughts on the Theory of the Firm; in: Journal of Institutional and Theoretical Economics, Vol. 149, pp. 365 - 369

Alchian, A./Demsetz, H. (1972): Production, Information Costs, and Economic Organization; in: American Economic Review, Vol. 62, pp. 777 - 795

Allen, F./Gale, D. (1997): Comparative Financial Systems: Competition vs. Insurance; unpublished manuscript; Philadelphia

---

53 The evocative German terms coined by Schneider (1990) and revived by Elschen (1995, p. 205) for the conflicting positions are *Kernforschung* [literally: nuclear research] for the research that focuses on the central issues and is located at the centre of the discipline, *Ramschladen* [literally: junk shop] for the collection of unintersting bits and pieces, and *Dünnaufguß* [literally: weak brew] for the watered-down version of the main lessons of the specialised subfields.

Baker, G./Gibbons, R./Murphy, K.J. (1997): Implicit Contracts and the Theory of the Firm; Working Paper; Harvard Business School; Boston, MA

Barney, J. (1991): Firm Resources and Strategic Competitive Advantage; in: Journal of Management, Vol. 17, pp. 99 - 120

Berle, A.A./Means, G.C. (1932): The Modern Corporation and Private Property; New York

Brickley, J.A./Smith, C.B./Zimmerman, J.L. (1997): Managerial Economics and Organizational Architecture, Chicago et al. 1997

Chandler, A.D. (1962): Strategy and Structure; Cambridge, MA

Coase, R.H. (1937): The Nature of the Firm; in: Economica, N.S., Vol. 4, pp. 386 - 405

Collis, D.J./Montgomery, C.A. (1997): Corporate Strategy - Resources and the Scope of the Firm; Chicago et al.

Demsetz, H. (1991): The Theory of the Firm Revisited; in: Williamson, O.E. /Winter, S. (eds.): The Nature of the Firm - Origin, Evolution and Development; New York

Dunning, J.H. (1988): The New Style Multinationals - Circa the late 1980s and early 1990s; in: Dunning, J.H. (ed.): Explaining International Production; London; pp. 327 - 347

Elschen, R. (1995): Was ist das Allgemeine in der "Allgemeinen Betriebswirtschaftslehre"?; in: Elschen, R./Siegel, T./Wagner, F. (eds.): Unternehmenstheorie und Besteuerung, Festschrift für D. Schneider; Wiesbaden; pp. 203 - 227

Fama, E. (1980): Agency Problems and the Theory of the Firm; in: Journal of Political Economy, Vol. 88, pp. 288 - 307

Fama, E./Jensen. M. (1983a): Separation of Ownership and Control; in: Journal of Law and Economics, Vol. 26, pp. 301 - 326

Fama, E./Jensen. M. (1983b): Agency Problems and Residual Claims; in: Journal of Law and Economics, Vol. 26, pp. 327 - 349

Franks, J./Mayer, C. (1995): Ownership and Control; in: Siebert, H. (ed.): Trends in Business Organization: Do Participation and Co-operation Increase Competitiveness?; Tübingen; pp. 171 - 195

Grossman, S./Hart, O. (1986): The Costs and Benefits of Ownership: A Theory of Vertical and Lateral Integration; in: Journal of Political Economy, Vol. 94, pp. 691 - 719

Gutenberg, E. (1929): Die Unternehmung als Gegenstand betriebswirtschaftlicher Theorie; Berlin et al.

Gutenberg, E. (1951/1983): Grundlagen der Betriebswirtschaftslehre, Vol. 1: Die Produktion; 1st edition 1951; 24th edition 1983; Berlin et al.

Gutenberg, E. (1955/1984): Grundlagen der Betriebswirtschaftslehre, Vol. 2: Der Absatz; 1st edition 1955; 17th edition 1984; Berlin et al.

Gutenberg, E. (1969/1980): Grundlagen der Betriebswirtschaftslehre, Vol. 3: Die Finanzen; 1st edition 1969; 8th edition 1980; Berlin et al.

Gutenberg, E. (1958): Einführung in die Betriebswirtschaftslehre; Wiesbaden

Gutenberg, E. (1962): Unternehmensführung - Organisation und Entscheidungen; Wiesbaden

Gutenberg, E. (1989): Zur Theorie der Unternehmung: Schriften und Reden von Erich Gutenberg; H. Albach (ed.); Wiesbaden

Hackethal, A./Tyrell, M. (1998): Complementarity and Financial Systems – A Theoretical Approach; Finance Working Paper, Johann Wolfgang Goethe-Universität; Frankfurt/Main, (revised English version)

Grochla, E. (ed.)(1990): Handbook of German Business Management; Stuttgart

Hart, O. (1993): An Economist's View of Fiduciary Duties; London School of Economics Discussion Paper; London

Hart, O. (1995): Firms, Contracts and Financial Structure; Oxford

Heinen, E. (1962): Die Zielfunktion der Unternehmung; in: Koch, H. (ed.): Zur Theorie der Unternehmung; Festschrift zum 65. Geburtstag von Erich Gutenberg; Wiesbaden

Heinen, E. (1976): Grundfragen der entscheidungsorientierten Betriebswirtschaftslehre; Munich

Holmström, B./Milgrom, P. (1991): Multitask Principal-Agent Analyses: Incentive Contracts, Asset Ownership, and Job Design; in: Journal of Law, Economics and Organization, Vol. 7 (Special Issue), pp. 24 - 52

Holmström, B./Milgrom, P. (1994): The Firm as an Incentive System; in: American Economic Review, Vol. 84, pp. 972 - 991

Holmström, B./Tirole, J. (1989): The Theory of the Firm; in: Schmalensee, R./ Willig, R. (eds.): Handbook of Industrial Organization, Vol.1; Amsterdam et al.; pp. 61 - 133

Jensen, M. (1983): Organization Theory and Methodology; in: Journal of Accounting Research, Vol. 58, pp. 319 - 339

Jensen, M./Meckling, W. (1976): Theory of the Firm: Managerial Behavior, Agency Costs and Ownership Structure; in: Journal of Financial Economics, Vol. 3, pp. 305 -360

Knobling, P. (1999: Die Interdependenz von Unternehmensverfassung und Unternehmensfinanzierung bei börsennotierten Aktiengesellschaften; Frankfurt/Main (forthcoming)

Köhler, R. (1966): Theoretische Systeme der Betriebswirtschaftslehre; Stuttgart

Kosiol, E. (1966): Die Unternehmung als wirtschaftliches Aktionszentrum; Reinbek bei Hamburg

Kreps, D. (1990): A Course in Microeconomic Theory; New York et al.

Kreps, D. (1997): Human Resource Management: A Strategic Approach; unpublished manuscript; Stanford

Laux, C. (1996): Kapitalstruktur und Verhaltenssteuerung; Wiesbaden

Lincoln Electric Company (1975): Harvard Business School, Case Study No. 376-028

Machlup, F. (1967): Theories of the Firm: Marginalist, Behavioral, Managerial; in: American Economic Review, Vol. 57, pp. 1 - 33

Milgrom, P./Roberts, J. (1990): The Economics of Modern Manufacturing: Technology, Strategy and Organization; in: American Economic Review, Vol. 80, pp. 511 - 528

Milgrom, P./Roberts, J. (1992): Economics, Organization and Management; Englewood Cliffs, NJ

Milgrom, P./Roberts, J. (1995): Complementarities and Fit: Strategy, Structure and Organizational Change in Manufacturing; in: Journal of Accounting and Economics, Vol. 19, pp. 179 - 208

Neus, W. (1997): Verrechnungspreise - Rekonstruktion des Marktes innerhalb der Unternehmung?; in: Die Betriebswirtschaft, Vol. 57, pp. 38 - 47

Nicklisch, H. (1928): Grundfragen für die Betriebswirtschaftslehre; Stuttgart

Ordelheide, D./Rudolph, B./Büsselmann, E. (eds.) (1991): Betriebswirtschaftslehre und ökonomische Theorie; Stuttgart

Peteraf, M.A. (1993): The Cornerstones of Competitive Advantage: A Resource-Based View; in: Strategic Management Journal, Vol. 13, pp. 179 - 191

Picot, A./Dietl, H./Franck, E. (1997): Organisation: Eine ökonomische Perspektive; Stuttgart

Porter, M. (1980): Competitive Strategy; New York

Porter, M. (1985): Competitive Advantage; New York

Porter, M. (1994): Toward a Dynamic Theory of Strategy; in: Rumelt, R./Schendel, D./Teece, D. (eds.): Fundamental Issues in Strategy - A Research Agenda; Boston, MA

Schauenberg, B. (1993): Theorien der Unternehmung; in: Wittmann, W. et al. (eds.): Handwörterbuch der Betriebswirtschaftslehre, 5th edition, sub-volume 3; Stuttgart; columns 4168 - 4182

Schauenberg, B./Schmidt, R.H. (1983): Vorarbeiten zu einer Theorie der Unternehmung; in: Kappler, E. (ed.): Rekonstruktion der Betriebswirtschaftslehre als ökonomische Theorie; Spardorf; pp. 247 - 276

Schmidt, R.H. (1995): Die Grenzen der (Theorie der) multinationalen Unternehmung; in: Bühner, R./Haase, K./Wilhelm, J. (eds.): Die Dimensionierung des Unternehmens; Stuttgart; pp. 73 - 95

Schmidt, R.H. (1997): Corporate Governance: The Role of Other Constituencies; in: Pezard, A./Thiveaud, J.M. (eds.): Corporate Governance: Les perspectives internationales; Paris, pp. 61 - 74

Schmidt, R.H./Spindler, G. (1997): Shareholder-Value zwischen Ökonomie und Recht; in: Assmann, H.D. et al. (eds.): Wirtschaft- und Medienrecht in der offenen Demokratie, Festschrift für F. Kübler; Heidelberg; pp. 515 – 555

Schmidt, R.H./Spindler, G. (1998): Path Dependence, Complementarity and Corporate Governance: A Comment on Bebchuk and Roe; Working Paper Finance & Accounting, Johann Wolfgang Goethe-Universität Frankfurt

Schmidt, R.H./Terberger, E. (1997): Grundzüge der Investitions- und Finanzierungstheorie; 4th edition; Wiesbaden

Schmidt, R.H./Tyrell, M. (1997): Financial Systems, Corporate Finance and Corporate Governance; in: European Financial Management, Vol. 3, pp. 333-361

Schneider, D. (1985): Allgemeine Betriebswirtschaftslehre; 2nd edition; Munich

Schneider, D. (1990): Verfehlte Erwartungen an eine Allgemeine Betriebswirtschaftslehre in Lehre und Forschung; in: Die Betriebswirtschaft, Vol. 50, pp. 272 - 280

Schneider, D. (1993): Betriebswirtschaftslehre, Vol. 1: Grundlagen; Munich

Schneider, D. (1997): Betriebswirtschaftslehre, Vol. 3: Theorie der Unternehmung; Munich

Sweezy, Paul M. (1939): Demand under Conditions of Oligopoly, Journal of Political Economy, Vol. 47, pp. 568-573.

Shephard, R.W. (1953): Cost and Production Function, Princeton.

Terberger, E. (1994): Neo-institutionalistische Ansätze; Wiesbaden

Wernerfelt, B. (1984): A Resource-Based View of the Firm; in: Strategic Management Journal, Vol. 4, pp. 171 - 180

Wiedeking, W. (1995): Reengineering und Restrukturierung am Beispiel der Porsche AG; in: Schmalenbach-Gesellschaft (ed.): Reengineering - Kongreßdokumentation; Stuttgart; pp. 205 - 217

Williamson, O. (1975): Markets and Hierarchies: Analysis and Antitrust Implications; New York et al.

Williamson, O. (1985): The Economic Institutions of Capitalism; New York et al.

Winter, S.G. (1995): Four R's of Profitability: Rents, Resources, Routines and Replication; in: Montgomery, C.A. (ed.): Resource-Based and Evolutionary Theories of the Firm: Towards a Synthesis; Boston, MA; pp. 147 - 178

Wöhe, G. (1959): Methodologische Grundprobleme der Betriebswirtschaftslehre; Meisenheim

Wöhe, G. (1996): Einführung in die Allgemeine Betriebswirtschaftslehre; 1st edition 1960; 19th edition 1996; Munich

Womack, J.P./Jones, D.T./Roos, D.S. (1990): The Machine that Changed the World; New York

The "Unified Basis" as a Starting Point for Business Economic Analysis

Remarks on some core issues in the theory of the firm on the occasion of the centenary of the birth of Erich Gutenberg

W. Schüler[1]

Overview

- Erich Gutenberg took the firm's productivity relation as the "unified basis" from which he developed a self-contained, integrated theory of the firm. The transaction, the exchange of goods and services between economic agents, which is viewed in microeconomic theory as the "most fundamental unit of analysis" contrasts with Gutenberg's theory. This paper compares the two conceptions with special reference to their depiction of the firm as an organization.

- The basic assumptions lead to conceptions of the firm as a value-creating system on the one hand, and nexus of contracts on the other. In several areas the two conceptions are complementary. However, they differ radically in that the business economist cannot dispense with the assumption of a "disposition factor" – and this already begins in explaining the firm's existence.

- There are also significant differences in respect of the notion of a firm as an organization. In the case of a value-creating system, structure and behavior are analyzed and designed pre-eminently from the perspective of effectiveness. However, the view of the firm as a nexus of contracts concentrates on the efficient coordination of goods and services offered to, and by, that firm. Whilst the limits of the firm dominate the question of structure, the importance of trust for the management tasks seems to be an underestimated behavioral assumption.

Keywords: Theory of the Firm, Productivity Relation, Transaction

---

1 Prof. Dr. Dr. h.c. Wolfgang Schüler, former chair of business economics, especially management and organization, Otto-von-Guericke-University Magdeburg, P.O.B. 4120, D-39016 Magdeburg.

1 Introduction

Developing a theory of the firm from a single "unified basis" was the vision of Erich Gutenberg. He felt this as the challenge of his time noting that business economics had often encountered the objection, "that its subject-matter lacks the self-contained unified character of a great scientific conception", (Gutenberg [1967], p. 22f.). The foundation on which such a unification could be built was, in his view, the productivity relation determined within the firm: "The basic idea on which my conception of the firm is constructed ... is the conceptual interpretation of the production process as a combining process ... I believed that only in this way it would be possible, starting from a unified fundamental idea, to attain that systematic self-contained character and logic for my researches which I had in my mind as my final goal", (Gutenberg [1953], p. 334). Consequently, his three-volume "*Foundations of business economics*" ("*Grundlagen der Betriebswirtschaftslehre*") start with an analysis of production (volume 1). Using this foundation, he next deals with the sale of end-products (volume 2) and then with the financing of the liquidity gap between sales revenues and payments for factor inputs (volume 3). In this way he therefore realized his vision in a logically comprehensive manner.

Subsequently many proposals for placing other aspects at the center have been made. For instance, in Germany "marketing" replaced Gutenberg's "sales", and emerged with the pretension of being the genesis of all considerations and action within the firm. Later it was contended that investment (and financing) constituted the central entrepreneurial activity and that the firm should be viewed as a cash flow system. Finally it was argued that, with the progressive differentiation of the subject-matter, the more aesthetic ideal of a unified theory based on a single fundamental conception should be abandoned for pragmatic reasons.

Nevertheless, the question of a unified basic concept continues to haunt the discipline. Decades after Gutenberg's discourse on the "unified basis", and doubtless quite independently of him, an almost identical formulation, which can be traced back to Commons [1934], is thrown into the debate. Milgrom and Roberts refer to a "most fundamental unit of analysis", ([1992], p. 21). However, this time it is a matter of a unified basis of analysis for microeconomic theory in its entirety in a sense which would obviously comprise business economic theory of the German type, were Milgrom and Roberts acquainted with it. As the fundamental unit of analysis the authors adopt the transaction, the exchange of goods and services between two individuals acting as economic agents. But, in Gutenberg's concept, reference to a *fundamental* unit is justified by viewing the productivity relation as the real essence of the firm's existence and from which all other functions derive. In contrast, the Milgrom / Roberts concept emphasizes a more methodological perspective. Since all activities, which deal with goods and services as well as with financial matters, reduce to exchange relations, transactions, as tools which are independent of their contents, are seen to be fundamental.

The two alternatives lead to rather different perspectives of the firm. In Gutenberg's view, which, from a practical standpoint has implicitly remained up-to-date in applied analysis (from Porter's value creating chains to the business process oriented organizational design), one would today refer to the firm as a value creating system. On the other hand, as exchanges of goods and services are agreed upon in contracts, a firm can be viewed as a nexus of contracts. This is the perspective that takes pride of place in today's microeconomic theory.

The two basic concepts are examined below in respect both of their implications and their capacities to explain important phenomena. Also examined hereafter are the resultant insights into organizational structures and processes and the interrelationship between the two concepts in respect of the "unity of economics" as a program.

2 Understanding the Firm

2.1 The Firm as a Value Creating System

2.1.1 Basic Features of the Notion

Production and consumption are, along with exchange and saving, the basic activities of the "managing" man. This is the origin of the definition of firms as economic units with production, or more generally, the creation of values as their central aim. Simultaneously, their productive performance provides the social legitimation for the existence of firms which can be formed, without restrictions, also by individuals. Here the term production may be interpreted in a rather wide sense. Assuming goods are characterized not only by quality but also by quantity, time and place of availability, each transformation with respect to one of these parameters, e.g. also distribution, may be viewed as a productive operation.

Gutenberg's definition of the firm is substantiated by the principles of action that a firm pursues; in addition it has two levels. In his diction "works" *("Betriebe")* are economic units (1), which combine productive factors to produce new goods and services, whilst (2) conforming to economic principles and (3) attaining a financial equilibrium. Additionally, "firms" *("Unternehmen")* can themselves decide upon their activities with respect to profit maximizing expectations in contrast to those who, in a non-market economy, receive orders from central planning institutions. Thus, firms are characterized in particular by their ability to act autonomously in choosing their goals and realizing their plans.

In contrast, the traditional neoclassic theory characterizes the firm with a production function representing the given technology, and a set of possible alternative production plans. The remaining management problem is to find, and realize, the short-term profit maximum given by the cost function (determined implicitly by the production function) and the assumed market conditions. In particular the firm so defined is unaware of organizational problems and, as the sole decision maker, the entrepreneur forms and implements his intentions himself and alone.

Juxtaposed with the traditional view just outlined, the detailed analysis of the productivity relation in German business economics, and pre-eminently the Gutenbergian influence, have hardly been recognised in microeconomics as important developments. The Gutenbergian entrepreneur does not receive a heaven-sent production function and has to do more than simply choose a technology. He *combines* production factors and makes arrangements concerning each of them in respect of different conditions and their productiveness.

The production factors elaborated by Gutenberg – labor, production equipment, materials and supplies – are analyzed in his theory in detail. As opposed to the aggregative terms of microeconomics – labor, land and capital – it is only a short step to the persons supplying these factors. Apropos of the emphasis that was a feature of his day he notes: "The notion of factor combination leads immediately to the problems of human existence at the workplace with its frustrating consequences, but also in many cases to possibilities with which one can be delighted. This proximity to the firm's reality has caused me to conceive of the firm's process as a combination process and to choose it as the basis of my conception" (Gutenberg [1989], p. 75). Here something other than the purely formal production function construct that is known to neoclassical economics is obviously intended.

2.1.2 The "Disposition" Factor

New above all is Gutenberg's "disposition" factor, which embraces the entire array of managerial decision problems – from the setting of goals and planning, organization and operational decisions, to updating plans in response to the results of controls. "If ... firms in their capacities as individual phenomena are made the special subject of their own discipline, as in business economics, then the governance function, the exercise of which is a "disposition" task, cannot be omitted," (Gutenberg [1989], p. 67/68). Whilst the "disposition" factor does not appear explicitly in the production function, or in the corresponding cost function, it nevertheless influences their shape, as is readily apparent in the case of a reorganization.

That means, in contrast to the microeconomic view which because of its aggregative approach takes an external bird's-eye view, that here certain problems of detail are even perceived at all and viewed simultaneously from the inside. This has consequences both for the questions to be asked and for the answers to be given.

Thus from this perspective, for instance, the question of why firms exist at all is of no special interest. For if the individual who manages his own affairs has to produce, to perform something for his survival, the concept of the firm does not assume a multi-person basis which makes that relationship the focal point. From this worm's eye view, which is focused on the details of managerial decisions, the question of the conditions for the emergence of firms comes down to those of *autonomous acting*. Gutenberg discussed these conditions in his deliberations on the relations between the firm and the economic system.

Why and when firms emerge – from this viewpoint the question was answered realistically by analyzing the conditions of self-employment resulting from the economic, legal and administrative systems, i.e. the institutional framework, together with the characteristic features of the founders e.g., vision, motivation, ability, venturesome nature, etc. Consequently, Gutenberg ([1929], p. 11) regards the emergence of firms as a "conscious and creative human act", the result of man's creative power.

2.2 The Firm as a Nexus of Contracts

2.2.1 The Basic Concept

From a microeconomic viewpoint an economy is formed by a set of economic agents each of whom is equipped with a given bundle of goods and services, who enter an exchange process whilst aiming at a Pareto-optimal (and in this sense efficient) allocation of resources. This notion of an economic system should be understood in a most general manner. It should comprise the "economy as a whole" at the highest level as well as its subsystems, for example, a particular (partial) market or a firm; (cf. Milgrom / Roberts [1992], p. 19-20).

Each transaction is executed within a particular institutional framework which also embodies a so-called governance structure (Williamson). The latter helps to resolve contentious interpretations of contracts and therefore how far a party can pursue its claims. The transaction costs of an exchange depend not least on this institution. The central thesis says that for each transaction type – it is not necessary to discuss the features here in detail – the institutional framework leading to minimal transaction costs will be chosen.

The two most important institutional alternatives considered are markets and hierarchical firms. Market transaction costs comprise different components (costs of gathering information on potential parties to a contract and their standing, costs of concluding or modifying a contract, costs of conflicts and possible litigation, etc.). In the case of a firm, the costs of maintaining an hierarchical management system are treated as the most important transaction costs.

On this view, a firm emerges if at least two economic agents conclude that exchanging their goods and/or services under the roof of an enterprise would lead to lower transaction costs than if each continued to act alone in the market. Formally a firm thus results from contracts between agents. Following Jensen / Meckling [1976], a firm is viewed as a "nexus of contracts", which represents an alternative to the market as a mode of coordination.

2.2.2 Demarcating the Firm and Market

The foregoing implicit definition of the firm suffers from a lack of precision in that it has no significant feature such as, for example, the "disposition" factor, which indicates how to recognize any given set of contracts as a firm. This ultimately becomes a question of how the limits to the market, as the alternative coordinating institution, should be conceived, how this institution should work and what it is able to perform. Here it is necessary explicitly to differentiate between two variants which hitherto have been distinguished no more than implicitly in the literature, if at all.

The first variant starts from the immediately intuitive notion of coordination via the market through the price mechanism and the related information processes. Suppliers and demanders of goods and services are initially self-employed economic agents who find each other via the market. There are transaction costs on both sides and the conditions of exchange are determined by the market. The remaining question concerns the design of the contracts between the parties. The pre-eminent question is whether discrete performances should be agreed upon immediately; or, whether outline agreements should constitute a framework which enables one party to order discrete performances by the other which can be precisely specified later. This second case can be regarded as the genesis of a firm. Hart ([1990], p.159) describes the consequences of this viewpoint rather impressively: "The firm is simply a nexus of contracts, and there is therefore little point in trying to distinguish between transactions within a firm and those between firms; rather, both categories of transactions are part of a continuum of types of contractual relations, with different firms or organizations simply representing different points on this continuum". Perhaps even more lucid is the key formulation of Jensen / Meckling as cited also by Hart ([1990], p.159). Thus, viewing its contractual relations as an essential aspect of the firm "...serves to make it clear that the personalization of the firm implied by asking questions as 'what should be the objective function of the firm' ... is seriously misleading. *The firm is not an individual.* ... The 'behavior' of the firm is like the behavior of a market, i.e., the outcome of a complex equilibrium process", (cf. Jensen / Meckling [1976], p. 311).

In that the latter proposition treats the individuality of the firm as an absurdity, whilst the modern theory of management strongly emphasizes *corporate identity*, it can rightly be questioned whether such a concept can contribute to an understanding of reality. That the boundaries of the firm become problematical when use is made of the multiplicity of possible contractual arrangements is indisputable precisely because of the recent tendency to concentrate on core competences and the outsourcing of activities. On the other hand it is equally apparent that, for its very existence, a firm (as a whole) needs the "disposition" factor for which the market has *no* analogue at its disposal.

Therefore some authors (e.g. Salvatore [1996], p.8) start immediately with the second interpretation indicated above, namely, that the market is only able to serve as an *instrument* that is used also by individual economic agents (who are more explicitly described as *entrepreneurs*). They thus circumvent the logical-systematical, though hardly implementable, construction whereby *entrepreneurial behavior* is characterized as occuring within a firm only if it buys at least one of the inputs needed for its end-product(s) within the framework of an incomplete contract. The "disposition" factor that is peculiar to the *entrepreneur* also contains the productive-innovative element of management: without it no team production in the sense of Alchian / Demsetz [1972] would be planned, without it there would be no new products, the markets for which emerge only after they are launched.

2.2.3 Specifying the Concept of the Firm

The notion of the firm as "nexus of contracts" not only lacks any reference to the specific quality and the indispensable role of individual parties. Within microeconomics itself voices are also to be heard which emphasize that this approach doesn't contribute enough to answering the question of what a firm actually is. They contend that real progress results from the transition to interpreting the firm as a set of property rights. It then becomes possible to "identify a firm with all the non-human assets that belong to it", (cf. Hart [1990], p.160). This completes "the basic ingredients of a theory of the firm. In a world of transaction costs and incomplete contracts, ex-post residual rights of control are important because, through their influence on asset usage, they affect ex-post bargaining power and the division of ex-post surplus in a relationship", (cf. Hart [1990], p.161). Hart illustrates these statements – including the contention that the boundaries of a firm matter when contracts are incomplete – with several impressive examples, (cf. Hart [1990], p.160-164).

Furthermore in the search for greater precision it is helpful to consider the internal content rather than the formal character of the "nexus of contracts" which constitutes the firm. This means however that the idea behind the contracts is possibly more important for understanding the firm than the contracts themselves. In the same way Gutenberg in his day recommended that business administration should not halt at the accounting statements but should analyze the underlying facts and relationships which first manifest themselves in those statements only at the end of the entrepreneurial process.

What however is the essence of this network, what does microeconomic theory's great jump from the "firm as a production function" to the "firm as a nexus of contracts" really say? Fama ([1980], p. 289) describes it with one sentence: "The firm is viewed as a set of contracts *among factors of production*", (italicised by the author).

2.3 Comparison: Different Tasks for Firms and Markets

2.3.1 Complementary Nature of Concepts

Fama's formulation represents nothing more than the rediscovery of the factor combination stressed earlier by Gutenberg. Of course, in the context of contract design it appears in a new light. However, Gutenberg also had the individual offering the factor clearly in view. In this regard the proposition already cited above from "Rückblicke", (Gutenberg [1989] can again be mentioned. The expression "combining factors" *also* means designing contracts. On the other hand in Fama's formulation there is no hint of the role of the "disposition" factor. In his view this role coincides with that of the supplier of an elemental factor. This is therefore a question of supplementing Gutenberg's perspective, not of negating it.

Returning to our starting point, namely, the comparison of transaction and productivity relations as fundamental units of analysis; the implication is that both are needed and that the one cannot be a substitute for the other. Conceptual content and practical realization of a factor combination are the core tasks which are to be resolved by reference to *effectiveness* criteria (instead of *efficiency* criteria alone).

This is also valid if, following Engelhardt / Freiling ([1995], p. 903), it is assumed that the participation of the customer in the supplier's production process is generally necessary. One might accept this thesis as a plea for a perspective interpreting the firm's supply of goods and/or services in today's competitive conditions in a broad sense as those of service providers – it is indisputable that services require the contribution of an "external factor" by the customer. But it is less clear that "criticizing Gutenberg's system" (ibd.) had to start here. Combining factors as an act of "disposition" does not imply merely "the assumption of a rigid connection between input and output via a production function", (Engelhardt / Freiling ([1995], p. 904). Combining factors remains a central task of *firms* and not of markets even if "considering the interactive process between supplier and customer in detail" (ibid.) is assumed to be necessary for understanding the emergence of equilibria; under the same market conditions some firms survive, others fail.

On the other hand, the preparation of the factors and distribution of outputs constitute the transaction functions, the analysis of which has in fact experienced an essential enrichment from contract theory. But the mere existence of contracts regulating the receipt of inputs and delivery of outputs leaves open essential details of the real combination process as it is analyzed in Gutenbergian "traditional" business economics.

2.3.1 Market and Firm are not Alternatives

This reasoning demonstrates that the conceptual construct, which treats the institutions market and firm as alternative patterns of coordination and seeks to explain their separate emergence, is not logically defensible. Markets and firms have different tasks; for instance, no market is able to coordinate offers of goods like flour, eggs, milk, and raisins etc. and thereby produce a cake. An "entrepreneur," an individual, or a unit which organizes economic activity, is always needed to plan the productivity relations and use the market if need be. If the facts are precisely evaluated – perhaps to the extent of a quantitative modeling as, for example, in Malone [1988] – it becomes readily apparent that the true alternative to the production of complex outputs by firms as suppliers lies in the fact that the *demander*, rather than the market, takes on the "disposition" task. In some circumstances (cf. Engelhardt / Freiling [1995]) the "disposition" task of the production conception is resolved jointly by the supplier and demander. However, as an institution, the market is, of itself, capable of no more than the coordinating of the allocation of existing goods and services in the narrowest sense.

One of the few situations in which markets and firms appear, at least at first glance, more as substitutes than as complements is the well known "*make or buy*"-problem, i.e. the question of whether a firm should produce a necessary input itself or buy it via the market. This decision can, following Williamson [1975], perhaps be regarded most readily as the choice between the institutions "market" and "firm" as alternative forms of coordination, and thus the transaction can be interpreted as the more basic procedure. But even this *"make or buy"* problem emerges only from the perspective of an already *existing* firm. It is not therefore logically consistent to discuss the firm's existence from this standpoint and, as it were, to remove the initial assumptions in the course of the argument. The necessity of the "disposition" factor as the core of the firm, that is, the insight that production as a factor combination together with all the related administrative considerations (from strategic planning to cost minimizing operations management) constitutes more than simply the coordination of factor inputs, cannot be circumvented.

2.3.3 Necessity of Corporate Identity

This in fact is the clear counterpart to Jensen / Meckling. Their contention that the firm, like the market, neither has nor needs its own identity and objective function (from which, for example, the productivity relations are derived and, as necessary, modified), no longer refers to the firm that is of interest to the manager. Consequently something like "management" is apparently a completely empty and superfluous notion and everything connected with it, for example creating a corporate identity, must be obsolete. Of corporate strategy Williamson ([1991], p.76) concisely states "economy is the best strategy".

Other microeconomists however seem rather uneasy and are seeking to fill the gap between the latter implications on the one hand and reality on the other. Thus, for example, the index of the book by Milgrom / Roberts [1992] shows five entries referring to "*corporate culture*" and Kreps ([1990a], p. 766) states, "It should certainly come as no surprise that firms and other organizations carry reputations, or even that for some firms their reputation is as valuable an asset as they have". However, when Kreps addresses himself to the creation of reputation, he discusses the behavior of a single player, in a sequence of games, who cannot be equated with a firm defined as a nexus of contracts! The logical conflict is resolved only when – in the sense of the second alternative mentioned above – the individual can operate as a firm subject to the condition that s/he supplies only her(his) individual output of goods and/or services and enters no contracts on inputs whatsoever.

3 Organization

3.1 Organization as an Instrument of Value Creation

In contrast to the firm in traditional microeconomic theory, which is identified with a production function, the conception of the firm that is founded on the productivity relation knows not only the actual strategic planning objectives implicit in profit maximization but also the *organization* of the firm.

This organization can be regarded as an intangible mechanism, as an "apparatus for realizing the objectives which result from planning", (cf. Gutenberg [1951], vol. 1). Therefore one speaks of an instrumental, or functional, notion of organization. Organization in this sense is a means to an end; it is the decisive determinant of the manner in which the firm functions – in the terminology of modern systems theory, how the system "behaves". For Gutenberg the main issue of the organization is departmentalization and the rules for the designing of the firm's constituent processes. He distinguishes between general and case-related rules and explains the quantitative relation between them by reference to the so-called substitution law of the organization.

Here Gutenberg partly anticipates the decision theoretic view of organization developed later. The "organizational form" specified by Marschak and Radner [1972] consists of exactly one set of information and decision rules for each member of a team. It is incidentally also notable that Marschak / Radner devote about one third of their book to the analysis of the one-person team. Thus the one-person firm also has organizational problems and it says much for the elegance of this theory that it does not exclude this extreme case.

If several, or more, persons are involved, the rules also cover authority for action going beyond procedural matters. Here the core of the firm's organizational problem is seen as the formation and utilization of capacities for the handling of tasks resulting from its aspired total performance. In practice this aspect is, even today, seen to be eminently important. The organizational problem does not therefore lie first and foremost in the coordination of available factor inputs, but already in the defining and structuring of necessary internally produced inputs for which economic agents possibly need special training.

Consequently the organizational problem is here viewed by reference to an *effectiveness* criterion with the aim of attaining a high performance in relation thereto. If there are several solutions of comparable effectiveness, the most efficient should be chosen. This conception of the firm is always based on the idea that, in contrast to the market, there exists an organizational goal which is determined in the planning process from the interpretation of the value-creating task. How this process of forming intentions is itself to be organized – taking cognizance of possible modifications to the executive board's authority, e.g., via co-determination regulations – should be regarded as a question of the exogenous institutional and political framework.

Some macroeconomists (cf. e.g. Olson [1995]) emphatically contend that an organization founded by several persons owes its existence to the common interest of those founders. Hence it indeed pursues a common objective and an organizational interest! Consequently other persons dealing with the organization in different capacities, for instance as employees, are not its members and are therefore not entitled to participate in such intention-building processes.

In any case, Gutenberg perceived the firm's intention-building as an organizational problem. For him the existence of a "firm's centre of intention formulation" was indispensable. Of course this centre is not identical with the neoclassical entrepreneur and is not a sole decision-maker. Gutenberg worked very extensively on the question of "genuine" leadership decisions and their features – decisions then to be taken by the centre itself and not to be delegated to other levels of authority (Gutenberg [1962]). However, he made no distinction between owners acting as entrepreneurs and managers with entrepreneurial responsibilities.

3.2 Organization within the Nexus of Contracts

The new microeconomic theory also deals with organizational phenomena in respect both of the firm's structure and the design of certain functions.

Structural considerations are of course principally analyzed as questions of vertical integration, i.e. that depth of productive capacity which a firm realizes with a multi-stage value-creation process within its own limits. Transaction cost considerations may yield fruitful insights in analyzing the conditions under which, in a multi-stage process, a task should be performed by a self-supporting firm or under the common roof of a larger firm. The method can at least contribute to the explaining firm size and their size distribution.

The basic model of the inner structure of firms is always the hierarchy. Viewing the firm as an institutional framework for initiating and executing contracts; the hierarchy appears in the relation between a superior ("principal") giving orders and a subordinate ("agent") accepting orders. Hence, the organizational interest in the performing of tasks is mainly treated as an aspect of delegation. But the relationship between owners as principals and managers as agents is also the subject of intensive study.

Generally, and therefore also in the case of transactions executed via the market, the behavioral exchange assumptions that are supposed to be valid include the expectation that each party radically pursues his/her own interests. Adamant opportunism including not only slyness but also wilful deceit, lies and deception belong to the principles of action contemplated in this situation.

In view of the agent's opportunism and, additionally, because of informational asymmetry, the consequence of which is that the principal is able to observe the agent's actions only at prohibitively high costs (or not at all), the central problem turns out to be the question of an optimal contract design. Optimality means maximizing the principal's residual profit after paying the agent's reward – subject to the restriction that the reward should provide the agent with an incentive not only to enter a contract but also to perform his tasks to the best of his ability.

If coordination is understood as the real core of organization then institutions could be identified with organizations and transaction costs could be equated to organizational costs. Accepting this proposition allows transaction cost theory at least to be recognized as the foundation of an organization theory.

To examine this statement, the transaction as the "most fundamental unit of analysis" should be closely scrutinized. The hypothesis would be that alternative organizational designs, including those within the firm, are nothing more than different ways of exchanging the same goods and services. "Is it valid at least in the most elementary case…" it might be asked, "…to proceed from a comparison of functional and divisional organizational forms?" Williamson who, in this context refers to U and M-forms of the firm, indeed appears to take this view, (cf. e.g. Williamson [1975], ch. 8).

However, a closer look makes it clear that, even in both of these elementary structural alternatives, it is in no way the case that the same factor inputs are merely coordinated in different ways. The advantages of the functional organization lie in the superior economic efficiency in physical performance facilitated by specialization. On the other hand problems arise in the control process, at least in larger firms, because top management is also called upon to coordinate operational tasks. However, in adopting a divisional structure, the multiplying of individual functions, e.g., distribution, and therefore the foregoing of the operational effects of specialization, have, in the designing of a more efficient control system, to be juxtaposed with inter alia the advantages of positioning decision-makers nearer to the market. Thus, in the two cases different costs and different factor inputs are combined.

This means that the comparative evaluation of organizational forms cannot be based merely on the respective transaction and coordination costs; and, that production costs must also be included into the comparison. Malone [1988] points out that, furthermore, disturbance and break-down costs depend on the chosen organizational form and, consequently, should be taken into account in each comparison. Here again it is evident that the functioning of a productive system as an actual goal of organizational design goes well beyond the mere coordination issue.

3.3 Comparison: Incentive Problems as a New Subject-area

One of the most important results of the new institutional economics is that the role played by the organization has finally been perceived and acknowledged from this perspective (*"Organization matters"*, cf. Milgrom/Roberts [1992], ch. 1). The most important contribution undoubtedly lies in the analysis of the design of incentive systems within contracts of employment. Of special interest are the relations between owners and managers because it is contended that, unless the two are divorced, the existence of large joint stock companies, which are hardly influenced by individual shareholders, cannot be explained.

Gutenbergian business economics is at least no obstacle to this attempted micro-economic explanation. The perception of the management function, and the analysis of the implicit problems, are important; less significant is the question of who should resolve those problems. In any case Gutenberg does not commit himself to owners as managers and, at this stage, explicitly introduces the notion of "centre of business intention formulation" into his reasoning.

The recognition of possibly different motivations and interests on the part of owners and managers doubtless constitutes an essential contribution of modern microeconomic theory – the more so since Gutenberg preferred to distance himself from everything which even appeared to be no more than tangential to the neighbouring disciplines of psychology and sociology. Thus the modern economic theory of incentives certainly represents a significant enrichment of the body knowledge. However, it is no substitute for economic endeavors to resolve practical managerial issues. How management acts is of interest not only with regard to labor disutility and risk preferences.

As regards the order of magnitude of the "separation of ownership and management" however, it should be mentioned that the proportion of family businesses engaged in the value-creating process in Germany in which owners are engaged in management is estimated to be close to 70%.

The inter-personal relations within institutions which are assumed in microeconomic theory should be viewed critically. Especially within a firm, common action requires a common basis of confidence, so it is frequently argued. The "*corporate identity*" which is extremely important for external relations is, from this perspective, founded upon the common value system of the people acting within the firm. Establishing and maintaining this system represents one of the principal tasks of a responsible management. The significance of trust in the different cultures, which should not be underestimated, is also contrasted with the new microeconomic approach at the sociological level; cf. Fukuyama [1995]. Albach ([1993], p. 14) states in the same sense, "... trust is a highly cost efficient form of coordination in the firm"; and, "If 'modern' microtheory makes immoral behavior the starting point and cornerstone of its theorems, thereby treating the pathological case as the normal case of human behavior, the brutalising of morals should come as no surprise." ([1995], p. 1064). Economic practitioners argue similarly. Exactly where the institutional framework is not in good shape, as for instance in today's Russia, the persons entering contracts, and their trustworthiness, are much more important than contract content which, in the case of conflicts, is extremely difficult to enforce legally.

Finally, as mentioned above, explaining firm *structures* (in a sense going beyond integration perspectives) is difficult on the basis of current microtheory. A conception of organization costs that dispenses with production is evidently not sufficient for this purpose.

4 Conclusion – Routes to a "Modern" Theory

4.1 Integration of Approaches

A comparative analysis of two fundamental concepts of economic research might be summarized as follows. The new microeconomic theory, which is mainly endorsed with American contributions, has taken a significant leap beyond its precursors. Like the swing of a pendulum, it has gone from one extreme (understanding the firm as a production function) to the other (understanding the firm as a nexus of contracts) and now focuses on the transaction as the center of attraction. Thus the analysis indeed turns to topics hitherto totally ignored, the understanding of which amounts to a significant advance of the discipline.

On the other hand, these new developments (along with their enthusiastic reception in German business economics) take no account of the contributions of business economics in the German-speaking countries (especially the Gutenberg influence) which have scarcely been recognized in America. We have attempted to show that the Gutenbergian conception of the firm, in which output performance is treated as a central problem-area, contains much more than the neoclassical identification of the firm with a production function. The "disposition" factor in particular, which is peculiar to each individual firm is an indispensible feature that is not available in the market place as an alternative coordination mechanism.

It seems to follow that a basic concept of economic analysis needs both the input-output-transformation as core function and "raison d'être" of the firm as a system, as well as its input and output interfaces with the environment, i.e. the exchange of goods and services. Moreover, the Gutenbergian business economist would have no difficulty in interpreting the notion of factor combination so broadly that it also comprises the (contractual) modalities of factor procurement. He could therefore recognize a further development of Gutenberg's fundamental conception in the newer contractual theory rather than a renunciation.

This statement is supported by the possibility of further developing business economics without any serious dislocation. The discipline regards itself as a science of human behaviour in firms, that is of intra-firm decisions. The discipline cannot be content with an assumption which is perhaps satisfactory from a bird's eye perspective, namely, that the behavior of a firm is the result of a complex equilibrium process. More to the point is that a firm is preoccupied with the advantageous exploitation of existing disequilibria.

Consequently the firm has also to perceive and analyze the restrictions on action in different situations. In so doing it turns out, for instance, that firm size and structure depend not only on transaction costs but also on the predominant objectives and experiences of the actors. Thus at present a trend towards concentration on the so-called core business can be observed in many industries following a long period in which risk reduction through diversification found many adherents. The reason for concentrating is relatively remote from transaction cost categories. Almost always it is said that the firm made the mistake of entering a particular line of business without possessing the necessary basic knowledge. Something similar applies to the founding of a firm. Such a decision generally has more to do with the concrete situation, i.e. with the potentials, capabilities, risk preferences, and motivations of the founders etc., rather than with transaction costs.

Finally attention should be drawn to a further compatibility of the Gutenbergian conception with another newer development, namely, with a resource-oriented approach to the theory of the firm. While the origins of the approach, which stem from Penrose [1959], refer to the specifics of a firm's total resource combination as a source of its growth (nowadays one would say: as its competitive edge), the specific knowledge of its employees nowadays increasingly satisfies this role; cf. Conner / Prahalad [1996]. Both perspectives may well be interpreted as refinements of Gutenberg's factor combination, as is readily appreciated.

4.2 Modernity of the Theory

"One of the differences between the natural and social sciences lies in Newton's contention that, in the natural sciences, one generation of researchers stands on the shoulders of the preceding generation, while in the social sciences one generation treads in the preceding generation's face." Albach ([1993], p. 16) thus quotes the sociologist David Zeaman whose characterization of a form of modern thinking is also familiar in economics.

Of course science lives off modernity and theoretical advance; stagnation would be its death. However, the modest manner in which modest thinkers present their results as temporary findings is virtually an identity card. Just as, for example, Hart ([1990], p.166) finds his portrait of the firm "still, in many ways, [as] a caricature," Gutenberg was also conscious of "all scientific effort being always merely a passage – by no means fruitless but leading to results of a provisional nature", (Gutenberg [1989], p.107).

Progress and modernity are necessary. But implicit in the term modernity is also to be found a touch of fashion. Fashion needs no more than a large number of fans. It is often associated with the exerting of opinion-forming pressure through the use of such epithets as "old-fashioned" and "dated". There are also fashions of this kind in the field of scientific endeavor but fortunately there are also warning voices. "Microeconomists ..." and not only they, it might be added, "... have a tendency to overresearch 'fashionable' topics"; then maybe "they can be convinced by something because it is fashionable and not because it rings true", writes Kreps ([1990a], p. 8).

The newer micro economic theory has undoubtedly the potential to preclude the "fashion syndrome." It would stand comparison with business administration in the German speaking world that was extensively developed by, and after, Gutenberg because of its compatibility potential. Conversely, "traditional" business economists who have not forgotten the struggle over the foundations of their discipline will be pleased with the newly opened perspectives which do not require everything formulated hitherto to be thrown into the wastepaper basket.

But surely the "modern" microeconomic theory also finds itself in a state of transition, a "transitorium", in order to speak once again with Gutenberg ([1989], p.107). At least one dimension on which the need of a speedy revision is apparent, is the way it handles information.

Thus the strong emphasis on informational asymmetry in principal-agent relationships becomes questionable in workplace environments which are made transparent with workflow-systems – i.e. computer-aided information systems which track the sequence of operations and permit the continuous control of the rate of capacity utilization. Moreover, considering the present state of information and communication technology, it is somewhat anachronistic to conceive of information systems merely as suppliers of single parameter values in decision problems. Modern networked information systems offer much more and have a considerable influence on the development of economic structures. Evaluating this influence, Malone and Rockart ([1996], p.71) cite, for example, Williamson's hypothesis to the effect that a high proportion of external products and/or services requires greater coordination and therefore higher transaction costs and is thus less probable. They point out that this hypothesis is contradicted by the new information technology which specifically reduces external information costs.

Ergo: the propositions of scientific theory require a continuous critical reappraisal in the light of new insights and developments. However, as we attempted to show in the previous sub-section, Zeaman‘s “shoulder-model” could also be fruitfully applied in economics. A critical examination of the existing state of knowledge succeeds best if it focuses on the internal consistency and conclusive character of a predicative system of propositions and also upon the relationship of the latter to observable reality. Precisely that can be learned from Erich Gutenberg in which case there is no reason to be worried about the unity of economics.

References

Albach, H., Betriebswirtschaftslehre als Wissenschaft – Entwicklungstendenzen der modernen Betriebswirtschaftslehre, in: Albach, H./Brockhoff, K. (eds.), Die Zukunft der Betriebswirtschaftslehre in Deutschland, ZfB-Erg.-Heft 3[1993], 7-26

Albach, H., Verfall der Sitten? Editorial, in: Zeitschrift für Betriebswirtschaft 65[1995] 10, 1063-1065

Alchian, A.A. / Demsetz, H., Production, Information Costs, and Economic Organization, in: American Economic Review 62[1972], 777-795

Commons, J.R., Institutional Economics, Madison [1934].

Conner, K.R. / Prahalad, C.K., A Resource-based Theory of the Firm: Knowledge Versus Opportunisms, in: Organization Science, 7[1996]5, 477-501

Engelhardt, W. H. / Freiling, J., Die integrative Gestaltung von Leistungspotentialen, in: Zeitschrift für betriebswirtschaftliche Forschung 47[1995]10, 899-918

Fama, E. F., Agency Problems and the Theory of the Firm, in: Journ. of Political Economy, 88[1980]2, 288-307

Fukuyama, F., Konfuzius und Marktwirtschaft – Der Konflikt der Kulturen, München [1995]

Gutenberg, E., Die Unternehmung als Gegenstand betriebswirtschaftlicher Theorie, Berlin [1929], Reprint Frankfurt/M. u.a. 1980

Gutenberg, E., Grundlagen der Betriebswirtschaftslehre, 3 vol., Berlin u.a., vol. 1: Die Produktion, 1st ed.. [1951]

Gutenberg, E., Zum ”Methodenstreit”, in: Zeitschrift für handelswissenschaftliche Forschung, Neue Folge, 5[1953], 327-355

Gutenberg, E., Betriebswirtschaftslehre als Wissenschaft, 3. ed., Krefeld [1967]. (This is the text of an academic ceremonial address given at the university’s foundation celebration on May 22, 1957).

Gutenberg, E., Unternehmensführung: Organisation und Entscheidungen, Wiesbaden [1962]

Gutenberg, E., Rückblicke, in: Zur Theorie der Unternehmung, ed. by H. Albach, Berlin-Heidelberg-New York [1989], 1-109

Hart, O., An Economist's Perspective on the Theory of the Firm, in: Organization Theory, ed. by O.E. Williamson, New York-Oxford, [1990], 154-171

Holmström, B.R. / Tirole, J., The Theory of the Firm, Chapter 2 in: Handbook of Industrial Economics (ed. by R. Schmalensee / R. Willig), New York [1989]

Jensen, M.C. / Meckling, W.H., Theory of the Firm: Managerial Behavior, Agency Costs and Ownership Structure, in: Journal of Financial Economics, 3[1976], 305-360

Kreps, D. M., A Course in Microeconomic Theory, New York [1990a]

Kreps, D. M., Corporate Culture and Economic Theory, in: Perspectives on Positive Political Economy, ed. by J. E. Alt and K. A. Shepsle, Cambridge u.a. [1990b], 90-143

Malone, Th. W., Modeling Coordination in Organizations and Markets, in: Management Science, 33 [1987], 1317-1332

Malone, Th. W. / Rockart, J. F., Vernetzung und Management, in: Spektrum der Wissenschaft, Dossier 1, o.J. [1996], 68-75

Marschak, J. / Radner, R., Economic Theory of Teams, New Haven – London [1972]

Milgrom, P. / Roberts, J., Economics, Organization and Management, Englewood Cliffs [1992]

Olson, M., The Logic of Collective Action : Public Goods and the Theory of Groups, 16th print, Cambridge, Mass. [u.a.] : Harvard Univ. Press, [1995]

Penrose, E., The Theory of Growth of the Firm, Oxford [1959]

Picot, A. / Reichwald, R. / Wigand, R.T.: Die grenzenlose Unternehmung – Information, Organisation und Management, 2nd ed., Wiesbaden [1996]

Salvatore, D., Managerial Economics, New York u.a. [1996]

Williamson, O.E., Markets and Hierarchies: Analysis and Antitrust Implications, New York – London [1975]

Williamson, O.E., Strategizing, Economizing, and Economic Organization, in: Strategic Management Journal, 12[1991], 75-94

Summary

In this paper the input/output productivity relation on the one hand, and the transaction on the other, are juxtaposed as basic units of analysis in business- and microeconomic research. It is shown that the conception of the firm implicit in contract theory opens up some important additional perspectives but cannot replace the model of the firm as a value-creating system.

In Memory of Erich Gutenberg

H. Albach[1]

Overview

- Erich Gutenberg (1897 - 1984) was the most influential business economist of the post-war period. His "productivity relationship" has become the foundation of the modern theory of the firm.
- This theory is developed in his three volume path-breaking work "Principles of Management". The paper reviews Volume One: Production, Volume Two: Marketing, Volume Three: Financing in the light of modern developments.
- It is shown that Gutenberg's theory not only remains to be an important orientation for management but also a strong and vital building block for theoretical developments.

Keywords. Theory of the Firm, Production Theory, Marketing, Corporate Finance

1. Exactly 100 years ago, on the 13th of December 1897, Erich Gutenberg was born. No other German business economist has had anything approaching his impact on the development of German management science. Generations of students have studied his three volume work "Grundlagen der Betriebswirtschaftslehre" (Principles of Management). The influence of this pioneering work has been felt not only in Germany but also in Spain, Latin America, Japan and France. Gutenberg´s work in the 'fifties and 'sixties, and the textbooks on management, economics and law that he edited under the title "The Science of Economics" also influenced those students in the German Democratic Republic who had access to his works during the early years of that regime. This knowledge helped them to master the turnaround after German reunification and expedited the renaissance of management teaching after years of communism.

---

1 Professor Dr. Dr. h.c. mult. Horst Albach, WHU Koblenz – Otto Beisheim Graduate School of Management, 56179 Vallendar, Burgplatz 2, Germany, email: profalbach@aol.com

Gutenberg never intended to establish a school of thought when writing his books and articles. He wanted to create a strong and vital theory of the firm. His intention was to conceive a theory of the firm as an all-comprising theory reflecting all of the specialties that had developed in the field after the war. He made it quite clear that he understood management to be an integral part of economics, and, therefore, he stressed the unity of economics and management. A vital theory of the firm is never out of touch with reality and practice within firms. Therefore, he emphasized the transfer of theory into practice. For him, a vital theory of the firm is a theory which is oriented towards the problems of real firms and which contributes to the resolution of such problems, in practice.

On Gutenberg's 100th anniversary and 13 years after his death in Cologne on May 22, 1984, his students may proudly and frankly ask themselves the question: Do the foundations of the theory of the firm that Erich Gutenberg laid down still underpin the present edifice of theoretical research in management? Does Gutenberg's theory contribute to the solution of the problems presently facing our firms?

An attempt will be made to answer these questions by the 50 speakers delivering papers on the occasion of a memorial conference to be held by the Erich Gutenberg Society in Cologne on the 12th and 13th September 1997 with the title "The theory of the firm in research and practice". We attempt to answer these questions hereafter using the subjects of the three volumes of Gutenberg's "Principles" as the headings of the three parts of this paper:

- the theory of finance
- the theory of marketing
- the theory of production.

2. Whoever looks at the list of Nobel Prize winners in economics in recent years will find the names of Modigliani (1985), Miller (1990), Sharpe (1990), Markowitz (1990), Scholes (1997), Merton (1997). They have all contributed pioneering work which marks the progress of capital market theory. Their works have produced two very important insights:

- the financial sphere of the firm can be separated from the real sphere
- the capital market is not imperfect.

While the separation theorems of the older capital market theory assumed the capital market to be perfect, the more recent work on arbitrage theory has shown how the imperfections of the capital market can be overcome. Theses contributions have had a significant influence on management research in Germany. The theory of finance of the firm today is capital market theory. It has become a field of analysis very much separated from the real sphere of the firm. Therefore, it might seem that the dispute between Erich Gutenberg and Hans Linhardt about the methodological approach to the theory of finance of the firm had been decided in favor of Linhardt. However, this is not the case.

Erich Gutenberg's theory of the firm conceives of the financial sphere as being integrally linked to the sphere of production. The financing function is to maintain financial equilibrium in the firm and, accordingly, to maintain an uninterrupted production process. The sole objective of financial planning is to provide the finances required by the production process on a proper timely basis, i. e. in the periods when investment in the different productive assets has to be made. Of course, the financing process has to ensure that costs of capital are minimized subject to the time constraint of the production process. Gutenberg assumes the conditions of the various financial instruments (interest rate, amortization, duration) to be given by the capital market and by contracts with the banks. On the basis of this assumption Gutenberg derives a capital structure of the firm, consisting of equity, short term debt and long term loans, which is optimal for the company and for its asset structure. Asset structure and capital structure are simultaneously optimized and result in an optimal structure of the balance sheet.

Gutenberg's theory of finance is based on the experience of an imperfect capital market in which the interest rate for capital is not one price and where there is no perfect market for the risk inherent in firms. An optimal mix of financing instruments is based on the negotiations between the treasurer of the firm and the financial institutions with whom the firm does business.

Gutenberg's experience is still valid. The financing problems of large multinational corporations have, it is true, changed. These corporations have been able to loosen, or even dissolve, their close ties with their main bank under the influence of globalization and securitization. They use the international capital market to solve their financial problems. But there are millions of firms in Europe that are not quoted on stock exchanges and which therefore have to solve their financial problems on imperfect credit markets in Europe. The financial problems of start-up firms and small and medium-sized firms are closely related to the real production and distribution processes of these firms. Capital for them is a heterogeneous good which reflects the special services of the individual credit institute. Each individual credit institute is approached by firms with highly individual financial problems, and their financial package is customized to meet the individual demands of these firms. Modern capital markets theory, therefore, has not rendered obsolete Gutenberg's theory of corporate finance. On the contrary, it has underscored the importance of Gutenberg's financial theory. The problem is to negotiate with the bank, on an imperfect capital market, a mix of financing instruments which is tailored to investment projects and minimizes the cost of capital.

Negotiations between the firm and its main bank on imperfect capital markets are the subject of more recent developments in financing theory. Contract theory rather than production theory is, however, the general methodological background of these more recent developments. The problem is not how to finance production processes but how to analyze financing contracts in the face of information asymmetries and credit risks. The firm is modeled as an auctioneer who tries to meet his demand for loans by procuring it from the credit institute which makes the best offer. If one financial institute has better private information about the firm than another, it can make a better offer. Better information is provided to the financial institute if a director of the bank is a member of the board of the company, or if the bank holds a substantial share in the equity of the company. In such a case moral hazard problems between the firm and the banking institute are reduced. The firm would not dare use the loan for investments with a higher risk than those which underlay the credit application. Recent financing theory considers moral hazard to be a real problem and answers the question of how the bank deals with the risk of loan default because of the opportunistic behavior of its clients. In reality the bank will either not conclude a loan contract at all, or will ask for collateral equal to double the loan, or will require a risk-adjusted interest rate with the perceived credit risk which is commensurate.

On the basis of Gutenberg's financing theory such reasoning for concluding a loan contract on imperfect credit markets would appear to be rather strange if not pathological. Gutenberg's theory of finance is a theory of everyday life in the firm and not of exceptions. In a long term relationship between the firm and its main banks honoring contracts is normal, and defaulting on loans is the exception. It is in the best of the interest of the firm to fully inform its bank rather than to exploit information asymmetries.

3. In Gutenberg's theory of the firm, long-run relationships of trust are of paramount importance in the field of sales. Managing the relationships with customers using the marketing instruments of product design, distribution channels, advertising, information and price is the pre-eminent managerial task. All of these instruments serve one purpose, namely, to fulfil the wishes and the expectations of the customers to an ever greater extent and thereby bind the customer closer to the firm. The more the company succeeds in these endeavors, the larger is what Gutenberg has called the "acquisition potential" which measures the degree of closeness to the customers of the firm. More specifically Gutenberg understands by the "acquisition potential" the freedom to set prices which differ from, and exceed those of competitors. The more the firm can increase consumer

welfare, the competitiveness of its customers and, in the final analysis, the profits of its customers, the greater the acquisition potential. It is the superior service that characterizes the long-run relationship between the firm and its customers and which is the basis of its reputation in the market.

There is no doubt but that reputation also plays an important role in the "modern" theory of the firm. Here, reputation is essential because customers are afraid that they might not get a good product but a "lemon" if they do not buy from a firm with a reputation for trustworthiness. A supplier who is not known to the customer, because the relationship between them has not existed long enough to provide favorable experience, is not trusted. It is assumed that a new supplier exploits asymmetric information by charging prices which exceed the true value of the product. The customer, of course, wants to protect himself against this exploitation by the supplier. He does so by formulating his contract with the supplier in a manner which induces the supplier to make his private information public. Long-run contracts are a guarantee that the supplier has an interest in dealing fairly with the customer. If a long-run customer relationship with perfect sharing of information promises more profits, than does a sequence of short-run contracts with asymmetric information, the supplier serves his own interests if he treats the customer fairly.

Mutual trust has thus become an important economic factor in the modern theory of the firm. "Honesty is the best policy" is not just an admirable adage, but a mathematically proven theorem.

Modern marketing theory can therefore be considered as a scientific proof of normal behavior in the market. It is the normal case that Erich Gutenberg treats in his "Grundlagen der Betriebswirtschaftslehre" (Principles of Management). Gutenberg's doubly kinked demand curve, which later generations have termed the "Gutenberg demand function" can thus be seen as the origin of the theory of reputation capital which plays such a prominent role in contract theory today. There is no doubt but that Gutenberg's theory has proved to be most important for the practice of marketing, in attempts to improve the closeness to the customer and for managing customer relations on the basis of mutual trust.

4. In Gutenberg's theory of the firm, the product results from a productivity relationship between factor inputs into the firm's production process and its output. If this general concept is narrowed down to the "Gutenberg production function", his theory can be regarded as a monument to the methodological dispute of the 'fifties, namely, whether the factors of production can be substituted or whether they are "limitational". This dispute between Gutenberg and Mellorowicz centered on the question of whether the old S-shaped production function was a correct description of the productivity relationship in the firm; or, whether a linear

production function with fixed coefficients was a more appropriate description of industrial production. Gutenberg argued that factors of production can only be substituted within the technical limits of what he called a "factor consumption function" which describes the variation in the coefficients of production as a function of the speed or the intensity in use of technical equipment. This dispute has long been decided in favor of Erich Gutenberg.

However, Gutenberg was more ambitious when he developed the concept of a productivity relationship. He wanted to use this concept as a description of the firm in its entirety and the systematic interdependence of procurement, production and sales. Therefore, his concept of the productivity relationship is the basis of his general theory of the firm which is still valid. His production function is more than an engineering production function. It describes the complex relationships between the different factors of production and their contribution to the overall efficiency of the firm and provides the theoretical basis for monitoring factor usage.

The relationship between labor, as used in production, and fixed assets is at the core of Gutenberg's productivity relationship. Gutenberg assumes that management and employees have reached consensus about corporate objectives and that, therefore, conflicts about working conditions in the production process have already been resolved.

More recent developments in the theory of the firm have tried to view the firm not as a productivity relationship, but as a network of contracts between the firm and its customers, suppliers and employees. The management of the contractual relationship with customers was mentioned above and it is along the same lines that relationships with suppliers are studied. It may be questioned whether Gutenberg's understanding of the role of employees in the productivity relationship has been rendered obsolete by more recent advances in contract theory. Today the relationships between employees and the firm are treated as a principal-agent relationship. Employer and employee have different personal utility functions. It is, therefore, important to find contractual forms for these relationships which guarantee that these disparate objectives will not prove harmful or even disastrous to the firm. The labor contract may, therefore, provide for strict control of the efficiency of the worker, it may contain material and intangible incentives which co-ordinate the objectives of the employees with the objectives of the firm. The contract may, finally, help to provide the employee with the insight that it is in the long run personal interest of each employee to behave in a manner that is congruent with the firm's objectives.

Gutenberg's theory of the firm does not deny such possibilities. However, they are solved in the search process for new employees. Those employees who do not seem willing, or adequately equipped, to meet the objectives of the firm will not be hired. Consequently, all employees who have been hired will therefore behave optimally in the production process. Of course, persons will differ in their personal characteristics, and their efficiency will also depend on the work place, on their relationships with colleagues and on the mode of co-operation with the boss. Deficits in motivation and in communication are not overlooked but are assumed to have been appropriately resolved when production begins. This does not have anything to do with what some authors term "pre-contractual arrangements" but rather with a basic understanding of the nature of the firm as an economic institution.

One of the institutional arrangements which have been introduced to solve conflicts between labor and capital before they can result in serious difficulties in the production process is co-determination. Co-determination is one of the "system- related factors" which have an impact on the precise nature of decision processes in the firm. Gutenberg was a member of the Government Commission on Co-determination. In this capacity Gutenberg studied the advantages, but also the problems of co-determination. He never regarded the concept of harmony which is the foundation of the German Works Council Act as self-evident or generally valid. The Co-Determination Act solves conflicts by making co-operation between management and labor in managerial decisions mandatory. The interest of labor has to be taken into consideration because, if labor representatives disagree, entrepreneurial decisions become more expensive. Also, labor can influence the behavior of management before decisions are made. However, the final decision rests with capital. Thus the principle of autonomy of capital in decision making which, according to Gutenberg, is one of the decisive characteristics of the firm, remains untouched. Gutenberg's theory of the firm is thus still valid in practice today.

5. Erich Gutenberg studied economics with Professor Wolff in Halle and business administration with Professor Fritz Schmidt in Frankfurt. Therefore, the firm was for him an important institution within the institutional framework of the economy which comprises firms, households, markets, and the state. It is on this conceptual basis that Gutenberg tries to incorporate microeconomic production theory (and the supply of labor by households), microeconomic price theory (and the theory of the different market forms) and allocation theory in his theory of the firm. This includes corporate governance as well as the theory of business finance.

Today, firms are imbedded in a global economy. They offer their products in global competition. Management today cannot be effective unless it has a clear understanding of the interdependence of economies in a global world. Thus, Gutenberg's insistence on closer ties between economics and business administration has proved to be most important for the practice of management – despite the objections with this methodological reorientation of business administration that were raised against the first volume of Gutenberg's "Principles" immediately after its publication in 1951.

Gutenberg's theory is still today an important orientation for management. Modern controlling and process cost accounting cannot be understood without a deep insight into Gutenberg's production theory. Recent contributions to production theory founded on the insights of Gutenberg constitute the theoretical basis of modern controlling. Gutenberg's marketing theory, with its analysis of imperfect product markets, is the theoretical basis of today's marketing practice. Younger scientists have built on this basis and have studied the dynamic effects of applying such marketing instruments as pricing, product design, distribution channels, and advertising. Price management in practice, outlays on advertising and communication, empirical tests of markets and of consumer behavior all have their common basis in the marketing theory developed by Erich Gutenberg. While the problems, that Gutenberg dealt with in his theory of corporate finance, are, due to securitization and globalization, no longer the principal financial issues in large firms, start-up firms and fast growing small and medium-sized firms find a precise description of their problems in Gutenberg's financial theory together with guides to their practical resolution.

Gutenberg's theory of the firm is, on the occasion of his 100th birthday, a strong and vital building block. It is a good building block because, as experience has shown, subsequent generations of management scientists can build on it and thereby enlarge and enrich the body of theoretical knowledge. It is a good building block because it can integrate other methodological approaches into the theory of the firm. It is vital, because it helps practitioners to make good decisions and to maintain the competitiveness of German firms in global competition despite all the rigidities in our society and its legal framework.

Summary

The paper presents the most important aspects of Erich Gutenberg's theory of the firm and its three parts: Production, Marketing, and Financing. Gutenberg's theory of corporate finance conceives of the financial sphere of the firm as being integrally linked to the sphere of production. The financing function is to maintain financial equilibrium in the firm and accordingly to maintain an uninterrupted production process. Capital markets are incomplete, and, therefore, the capital structure of the firm matters.

In Gutenberg's theory of the firm, long-run relationships of trust are of paramount importance, particularly in marketing. His theory, presented as early as 1951, introduces the marketing variables product design, distribution channels, advertising, information and price as instruments that help the firm to get closer to the customer and to establish long-run transaction relationships. Managing the goodwill of such long-run relationships with relationship specific investments is the essence of the theory of marketing. These relationships are represented in a doubly-kinked demand curve, which, in oligopoly, leads to interesting multiple equilibria (secret price cutting oases).

Gutenberg's production theory builds on the assumption of a linear technology with intensity variations. This idea is represented in a production function with intensity dependent production coefficients. It is one of the major contributions of Gutenberg to have given an in-depth analysis of the determinants of efficiency of the inputs of each factor of production. Gutenberg's theory provides the economic framework for incorporating insights for organizational behavior, engineering, and labor economics.

Erich Gutenberg - His Work

Roots, Rise, Results+

H. Sabel[1]

Overview

- The problem discussed in this paper is to find the roots of the work of a real celebrity.
- The method used is the interpretation of the different tensions of life that guided Gutenberg to his tremendous work which is presented in the context of the development of „Betriebswirtschaftslehre".
- The enormous influence of person and work is shown in that the body of knowledge of modern „Betriebswirtschaftslehre" is founded on his „Grundlagen der Betriebswirtschaftslehre".

Keywords: Roots of a life, Sales, Finance, Investment, Organization, Methodology

Introductory Notes

If you want to honor a scientist, the first honor is to confess that many contributions have been written in his honor[2] and that many honorary doctorates[3] have been conferred upon him and you feel the burden of all of this.

+ Extended version of a lecture at the Federal Association of German Economists and Management Experts on the occasion of the hundredth birthday of Erich Gutenberg on December 8, 1997, at the University of Cologne. For a better understanding all literal quotations were translated by the author.

1 Professor Dr. Hermann Sabel, Institut für Gesellschafts- und Wirtschaftswissenschaften der Rheinischen Friedrich-Wilhelms-Universität Bonn, Betriebswirtschaftliche Abteilung III - Marketing, Adenauerallee 24-42, 53113 Bonn, Germany, email: Prof.Dr.H.Sabel@uni-bonn.de, URL: http://www.bwl3.uni-bonn.de

2 Cf. Albach, H.: Überwindung des Gegensatzes zwischen Volks- und Betriebswirtschaftslehre. Ein Überblick über die Entwicklung der letzten fünfzig Jahre. Zum achtzigsten Geburtstag von Erich Gutenberg, in: Frankfurter Allgemeine Zeitung, 13.12.1977, p. 12; Albach, H.: Allgemeine Betriebswirtschaftslehre. Zum

Being a disciple you are more or less biased and caught by the fascinating personality Gutenberg was, but you can take for granted that he always expected an independent judgment.

According to both points this contribution will have the peculiarity that the contending literal quotations, and it will content many, are entirely from Gutenberg except those of just one other.

1 The Roots of the Work

Place and spaces, time and periods lead life, what talents however there are. Cologne is where Gutenberg experienced the brilliance of his work which he consolidated here. It was at this place that he gave his famous university speech on the occasion of the university foundation celebration on May 22nd 1957 on „Betriebswirtschaftslehre as a science".[4] His lucid tripartite statement embraced his point of view on business management as a discipline applying to individual economic units[5], his roots to others, like Schmalenbach and Schmidt[6] whence he came and the theory that they as accounting management scientists had never really known.[7]

Gedenken an Erich Gutenberg, in: Zeitschrift für Betriebswirtschaft, 56. Jg. (1986), pp. 578-613; Albach, H.: Eine lebendige Theorie der Unternehmung. Zum 100. Geburtstag Erich Gutenbergs, in: Frankfurter Allgemeine Zeitung, No. 288, 11.10.1997, pp. 21/22; Henninger, C.: Jenseits von Soll und Haben, in: Frankfurter Allgemeine Zeitung, 13.12.1982; Jacob, H.: Praxisnahe Theorie der Unternehmung, in: Die WELT, 13.12.1972; Jacob, H.: Gutenbergs Konzeption überzeugt auch noch heute, in: Die WELT, 12.12.1977, p.11; Jacob, H.: Erich Gutenberg zum Gedächtnis, in: DIE BETRIEBSWIRTSCHAFT, 44. Jg. (1984), p. 651; Kilger, W.: Zum wissenschaftlichen Werk Erich Gutenbergs, in: Zeitschrift für Betriebswirtschaft, 32. Jg. (1962), p. 689; Kreikebaum, H.: Er hat eine ganze Generation von heute erfolgreichen Betriebswirten geprägt, in: Westfalen-Blatt, 13.12.1977, p. 288; Lücke, W.: Erich Gutenberg vollendet sein achtzigstes Lebensjahr, in: Angewandte Planung, Vol. 1, 1977, p. 139; Pfeil, G.-H.: Betriebswirtschaft auf neuen Wegen, in: Die WELT sprach mit Dr. Dr. h.c. Erich Gutenberg, in: Die WELT vom 18.12.1962, p. 8; Schüler, W.: Zum 85. Geburtstag von Erich Gutenberg, in: Betriebswirtschaftliche Forschung und Praxis, 34. Jg. (1984), p. 576; Seelbach, H.: Zum Tode von Erich Gutenberg, in: Das Wirtschaftsstudium, 13. Jg. (1984), pp. 355/356; Wöhe, G.: Erich Gutenberg zum Gedenken, in: Deutsches Steuerrecht, 23. Jg., No. 1/2 (1985), p. 6.

3 Cf. the documents about the honorary doctorate award, in: Albach. H. (Ed.): Zur Theorie der Unternehmung, Schriften und Reden von Erich Gutenberg. Aus dem Nachlaß, Berlin et al. 1989, pp. 285-289.

4 Cf. Gutenberg, E.: Betriebswirtschaftslehre als Wissenschaft, Kölner Universitätsreden 18, 3. ed., Krefeld 1967.

5 Cf. Gutenberg, E.: Die Unternehmung als Gegenstand betriebswirtschaftlicher Theorie, Berlin-Vienna 1929, preface.

6 Albach says, that it is true that Gutenberg noticed the great triple star of business management Schmalenbach, Schmidt, and Nicklisch, but that there is no doubt, that in

Here he filled students with enthusiasm, from here he guided the paths of his disciples, here he shaped many people who now have important responsibilities in the economy, trade and industry and in society at large. This is where he lived, where he died on May 22nd 1984 and this is where he is at rest.[8]

Life springs from tensions. He did not really love Cologne but he knew that Cologne was the faculty to which he belonged. It was not easy in this faculty; but it must still thank him today for the reputation to which he decisively contributed.

From the beginning of his life there was tension.[9] As a son of a businessman he was born on December 13th 1897 in Ostwestfalen. After his first war experience he studied natural sciences in Hannover because he was familiar to the world of machines and wanted to explain their interactions.

The study of natural sciences led him to the abstract beauty of the spheres of physics and the shells of chemistry and somehow he felt it was too to far away, perhaps because others wanted him to be closer. So after leaving Hannover and the natural sciences (he himself talked of a „breaking-off of the studies in Hannover"[10] in his handwritten curriculum vitae), he contracted with the paternal business to start there five years later and began to study economics in Würzburg[11]. He completed his studies in Halle as a Ph D graduate at the age of 24.[12] Of this young age he later said, „At the age of 24 or 25, neither the intellectual nor the professional development of a human being is finished."[13]

In his dissertation he again becomes conscious of the tension between theory and reality. He addresses himself to Thünen's isolated state as a fiction. The philosophy should resolve the tension between abstraction and reality in a way that is also formative for the future. This can readily be inferred from the last sentence of the dissertation. „Thünen is a practical man with pronounced theoretical talent who is

---

Gutenberg's opinion the work of Nicklisch provided the least support for „Betriebswirtschaftslehre". Albach, H.: Allgemeine Betriebswirtschaftslehre, loc. cit., p. 590.

7 Cf. Gutenberg, E.: Die Unternehmung als Gegenstand betriebswirtschaftlicher Theorie, loc. cit., preface.

8 Cf. Albach, H.: Allgemeine Betriebswirtschaftslehre, loc. cit., p. 596/597.

9 Cf. Gutenberg, E.: Eigenhändig geschriebener Lebenslauf, in: Albach, H. (Ed.): Zur Theorie der Unternehmung, loc. cit., pp. 281-283.

10 Cf. Gutenberg, E.: Eigenhändig geschriebener Lebenslauf, in: Albach, H. (Ed.): Zur Theorie der Unternehmung, loc. cit., p. 281.

11 Cf. for that purpose Gutenberg, E.: Rückblicke, in: Albach, H. (Ed.): Zur Theorie der Unternehmung, loc. cit., p. 1-118, here p. 6.

12 Cf. Gutenberg, E.: Eigenhändig geschriebener Lebenslauf, in: Albach, H. (Ed.): Zur Theorie der Unternehmung, loc. cit., p. 281.

13 Gutenberg, E.: Betriebswirtschaftslehre als Wissenschaft, loc. cit., p. 37.

totally aware of the danger of exceeding the limit of the allowable when using the isolating method."[14]

Gutenberg is evidently also aware of this danger. He discovers regularities and models but they are to far removed from the machines in which he is interested. He discovers that individual machines are as short-lived as the paternal firm to which he has no further rights of entry.[15] So he studies business management in Frankfurt and obtains his Habilitation in Münster for dealing with an issue which had brought his life to a head, namely, „The firm as the subject of managerial theory".[16] His intention is to examine, „...what all this managerial theory is supposed to mean, especially the manner in which the enterprise as an economic unit can be the subject of a theory"[17].

The answer ripens by departing from the problem, on one hand by positive experience in auditing and as the incumbent of his first chairs; and, on the other from further military service and experience of the divided Germany from Jena and Breslau via Marburg to Frankfurt to the professorship of Fritz Schmidt and the teaching of Lorey with whom he studied mathematics as a student.[18]

2 The Development of the Work

What is the answer? An enormous work: The fundamentals of business management.[19] How did he find it? From tension. A productive tension toward political

---

14 Gutenberg, E.: Thünens isolierter Staat als Fiktion, 4. Band der Bausteine zu einer Philosophie des „Als-ob", edd. H. Vaihinger and R. Schmidt, Munich 1922, p. 103.

15 Cf. Gutenberg, E.: Eigenhändig geschriebener Lebenslauf, in: Albach, H. (Ed.): Zur Theorie der Unternehmung, loc. cit., p. 281.

16 Gutenberg, E.: Die Unternehmung als Gegenstand betriebswirtschaftlicher Theorie, loc. cit.

17 Gutenberg, E.: Die Unternehmung als Gegenstand betriebswirtschaftlicher Theorie, loc. cit., preface.

18 Cf. note 48 in Albach, H.: Die Betriebswirtschaftslehre: Eine Wissenschaft, in: Albach, H. (Ed.): Zur Theorie der Unternehmung, loc. cit., pp. 213-280, here p. 270.

19 Gutenberg, E.: Grundlagen der Betriebswirtschaftslehre, 1. Band, Die Produktion, 24., unchanged ed. (Enzyklopädie der Rechts- und Staatswissenschaft, Abteilung Staatswissenschaft), Berlin - Heidelberg - New York 1983; Gutenberg, E.: Grundlagen der Betriebswirtschaftslehre, 2. Band, Der Absatz, 17. ed. (Enzyklopädie der Rechts- und Staatswissenschaft, Abteilung Staatswissenschaft), Berlin - Heidelberg - New York 1984; Gutenberg, E.: Grundlagen der Betriebswirtschaftslehre, 3. Band, Die Finanzen, 8., enlarged ed. (Enzyklopädie der Rechts- und Staatswissenschaft, Abteilung Staatswissenschaft), Berlin - Heidelberg - New York 1980.

economy[20], an inevitable, though unintended, tension toward some exponents of business administration[21], and a demanding experience-based tension toward management practice.[22]

Although he knew firms profoundly and understood the „theory of the firm" very well, one thing was too close and the other too far away because he began with machines, with production. His view had both focus and depth of focus.

The focus of his attention was the combination process whereby productive factors yield products. When he discovered it, he realized that the answer lay in three important attributes. First of all, a new system of productive factors needed to distinguish between those that are combined and others that are combinable. Second, a new non-substitutional production function which does not affect the different consumption-orientated adapting processes was necessary. Third, a troublesome multiproduct perspective was necessary because the elegant model of the single-product firm broke down in practice.

What was his concern regarding business management as a science? He wanted „to examine whether the original relation between factor input and factor output, namely, the firm's productivity relation, could be used as the basis for a reference system in which all business processes find their natural order"[23].

How did he arrive at this natural order? Through his depth of focus. Gutenberg himself offered his opinion on the kinds of methods business management should use to solve problems. He commented on all methods, except for the first, which is about gaining a knowledge of the facts. He enumerated α to δ as an answer to the question of a basis for a knowledge of the facts, beginning with α, „on own experience and expertise"[24]. This experience and expertise therefore is a guiding principle for causal and final analysis and for analysis in accordance with the methods of

20 Gutenberg, E.: Rückblicke, in: Albach, H. (Ed.): Zur Theorie der Unternehmung, loc. cit., p. 22. Although being favorably disposed to this new and developing area of economics, -I was indeed a management scientist lived with my personal scientific tension and that of my discipline.

21 Gutenberg, E.: Rückblicke, in: Albach, H. (Ed.): Zur Theorie der Unternehmung, loc. cit., p. 143. I don't know whether the representatives of business management of that time were familiar with the field of economics and its quantitative methods. You can hardly take that as read. But given some of them were familiar with it, it is still obscure to me, why they didn't use this apparatus which was tailored to the dealing of microeconomic problems.

22 Gutenberg has felt this tension in the days of National Socialism as well as before and afterwards. Cf. Albach. H.: Die Betriebswirtschaftslehre: Eine Wissenschaft, loc. cit., pp. 253foll.

23 Gutenberg, E.: Betriebswirtschaftslehre als Wissenschaft, loc. cit., p. 25.

24 Gutenberg, E.: Betriebswirtschaftslehre als Wissenschaft, loc. cit., p. 28.

the social sciences. On which word can one fix this guiding principle? I think on representation[25].

It very often happens that the author himself is unaware of a central concept because he knows so much about it. Thus, the entry „representation" is not to be found in the index of the volume on production. But the structure of the work shows a typical irregularity. All headings are formulated substantivally . Only the decisive part, that leads to the Gutenberg production function, is stated in interrogative form. „Is the law of diminishing returns (the type A production function) representative for the industrial production?"[26]

What Gutenberg here explicitly demands from the question had always been an implicit preoccupation. Already in the preface to the first edition he stated, "I have tried to develop the problems of this book from the fullness and diversity of the observable circumstances. Simultaneously, I have endeavoured to use the analytical apparatus of modern theory in this book to reflect the nature of the items investigated in a justifiable and effective manner."[27]

According to Gutenberg a model is justifiable and effective, if its „assumptions correspond with the technical conditions of industrial production."[28] And then he spread out examples from α to δ, that lead to the conclusion, "that the type A production function, the law of diminishing returns, is not representative of industrial production. We must therefore search for another law of combination."[29]

Without having reflected upon it, the academics in business management actually believed that their approaches were already sufficiently for representative, but were unaware of the precision of Gutenberg`s approach. Gutenberg did not really mind the elegance of mathematics of the law of diminishing returns. On the contrary, he embellished it. He was perturbed by the fact that, in many of the firms he had audited, limitational relationships governed the inputs of the factors of production.

The academics in business management, especially Mellerowicz with whom Gutenberg was not in dispute, were disturbed by the mathematics. It was described as a clash over economic methods and Gutenberg did not actually mind because he was a gentleman. He said: „Everybody, who adheres to the German university

---

25 He may have found this word in connection with Marshall's representative firm, but he used it in a sense that was totally different from the meaning of the typical, average firm. So he concluded: Gutenberg, E.: Rückblicke, in: Albach, H. (Ed.): Zur Theorie der Unternehmung, loc. cit., p. 27. There were just a few suggestions in Marshall's represantative firm regarding my special intentions and ideas.

26 Gutenberg, E.: Grundlagen der Betriebswirtschaftslehre, 1. Band: Die Produktion, 21. ed, Berlin - Heidelberg - New York, 1975, p. 303.

27 Gutenberg, E.: Die Produktion, loc. cit., p. VI.

28 Gutenberg, E.: Die Produktion, loc. cit., p. 318.

29 Gutenberg, E.: Die Produktion, loc. cit., p. 325.

tradition will understand that I refuse to discuss in the same tone of personal aggressiveness, that Mellerowicz is using in his dealings with me."[30]

In this exchange Mellerowicz reproached him for taking a new direction in management science and for many other things of both a specific and general nature, that is, in respect both of the concept in its entirety and its details; and, that in the case of the latter, he unnecessarily introduced new terms,[31] Gutenberg's reply was, "According to prevailing methodical opinion, terms are, in the nature of things, only a means to an end, not an end in itself, therefore not yet knowledge, but an instrument for use in the process of gaining knowledge."[32]

In this sense he also raised the question of representation in two other significant functional areas, namely, sales and finance. Here also, his own far-reaching experience and expertise led him to new models. What was the motive for such a depth of focus? It was probably the desire only to designate as a theory that which had passed the test of his own experience.

Precisely for the case of the double-kinked demand curve in the sales area there is a Gutenberg text which is typical in the sense of "representation," even though that word also does not appear there. "Whilst I was preoccupied with pricing observations and related considerations, I was coincidentally witness to a conversation between two gentleman in a firm which produced neckties, or distributed them wholesale. I can no longer remember the exact details. It happened in the mid-thirties when I was called to the firm, which was domiciled in the Krefeld or Mönchengladbach area, to deal with a taxation issue. The firm was generally dealt with by our place of business in Cologne, but as there was nobody available there who could take over the tax consultation, I helped out. It was not a big firm. The conversation - I mean the one between the owner of the firm and an employee - concerned the pricing of neckties. The employee calculated the price in accordance with the usual cost-based pricing formula that I mentioned above. Then I heard the owner of the firm saying (this is the gist): But for this necktie we can easily ask for a higher price. It has an especially attractive design and will readily find a customer. When the owner suggested a higher price, the employee said: but we cannot go higher because of the danger that we will be drawn into a price category in which better neckties are offered to customers."[33] So much for Gutenberg's experience.

How does Gutenberg transfer this experience into theory? "Unimportant though this minor result is - at that time it was really on my mind because the price be-

---

30 Gutenberg, E.: Zum Methodenstreit, in: Zeitschrift für handelswissenschaftliche Forschung, NF, 5. Jg. (1953), pp. 327-355, here p. 327.

31 Cf. Gutenberg, E.: Zum Methodenstreit, loc. cit., p. 327.

32 Gutenberg, E.: Zum Methodenstreit, loc. cit., p. 328.

33 Gutenberg, E.: Rückblick auf die Betriebswirtschaftslehre des Absatzes, in: Zeitschrift für Betriebswirtschaft, 55. Jg. (1985), pp. 1200-1213, here p. 1210.

haviour that I here encountered in a market that was characterized by product differentiation and buyer preferences, could not be explained with the Cournot model. In any case, because of my preoccupation with classical microeconomic theory, or perhaps because I had recently become aware of it due to increasing experience and observation in this field, I concluded that product differentiation needed a price-sales function which differed from those to which I was accustomed. So I arrived at the double-kinked demand curve."[34] This tension between economic model and personal experience lead to a new microeconomic price theory.

This double-kinked price-sales function, which results from a mixture of a polypoly and monopoly, and combined with partial interdependence, also the oligopolistic model is, from today's point of view, explained by the fact that, in addition to price, other instruments can influence sales volume. He examined all of these instruments in detail, and in combination, in respect of various conditions and effects because he could not reconcile with his own experience that everything could be reduced to price when in reality the overriding importance of other sales policy instruments was undeniable.

The stringency of Gutenberg's "representation" requirement resembles Popper's demand for falsification[35]. It is possible to regard his claim as an expression of Popper; since everything that is not representative can easily be falsified, but should not be chosen as a hypothesis because the goal is the representative hypothesis, which is not falsified yet and falsifies the one which is not representative designating it as a special case of such markets where only the price is relevant and the expected price-sales function cannot be falsified. This of course remains to be a special case facing the varied heterogeneity of the markets.

Since he did not shrink from applications for these heterogeneous markets, he published a volume entitled Sales planning in practice. In the preface he gives as the justification for this volume. „Practical experiences I have gained in this field has shown me that no area of planning has such an abundance and diversity of forms, variants and unresolved questions as sales planning."[36] He ended this volume with a contribution apostrophizing sales planning as a means of the corporate policy and, in this way, integrated it into the whole.[37]

Finance led him back to balance sheets. He knew them from the theory of Schmidt and from professional accountancy practice. Capital theory he knew from eco-

---

34 Gutenberg, E.: Rückblick auf die Betriebswirtschaftslehre des Absatzes, loc. cit., pp. 1210/1211.

35 Cf. Popper, K.: Logik der Forschung, 6., improved ed., Tübingen 1976, pp. 47foll.

36 Gutenberg, E.: Vorwort des Herausgebers, in: Gutenberg, E. (Ed.): Absatzplanung in der Praxis, Wiesbaden 1962, p. 7.

37 Cf. Gutenberg, E.: Die Absatzplanung als Instrument der Unternehmensführung, in: Gutenberg, E. (Ed.): Absatzplanung in der Praxis, loc. cit., pp. 285-320.

nomics. In the case of finance and investment, his difficulty was that accounting practice too close and that classical capital theory was too distant. In both cases the question of representation again arose.

He realized that, within the sphere of finance, the golden balance sheet rule would not be the representative solution, as the following paragraph shows. „Only when the capital structure that complies with the golden balance sheet rule is simultaneously the most cost-effective, will this rule for structuring debt capital not contradict the principle of cost minimization in enterprise's financial sphere. How often this condition can be found in corporate practice is a question which is not discussed any further here. It may however be assumed that this condition is not the rule."[38]

Apropos of capital theory he asks, "Can the accelerator principle, more precisely, the investment function expressed by this principle, really be considered to be representative of the behavior of firms in respect of their investment decisions?"[39] To answer he fell back on his method α to δ, systematic questioning, and presented the first empirical investigation into the investment decisions of German industrial firms. He revealed investment determinants differing from the accelerator principle.[40]

However, this investigation did not lead to a theory of finance. His intention was to represent the core of the relationship between capital requirements and capital covers which, for their part, were to derive from the tangible processes of production and sales. „Thus the processes taking place in the financial sphere are moved into the firm as a total system from which they are fundamentally immovable."[41] They also shouldn't get out of this so that the firm can rise on a common foundation in its natural order and the monumental work of the fundamentals of business management completes itself - but not yet the whole work.

This firm brought Gutenberg back to a question of which, despite all machines, functions and representations, he really never lost sight, but which he had not yet formulated theoretically. Already in his doctoral thesis he had written, "The realm of the human soul extends so far and the possibilities of its influences and dependencies are so great."[42]

Somewhat so great can only then be formed to a contemplation of models of firms[43] which he has characterized by system indifferent and system related facts if

---

38 Gutenberg, E.: Die Finanzen, loc. cit., pp. 287/288.

39 Gutenberg, E.: Untersuchungen über die Investitionsentscheidungen industrieller Unternehmen, Cologne und Opladen 1959, p. 14.

40 Cf. Gutenberg, E.: Untersuchungen über die Investitionsentscheidungen, loc. cit., pp. 36-160.

41 Gutenberg, E.: Die Finanzen, loc. cit., p. 2.

42 Gutenberg, E.: Thünens isolierter Staat als Fiktion, loc. cit., p. 90.

43 Cf. Gutenberg, E.: Die Produktion, loc. cit., pp. 457-486.

one accepts that there are „meta economic forces and processes which determine form and shape of economic execution."[44] As regards individual economic units it must be recognized that within a firm there are three centers of decision making and then reality as a member the Codetermination Commission must also be experienced. "The bitterness of the debate about a modification to corporate governance which we have experienced in recent years reveals that it was not a commercial matter but a political issue."[45]

Economically he always struggled for the organization, published a monolith „business administration - organization and decisions"[46] and, whilst not developing a model, promulgated a general law, namely, the substitution law of the organization.

In this case he probably also orientated himself with his representational guideline. He would have felt it improper to squeeze a such an extensive realm into the narrow confines of a model; from an early stage he was always well aware that every method has its limitations.

Perhaps the substitution law of the organization was only little appreciated because it was actually not a model but rather more of a general tendency. For this reason it has greater explanatory power and also explains such phenomena as the substitution of many letters as a case-by-case regulation with the general rule of the Latin alphabet, at least in information technology. As president of the German-Japanese Society, Gutenberg would have been pleased to learn that Japanese word processing systems operate with a horizontal typewriter keyboard which is overlaid with both kana and the alphabet; for text input however, the Japanese use the alphabet.[47]

The tension between him and management was productive in various ways. Whatever he perceived as an item of economic theory, the related phenomena caused a kind of friction. But he was through and through a scientist which is probably best demonstrated by the following quotation, with which he almost ended his university speech, "All this with the goal of knowing how to govern management, to prevent it from becoming high-handed instead of playing its part as a servant which it is destined to do in people's life.-"[48]

This statement, which ends with a dash, is, concise though it may be, a better reflection of Gutenberg's experience with management than is his handwritten curriculum vitae, in which the practical experience ends with the fact that he was a

---

44 Gutenberg, E.: Betriebswirtschaftslehre als Wissenschaft, loc. cit., p. 10.

45 Gutenberg, E.: Betriebswirtschaftslehre als Wissenschaft, loc. cit., p. 11.

46 Cf. Gutenberg, E.: Unternehmensführung - Organisation und Entscheidungen, Wiesbaden 1962.

47 Cf. Coulmas, F.: Wie das Alphabet nach Japan, in: Spektrum der Wissenschaft, November 11/1994, pp. 90-100, here p. 100.

48 Gutenberg, E.: Betriebswirtschaftslehre als Wissenschaft, loc. cit., p. 38.

member of the Board of Executive Directors of the Deutsche Wirtschaftsprüfungs AG (audit company) in Essen.[49]

Being a scientist, who in the sense of Popper feels obliged to serve humanity,[50] it was obviously very important to him, that management science should serve in the same way by preventing management from making high-handed mistakes; otherwise management might perform a disservice to humanity. Gutenberg must have seen much arrogance and it would have contradicted his habit of drawing inferences from his own experience were he not to have made this concise statement.

3 The Influence of Person and Work

Thanks to Erich Gutenberg, general business management can be found in in Germany[51], Japan[52], and Spain. The publication of translations[53] of parts of his work in Afghan, English, French, Italian, Japanese, and Spanish attests to his international importance. The syllabus of students in business management stems partly from

---

49 Cf. Gutenberg. E.: Eigenhändig geschriebener Lebenslauf, in: Albach, H. (Ed.): Zur Theorie der Unternehmung, loc. cit., p. 282.

50 Cf. Popper, K.: Alles Leben ist Problemlösen, 7. ed., Munich - Zurich 1995.

51 The topic „Expectations from a general business management from the perspectives of research an teaching" was discussed by the participants of a panel discussion, H. Albach (chairman), J. Bloech, E. Dichtl, G. Schanz, H. Schierenbeck, D. Schneider, and G. Vogelsang, which took place in 1989 at the 51st Scientific Annual Conference of the managing committee of the society of university teachers for business in Münster. Cf. Podiumsdiskussion, in: Adam, D.; Backhaus, K.; Meffert, H.; Wagner, H. (Ed.): Integration und Flexibilität, Wiesbaden, 1990, pp. 137-180. The result was, not surprisingly, undecided. While the chairman summarizes: Albach, H.: Podiumsdiskussion, loc. cit., pp.179/180, We surely will experience an interesting development of General Business Management), the organizers conclude in their preface: Adam, D.; Backhaus, K.; Meffert, H.; Wagner, H.: Vorwort, in: Adam, D.; Backhaus, K.; Meffert, H.; Wagner, H. (Ed.): Integration und Flexibilität, loc. cit., p. 6. In a discipline, in which today fruitful dispute and exchange of ideas are rather an exception than a rule in contrast to the 20s and 50s, an attempt of disussion seems to be positive because it has stimulated many colleagues to think once again about General Business Management.

52 Although Gutenberg provides an admirable sensitive analysis of Japanese firms, which was indeed highly esteemed by many Japanese, there was a very unsensitive misunderstanding founded in the forced spirit of age which is expressed in Nagaoka's question. Cf. Gutenberg, E.: Über japanische Unternehmen, Wiesbaden 1960; Nagaoka, K.: Brauchen wir eine neue Betriebswirtschaftslehre? Aus der Sicht der japanischen Kritischen Betriebswirtschaftslehre, working papers of the economic sciences department at the comprehensive university of Wuppertal, Wuppertal 1979, No. 35.

53 Cf. the 21 contributions in the index of publications of Gutenberg in Albach, H. (Ed.): Zur Theorie der Unternehmung, loc.cit., pp. 291-299.

his own work but even more so from the work of those that were directly influenced by him.

No field of research has released such a huge flood as has production. After the type A production function was superseded by Gutenberg's type B production function and freedom reigned, many others followed with an array of production functions requiring the first quarter of the alphabet.[54] These production functions were the foundations of single-stage, multistage, static and dynamic production theory for single-product and multiproduct firms.[55] Program planning and opera-

---

[54] Cf. production function type C at Heinen (Heinen, E.: Betriebswirtschaftliche Kostenlehre, Kostentheorie und Kostenentscheidungen, 6. ed., Wiesbaden 1983), production function type D (Kloock, J.: Betriebswirtschaftliche Input-Output-Modelle. Ein Beitrag zur Produktionstheorie, Wiesbaden 1969; Kloock, J.: Zur gegenwärtigen Diskussion der betriebswirtschaftlichen Produktions- und Kostentheorie, in: Zeitschrift für Betriebswirtschaft, 39. Jg. (1969), Ergänzungsheft I, pp. 49-82), production function type E (Küpper, H.U.: Dynamische Produktionsfunktion der Unternehmung auf der Basis des Input-Output-Ansatzes, in: Zeitschrift für Betriebswirtschaft, 49. Jg. (1979), pp. 93-106), production function type F (Matthes, W.: Dynamische Einzelproduktionsfunktion der Unternehmung. Report No. 81 of the Seminar for General Business Management and Planning, 2. ed., Cologne 1986).

[55] Cf. Albach, H.: Zur Verbindung von Produktionstheorie und Investitionstheorie, in: Zur Theorie der Unternehmung, edd. H. Koch, Wiesbaden 1962, pp. 137-203; Bohr, K.: Zur Produktionstheorie der Mehrproduktunternehmung, Cologne et al. 1967; Dellmann, K.: Betriebswirtschaftliche Produktions- und Kostentheorie, Wiesbaden 1980; Dinkelbach, W.: Zum Problem der Produktionsplanung in Ein- und Mehrproduktunternehmen, Würzburg - Vienna 1964; Dinkelbach, W.; Rosenberg, O.: Erfolgs- und umweltorientierte Produktionstheorie, 2. ed., Berlin - Heidelberg 1997; Fandel, G.: Produktion I: Produktions- und Kostentheorie, 3. ed., Berlin et al. 1993; Kilger, W.: Produktions- und Kostentheorie, Wiesbaden 1958; Kistner, K.P.: Produktions- und Kostentheorie, 2. ed., Heidelberg 1993; Kloock, J.: Betriebswirtschaftliche Input-Output-Modelle, loc. cit.; Knolmayer, G.: Der Einfluß von Anpassungsmöglichkeiten auf die Isoquante in Gutenberg-Produktionsfunktionen, in: Zeitschrift für Betriebswirtschaft 53. Jg. (1983), pp. 1122-1147; Küpper, H.U.: Interdependenzen zwischen Produktionstheorie und der Organisation des Produktionsprozesses, Berlin 1980; Lassmann, G.: Die Produktionsfunktion und ihre Bedeutung für die betriebswirtschaftliche Kostentheorie, Cologne et al. 1958; Lücke, W.: Produktions- und Kostentheorie, 3. ed., Würzburg 1973; Luhmer, A.: Maschinelle Produktionsprozesse. Ein Ansatz dynamischer Produktions- und Kostentheorie, Opladen 1975; Pressmar, B.D.: Kosten- und Leistungsanalyse im Industriebetrieb, Wiesbaden 1971; Schüler, W.: Prozeß- und Verfahrensauswahl im einstufigen Einproduktunternehmen, in: Zeitschrift für Betriebswirtschaft 43. Jg. (1973), pp. 435-458; Schweizer, M.; Küpper, K.U.: Produktions- und Kostentheorie der Unternehmung, Reinbek 1974; Troßmann, E.: Grundlagen einer dynamischen Theorie und Politik der betrieblichen Produktion, Berlin 1983.

tions scheduling[56] became possible and everything could be captured by standard marginal costing and contribution costing[57].

Consideration of the instruments of sales policy led to monographs on each instrument[58], on the double-kinked demand curve in competition theory[59] and into empiricism[60] and competition policy[61]. But the book was always entitled Sales.

---

56 Cf. Adam, D.: Produktionsmanagement, Wiesbaden 1992; Albach, H.: Produktionsplanung auf der Basis technischer Verbrauchsfunktionen, in: Arbeitsgemeinschaft für Forschung des Landes Nordrhein-Westfalen, No. 105, Cologne and Opladen 1962; Jacob, H.: Die Planung des Produktions- und Absatzprogrammes, in: Industriebetriebslehre, hrsg. v. Jacob, H., 4. ed., Wiesbaden 1990, pp. 405-590; Kern, W.: Industrielle Produktionswirtschaft, 5. ed., Wiesbaden 1992; Kilger, W.: Optimale Produktions- und Absatzplanung, Opladen 1973; Kistner, K.P.; Steven, M.: Produktionsplanung, 2. ed., Heidelberg 1993; Küpper, H.U.: Ablauforganisation, Stuttgart et al. 1981; Sabel, H.: Programmplanung, kurzfristige, in: HWProd, edd. Kern, W., Stuttgart 1979, col. 1686-1700; Schneeweiß, Ch.: Einführung in die Produktionswirtschaft, 6. ed., Berlin u.a. 1997; Seelbach, H.: Ablaufplanung, Würzburg 1975; Zäpfel, G.: Produktionswirtschaft - Operatives Produktionsmanagement, Berlin et al. 1982.

57 Cf. for example Kilger, W.: Flexible Plankostenrechnung und Deckungsbeitragsrechnung, 10. ed., Wiesbaden 1993; Riebel, P.: Einzelkosten- und Deckungsbeitragsrechnung, 7. ed., Wiesbaden 1994, and many more.

58 Cf. Jacob, H.: Preispolitik, 2. ed., Wiesbaden 1971; Dichtl, E.: Die Beurteilung der Erfolgsträchtigkeit eines Produktes als Grundlage der Gestaltung des Produktionsprogramms, Berlin 1970; Sabel, H.: Produktpolitik in absatzwirtschaftlicher Sicht, Wiesbaden 1971; Brockhoff, K.: Produktpolitik, 3., upriched ed.., Stuttgart 1993; Behrens, K.: Absatzwerbung, 2. ed., Wiesbaden 1976; Böcker, F.: Der Distributionsweg einer Unternehmung, Berlin 1972; Schmalen, H.: Kommunikationspolitik, 2. ed., Stuttgart et al., 1992.

59 Cf. Albach, H.: Das Gutenberg-Oligopol, in: Koch, H. (Ed.): Zur Theorie des Absatzes, Wiesbaden 1973, pp. 9-33; Albach. H.: Unternehmen im Wettbewerb: Investitions-, Wettbewerbs- und Wachstumstheorie, Wiesbaden 1991; Albach, H.: Über Informationsmonopole, in: Zeitschrift für Betriebswirtschaft, 62. Jg. 1992, pp. 1055-1068; Albach, H.: Die Bedeutung neuerer Entwicklungen in der Wettbewerbstheorie für die strategische Unternehmungsführung, in: Ordelheide, D.; Bern, R.; Büsselmann, E. (Ed.): Betriebswirtschaftslehre und ökonomische Theorie, Stuttgart 1991, pp. 255-272; Albach, H.: Global Competition among the Few, No. 40 der Swedish School of Economics and Business Administration Research Reports, Helsingfors 1997; Sabel, H. et al.: Zur Diskussion des Gutenberg-Oligopols, in: Zeitschrift für Betriebswirtschaft, 46. Jg. (1976), pp. 205-224.

60 Cf. Hruschka, H.: Schätzung und normative Analyse ausgewählter Preis-Absatz-Funktionen, in: Zeitschrift für Betriebswirtschaft, 67. Jg. (1997), pp. 845-864; Wied-Nebbeling, S.: Zur Preis-Absatz-Funktion beim Oligopol auf dem unvollkommenen Markt. Empirische Evidenz und theoretisch-analytische Probleme der Gutenberg-Funktion, in: Jahrbücher für Nationalökonomie und Statistik, Vol. 198 (1983), pp. 123-144.

61 Cf. Albach, H.: Protektion, Protektionismus, Preis- und Innovationswettbewerb, in: Gewerblicher Rechtsschutz und Urheberrecht, Vol. 4 (1992), pp. 238-239; Albach,

Gutenberg simply did not want to become friends with marketing, probably because he regarded it as a fashion.

He never was modernistic but always modern. He liked and possessed modern art, was personally acquainted with some of its exponents, and was himself on the verge of being a talented contributor.[62] Although he might have esteemed Beuys' early drawings he was sure that he had not to like him, because of the idea that indeed everyone is an artist which appears to him suspect, because it is not human.

He was probably the last nobleman and, like Max Planck was searching for something new by staying indebted to the old,[63] never the new at all costs, especially if it was simply fashionable. In modern terminology he was never "method driven" but always "problem driven". He never would have understood that a problem could be bent to fit a given method.

First and foremost he would not have understood that there is only the 'bad slave" but not also the "good slave"[64] or only the "good-for-nothing servant" and not also the "good and faithful servant".[65] Second, he would not have comprehended why so many disciples of the so called new theory do not continue reading the text: Thus, in both cases, the master, after discovering opportunistic behavior, cuts the slave "into pieces"[66] and throws "the servant into the utmost darkness"[67], where both of them will "howl and grind on their teeth"[68] which is heard and proclaimed by the those present. Third, he would not have understood that they only adopt the agency theory approach because they do not mind that nearly any set of assumptions leads to nearly any set of results;[69] and, that it would be rather disturbing for them if they had to give up the elegance of the unity of the models.

In all three cases Gutenberg would have raised the representational issue. In the first case Gutenberg would have been happy to hear about the important works of Reinhard Selten in the field of experimental economics who concludes that human behavior is highly likely to be characterized by fairness. In the second case he

---

H.: Wettbewerbspolitik und globale Strategien für intelligente Produkte, in: Krystek, U.; Lück, J. (Ed.): Führungskräfte und Führungserfolg, Wiesbaden 1995, pp. 51-69.

62 Cf. Albach, H.: Die Betriebswirtschaftslehre: Eine Wissenschaft, loc. cit., pp. 264/265.

63 Cf. Speicher, Chr.: Dem Alten verhaftet, dem Neuen verpflichtet. Zum 50. Todestag von Max Planck, in: Neue Züricher Zeitung, No. 227, 01.10.1997, p. 65.

64 Cf. Matthew 24, 45.

65 Cf. Matthew 25,14-15.

66 Cf. Matthew 24, 51.

67 Cf. Matthew 25, 30.

68 Cf. Matthew 24, 51 and 25, 30.

69 Cf. Franke, G.: Agency-Theorie, in: Enzyklopädie der Betriebswirtschaftslehre I: Handwörterbuch der Betriebswirtschaft, Teilband 1, 5. ed., edd. Wittman, W.; Kern, W.; Köhler, R.; Küpper, H.U.; von Wysocki, K., Stuttgart 1993, col. 37-49, here, col. 48.

would have chosen another formulation of the problem because every human has a history which can be assessed, because control is a matter of course in business management, and because information about deficient behaviour is spread not only by journalists who love "bad news". That he would have regarded the method-driven approach as inadmissible is nowhere plainer than in the introduction to his university speech, "Work on the problem, and around the problem, was, and remains, the only genuine scientific posture irrespective of where the scientific thinking leads and of whether its results are of practical relevance. Conversely, in providing practically useful results the scientific character of the underlying effort itself cannot be questioned."[70]

He could not oppose the utilization of results because he was almost driven to focus scientific interests on the aim of "...preventing the forces driving the economy from getting out of control and thereby destroying instead of constructing "[71].

The scientific consequence also prevented him from taking seriously the diversity of paradigms which, appearing and vanishing with the changing spirit of the age, come and go, because it would have contradicted his humanistic world view of life. The conception that a firm is a nexus of contracts and, as such, loses its identity, would also have contradicted his understanding of the firm.[72], [73] "Thus it is clear that the principle of profitability, which dominates the typical firms that characterize a market economy, is fashioned from liberalism and natural law"[74], and: The "multi-shaped world of firms is rooted in the intellectual substance of past and present approaches to the order of life."[75] Although he realized the continuos change of such approaches to life he never would have accepted a break consisting of denying reality.

In this view of life he was in agreement with those with whom he cultivated exchanges, namely, with Wilhelm Kromphardt and Eduard Willeke, with Erich Preiser and Erich Schneider, with Fritz Neumark and Heinz Sauermann, with René König and Theodor Schieder.

Whatever he did he tried to recognize regularities in the Greek sense of theory as an idea of finding beauty in understanding the unity of the solution to a problem and to be human.

---

70 Gutenberg, E.: Betriebswirtschaftslehre als Wissenschaft, loc. cit., p. 5.

71 Gutenberg, E.: Betriebswirtschaftslehre als Wissenschaft, loc. cit., p. 9.

72 Cf. Jensen, M.C.; Meckling, W.H.: Theory of the Firm: Management Behavior, Agency Costs and Ownership Structure, in: Journal of Financial Economics, Vol. 3 (1976), pp. 305-360.

73 „Das Unternehmen ist kein Individuum", Jensen, M.C.; Meckling, W.H.: loc. cit., p. 311.

74 Gutenberg, E.: Betriebswirtschaftslehre als Wissenschaft, loc. cit., p. 12.

75 Gutenberg, E.: Betriebswirtschaftslehre als Wissenschaft, loc. cit., p. 12.

When someone takes his shining place in history it is worth commemorating and the eulogist counts himself lucky to have honored the one in a way the esteemed might have accepted it given his personal modesty, although he could have been proud in building a work which his following decisive sentence could be applied on: „Only when it has become possible to make a constituent part of the integral whole meaningful is science instructive."[76] This sentence itself honors a real celebrity.

Literature

Adam, D.: Produktionsmanagement, Wiesbaden 1992

Adam, D.; Backhaus, K.; Meffert, H.; Wagner, H.: Vorwort, in: Adam, D.; Backhaus, K.; Meffert, H.; Wagner, H. (Ed.): Integration und Flexibilität, Wiesbaden, 1990

Albach, H.: Produktionsplanung auf der Basis technischer Verbrauchsfunktionen, in: Arbeitsgemeinschaft für Forschung des Landes Nordrhein-Westfalen, No. 105, Cologne and Opladen 1962

Albach, H.: Zur Verbindung von Produktionstheorie und Investitionstheorie, in: Zur Theorie der Unternehmung, ed. H. Koch, Wiesbaden 1962, pp. 137-203

Albach, H.: Das Gutenberg-Oligopol, in: Koch, H. (Ed.): Zur Theorie des Absatzes, Wiesbaden 1973, pp. 9-33

Albach, H.: Überwindung des Gegensatzes zwischen Volks- und Betriebswirtschaftslehre. Ein Überblick über die Entwicklung der letzten fünfzig Jahre. Zum achtzigsten Geburtstag von Erich Gutenberg, in: Frankfurter Allgemeine Zeitung, 13.12.1977, p. 12

Albach, H.: Allgemeine Betriebswirtschaftslehre. Zum Gedenken an Erich Gutenberg, in: Zeitschrift für Betriebswirtschaft, 56. Jg. (1986), pp. 578-613

Albach, H. (Ed.): Zur Theorie der Unternehmung, Schriften und Reden von Erich Gutenberg. Aus dem Nachlaß, Berlin et al. 1989

Albach, H.: Die Betriebswirtschaftslehre: Eine Wissenschaft, in: Albach, H. (Ed.): Zur Theorie der Unternehmung, Schriften und Reden von Erich Gutenberg. Aus dem Nachlaß, Berlin et al. 1989, pp. 213-380

Albach, H.: Die Bedeutung neuerer Entwicklungen in der Wettbewerbstheorie für die strategische Unternehmungsführung, in: Ordelheide, D.; Bern, R.; Büsselmann, E. (Ed.): Betriebswirtschaftslehre und ökonomische Theorie, Stuttgart 1991, pp. 255-272

Albach, H.: Unternehmen im Wettbewerb: Investitions-, Wettbewerbs- und Wachstumstheorie, Wiesbaden 1991

---

[76] Gutenberg, E.: Betriebswirtschaftslehre als Wissenschaft, loc. cit., p. 38.

Albach, H.: Über Informationsmonopole, in: Zeitschrift für Betriebswirtschaft, 62. Jg. (1992), pp. 1055-1068

Albach, H.: Protektion, Protektionismus, Preis- und Innovationswettbewerb, in: Gewerblicher Rechtsschutz und Urheberrecht, Vol. 4 (1992), pp. 238-239

Albach, H.: Wettbewerbspolitik und globale Strategien für intelligente Produkte, in: Krystek, U.; Lück, J. (Ed.): Führungskräfte und Führungserfolg, Wiesbaden 1995, pp. 51-69

Albach, H.: Global Competition among the Few, No. 40 of the Swedish School of Economics and Business Administration Research Reports, Helsinfors 1997

Albach, H.: Eine lebendige Theorie der Unternehmung. Zum 100. Geburtstag Erich Gutenbergs, in: Frankfurter Allgemeine Zeitung, No. 288, 11.10.1997, pp. 21/22

Behrens, K.: Absatzwerbung, 2. ed. Wiesbaden 1976

Böcker, F.: Der Distributionsweg einer Unternehmung, Berlin 1972

Bohr, K.: Zur Produktionstheorie der Mehrproduktunternehmung, Cologne et al. 1967

Brockhoff, K.: Produktpolitik, 3., extended ed., Stuttgart 1993

Coulmas, F.: Wie das Alphabet nach Japan, in: Spektrum der Wissenschaft, November 11/1994, pp. 90-100

Dichtl, E.: Die Beurteilung der Erfolgsträchtigkeit eines Produktes als Grundlage der Gestaltung des Produktionsprogramms, Berlin 1970

Dellmann, K.: Betriebswirtschaftliche Produktions- und Kostentheorie, Wiesbaden 1980

Dinkelbach, W.: Zum Problem der Produktionsplanung in Ein- und Mehrproduktunternehmen, Würzburg - Wien 1964

Dinkelbach, W.; Rosenberg, O.: Erfolgs- und umweltorientierte Produktionstheorie, 2. ed., Berlin - Heidelberg 1997

Fandel, G.: Produktion I: Produktions- und Kostentheorie, 3. ed., Berlin et al. 1993

Franke, G.: Agency-Theorie, in: Enzyklopädie der Betriebswirtschaftslehre I: Handwörterbuch der Betriebswirtschaft, Teilband 1, 5. ed., edd. Wittman, W.; Kern, W.; Köhler, R.; Küpper, H.U.; von Wysocki, K., Stuttgart 1993, col. 37-49

Gutenberg, E.: Thünens isolierter Staat als Fiktion, 4. Band der Bausteine zu einer Philosophie des „Als-ob", edd. H. Vaihinger und R. Schmidt, München 1922

Gutenberg, E.: Die Unternehmung als Gegenstand betriebswirtschaftlicher Theorie, Berlin-Vienna 1929, unv. Nachdruck 1997

Gutenberg, E.: Zum Methodenstreit, in: Zeitschrift für handelswissenschaftliche Forschung, NF, 5. Jg. (1953), pp. 327-355

Gutenberg, E.: Untersuchungen über die Investitionsentscheidungen industrieller Unternehmen, Cologne und Opladen 1959

Gutenberg, E.: Über japanische Unternehmen, Wiesbaden 1960

Gutenberg, E.: Die Absatzplanung als Instrument der Unternehmensführung, in: Gutenberg, E. (Ed.): Absatzplanung in der Praxis, Wiesbaden 1962

Gutenberg, E.: Unternehmensführung - Organisation und Entscheidungen, Wiesbaden 1962

Gutenberg, E.: Vorwort des Herausgebers, in: Gutenberg, E. (Ed.): Absatzplanung in der Praxis, Wiesbaden 1962

Gutenberg, E.: Betriebswirtschaftslehre als Wissenschaft, Kölner Universitätsreden 18, 3. ed., Krefeld 1967

Gutenberg, E.: Grundlagen der Betriebswirtschaftslehre, 1. Band: Die Produktion, 21 Auflage, Berlin - Heidelberg - New York, 1975

Gutenberg, E.: Die Grundlagen der Betriebswirtschaftslehre. 3. Band: Die Finanzen, 8., extended ed., Berlin - Heidelberg - New York 1980

Gutenberg, E.: Rückblick auf die Betriebswirtschaftslehre des Absatzes, in: Zeitschrift für Betriebswirtschaft, 55. Jg. (1985), pp.1200-1213

Gutenberg, E.: Eigenhändig geschriebener Lebenslauf, in: Albach, H. (Ed.): Zur Theorie der Unternehmung, Schriften und Reden von Erich Gutenberg. Aus dem Nachlaß, Berlin et al. 1989; pp. 281-283

Gutenberg, E.: Rückblicke, in: Albach, H. (Ed.): Zur Theorie der Unternehmung, Schriften und Reden von Erich Gutenberg. Aus dem Nachlaß, Berlin et al. 1989; pp. 1-118

Heinen, E.: Betriebswirtschaftliche Kostenlehre, Kostentheorie und Kostenentscheidungen, 6. ed., Wiesbaden 1983

Henninger, C.: Jenseits von Soll und Haben, in: Frankfurter Allgemeine Zeitung, 13.12.1982

Hruschka, H.: Schätzung und normative Analyse ausgewählter Preis-Absatz-Funktionen, in: Zeitschrift für Betriebswirtschaft, 67. Jg. (1997), pp. 845-864

Jacob, H.: Preispolitik, 2. ed., Wiesbaden 1971

Jacob, H.: Praxisnahe Theorie der Unternehmung, in: Die WELT, 13.12.1972

Jacob, H.: Gutenbergs Konzeption überzeugt auch noch heute, in: Die WELT, 12.12.1977, p.11

Jacob, H.: Erich Gutenberg zum Gedächtnis, in: DIE BETRIEBSWIRTSCHAFT, 44. Jg. (1984), p. 651

Jacob, H.: Die Planung des Produktions- und Absatzprogrammes, in: Industriebetriebslehre, edd. H. Jacob, 4. ed., Wiesbaden 1990, pp. 405-590

Jensen, M.C.; Meckling, W.H.: Theory of the Firm. Management Behavior, Agency Costs and Ownership Structure, in: Journal of Financial Economics, Vol. 3 (1976), pp. 305-360

Kern, W.: Industrielle Produktionswirtschaft, 5. ed., Wiesbaden 1992

Kilger, W.: Zum wissenschaftlichen Werk Erich Gutenbergs, in: Zeitschrift für Betriebswirtschaft, 32. Jg. (1962), p. 689

Kilger, W.: Optimale Produktions- und Absatzplanung, Opladen 1973

Kilger, W.: Produktions- und Kostentheorie, Wiesbaden 1958

Kilger, W.: Flexible Plankostenrechnung und Deckungsbeitragsrechnung, 10. ed., Wiesbaden 1993

Kistner, K.P.: Produktions- und Kostentheorie, 2. ed., Heidelberg 1993

Kistner, K.P.; Steven, M.: Produktionsplanung, 2. ed., Heidelberg 1993

Kloock, J.: Betriebswirtschaftliche Input-Output-Modelle, Ein Beitrag zur Produktionstheorie, Wiesbaden 1969

Kloock, J.: Zur gegenwärtigen Diskussion der betriebswirtschaftlichen Produktions- und Kostentheorie, in: Zeitschrift für Betriebswirtschaft, 39. Jg. (1969), Ergänzungsheft I, pp. 49-82.

Knolmayer, G.: Der Einfluß von Anpassungsmöglichkeiten auf die Isoquante in Gutenberg-Produktionsfunktionen, in: Zeitschrift für Betriebswirtschaft, 53. Jg. (1983), pp. 1122-1147

Kreikebaum, H.: Er hat eine ganze Generation von heute erfolgreichen Betriebswirten geprägt, in: Westfalen-Blatt vom 13.12.1977, p. 288

Küpper, H.U.: Dynamische Produktionsfunktion der Unternehmung auf der Basis des Input-Output-Ansatzes, in: Zeitschrift für Betriebswirtschaft, 49. Jg. (1979), pp. 93-106

Küpper, H.U.: Interdependenzen zwischen Produktionstheorie und der Organisation des Produktionsprozesses, Berlin 1980

Küpper, H.U.: Ablauforganisation, Stuttgart et al. 1981

Lassmann, G.: Die Produktionsfunktion und ihre Bedeutung für die betriebswirtschaftliche Kostentheorie, Cologne et al. 1958

Lücke, W.: Produktions- und Kostentheorie, 3. ed., Würzburg 1973

Lücke, W.: Erich Gutenberg vollendet sein achtzigstes Lebensjahr, in: Angewandte Planung, Band 1, 1977, p. 139

Luhmer, A.: Maschinelle Produktionsprozesse. Ein Ansatz dynamischer Produktions- und Kostentheorie, Opladen 1975

Matthes, W.: Dynamische Einzelproduktionsfunktion der Unternehmung. Report No. 81, Seminar for General Business Management and Business Management Planning, 2. ed., Cologne 1986.

Nagaoka, K.: Brauchen wir eine neue Betriebswirtschaftslehre? Aus der Sicht der japanischen Kritischen Betriebswirtschaftslehre, Arbeitspapiere des Fachbereichs Wirtschaftswissenschaft der Gesamthochschule Wuppertal, Wuppertal 1979, No. 35

o.V.: Podiumsdiskussion, in: Adam, D.; Backhaus, K.; Meffert, H.; Wagner, H. (Ed.): Integration und Flexibilität, Wiesbaden, 1990, pp. 137-180

Pfeil, G.-H.: Betriebswirtschaft auf neuen Wegen, in: Die WELT sprach mit Dr. Dr. h.c. Erich Gutenberg, in: Die WELT, 18.12.1962, p. 8

Popper, K.: Logik der Forschung, 6., improved ed., Tübingen 1976

Popper, K.: Alles Leben ist Problemlösen, 7. ed., Munich - Zurich 1995

Pressmar, B.D.: Kosten- und Leistungsanalyse im Industriebetrieb, Wiesbaden 1971

Riebel, P.: Einzelkosten- und Deckungsbeitragsrechnung, 7. ed., Wiesbaden 1994

Sabel, H.: Produktpolitik in absatzwirtschaftlicher Sicht, Wiesbaden 1971

Sabel, H. et al.: Zur Diskussion des Gutenberg-Oligopols, in: Zeitschrift für Betriebswirtschaft, 46. Jg. (1976), pp. 205-224

Sabel, H.: Programmplanung, kurzfristige, in: HWProd, edd. Kern, W., Stuttgart 1979, col. 1686-1700

Schmalen, H.: Kommunikationspolitik, 2. ed., Stuttgart et al., 1992

Schneeweiß, Ch.: Einführung in die Produktionswirtschaft, 6. ed., Berlin et al. 1997

Schüler, W.: Prozeß- und Verfahrensauswahl im einstufigen Einproduktunternehmen, in: Zeitschrift für Betriebswirtschaft, 43. Jg. (1973), pp. 435-458

Schüler, W.: Zum 85. Geburtstag von Erich Gutenberg, in: Betriebswirtschaftliche Forschung und Praxis, 34. Jg. (1984), p. 576

Schweizer, M.; Küpper, K.U.: Produktions- und Kostentheorie der Unternehmung, Reinbek 1974

Seelbach, H.: Ablaufplanung, Würzburg 1975

Seelbach, H.: Zum Tode von Erich Gutenberg, in: Das Wirtschaftsstudium, 13. Jg. (1984), pp. 355/356

Speicher, Chr.: Dem Alten verhaftet, dem Neuen verpflichtet. Zum 50. Todestag von Max Planck, in: Neue Züricher Zeitung, Nr. 227, 01.10.1997, p. 65

Troßmann, E.: Grundlagen einer dynamischen Theorie und Politik der betrieblichen Produktion, Berlin 1983

Wied-Nebbeling, S.: Zur Preis-Absatz-Funktion beim Oligopol auf dem unvollkommenen Markt. Empirische Evidenz und theoretisch-analytische Probleme der Gutenberg-Funktion, in: Jahrbücher für Nationalökonomie und Statistik, Bd. 198 (1983), pp. 123-144

Wöhe, G.: Erich Gutenberg zum Gedenken, in: Deutsches Steuerrecht, 23. Jg., Heft 1/2 (1985), p. 6

Zäpfel, G.: Produktionswirtschaft - Operatives Produktionsmanagement, Berlin et al. 1982

Summary

Gutenberg is the founder of the so called „Betriebswirtschaftliche Theorie". He has been inspired by the fact that the theory of the firm did not cover all problems from the point of view of an individual firm. There have been lots of followers. But nowadays his concept is questioned by other theories which would have never been accepted by him regarding his strict orientation on problems rather than on methods. To follow the way of problem orientation he proposed a methodological guidance: the concept of representativity, which can be seen as analogous to Popper's scientific claim of being accessible to falsification. In integrating new models for each sector respectively to a whole he erected a coherent building of the firm made up of the sectors of production, sales, and finance. Regarding the organization, and being aware of its complexity as well as the limitations of all methods, he confined himself on developing just one rule, the rule of substitution, meaning the substitution of different rules for single cases by a general one for every case. By this he grasped the whole firm, the theory of which we owe him. That is the greatest honor.

The Impact of Gutenberg's Theory of Organisation upon Modern Organisational Conceptions

H. Kreikebaum[1]

Overview

- In the light of the diversity of modern conceptions of organisational theory and practice, an analysis of Gutenberg's influence on modern organisational thinking, with special reference to the status quo of today's organisational practice, presents an important challenge.
- We first investigate how Gutenberg's thinking has been perceived in modern organisational theory. Thereafter we analyse whether his proposals constitute an appropriate solution to today's organisational problems.
- The impact on modern organisational research is analysed on the basis of Gutenberg's new organisational structures, which resulted from changes in technological and economic conditions and by reference to Gutenberg's organisational theory.
- We demonstrate how Gutenberg's considerations can be applied to solve two important practical problems, namely, the delineation of power between the executive board of directors and the supervisory board, and the principle of substitution in organisation.

Keywords. Organizational Theory, New Institutional Economics, Modern Organizational Conceptions

---

1 Prof. Dr. Hartmut Kreikebaum, Lehrstuhl für Industriebetriebslehre, Johann Wolfgang Goethe-Universität Frankfurt am Main, Postfach 11 19 32, 60054 Frankfurt am Main

1 Introduction

1.1 Problem Definition

When Erich Gutenberg developed his theory of organisation within the framework of his system of directing factors some forty years ago, it appeared just as unconventional and innovative as contemporary organisational concepts. In the meantime new organisational theories have been developed and, due to structural changes in technological and economic conditions, entirely new structures and processes.

Gutenberg presented his theory in such a distinct and colourful manner that it can readily be recapitulated. More complex is a portrayal of a summary of contemporary theories of organisation. Even more demanding is an analysis of Gutenberg's noticeable impact on modern organisations. However, this impact accounts for the relevance of the central topic.

It can be illustrated with the following two leading questions:

1. What are the impacts of Gutenberg's thinking on modern theories of organisation? Does he, for example, provide a direct line of thought to organisational economics? Alternatively, where can Gutenberg's approach be found within modern organisational research in respect of both methodology and content?
2. How "modern" in the sense of a "timeless" meaning are Gutenberg's concepts of organisational practice? Do they provide starting-points for analysing, explaining and coping with the dynamic and structural change that is currently taking place within corporate organisations?

The answers to these questions depend on what is understood by "modern approaches" to organisational theory and practice. This means that they are subjective by definition. However, there can be no doubt the rate of change within the last two decades in the spectrum of organisational responsibilities has rarely been exceeded hitherto. The new challenges to the theory and practice of organisation are caused by radical changes in structural, technological and economic conditions. Globalisation on the one hand, and the development of information technology and the revolution in the accumulation of knowledge on the other should be stressed at this point.

1.2 The Organisation within Technological and Economic Structural Change

- Globalisation of Markets

The trend towards a world-wide adaptation to customer needs, that may be observed in various industries, can be considered as the main cause of changes in demand conditions.[2] Global product and market strategies are not only being pursued by large-scale, but also increasingly by small and medium-sized businesses. Today one third of world trade is handled between the different units of internationally operating businesses and a further third between global players.

The restructuring of operations includes new challenges to competitive strategies and the shaping of organisations. The construction of new production capacities in foreign countries has considerable organisational and personnel consequences. The global players must redefine their position within world-wide competition and develop an integrated global vision. Simultaneously they are forced to adapt their decision structures to the global, regional and local demand, resource and competitive conditions. This process requires a fundamental re-appraisal of governance structures and of the efficient cross-linking of world-wide activities. One result of the globalisation is hybrid organisational structures which, depending on the circumstances, combine product-oriented, functional and customer-related configuration elements.

- Information and Communication Technology

The influence of information and communication technology on the shaping of organisations cannot be emphasized greatly enough. Data transmission networks, as well as integrated data bases, significantly improve coordination and integration within global firms. The use of task-oriented information and communication technology causes a modularization of companies.[3] The development of simplified and individualised information and communication technology systems supports the trend towards customer-oriented organisation structures and processes. The world-wide linkage of organisational activities reveals, amongst other things, the trend-like increase of external cooperations through strategic alliances and joint ventures of transnational corporations.

Furthermore, the new technologies provide the means for an interactive application, the interactive use of different types of media and an increased efficiency of the communication process within the company. A higher integration of information and communication technology at the international level leads to a tendency

---

2 This tendency of "converging commonality" was initially described by Levitt, 1983.

3 See Picot/Reichwald/Wigand 1996, pp. 247-259.

towards a greater international spread of human resources as well as to the reinforcing of local autonomy in decision making.[4]

Summing up; new organisational structures develop through profound changes in competitive structure, in the innovation potential of information and communication technology and because of the radical change in values within society and the world of labour. The modularization of companies, that developed through flat hierarchical organisation structures, the development of symbiotic organisations and hybrid forms of cooperation as well as the evolution of virtual corporations, all represent the new organisational structures that provide the means for the organisation to face the challenges caused by the changed general economic setting. In addition, through modularization, corporations more effectively overcome the restrictions that are pre-set by the scarcity of resources, lack of knowledge and spatial distance. [5]

2 An Overview of Gutenberg's Concept of Organisation

Gutenberg initially discusses organisational problems in the first volume of his series "Grundlagen der Betriebswirtschaft" (Fundamentals of Business Administration):[6] His book "Unternehmensführung" (Management) should also be mentioned.[7] As Gutenberg's organisational concept is well-known, the following description is reduced to a brief summary of the fundamental elements of his theoretical approach.

1. Organisation as the task of the directing factor

The "directing factor" controls the entire operating activities. It is composed of an irrational (individual) layer, a rational layer (planning) and an implementation layer (organisation). The function of the organisation is to execute and implement the planning of the general business process (instrumental character, organisation as a means to an end). The coordination of large departments represents a typical executive decision.

2. Basic conditions of organisational design

The assignment of tasks to units of responsibility (persons taking business-decisions) arises under three conditions: capacity, quality and conformity. Congruence must exist between assignment, authority and responsibility. Within the process of

---

4 See Schober 1996, p. 42.

5 See in detail Picot/Reichwald/Wigand 1996.

6 See Gutenberg 1983.

7 See Gutenberg 1962.

delegating decision making powers to a person or an organisational unit, the question of integration intensity and discretion of these administrative units is of relevance. In the individual case it is determined through personnel and functional conditions.

3. Influences of the informal on the formal organisation

The formal corporate organisation consists of the organisational structure, of open and bound forms of cooperation, the information system and the substitution principle of the organisation. Within, and beside, the formal organisation, informal relationships and groups develop and influence the business operations. The informal organisation improves the efficiency of the communication system, e. g., through additional information, but may also block and delay a planned reorganisation, for example through resistance.

4. Hierarchy and Team Structures

According to Gutenberg, the line system represents the hierarchy of responsibilities (principle of the unity of command). Additionally, the functional system of responsibilities (Taylor) and the line-staff system is required. Teams are necessary to ensure the multi-functional cooperation of the administrative units.

5. Relationship between Information and Decision

The different forms of information may be subsumed into information for decision-making purposes and information that is not decision-relevant (e. g. stimulating or reporting information). Gutenberg emphasised the interdependencies between the organisational decision-making process and the information system from the perspective of optimisation, to the same extent as the relationship between communication and forms of organisational structure.

Summing up this necessarily simplified overview; it may be stated that Gutenberg's organisational conception elaborated a variety of organisational matters in a manner which, both conceptually and in individual respects, was outstanding at the time.

3 Gutenberg's Reception within Economic Theories of Organisation

3.1 "Modern" Approaches to Organisation Theory

Here, modern approaches to organisational theories means economic theories of organisation.[8] Their common element is that they all view organisations from an economic perspective. Their roots can be found in various approaches to organisational research, beginning with the analysis of the division of labour and the advantages of specialisation by Adam Smith; and extending to Taylorism and motivation theories. The latter were followed by the incentive/contribution theory first developed by Barnard which was extended by March and Simon and continued by the contingency approach and the team theory developed by Marschak and Radner. Economic theories are based on methodological individualism, i. e., the assumption that organisational acting is determined by individual decisions and that individuals maximise their personal utility, which may be to the benefit of others (altruism), but also at the expense of others (opportunism).

Economic theories may be distinguished further by additional statements on the information level of the organisational member. Neo-classical theory and industrial economics are based on the working hypothesis that information is complete and that actors' behaviour is entirely rational. Yet neo-institutional approaches suggest that the rationality of decision-makers is limited, and that they try to compensate this through the design of institutions.[9]

Neo-classical microeconomics is oriented towards the model of the competitive market. The connection to organisational aspects may be made through the examination of the competitive organisation and an analysis of the results of the market process based on different performance criteria, e. g. efficiency of resource allocation or the general efficiency of production economics.[10] The conception of a decision-oriented organisation theory developed against this background focuses on the following problems:[11]

- The reduction of complexity within the decision-making process;
- The decision and coordination process within groups;
- The basic pattern of coordination of short- and long-term decisions;

---

8 For the following, see Picot/Dietl/Franck 1997.

9 See Franck 1995, p. 21.

10 See Picot/Dietl/Franck 1997, pp. 43-53.

11 See especially Laux/Liermann 1997.

- Hierarchical organisational concepts as a system of task-related, organisational or communicative decisions;
- The formulation of explicit and implicit behavioural norms as the core problem of organisational design;
- Compatibility features and their improvements;
- Theoretical decision models of organisation, e. g. team theory and delegation value concept.

The neo-institutional theories of business structure may roughly be divided into three classes: the property rights theory, the transaction cost theory, and the principal agent theory.[12] In contrast to the neo-classical model, all three approaches have in common that the organisation is viewed as a nexus of contracts. The different concepts partially overlap. For several years an attempt has been made to combine organisation theory with transaction cost theory and the general theory of law to spawn a theory of "new economics of organisation".[13] The new economics of organisation theory basically adopts Williamson's perspective of the firm as a governance structure.[14]

The property rights theory focuses on the rights of action and disposition of the economic actors. Based on the corporate legal structure, those rights are determined by organisational regulations. Business organisation develops through the delegation of rights of action and disposition from the executive board to other organisational members. In conjunction with the closely related transaction cost theory, an examination is made of the effects on efficiency of the varying distribution of property rights between the decision-making units and the interest groups within the organisation. The search for an almost complete clustering of rights helped to overcome the division of disposition and execution propagated by Taylor. Individual units of responsibility and autonomous working groups are empowered to decide what is required in order to fulfil their functions. Through the concentration of property rights (partially) autonomous modules develop at different levels of the organisation, e. g., profit centres and cost centres.[15]

Transaction cost theory examines the transaction and coordination processes that develop between individual decision-makers and institutions through the transfer of rights of disposition and their costs. Of special interest for the theory of organisation are concepts relating to the explanation and design of the "right" division of labour, or concerning the minimisation of interdependencies between the subtasks, the simplification of know-how transfer between the units of responsibility and the allocation of subtasks to the units of responsibility (centralisation/decentralisation)

---

12 See for details Picot/Dietl/Franck 1997, pp. 53-94.

13 See Wieland 1996, p. 95, pp. 113-132.

14 See among others Williamson 1993.

15 See Franck 1995.

according to their special field (core competencies). The central organisational problem is the development of coordination and motivation mechanisms for the minimisation of transaction costs.[16] Between the coordination through the market and through hierarchy[17] various forms of cooperation can be found.[18]

Principal agent theory is concerned with the reduction of the asymmetry of information between principal and agent. In addition to the methods of signalling, screening and self-selection, the interest of the agent can be aligned with that of the principal through appropriate incentive and sanction systems. They seem appropriate not only in respect of horizontal or vertical coordination, but also for the regulation of the internal relationships between the managerial unit and employees as well as between owners and managers.

There are manifold interdependencies between the above-mentioned approaches.[19] Thus, the existence of transaction costs has a considerable influence upon the distribution of property rights. Besides the welfare profits and losses, they represent a further criterion for the assessment of varying distributions of rights of disposition. As both measures tend toward parallel conclusions in their assessment of external effects, the relationships between the transaction cost theory and the property rights theory can only be considered as generally complementary.[20]

In contrast to the relationship between transaction costs and property rights transaction cost theory and principal agent theory tend to conflict. This may result from the fact that different areas have been examined by reference to specific efficiency criteria. However, unlike property rights theory, transaction cost and principal-agent concepts consider the institutional framework as given. The three approaches constitute an instrument which, on the one hand, facilitates an examination of the efficiencies of institutions and, on the other, of the coordination of relationships that determine performance.[21] The profitability of a certain theoretical concept must ultimately be assessed within the actual organisational decision process.

In brief it can be stated that "modern" organisation theory presents itself as a "wild mixture". The decision-oriented approach proves to be more prevalent.[22] It combines both behavioural findings and components of economic approaches.

---

16 See extensively Picot/Dietl/Franck 1997, pp. 66-81.

17 Williamson 1990, pp. 1-25.

18 See the example of the decreasing degree of vertical integration for different decision alternatives of optimising production depth described by Picot/Dietl/Franck 1997, pp. 91-94.

19 See in detail Picot/Dietl/Franck 1997, pp. 91-94

20 For this chapter, see Picot/Dietl/Franck 1997, p. 92.

21 See the detailed comparison of neo-institutional concept in Picot 1991a, pp. 153-156.

22 The decision-related approach is described in detail by Frese and Laux. See Frese 1995, pp. 4-7, and Laux/Liermann 1997.

3.2 Gutenberg's Conception from the Perspective of Modern Organisation Theory

Gutenberg's conception can be considered as a "modern" approach for his era. As described below, his ideas and concepts were subsequently taken up and extended in the later works of other authors. The integration of organisational issues into microeconomics and the theory of organisation are cases in point, just as his openness to behavioural research.

The integration of the organisation into the *system of directing factors* pointed the way ahead to the later discussion of governance structures. In addition it was Gutenberg who made the application of the principal agent theory possible, by calling for the coordination of large departments as an executive decision that can not be delegated. Moreover, the search for an adequate complexity of organisations, that appears to be the focus of current organisational research, is implicit in Gutenberg's demand for the avoidance of an "under" or "over" organisation.

Gutenberg's perspective of the instrumental character of the organisation also predominates within normative decision-oriented organisation theories. The aim of an organisation is ultimately to take the "good" object decision. All organisational and communicative decisions of a managerial authority directly or indirectly serve this purpose.

The *basic problem of organisational design* lies in the controlling of decisions at different levels of the organisational hierarchy in order to meet predefined goals and objectives. The subjects of this controlling process are the operating activities (tasks) and directing activities. Different decision-making levels are in charge of the controlling process depending on the nature and scope of the tasks. For example, the establishment of a departmental structure, and the distribution of managerial tasks, are managerial responsibilities. This is especially relevant for organisational decisions, e. g., on the form of departmentalisation and on the number of hierarchical levels, but also for the selection of executives.

Compatibility of requirement is the instrument with which the decision-oriented organisation theory examines the correspondence between the demands on the managers' unit and their directing possibilities and characteristics.[23] Compatibility of requirement of directing tasks can not be measured objectively, because their outstanding features prove to be low structuration, high variability and a large number of decision tasks. Compatibility of incentives ensures that the ultimate unit of responsibility pursues goals that do not contradict those of the organisation.

---

23 See in detail Laux/Liermann 1997, pp. 239-244.

New organisation theories discuss the analysis and synthesis of tasks on the basis of transaction costs.[24] The assignment of competence to administrative units follows the principles of property rights theory by minimising the welfare losses that result from external effects and transaction costs. As an "economic theory of delegation"[25] the principal-agent theory provides detailed information on the risks and instruments of delegation. The risks for the principal arise from the asymmetrical information of the principal on the characteristics and intentions of the agent (hidden characteristics, hidden action and hidden intentions).

Gutenberg's research on the *effects of the informal upon the formal organisation* follows behavioural statements within the literature, but he was also able to base his findings on extensive experience during his versatile working life. He was acquainted with a world of economic agents who are far from perfect and interact with a high degree of dependence on the basis of bounded rationality and morals. Gutenberg takes up the social psychological approach of Simon and other exponents of behavioural theory. He stresses the necessity of organisational search and learning processes and discusses organisational uncertainties that result from the existence of informal group development and communication. Within decision-oriented organisation theories the discussion of the effect of informal and formal activities was widely replaced with discussion of the problem of collective decision making within groups.[26]

Gutenberg considers the close connection between *hierarchy and organisation* as the constitutive element of the company organisation structure, but he also considers it necessary to integrate team-like structures into the institutional decision-making process.[27] For Gutenberg, teams play an important role within the information structure of a decentralised decision-making process. Their advantages lie for him within the common interests and common goals of the team members and the organisation. This approach is taken up in modern versions of team theory. It has also given important impulses to the development of the delegation value concept that provides the means for solving delegation problems. In contrast to Marschak's original assumptions, on which Gutenberg based his concepts, conflicts between team members and objectives that are set by the institution, are nowadays not excluded, but explicitly taken into consideration. The delegation value concept developed by Laux even involves the case, in which the institution

---

24 The three principles determining specialisation are described by Picot/Dietl/Franck 1997, p. 166.

25 Picot/Dietl/Franck 1997, p. 85.

26 See for example Frese 1995, pp. 170-178.

27 The link can also be found in newer proposals for the implementation of organisations with a low degree of hierarchy. They are obviously based on the assumption that the real antithesis is not hierarchy - market, but hierarchy - anarchy. See in detail Wieland 1996, pp. 36-42.

possesses uncertain expectations about the level of information of the potential decision-making authorities, and the conclusions drawn from this state of affairs.[28]

Team theory examines the effects of various forms of information search and transfer based on the division of labour and upon team performance which depends on alternative rules for action from individual team members. The objective of the investigation is the simultaneous optimisation of the information structure of the team and the rules for action on the part of team members.[29]

In the context of an economic examination of the relationship between *information and decision*, Gutenberg discusses the optimal information and decision rules for the selection of marketing policy parameters. He also examines the consequences of the analysis of communication structures and studies the relationship between information costs and decision coordination.[30] He concludes: "No matter how we look at it, starting from Marschak, the incompatibility of the preference structures of decision centres and the incompleteness and inaccuracy of information systems are the pre-eminent current theoretical questions on the relationship between information and decision within organisation studies".[31]

4 Gutenberg's view of the interdependence of organisational theory and practice

Gutenberg's concept of organisation influenced modern organisation theory as well as organisational practice. Its focus centres upon the internal structure of the firm. The prevailing elements of his organisational concept are: the theoretical orientation towards the microeconomic model of the market (factor markets and product markets) on the one hand, and the consequent emphasis on the relevance of practice on the other. It is Gutenberg's objective to bring the variety of existing forms of organisation into a conceptual order. However, he resists the temptation to offer *ad hoc* practical solutions. On the contrary, he weighs up the pros and

---

28 See Laux 1979a, and Laux/Liebermann 1997.

29 "The coordination models based upon team theory undoubtedly represent at present the most differentiated and affirmative approach to mathematical organisation theory". Frese 1992, p. 224. Nevertheless, not all expectations regarding the efficiency of analytical models, especially those of interorganisational coordination, have been fulfilled. See Vornhusen 1994, p. 21.

30 Gutenberg adopts Albach's approach to the differentiation of information types and the conclusions regarding optimal information and communication systems. See Albach 1961. The problems related to the coordination of organisational decisions are examined in detail by Hax. See Hax 1965, and Hax 1969.

31 See Gutenberg 1983, p. 288.

cons of an organisational alternative in a very fundamental way and does not chosse a specific solution at first sight.

Gutenberg's understanding of the interdependence of theory and practice is principally shared by modern organisational theory. The neo-institutional concepts examine the possible impact of modern organisation theory upon practice. Insights provided by property rights theory and by principal-agent theory, for instance, can be transferred to interfirm cooperation as well as to virtual organisation and holding structures. Transaction cost theory can also be applied to these structures, but also to the concept of lean organisation and business reengineering.

Gutenberg strongly emphasises two basic assumptions:

- Organisational decisions represent voluntary actions that must be constantly executed in order to direct the development, and preservation, of the company. A comparison with a natural growth model is unnecessary, because such an organic process is in contrast to voluntary actions in organisations.
- Organisational decisions necessitate a commitment from top management. This is explicitly true for the coordination of important subsystems and for all organisational measures that are required for the planning and implementing of genuine management decisions. Management as a central authority must ensure that conflicts between the genuine decisions and opposing decisions at lower management levels do not demand too much of the management group. Top management is also responsible for guaranteeing cohesion between the central level of hierarchy, and the other levels, through adequate rules of delegation and task assignment.

Understandably, Gutenberg and other contemporary researchers took no account of responses to globalisation such as strategic alliances and dynamic networks as subjects of organisation theory, but, in dealing with problems of internal coordination as a main task of top management, Gutenberg also envisages strategic network constructs. They differ from a polycentric organisation with many decentralised units in the construction of focal companies (hub firms), which can principally be controlled from the top.[32]

Two practical examples demonstrate Gutenberg's high degree of "modernity" for that era.

In his fundamental comments on the relationship between the German and the U. S. American board system, Gutenberg also treats the specific problems of the supervisory board by reference to its historical evolution and in the light of the current critical discussion of the present legacy. He concludes that the supervisory board can barely fulfil its legal functions, namely, efficiently monitoring the executive officers. The members of the supervisory board are no longer able to

---

32 See Sydow 1993, p. 80, and Jarillo/Martinez 1988.

exert this control due to company magnitudes and the complexity of the monitoring function. Based upon his own empirical research into investment decisions in various fields of business, Gutenberg demonstrates that the originally intended division of authority between the executive board of directors and the supervisory board has become obsolete by defining business decisions that are subject to the approval of the supervisory board. His conclusion is as courageous as convincing: “If the supervisory board extends its monitoring competence, actively participates in formulating business policy and executes operating decisions, it should be described as what it is, an agency that participates in the decision-making process of the company.”[33] An examination of the present state of corporate governance makes it difficult to avoid the conclusion that Gutenberg's propositions and conclusions are still as relevant and topical as they were 35 years ago.[34] Although today they are discussed in terms of another theoretical instrument, that is the dilution of property rights on behalf of the board of directors (executive board). This does not change, however, the complex and controversial situation as such.

The second example refers to the "principle of organisational substitution", i. e., the tendency to replace individual (case by case) regulations with general regulations whenever the procedures are identical and periodical. In Gutenberg's words: “The tendency towards general rules increases with decreasing variability of cases.”[35] In defining this principle Gutenberg was led by plausibility considerations as well as by a critical view of the multitude of antagonistic principles of organisation. He demonstrates that the narrowing of autonomy on the lower echelons of hierarchy is compensated by an increase in autonomy and responsibility on the upper levels. Simultaneously Gutenberg attempts to determine the "optimum of the unconfined and constrained design" of organisational rules for specific tasks.[36] In other words he examines the problem of the optimal duration of a rule taking into consideration the transitional period for changing a rule.[37] It also applies to the process of substituting existing general rules with new general rules in companies with a high degree of organisation.[38] Weimer proposes to "search for the optimum" by determining the efficiency of a rule. The transaction cost theory and the principal agent theory constitute his methodological basis. The core of the latter represents the theory of delegation,[39] which has been established by Laux as the theory of delegation value. Transaction costs are reflected in organisational cost comparisons or in capital expenditure accounts.[40] They focus

---

33 See Gutenberg 1962, p. 43.

34 See Albach/Albach 1989, p. 434, p. 113; and Frese 1987, pp. 315-320, pp. 374-383.

35 See Gutenberg 1962, p. 145, and Gutenberg 1983, p. 240.

36 See Gutenberg 1983, p.242.

37 See Kreikebaum 1975.

38 According to Albach a transition type of substitution process implies that old generally regulated decision processes gradually run out.

39 See Laux 1979.

40 See Weimer 1988, p. 16.

upon the type of coordination. A transaction indicates the organisational task that is to be performed. Transaction costs arise, e. g., if organisational uncertainty has to be replaced by a specific type of coordination. According to Weimer it is possible to establish the law of organisational substitution which Gutenberg originally defined for plausibility reasons within the framework of microeconomics.

Gutenberg's thinking enriches modern organisational practice through his focus on the reduction of organisational uncertainty. The knowledge gained from case by case rules can be learned within the organisation and thereby institutionalised through the implementation of general rules.[41] The process of generating learning profits reduces organisational information asymmetry and becomes an important function of corporate management.

5 Outlook

In his scientific work Gutenberg was also determined to describe, and explain, real economic facts in a theoretically sound manner. He did not make himself dependent on the multiplicity of practice, but insisted on the right to formulate independent theoretical goals and methods. It is this ambivalent attitude towards its research object that is also true for modern organisation theory. There has been a trend, however, towards empirical research methods following Popper's influence.

Gutenberg's theoretical conception and methodology anticipated how the modern organisation can deal with its problems in a significant way. The "dilemma of organisation" results from the fact that the complexity of organisational problems, which are to be resolved, exceeds the individual organisation member's capacity. It consequently has to be reduced by the decomposition of tasks and delegation to other organisation members. This process, however, shifts the complexity from subject-related decisions to organisational decisions. Consequently exact recommendations run up against limits.[42] This result of modern organisation theory also confirms Gutenberg's strategy recommendation, namely, always to base the search for solutions to practical problems on a comprehensive theoretical framework.

Summary

The organisational concept designed by Gutenberg has proven its theoretical robustness and practicability and has certainly influenced modern organisational theory in respect of both content and method. Improvements in the resolution of

---

41 See Weimer 1988, p. 134.

42 See in detail Laux/Liebermann 1997, pp. 26-28.

real organisational challenges must also be credited to this work. But it should be noted that the influences of theory on business practice are of a rather indirect and mediating nature. Securing the immediate practical application of his organisational concept was not Gutenberg's prime objective. However, on the basis of selected examples it can be shown, that his proposals have extended their sphere of influence to modern organisation theory and concepts to a much greater extent.

References

Albach; H. (1961): Entscheidungsprozeß und Informationsfluß in der Unternehmensorganisation. In: Aghte, K./Schnaufer, E. (ed.): Organisation. TFB Handbuchreihe erster Band. Berlin - Baden-Baden, pp. 355-402.

Albach, H./Albach R. (1989): Das Unternehmen als Institution. Rechtlicher und gesellschaftlicher Rahmen. Eine Einführung. Wiesbaden.

Franck E. (1995): Die ökonomischen Institutionen der Transportindustrie: Eine Organisationsbetrachtung. Wiesbaden.

Frese, E. (1987): Unternehmensführung. Landsberg am Lech.

Frese, E. (1992): Organisationstheorie: Historische Entwicklung - Ansätze - Perspektiven, 2. Auflage, Wiesbaden.

Frese, E. (1995): Grundlagen der Organisation. Konzept - Prinzipien - Strukturen, 6. Auflage, Wiesbaden.

Gutenberg, E. (1962): Unternehmensführung. Organisation und Entscheidungen. Wiesbaden.

Gutenberg, E. (1983): Grundlagen der Betriebswirtschaftslehre. Band 1: Die Produktion. 24. Auflage, Berlin - Heidelberg - New York.

Hax, H. (1965): Die Koordination von Entscheidungen. Köln 1965.

Hax; H. (1969): Die Koordination von Entscheidungen in der Unternehmung. In: Busse von Colbe, W./Meyer-Dohm, P. (ed.): Unternehmerische Planung und Entscheidung. Bielefeld, p. 39-70.

Jarillo, J.C./Martinez, J.L. (1988): Benetton S.p.A., Case Study, Harvard Business School. Boston.

Kreikebaum, H. (1975): Die Anpassung der Betriebsorganisation. Effizienz und Geltungsdauer organisatorischer Regeln. Wiesbaden.

Laux, H. (1979): Der Einsatz von Entscheidungsgremien. Grundprobleme der Organisationslehre in entscheidungstheoretischer Sicht. Berlin - Heidelberg - New York.

Laux, H. (1979a): Grundfragen der Organisation. Delegation, Anreiz und Kontrolle. Berlin - Heidelberg - New York.

Laux, H./Liermann, F. (1997): Grundlagen der Organisation. Die Steuerung von Entscheidungen als Grundproblem der Betriebswirtschaftslehre. 4. Auflage, Berlin - Heidelberg - New York.

Levitt, Th. (1983): The Globalization of Markets. In: Harvard Business Review 61, No. 3, pp. 92-102.

Marschak, J./Radner, R. (1972): Economic Theory of Teams, London.

Picot, A. (1991a): Ökonomische Theorien der Organisation - Ein Überblick über neuere Ansätze und deren betriebswirtschaftliches Anwendungspotential. In: Ordelheide, D./Rudolph, E./Büsselmann, E. (ed.): Betriebswirtschaftslehre und Ökonomische Theorie. Stuttgart, pp. 143-170.

Picot, A./Dietl, H./Franck, E.: (1997): Organisation. Eine ökonomische Perspektive. Stuttgart.

Picot, A./Reichwald, R./Wigand, R.T: (1996): Die grenzenlose Unternehmung: Information, Organisation und Management. Wiesbaden.

Schober, F. (1996): Interdependenzen von Unternehmensstrategie und Informations- und Kommunikationsstrategien . In: Zeitschrift für Betriebswirtschaft 66, pp. 29-48

Sydow, J. (1993): Strategische Netzwerke: Evolution und Organisation. Wiesbaden.

Tapscott, D. (1996): Die digitale Revolution. Verheißungen einer vernetzten Welt - die Folgen für die Wirtschaft, Management und Gesellschaft. Wiesbaden.

Vornhusen, K. (1994): Die Organisation von Unternehmenskooperationen: Joint Ventures und strategische Allianzen in der Chemie- und Elektroindustrie. Frankfurt am Main.

Weimer, Th. (1988): Das Substitutionsgesetz der Organisation. Eine theoretische Fundierung. Wiesbaden.

Wieland, J. (1996): Ökonomische Organisation, Allokation und Status. Tübingen.

Williamson, O. E: (1990): The Firm as a Nexus of Treaties: an Introduction. In: Aoki, M./Gustafsson, B./Williamson O. E. (ed.): The Firm as a Nexus of Treaties. London, pp. 1-15.

Williamson, O. E: (1993): The Evolving Science of Organization. In: Journal of Institutional an Theoretical Economics, Vol. 149 (1), pp. 36-63.

Shareholder Value-Oriented Management in the Light of Gutenberg´s Theories

G. Obermeier[1]

Overview

- The theory and practice of "shareholder value-oriented management" has recently received close attention. However, this approach is by no means completely new. The theoretical foundations were already laid down in Gutenberg's work on corporate management, which today appears more current than ever.
- The theoretical background and developments which have led to increased shareholder value-orientation are described.
- A major element of shareholder value-oriented corporate management is the implementation of an appropriate organisational structure. This paper describes the characteristics which a group structure should have.
- A strategic management holding company is presented as an appropriate vehicle, whose core functions are substantially the same as those described by Gutenberg as "true" managerial decisions which cannot be delegated.

Shareholder Value, Corporate Management, Organisation Structure, Holding Company Concept.

1 Introduction

Ladies and Gentlemen, I was delighted to receive an invitation to speak on the occasion of the 100th anniversary of Erich Gutenberg's birth. As a representative of corporate Germany it is my intention today to demonstrate the connection between modern shareholder value-oriented methods of corporate management with Erich Gutenberg's traditional management teaching. Recently, and in my

---

1 Dr. Georg Obermeier

opinion justifiably, the topic of "value-oriented corporate management" has received a great deal of attention, both in literature of business administration and in corporate practice. Therefore, I also want to use the opportunity today to address this theme, in particular because Erich Gutenberg was concerned with organisational and leadership problems, above all in his thesis entitled "Unternehmensführung, Organisation und Entscheidung" which was published in 1962 and which today appears to be more topical than ever. It is remarkable that the conditions described by Gutenberg more than 35 ago, i.e. the problems arising from the conflict between ownership and management, as well as the solutions proposed by him, are still reflected in current contributions to management theory. I now want to discuss this in more detail.

2 Shareholder value-orientation as a key criterion for corporate management

2.1 Need for shareholder value-orientation

2.1.1 Change in environmental conditions

Over the past few years there have been fundamental changes in politics and the economy, to an extent never seen before. As a result of rapid technological change, increasing globalisation of markets and the related growth of corporations, the opportunities for a business to raise capital have become a major strategic success factor. The relationship of corporations to financial markets has been given a new dimension. This change has given a new impetus to the interaction between shareholders and their corporations, particularly in the case of quoted companies. Whereas in the past shareholders' behaviour tended to be rather passive (this was emphasised by the well-known phrase "shareholders are stupid and cheeky"), shareholders tend to be more critical nowadays. This change in behaviour is also demonstrated by the current discussion of corporate governance, which gives increased consideration as to whether to expand the German supervisory board's („Aufsichtsrat") statutory responsibilities. Under this concept, in addition to its control function the „Aufsichtsrat" (German supervisory board) would be more involved in the corporate decision-making process. In other words, the debate on corporate governance is tending to move in the direction of an American management structure, which Gutenberg already felt to be better than the two-tier management organisation of German stock corporations.[2] However,

2 See Gutenberg, E. (1962), p. 25 et seq.

this debate has not nearly reached a conclusion in Germany. In future, domestic as well as large foreign institutional investors will be active participants on the German capital markets. This is because, in view of the increasingly critical condition of the German state pension scheme, professional fund managers are now receiving more and more cash in the form of private pension contributions. These funds must be invested as profitably, and with as low a risk, as possible on capital markets. In view of the large volume of assets controlled by these fund managers they will use their not inconsiderable influence in order to enforce their interests. Their aim is to achieve a substantial increase in value of their equity portfolios.[3] Whether shareholder value will be created or diminished has thus become a far more important factor in management's decision-making process, at least for public companies. The theoretical foundations for these developments were laid many years ago. Gutenberg already paid close attention to the relationship between shareholders and their companies. The following capital market theories are based on his considerations.[4]

2.1.2 Theoretical background

An investor can choose between a large number of investment alternatives on the capital market. The deciding factors for making an investment decision are risk and return. The more favourable these two measurements are for one investment in comparison to alternative investments, the more readily the investor will be inclined to invest in the asset concerned.[5] Using this capital market mechanism, resource capital will thus always be put to optimum use from the point of view of the capital market investor. A company, or group, will thus only receive funds from the capital market if risks and return are sufficiently attractive.[6] This assumes that the company or group is successfully managed in terms of adding value. Only companies with high profit potential can fulfil shareholders' requirements over a period time. If this is not the case the company will lose existing and potential investors. The inevitable result is that its share price falls which, in turn, leads to an increase in the cost of raising additional equity and third-party capital.[7] The lower the stock exchange share price the lower the issue price for new shares, so that the amount of cash per share which can be raised declines with the fall in the current share price.[8] Furthermore, the opportunities of obtaining third-party funds decline with falling share prices. Creditors often evaluate the creditworthiness of companies on the basis of their stock exchange price. If share prices reflect growth in a company's value, a creditor assumes that the company is in a position to pay interest on additional third-party funds and subsequently repay the principal. The

3 See Müller, M. (1997).

4 See Gutenberg, E. (1969), p. 201 et seq.

5 See Gutenberg, E. (1969), p. 201.

6 See Klaus, H. (1994), p. 133.

7 See Adam, J. (1987), p. 106 f.

8 See Klaus, H. (1994), p. 134 f.

lower the share price the more negatively the creditworthiness of the company is evaluated. In extreme situations, third-party capital can either not be raised at all, or only at high interest rates.[9]

In view of this, share price performance has more then ever become a major strategic success factor. It has therefore become essential for corporate and group management to create shareholder value. Value-added thinking must take centre stage in corporate decision-making, involving maximum enhancement of share price and maximisation of shareholders' return on investment through dividends and share price increases.

2.2 Elements of shareholder value-oriented corporate management

The key issues on shareholder value-oriented corporate management in the literature relate to the measurement of shareholder value and its increase, the determination of major value drivers, the definition of appropriate ratios and relevant planning and reporting systems.

2.2.1 Increase shareholder value

Shareholder value is calculated as the difference between the value of a company and the value of its third-party capital. In turn, the value of the company is based on the present value of operating cash flows during the forecast period, the residual value, which represents the present value of the corporation for the period after the forecast period and, as a third element, the present value of non-operating assets. This last item includes, for example, marketable securities and other investments which can be disposed of and which represent a value which is not included in operating cash flows and which can thus be separately calculated.[10]

The key to the calculation of shareholder value is the forecast of future cash flows, being the difference between operating cash receipts and payments. These cash flows are discounted to their present value using an appropriate cost of capital. Determining the major valuation parameters, the so-called value drivers or value-creating factors, is of key importance for estimating operating cash inflows and outflows. These are primarily revenue growth, profit margins, income tax rates, capital expenditures and, naturally, capital costs and the length of the forecast period.[11] In order to calculate their present value the estimated cash flows are discounted at a cost of capital equal to the weighted average cost of third party and

9 See Picot, A. / Michaelis, E. (1984), p. 263.

10 For this section see Rappaport, A. (1995), p. 53 f.; Bühner, R. (1990), p. 35 f.

11 See Rappaport, A. (1995), p. 53 et seq.; Bühner, R. (1990), p. 35 et seq.

equity capital.[12] The weighted average cost of capital reflects returns required on both third-party capital and equity capital.[13] The estimated cost of capital is essential in order to determine the minimum return, or marginal rate, which must be received from new capital expenditures. Expenditures which achieve a return higher than the cost of capital ("economic value added") serve to create value, whereas expenditures which provide a return lower than cost of capital lead to a decline in value.[14] Gutenberg dealt extensively with the problem of determining the cost of capital and its importance for management decision-making.[15] Gutenberg concentrated on examining the influence which financial risk has on the structure of capital.[16] Of great interest are his descriptions of different costs of capital.[17] In particular, his work on the Modigliani and Miller hypothesis, namely,that the capital cost curve is independent of a company´s debt-ratio is extremely impressive, as he treats the problem from a practical point-of-view.[18] Overall it can be seen that the foundations of modern thinking on shareholder value-oriented corporate management is to be found in well-known theories and models. There are strong parallels between traditional capital expenditure calculations and capital market theory. What is new is that the key to shareholder value-oriented corporate management is determining shareholder value-creating factors from a uniform economic and financial approach in order to manage the corporation or group.

2.2.2 Planning and reporting system

A shareholder value-oriented corporate management, which concentrates on maximising the return on equity via dividends and share price increases, requires a departure from traditional performance indicators based on the accounting records and an increased concentration on measurements of return based on cash flows.[19] It is therefore essential that a reporting structure be directed towards return on investment. Ratio systems, particularly those which serve to integrate capital market implications such as Economic Value Added (EVA), CFROI and benchmarking, play an increasingly important part in the current discussion on efficient corporate management.

Allow me to go into more detail on the theme of quantitative objectives set by the parent company for its operating units, or benchmarking. The financial community is particularly persistent in its demands for companies to publish such figures,

12 See Rudolph, B. (1986), p. 892 et seq.

13 See Bühner, R. (1990), p. 41; Rappaport, A. (1995), p. 59.

14 See Bühner, R. (1990), p. 41.

15 See Gutenberg, E. (1969), p. 201.

16 See Gutenberg, E.. (1969), p. 199 et seq.

17 See Gutenberg, E. (1969), p. 208 et seq.

18 See Gutenberg, E. (1969), p. 208 et seq.

19 See Rappaport, A. (1995), p. 19 et seq.; Bühner, R. (1990), p. 13 et seq.; Copeland, T./ Koller, T./ Murrin, J. (1993), p. 50 u. 96 et seq.

which serve in practice as an external evaluation of the determination of management to achieve its objectives. From a practical point-of-view I would like to point out at this stage that quantitative performance indicators and, above all, benchmarking contribute to the early identification of weaknesses and strengths in performance and in a portfolio, and thus serve an important function. But it should also not be forgotten that a one-sided analysis only represents "half the truth". In addition, there are invisible "soft facts", such as growth potential of the market, the competitive situation and options related to projects, which play an important role. A truly rational corporate decision can only be made on the basis of an analytical evaluation after including these qualitative components.

But successful implementation of a shareholder value-enhancement concept is not achieved merely with the implementation of an appropriate reporting system. Reporting instruments which concentrate on return on investment cannot replace corporate management in the true sense. The establishment of an appropriate organisation structure is of no less importance.

2.2.3 Organisational structure

In general it must be appreciated that shareholder value-orientation is not merely reflected in the correct calculation of key performance indicators, and that an appropriate underlying philosophy must be established at all levels in the company. It thus follows that, in addition to the more technical matters, a change to shareholder value-oriented management requires the establishment of appropriate, efficient and flexible organisational structures together with a "value added culture" at all levels within the company and, above all, in the more complex structures which arise in a group of companies. Gutenberg emphasised the paramount importance of the implementation of an appropriate organisational structure for top management: "It is clear that the determination of the most appropriate organisational structure is of great importance, particularly for the highest management body within the company which has the powers to delegate responsibility and call to account those to whom it has given responsibility."[20]

---

20 Gutenberg, E. (1962), p. 11 (translated by the author).

3 Requirements for a group value-based management and organisation

3.1 Structure influenced by strategy

The increasing complexity of management tasks, globalisation of markets and constantly changing economic and social structures require permanent change in organisations and group structures which are often mature. A shareholder value-oriented corporate management is expected to concentrate rigorously on areas in which the company or group has core competences. The main principle is to establish competitive advantage based on the organisation's core competences.[21] In this connection, shareholder value-orientation means that nothing should stop the removal of weaknesses, or of established structures, to the extent that they hinder the achievement of the maximum return on investment. Divestitures of business units which do not provide an adequate rate of return, and of businesses which do not contribute to the strategic value-added concept, are just as relevant as the outsourcing of service functions or the establishment of strategic alliances and the acquisition of promising business segments.[22] Chandler's well-known principle of "structure follows strategy" has thus currently assumed great importance.[23]

3.2 The necessity of a decentralised organisational structure

In times of growing market insecurity structures are needed which encourage flexibility and innovation to facilitate rapid reactions to new market developments. A decentralised group management concept is one possibility. By means of a decentralised structure, the advantages which can be achieved in the market place can be grasped easier by quick reactions and timely development and marketing, than the advantages which can normally be achieved with a centralised group structure. Centralised forms of group organisations are primarily aimed at achieving synergies. However, in practice it has been shown that it is only possible to realise synergies to a small extent, so that the expected advantages are only partially achieved. A decentralised organisational structure which enables quicker and flexible reactions to a dynamic environment is thus much more promising. With an increased decentralisation of decision-making to individual business segments, the focus must be on managing and controlling individual segments, so that in extreme cases the realisation of synergies is limited to achieving financial advantage. This is not to be underestimated. The group parent

---

21 See Bühner, R. (1990), p. 72.

22 See Bühner, R. (1990), p. 102 f.

23 See Chandler, A. D., Strategy and Structure, Cambridge, Massachusetts 1962.

company can normally obtain better financial conditions by means of bundling and can then pass these on to its subsidiaries and business segments. In order to satisfy these requirements it is sufficient to have a relatively small headquarters staff to manage and control the business segments.[24]

3.3 Basic principles for a group organisation

In order to organise and lead a group effectively from a shareholder value-orientation perspective the following basic principles must therefore be met:[25]

- Responsibilities and reporting areas must be in conformity with each other within the management system.
- Clear "market-oriented" rules should be applied within the organisation so that the company can concentrate on its position vis-à-vis its external competition and not be distracted by internal conflict with another department or with head office. In addition, there should be no cross-subsidies between the business segments.
- The organisation should attempt to achieve a "small business mentality", in which innovation and closeness to the market, and therefore the appropriate incentives are encouraged.
- The organisation should be transparent and have the flexibility to be able to restructure and regroup.

Group head office is responsible for managing and controlling the individual business segments. The aim is to manage the cash flows of each business segment, in order to generate an internal rate of return on capital in excess of the cost of capital. In order to achieve this goal, the internal rate of return on capital employed in all business segments should be general knowledge. There must therefore be transparency as to the contribution to added value made by all business segments. Only then can the potential to add value to individual business segments be applied optimally. In addition, this prevents value-enhancing business segments subsidising value-destroying business segments over the long term. Cross-subsidies between the various segments, and the related danger of an incorrect allocation of resources can thereby be eliminated.

The foregoing basic principles suggest the following conclusions.

- As a multilayered organisation hinders transparency, a simple structure should be adopted.[26]

---

24 See Bühner, R. (1990), p. 107.

25 See Bühner, R. (1990), p. 104.

26 See Stewart III, B. C. / Glassmann, D. M. (1988), p. 86.

- The value enhancement of business segments should not be evidenced by traditional accounting ratios. The theoretically ideal success factor is the present value of cash flows generated from business segments.[27]
- Funds should be allocated using internal interest rates. Thus, funds will be allocated to those business segments which add the greatest amount of value.[28]
- Generally it is necessary to turn from profit-centre thinking to value-centre thinking.

4 Application of Gutenberg´s theories to a modern holding company function

4.1 The holding company concept

Considerations of a shareholder value-oriented corporate management style lead to a decentralised organisation of business segments and thus, if this is applied to a group, to the implementation of a management holding company structure or, even better, to a strategic management holding company structure.

management holding company structure describes a corporate structure in which the actual business operations are carried out by a number of legally independent (sub-segment) companies.[29] The concept of a strategic management holding company structure includes a systematic delegation of duties from the group management parent company to the legally independent corporate segments. The uniform management of the group is carried out by the executive board of the parent company using a group-wide strategy. The responsibilities of the operating companies include all operational steps and decisions which stem from group strategy and are of importance for the results.

In contrast to this structure, in a traditional group structure the parent company is itself a player on the market with its own products.[30] As a group parent company, a holding company cannot, by definition, be an operating company. Its only task is to manage the group.[31] Whereas a financial holding company limits the management functions of the parent company to purely financial aspects, the concept of a strategic management holding company goes considerably further. Above all, it is distinguished by the ability of the parent company to co-ordinate

27 See Copeland, T./ Koller, T./ Murrin, J. (1993), p. 96 et seq.

28 See Bühner, R. (1990), p. 112

29 See Bühner, R. (1990), p. 116.

30 See Urban, C. (1990), p. 42.

31 See Obermeier, G. (1992), p. 456.

its subsidiary companies.[32] It takes "real", rather delegated, management decisions which are explained more fully below.

The advantages of a holding company organisation in relation to a shareholder value-oriented corporate management structure are clear. They consist principally of the following:

- New companies can be integrated relatively quickly and without friction as, normally, their independence and corporate culture remain substantially unaffected.
- On the other hand, the holding company organisation facilitates a higher flexibility in respect of portfolio optimisation which therefore does not necessitate a costly and strife-ridden process of separation from individual segments.
- Powers and responsibility are clearly personified and defined within a holding company group. This high level of transparency permits an efficient control and measurement of the contributors to the success of the group.

4.2 Duties of the strategic management holding company

A strategic management holding company is typified by a systematic delegation of duties between the parent company's group management and the legally independent business units. The responsibilities of the parent company are deliberately limited to major core functions and genuine management duties. Gutenberg analysed the "real" management functions in detail in his paper entitled "Unternehmensführung, Organisation und Entscheidungen" („Business management, organisation and decisions").[33] The topicality of this description is striking. These are precisely the duties which today should be the responsibility of a modern strategic management holding company which aims to administer a shareholder value-oriented corporate management system.

Gutenberg sees "real" management decisions as having three characteristics. They are crucially important for the net assets and earnings position, and hence the position, of the company and its very existence. They can only be taken in the context of the company in its entirely and, in the interests of the company, cannot be delegated.[34] Gutenberg believes that real management decisions include the following issues:

32 See Obermeier, G. (1992), p. 456; Bühner (1990), p. 116.

33 See Gutenberg, E. (1962), p. 59 et seq.

34 See Gutenberg, E. (1962), p. 59-61.

"1. Determining corporate strategy from a broad perspective

2. Co-ordinating the large operating units

3. Removing problems within on-going operating processes

4. Taking business decisions of unusual operating importance

5. Filling management positions within the organisation"[35]

Gutenberg's description of corporate strategy determination from a broad perspective sets out what today is summarised in the phrase "determining corporate strategy". With respect to the duties of a strategic management holding company structure, this means laying down the group's strategic foundations. This involves determining a budget portfolio and the related fundamental actions to be taken on the basis of the existing portfolio, by concentrating on core competencies with the aim of adding shareholder value.

According to Gutenberg, the duties of co-ordinating operating divisions include the determination of sub-tasks based on the interests of the entire corporation.[36] If this idea is applied to the strategic management holding company concept, the entire success of the group is to be maximised by means of an optimum allocation of financial resources. The allocation of resources is thus a medium for applying group-wide investment and financing strategy with which the research, development and capital expenditures of the entire corporate group are determined. The co-ordination of business units and exercising of uniform management are implemented via financial and capital expenditure strategy.[37]

Gutenberg explains that the elimination of problems in the on-going operating process is also a "real" managerial task. By this he means problems whose origins lie in personnel or operating areas and which cannot be resolved without action from top management, as no other employees have the authority to restructure the organisation.[38] This function can also be delegated to the strategic management holding company. It should then undertake active crisis management, or at least support subsidiary companies in crisis situations. This is a case-by-case instrument of group management as defined in the terminology of Gutenberg's "Substitutionsgesetz der Organisation" (Substitution law of the organisation).[39] Here it is stated that, from case to case, individual rules should be replaced by general regulations if the events take place often enough. As, by definition, a "crisis" is not an on-going situation, it will, of necessity, only be subject to case-by-case rules, i.e. temporary crisis management. On the other hand, for certain

35 Gutenberg, E. (1962), p. 61 (translated by the author).

36 See Gutenberg, E. (1962), p. 69.

37 See Obermeier, G. (1992 a); p. 106 f.

38 See Gutenberg, E. (1962), p. 72.

39 See Gutenberg, E. (1962), p. 144 et seq.

problems which occur more often, group management must issue uniform instructions and list the action to be taken.

According to Gutenberg, the fourth task of management covers business decisions of unusual operating importance. Transactions and steps of unusual importance are those that cannot be undertaken without the authority and competence of management. They exceed the level of responsibility that can be delegated to a functional head or operations manager. In the event of error, or the failure of such transactions, considerable financial losses can occur which damage the company and, in extreme cases, endanger its very existence.[40] If applied to the strategic management holding company concept, these are again typical functions which it must fulfil. As the objective is the strategic and operating optimisation of the entire group, group management must determine those of the segment-related transactions and measures that are so unusually important that they cannot be delegated solely to the respective CEOs of the groups subsidiary companies. To be effective, these decisions require the agreement of group management in their functions as shareholders on the supervisory boards, or at annual general meetings, of the subsidiary companies. Their approval is in no case to be seen as a formality. Gutenberg explicitly noted "that the transactions requiring approval and which need the approval of the supervisory board are real management decisions in the economic sense of the word."[41] In summary, it can thus be concluded that, if used efficiently, the instrument of „transactions requiring approval“ contributes to the application of shareholder value-oriented policy and, in particular, to portfolio optimisation.

Gutenberg names the filling of management positions in companies as the fifth and last "real" management decision.[42] The use, and selection, of appropriate management is of great importance for the successful implementation of the strategic management holding company concept. In order to implement strategies successfully it is essential to place appropriate management personnel in key positions and to develop management potential. A strategic understanding of the company, and its tasks, is particularly required from management in key positions. Furthermore, management must be able to react quickly and flexibly to changes in its environment. Above all, managers are also required to understand the group's philosophy and to identify with the aims of the entire group.[43] Support mechanisms which stimulate compatible motivation are also required. Success-based forms of remuneration for managerial performance are necessary for a shareholder value-oriented managerial system.[44]

---

40 See Gutenberg, E. (1962), p. 73.

41 Gutenberg, E. (1962), p. 43 (translated by the author).

42 See Gutenberg, E. (1962), p. 74 f.

43 See Obermeier, G. (1992 a), p. 107 f.

44 See Bühner, R. (1990), p. 123 et seq.

Literature

Adam, J. (1987): Eigentumsstruktur und Unternehmenseffizienz, Rheinfelden 1987.

Bühner, R (1990): Das Management-Wert-Konzept, Strategien zur Schaffung von mehr Wert im Unternehmen, Stuttgart 1990.

Chandler, A. (1962): Strategy and Structure, Cambridge, Massachusetts 1962.

Copeland, T. / Koller, T. / Murrin, J. (1993): Unternehmenswert, Methoden und Strategien für eine wertorientierte Unternehmensführung, Frankfurt am Main, New York 1993.

Gutenberg, E. (1962): Unternehmensführung, Organisation und Entscheidungen, Wiesbaden 1962.

Gutenberg, E. (1969): Grundlagen der Betriebswirtschaftslehre, Dritter Band: Die Finanzen, Third Edition, Berlin, Heidelberg, New York 1969.

Klaus, H. (1994): Gesellschafterfremdfinanzierung und Eigenkapitalersatzrecht bei der Aktiengesellschaft und der GmbH, Frankfurt am Main et al. 1994.

Müller, M. (1997): Das Kapital macht Druck, Pensionsfonds und Investmentgesellschaften mischen sich zunehmend in die Geschäftspolitik deutscher Aktiengesellschaften ein, in: Die Zeit of 10/24/1997.

Obermeier, G. (1992): Strategisches Konzern-Controlling, in: Matheis, R. (Ed.): Erfolgsmanagement 2000, Konzepte für Menschen, Märkte und Unternehmen, Wiesbaden 1992.

Obermeier, G. (1992 a): VIAG - Vom Staatsunternehmen zur Management-Holding, in: Schulte, C. (Ed.): Holding Strategien: Erfolgspotentiale realisieren durch Beherrschung von Größe und Komplexität, Wiesbaden 1992.

Picot, A. / Michaelis, E. (1984): Verteilung von Verfügungsrechten in Großunternehmungen und Unternehmenesverfassung, in: ZfB 1984, pp. 252-272.

Rappaport, A. (1995): Shareholder Value, Wertsteigerung als Maßstab für die Unternehmensführung, Stuttgart 1995.

Rudolph, B. (1986): Neuere Kapitalkostenkonzepte auf der Grundlage der Kapitalmarkttheorie, in: Zeitschrift für betriebswirtschaftliche Forschung, Vol. 38, 1986, pp. 892-898.

Stewart III, B. C. / Glassmann, D. M. (1988): The Motives and Methods of Corporate Restructuring: Part II, in: Journal of Applied Corporate Finance, Vol. 2, 1988, pp. 79-88.

Urban, C. (1990): Ein Unternehmen im Aufbruch: Strategie, Organisation und Controlling bei Siemens, in: Horváth, P. (Ed.): Strategieunterstützung durch das Controlling: Revolutionen im Rechnungswesen?, Stuttgart 1990.

Summary

A shareholder value-oriented corporate and group management concept requires an appropriate, flexible organisational structure together with a "value-added culture". In view of the increasing complexity of managerial tasks as a result of dynamic growth, and the rapid change in economic and social conditions, the concept of a strategic management holding company is shown to be an ideal group structure. The managerial tasks which are fulfilled by a strategic management holding company are substantially the same as the functions which Gutenberg describes as "real" management decisions. They cannot be delegated and are to be seen from the overall perspective of the group, which is fundamental to a shareholder value-oriented management concept. There are thus grounds for concluding that Gutenberg´s work is as relevant as ever and that it can rightly be described as one of the "classics of economics".

Part II: Managerial Functions

Where do we Stand in the Theory of Finance? A Selective Overview with Reference to Erich Gutenberg

J. P. Krahnen[1]

Overview

- An attempt is made to survey key topics currently discussed in the Theory of Corporate Finance. Rather than being comprehensive, the focus is on the role of corporate control in evaluating financial policy. The paper develops the theme and discusses recent objections against the role of the takeover market, and relationship lending as efficient instruments of corporate control.
- In addition, the contributions of a Erich Gutenberg, an influential German business economist who, back in the fifties, opened up business studies to rigorous economic analysis, are critically reviewed. Special emphasis is given his model of corporate objectives, and the concept of corporate financial equilibrium. Recent models of corporate control emphasizing the possibility of autonomous mechanisms of internal control, are found to address quite similar questions.
- To date, our empirical knowledge on what corporate control really means is severely limited. To improve our understanding, and to allow a test of predictions derived from the large theoretical literature, more emphasis has to be given to pain-staking, empirical studies on the role of capital markets and financial intermediaries.

Keywords: Corporate finance, Incomplete contracts, Corporate control mechansisms, Early contributions by Erich Gutenberg.

---

1 Professor of Finance, Goethe-Universität Frankfurt; Director, CFS Center for Financial Studies, Frankfurt; Research Fellow, CEPR Centre for European Policy Research, London. eMail: krahnen@wiwi.uni-frankfurt.de

1 Introduction

Describing the current state of the theory of finance is no easy task. A field of study which, when Gutenberg's *Einführung in die Betriebswirtschaftslehre* appeared in 1958, seemed largely descriptive and self-contained, has since undergone a turbulent and rapid development. As it has evolved, an increasing use of microeconomic models and approaches has led to an understanding of the subject as one whose main purpose is to provide explanations; and, the classical business economics emphasis on description and recommendations for corporate design and management solutions has been relegated to the background. Erich Gutenberg's comprehensive analysis of corporate finance in the third volume of his *Grundlagen* appeared in 1968. Whilst this work gives a new emphasis to numerous aspects of the subject, its general tenor is firmly rooted in the classic understanding of what business economics (or business administration - I use these terms interchangeably) is basically about.

There can scarcely be a domain of business economics that would claim to owe less to the tradition of Erich Gutenberg than the modern theory of finance. However in the present essay I question this general preconception, and demonstrate that current research in certain areas of finance has reached a point at which it comes very close to what I consider to be the Gutenbergian view of an enterprise, namely an entity with autonomous interests.

For this reason, it seems useful to preface my selective overview with a discussion of Gutenberg's ideas themselves. The intention is to elaborate a number of fundamental differences and some, to my mind at least, remarkable parallels between Gutenberg and current research in the area of finance. The following sections focus on two current and, in my view, crucial questions of finance, namely the building of long-term financial relationships and the design of effective corporate governance structures that enable owners to exercise control, i.e. to monitor the activities of managers.

What I am not attempting to do is to provide a comprehensive overview of investment and the theory of finance in general. For one thing, several comprehensive surveys of this kind have recently appeared (Franke 1993, Brennan 1995, Merton 1995, Shanken/Smith 1996), so that a further attempt could hardly be expected to contribute anything new. Moreover, given the abundance of issues addressed and methods currently being pursued under the heading "Finance", a complete overview would seem (to me) to be more of a hindrance than a help in tracing trends in recent research. My selection is a reflection of my main interests; and hopefully it will also make it easier to draw the connection to Erich Gutenberg, which is what concerns us here, into sharper focus.

Viewed from a distance, the current research into investment and finance appears to be dealing with a broad, loosely-meshed network of individual topics. Even from afar, it is not difficult to recognise that adjacent knots in this net represent interconnected sets of themes. The sets of themes addressed by the theory of finance are dominated by questions relating to the design of explicit, and implicit, contractual arrangements between investors and enterprises. In this context, the discussion focuses particularly on individual forms of financing in situations characterised by asymmetric information, as well as on alleviating the resultant incentive problems.

An incomplete list of corporate finance themes includes determinants of optimal capital structure and optimal dividend policy; problems associated with specific forms of financing, in particular debt and equity capital under asymmetric information; but also the characteristics of various forms of internal finance; and in addition, the role of mechanisms designed to mitigate the incentive problems that have been identified: monitoring, bonding, self-selection and screening.

A second major area of study is investment and capital market theory, whose practice-oriented significance is often more impressive than that of corporate finance. This second domain includes portfolio theory, capital market theory and option pricing theory, as well as models designed to explain interest rate structures and exchange rate movements. Studies grounded in investment theory have provided a decisive impetus for corporate financial management and for the development of markets, especially those in which derivative products are traded. As an example, one might cite research into the measurement and control of portfolio risks, where the portfolios in question are the entire assets of a bank (including equity and debt securities, as well as derivatives, in particular swaps and options).

The link between corporate finance and investment-related themes is the theoretical and empirical analysis of institutions in the financial markets, i.e. the analysis of financial intermediaries such as banks, insurance companies and unit trusts (mutual funds). The list could also be extended to include stock exchanges. There exist today, grouped under the heading "market microstructures", independent programmes of research into the optimal characteristics and the informational efficiency of various forms of market organisation, in particular dealer and auction markets.

As a methodology, empirical studies have gained in importance in recent years, and occasionally experimental studies on subjects such as market microstructure are published. The profusion of different fields of study (and the above is by no means a complete list) and their substantial and growing importance within economic research as a whole is underscored not least by the fact that between

1990 and 1997 no fewer than five Nobel prizes were awarded to financial economists.

Figure 1: Theory of Finance

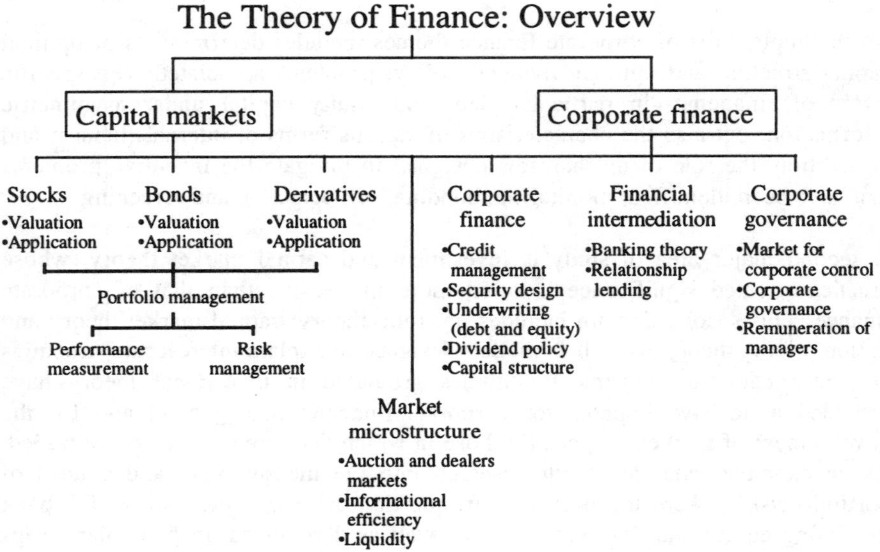

Against this background, the purpose of the present paper is to select a number of "knots" in the "network" referred to above, nodal points that fall into the "theory of finance" category, and to indicate the links between these nodal points. It is not possible to discuss here the history of the ideas that underpin financial research, and the development of those ideas over the past four decades. Instead I refer the reader to my essay on "Finanzierungstheorie zwischen Markt und Institution". In Krahnen (1993a) the development of financial theory is presented as a series of pendulum swings between a primarily market-oriented and a primarily institution-oriented approach. This duality of market versus institution is also evident in recent writings on market microstructure (Spulber 1995) and banking theory (Bhattacharya/Thakor 1993).

2 Erich Gutenberg's *Finanzen* and modern theory of finance

The outstanding impression left by Gutenberg's *Finanzen* is that all financing problems are derivative: the protagonist throughout Gutenberg's oeuvre is production – be it in the modelling of production, the optimisation of the production process or the accentuation of product policy. All other functions of a business operation are of secondary importance, being subordinate to production. This allocation of roles is particularly clear in the case of finance. Volume III of the *Grundlagen* is structured along very similar lines to the first volume, *Die Produktion*, and also uses largely the same terminology. The main thrust of Volume III is to link the decision-making problems in the sphere of production to their respective effects in terms of liquidity and finance. The arguments Gutenberg adduces here consistently move in the same direction: they proceed from the opportunities for production to the financial effects, which, although they can be conceived of as separate sub- optimisation problems, remain nonetheless dependent on the given production-related decisions.[2]

Present-day theory of finance takes a radically different approach. It has become a comprehensive theory of decision-making within enterprises, and its models seek to establish links between the claims and behaviour of all the parties involved in the enterprise in terms of Pareto-optimal agreements. Production issues, if considered at all, appear in a highly condensed form, e.g. in the sense of a postulated production function or postulated alternative investment projects, and thus play no more than a peripheral role. To better appreciate the transformation that has taken place in the relative importance the theory of finance attaches to the various elements involved, let us imagine for a moment that a company's value added is represented by a vehicle. In Gutenberg's time, financial managers were perceived as petrol pump attendants who filled up the corporate vehicle with the liquidity it needed to run on. From a present-day viewpoint, financial managers are seen as having traded in their pump attendant's uniform for a chauffeur's cap. Their task is now to direct and control the company's creation of value added and therefore – to retain the vehicle image – they now have their hands on the steering wheel.

2 An exception to this rule is the treatment of unusual situations, such as bankruptcy or reorganisation, where the financing side is also said to have consequences for the production-related decisions.

When reading *Finanzen*, three characteristics stand out which, taken together, also underscore the supportive, ancillary role of financial management in a world that is primarily governed by the imperatives of production.[3]

First, optimal corporate financing policy is a function of the firm's capital needs, its capital fund and the co-ordination of these two factors. These three elements also form the subjects of Parts I, II and III respectively of the third volume of *Grundlagen der Betriebswirtschaftslehre*. Here, the supply of, and demand for capital are developed as two mutually independent functions, which are derived primarily from the exigencies of the production process.[4] Against this background, Part III then deals with the co-ordination of the two in the sense of an elaborate simultaneous planning process which also attempts to capture in precise detail the temporal dimension of the production process. As is customary in models of integrated investment planning, the underlying cash flows of the investment alternatives and financing alternatives are assumed to be independent of one another. In isolating the optimisation problem at the level of the individual enterprise, simultaneous planning models refrain from any explicit attempt to model the lender/investor's rationale, his objectives and his constraints. As a programme for research, this view has consistently been superseded by one which focuses on the endogenous nature of capital needs and the supply of finance (see Weingartner 1979 and Krahnen 1993).

Second, Gutenberg's research programme presents the enterprise as an autonomous unit, i.e. largely independent of the stakeholders (owners, creditors, employees, etc.) which have become such an integral feature of today's discourse. In particular, there is no special orientation towards the interests and goals of any one group, e.g. shareholders (see, for example, Gutenberg 1980, p. 148[5]). This assumption by Gutenberg presumably coincides with the view taken within large firms even today – despite an increasing tendency to express the enterprise's commitment to maximising shareholder value. In contrast, the dominant view

---

3 The dominance of non-monetary considerations in Gutenberg's works can also be explained with reference to the historical period in which he was writing, a period in which the problems of a war economy and of economic reconstruction played a particularly important role.

4 Gutenberg had already set forth a tentative version of this interpretation in his review of Polak's influential survey of the "basic features of finance", *Grundzüge der Finanzierung*. See Gutenberg 1927.

5 Here he writes, for example: „...es lassen sich ohne Zweifel Fälle aufweisen, in denen das Verhalten von Großaktionären und Inhabern von Einzelfirmen und Personengesellschaften gegen das Interesse des Unternehmens, seine Sicherheit und seine Entwicklung verstoßen hat" [...instances can undoubtedly be identified in which the behaviour of major shareholders and owners of sole proprietorships and unincorporated firms has run counter to the interests of the firm, its security and its development] (emphasis added).

underlying today's theoretical models of contractual relationships is that there are no interests of the *enterprise as such*, i.e. a co-ordinated set of goals pursued by various actors, as discrete from their own respective individual interests. Generally speaking, the constellation of interests of one group, namely the shareholders, are postulated as the given objective function (of the principal), and an attempt is then made to minimise the degree of deviation from these objectives by optimising the design of the contracts concluded with the agent or agents.[6]

Third, the guiding principle underlying the process of co-ordination between capital needs and the so-called capital fund in Gutenberg's third volume is the need to ensure that a permanent "financial equilibrium" is maintained. This term implies that the cash inflow must at all times be at least equal to the outgoing payments that simultaneously fall due. The notion of a financial equilibrium first appears in Gutenberg's review of Polak's "Grundzüge der Finanzierung mit Rücksicht auf die Kreditdauer" (see Gutenberg 1927). In the context of simultaneous planning models, the stipulation of a financial equilibrium for any time t translates into an inequality which compares the cumulative volume of a firm's cash inflow up to time t with the volume of its outgoing payments during the same period. (For details, see Gutenberg 1980, pp. 272-277.) Gutenberg broadens the concept of financial equilibrium to include situations of uncertainty. The term "financial elasticity" is used to denote options for adjustment in cases where actual values differ from target values. Financial reserves should be available for such contingencies, he argues (see Gutenberg 1980, Chapter 14).

The basic situation assumed by Gutenberg – that of the enterprise as an entity with autonomous interests was probably shaped to some degree by his own experiences in a mechanical engineering firm when, in the 1920s, he was being prepared to assume management responsibility for his father's agricultural machinery factory.[7] Gutenberg's notion of the (autonomous) interests of the firm was thus not naive,

6 Although the shareholders' objectives are normally assumed to dominate (because they are regarded as residual claimants), there is no logical imperative that necessarily precludes the dominance of the objectives of any other group of actors, e.g. those of managers (employees). For a legal perspective on this question, see Schmidt/Spindler 1997; see also the explanation of the management function (labelled "dispositiver Faktor" by Gutenberg), i.e. the people who perform management functions, e.g. regarding an optimal design of a company's input-output relationship in Albach 1989, pp. 67-72.

7 He never actually assumed this entrepreneurial role because the firm was liquidated in 1925, enabling Gutenberg to continue his academic career. See Albach 1989, Chapter 1.

as is evidenced by his discussion of conflicting interests between management and owners (Gutenberg 1951, pp. 381-383).[8]

From the standpoint of today's dominant theory of the firm, the notion of the enterprise as an entity with autonomous interests appears not merely to be a relic from a bygone age, but is indeed a veritable counterpoint to a stakeholder-oriented model of the firm. In the stakeholder model, corporate goals can be derived from the constellations of persons and groups that are part of, or connected with, the company. Ultimately, owners – or shareholders – make their impression on corporate decisions by virtue of their role as residual claimants. The interests of all other parties, in particular those of the firm's employees and creditors, enter into the optimisation programme in the form of constraints. Viewed from this angle, the drive for financial equilibrium appears to be more of an incentive problem than a useful constraint for the firm's optimisation programme. This reassessment of the financial equilibrium is a consequence of an orientation towards the market value of the firm, which has become the generally accepted practice today. Maximising market value may be accompanied by financial equilibrium, but it does not have to be. In particular, when a corporate strategy geared towards maximising market value leads to (partial) liquidation, the equilibrium condition can and should be violated in the interests of market value maximisation. If, nonetheless, priority is accorded to financial equilibrium, the outcome is a variation of the overinvestment problem described in Hart (1995). Thus, today financial equilibrium is not "economically correct", either as a goal or as a constraint. For a more detailed discussion of this point, see Wagner (1997).

For the past 20 years, the theory of finance has been dominated by principal-agent models aimed at optimising the realisation of owners' interests in a situation characterised by asymmetric information or incomplete contracts. The notion of an enterprise with autonomous interests of its own is alien to these models. Nonetheless, the principal-agent models allow for conflicts of interest between owners and management, e.g. over the efficient liquidation of the firm's assets. In the more recent incomplete contract models, the interests of management are oriented (at least in part) towards the so-called private benefits of control, a term which refers to the additional benefits derived from expanding the resources controlled by the management. These benefits continue to accrue even when the firm's capital base has been expanded beyond its optimal level. And under such circumstances, unrestrained management decisions can lead to, for example, inefficient liquidation decisions. Or, conversely, units of the company that earn a below-market return may be retained even though they reduce shareholder value. This occurs because the expansion of the capital base, which promises to increase

---

8 I thank Albrecht Dietz for drawing my attention to this element of Gutenberg's work. It is however notable that the incentive-oriented view of the firm was not systematically integrated into the rest of his writings.

their private benefits, makes inefficient investments appear attractive in the eyes of the management.

In this situation, an optimal financing structure can force management to take liquidation decisions that are optimal from the point of view of the shareholders. For example, in the model devised by Hart (1995, Chapter 6), imposing the condition of a sufficiently high level of debt ensures that control shifts to the creditors in states of the world in which there is a danger of an inefficient perpetuation of the firm by the management.

The theoretical and empirical literature largely tends to view financing agreements from the point of view of management control (the control paradigm). The design of individual contracts, or of a portfolio of such contracts (capital structure), serves to overcome the divergence between the goals of investors and management in a cost efficient manner. A number of developments in the theory of finance which call the control paradigm into question are outlined in the following pages. The situations analysed include some in which shielding the firm to a certain degree against direct, market value-induced intervention by the shareholders proves to be advantageous. In my view, they reveal tendencies towards an approach which postulates the existence of a firm's autonomous interest in securing its own survival. And I interpret this as evidence of a shift towards the notion of financial equilibrium as a goal to be pursued by an enterprise. In contrast to Gutenberg's concept, however, here it is compatible with the superordinate idea of market value maximisation – and is therefore a tenable argument even when applied to a competitive market environment.

Finally, it should be pointed out that the three characteristics of Gutenbergian financial theory referred to here, namely the exogenous nature of the supply of, and demand for, capital, the autonomous nature of the interests of the firm, and concentration on financial equilibrium, are inter-connected. From a present-day standpoint, they are three features of a corporate management that acts under highly competitive conditions, takes decisions on a basis that is largely detached from the interests of its present shareholders, and, finally, takes account of a long-term survival interest as a strict constraint on its investment decisions.

3 Control as an issue for the theory of finance

The purpose of this section is to present some recent ideas on management control exercised via financial instruments. The underlying intuition is based on a recently published study by Martin Hellwig on corporate finance (see Hellwig 1997). Three "channels" of control are referred to, corresponding to the classic division of financing into equity capital and debt capital (as the two forms of external finance) and internal finance.

3.1 The market for equity capital

In the 1980s and early 90s, the notion of corporate control via the market for company shares was the subject of intensive theoretical and empirical investigation. Scepticism regarding the efficiency of a market for corporate control, which was expressed in the early works on the subject by Grossman/Hart 1980 and Stiglitz 1972, was countered by overwhelming evidence of increased market value realised through, for example, hostile take-overs (see Jensen/Ruback 1983). Later studies suggest that an increase in the market value of stocks may be the result of a redistribution at the expense of unprotected stakeholders (especially employees) (Shleifer/Summers 1988). It is also claimed that the effectiveness of the market for corporate control is significantly impaired by the countervailing activities of entrenched corporate administrations which have been able to set up protective devices ("poison pills") to make take-overs more difficult (see also Jensen 1991).

In the theoretical literature Harris/Raviv (1988) and Grossman/Hart (1989) examine the conditions under which the market for corporate control functions, a market which is particularly likely to be activated by changes induced by management. In a model of incomplete contracts with private benefits of control for management, the authors show that widely dispersed share ownership creates optimal incentives for a take-over if, in order to acquire a majority of the voting shares, it is also necessary to buy up the majority of cash flows. The optimality condition derived from this model corresponds to a corporate governance structure in which each share certificate entitles the holder to precisely one vote ("one share-one vote").

The optimal control structure of a firm is different from this if the private benefits of control for some shareholders are very large. This would conceivably be the case in a family business, for example. Here, Grossman/Hart's 1988 analysis predicts that second-class shares with limited voting rights will be issued. This practice, as manifested in the issue of non-voting preferential shares, is quite common in a number of European countries, though not in the United States. For Italy it is possible to demonstrate a statistically significant correlation between the size of the price discount for non-voting shares and the percentage of voting shares in the hands of a single person or a single family (Zingales 1995). This can be interpreted as an indication that corporate control via the market for equity capital is not very effective.

On the whole it would appear that the market for equity capital can only temporarily be an effective instrument of corporate control, and only in a small number of countries (Hellwig 1997).

3.2 Long-term credit relationships and corporate control

3.2.1 The significance of relationship lending in the theory

Relationships (between companies and their regular banks or "house banks") are a key concern of contemporary research, both theoretical and empirical, because they facilitate a particularly lucid demonstration of the market-versus-institution duality (Allen/Gale 1995, Rajan 1996, Holmström/Tirole 1996). Let us briefly examine why this is so. Even from the most cursory appraisal of external corporate finance it is immediately apparent that debt capital can be provided both via markets and via intermediaries. Debt capital is supplied via markets in the form of bonds, whereas debt capital via intermediaries typically takes the form of bank loans. Many observers, particularly those who focus on the Anglo-Saxon capital markets, have noted that market-traded bonds have been gaining ground recently, while bank-intermediated credit finance has experienced a corresponding decline (Hellwig 1991, Edwards/Mishkin 1995, Domanski 1997, Berlin/Mester 1997).

The question of a possible "Obsolescence of Commercial Banking" (Miller 1996) is an obvious one to ask. That intermediaries are likely to be pushed back still further is indicated, among other things, by the positive returns to scale that are expected to come from centralised credit assessment by rating agencies, as a substitute for decentralised assessment by several banks. Furthermore, market-traded bonds permit a superior risk allocation, and, thanks to daily valuation and realisation on the exchanges, they offer a high degree of liquidity and rapid information revelation.

In this context, the theoretical literature has devoted particular attention to the opportunities and risks associated with the renegotiation of multi-period loan agreements. Incentive-compatible contracts are determined which on the one hand prevent renegotiation (e.g. Stiglitz/Weiss 1983), or, on the other, intentionally provide for renegotiation as a possible means of sequential incentive creation (e.g. Hart/Moore 1988). Comparisons of market-oriented long-term bond financing with intermediary-oriented long-term credit relationships are characterised by two main arguments in the literature.

Dewatripont/Maskin 1995 see the advantages of bond financing in the certainty of being able to avoid renegotiation. The argument runs as follows: if debt finance is provided not via the market but by a person or an intermediary, and if the borrowing enterprise in question runs into difficulties that prevent it from repaying the credit on schedule, the lender is caught in a classic "lock-in" situation. The credit it disbursed now constitutes sunk costs, while the borrower can renegotiate. It is now in the lender's own interests to agree to, say, an additional loan, a remission of interest or a repayment deferral, if by doing so, it makes repayment at some later date more likely. The inefficiency of this process derives from the fact that, when the loan is first issued, the borrower already knows it can renegotiate if it encounters problems later, and thus may from the very beginning, have an incentive to invest suboptimally. A single lender would find it difficult to signal credibly at the start of such a relationship that it would not be willing to renegotiate. In contrast, in the case of a bond traded in the market with a large number of anonymous bond-holders there is virtually no chance of successful renegotiation. Even if the holders of the bond were known, the free-rider problem creates an incentive for every bond-holder to abstain from the renegotiations and thereby uphold the full value of his or her claim.

The counterposition emphasises the freedom of action under uncertainty that arises as a consequence of renegotiation. Supporters of this argument apply it in particular to the special nature of the financing relationship between lenders and their clients, and stress the positive aspects of the opportunity to renegotiate in this context (see Breuer 1994, Berlin 1996, Rajan 1996). In relationship lending there is a special bond of trust which may have evolved through the lender's many years of dealings with this contractual partner, as well as through the lender's being especially well informed about the qualities of the borrower and its projects. In any case, so the hypothesis runs, superior information creates a basis for trust which can, in effect, bind the borrower to the lender in a reversal of the lock-in situation described above.

This is so because the cancellation of a loan could also signal to uninformed competing lenders that this was a borrower with a bad project, as a consequence of which they would impose correspondingly strict terms on any loan they might grant to that particular firm, or indeed the firm may not receive a loan at all. In this situation the relationship bank or "house bank" can offer an implicit insurance without having to fear that the borrower will try to exploit its position. This insurance may consist in the bank's willingness to extend the term of the loan if the borrower runs into acute liquidity problems, or to waive interest and principal payments without making use of its right to sue for bankruptcy. In return for this service, the borrower pays an insurance premium which may take the form of a larger margin (to be paid later) or large commission fees on additional (future) business (cross-selling). In terms of pricing policy, this is an intra- or intertemporal cross subsidy. Under these conditions, financing through an intermediary represents a means of smoothing the supply of liquidity to firms. In order to be able to serve as a buffer in this respect, banks must themselves be protected against shocks. In this connection, Berlin/Mester (1997) emphasise the role of interest inelastic core deposits (i.e. savings deposits subject to statutory withdrawal notice).

It is worth dwelling for a moment on the question of why the smoothing effect on payment flows that is associated with relationship finance should be efficient. One reason is that it allows observers to distinguish between transitory and permanent idiosyncratic, i.e. firm-specific, shocks. Relationship lenders, which are comparatively well informed, are in a position to identify transitory shocks more reliably than uninformed sources of capital (e.g. investors in the bond market), who will not be able to distinguish between transitory and permanent problems and therefore will not be able to adjust their lending terms and conditions (interest rate, collateral, volume) accordingly.

This situation, taking idiosyncratic shocks into account, provides a starting point for a positive theory of financial relationships. At this stage it should be noted that liquidity buffers cannot always be made available on the basis of public information, i.e. information to which the market has access, and that, therefore, the provision of insurance by an intermediary based on private information can be of value.

3.2.2 Empirical significance of relationship lending

Can the existence of this insurance function in the context of financial relationships be demonstrated empirically? Under what conditions can it evolve in competitive markets? The answer to these questions follows directly from the question of the "Obsolescence of Commercial Banking" referred to earlier. Insofar as, under competitive conditions, credit relationships evolve in which the borrower is locked in and profit expectations are positive, relationship banks will not (and cannot) be squeezed out of the market.

In the past, systematic empirical research into the question of credit finance has failed mainly because of a lack of relevant data. However, there are now usuable data for a number of countries. In one of the first event studies on the significance of credit finance, James (1987) finds in the U.S. stock market a positive risk-adjusted excess return on the shares of firms that announce the granting of a bank loan. Follow-up research by Lummer/Mitchell (1989) and James/Wier (1990) demonstrates that a significant wealth effect occurs when the extension of an existing credit relationship is announced, but not when a first-time loan is granted.

These authors interpret this result as an indication of the significance of relationship lending. According to this view, a decision to extend a credit relationship is based on information that the bank has been able to acquire during the course of the preceding business relationship. A decision to extend can therefore be interpreted as a decision backed by information which is superior and private, i.e. the details are not known to the market. Under these circumstances, an announcement of the extension of a credit relationship can be regarded by the market as a positive signal of quality (in the sense of a low default probability), which causes the value of that firm's equity to rise. The difference between an extension and the granting of an initial loan lies in the fact that a first-time loan is not based on private information, since even the credit assessment of a bank can, as a rule, only draw on public information.

A series of studies in the United States have been based on extensive new data sets on the terms and conditions of loans issued to small and medium-sized enterprises. Petersen/Rajan (1994) apply the results of a theoretical study by Diamond (1991) on the acquisition of reputation in bond markets, taking the length of an uninterrupted business relationship between bank and firm and the diversity of the business relationship with the lender (cross-selling) as proxies for the strength of a relationship.

Using data on the most expensive form of finance in each case, namely trade credit, the authors find that the relationship variables have a significant impact. They interpret this finding as corroboration of the hypothesis on credit rationing advanced by Stiglitz/Weiss (1981).

In contrast, they find no correlation between their relationship proxy and the interest margin agreed upon in the credit contract. In a parallel study using the same data set but this time applied to lines of credit, Berger/Udell (1995) find that borrowers with longer contractual relationships pay lower interest margins and have to furnish less collateral. However, both of these studies leave open the question of whether the observations are indeed an effect of relationship lending, or whether they merely reflect a learning effect based on long-standing customer relationships which applies equally to normal banking relationships and to "house bank" relationships, similar to the experience rating with which we are familiar from the insurance business.

A recently concluded investigation allows us to differentiate for the first time between house-bank and normal banking relationships based on a data set for the

Federal Republic of Germany (Elsas/Krahnen 1998). This involves the self-assessment of credit department managers with regard to the "relationship" quality of individual loans chosen at random from their loan portfolios.[9] One of the insights to emerge from this survey was that the length of the business relationship, which in previous experiments had been used as a discriminatory criterion, is an imprecise proxy for the existence of a "house bank"-type relationship. It turns out that the median length of business relationships between borrower and bank is indeed about the same for house bank relationships as for normal banking relationships, the difference being not statistically significant. Thus the duration of a credit relationship cannot be a precise discriminatory criterion for relationship lending.

The hypothesis was tested which claims that, where there is a perceptible change in the client's credit standing, the house bank assumes an insurance function (Rajan 1996) insofar as it does not reduce the absolute volume of the finance it provides, and in fact increases it in relative terms. In contrast, normal banks in the same situation will, according to this hypothesis, reduce their financial commitments in both absolute and relative terms. A panel regression for the German data set confirms the hypothesis that house banks perform an implicit insurance function and finds no such characteristics for normal banks. For the purposes of this investigation, changes in the banks' internal rating of their customers were taken as an indicator of a perceptible change of credit standing.

However, this does not answer the question of how the insurance service provided by a house bank is remunerated. As yet, no conclusive data are available that would enable us to verify the hypothesis of intra- or intertemporal cross subsidies. However, there is also reason to doubt whether the internal customer costing data needed for earnings-oriented relationship management *could* be made available.

Empirical interest in the structure of credit relationships has been growing recently, and it is to this area of research that we must turn in order to obtain empirical evidence of the existence of an economic value of relationship lending. Theorists have offered a large number of possible explanations, most of which are derived essentially from the private information capital referred to at the beginning of this section, which the lender accumulates during its long-lasting relationship with its client and which, in terms of content, extends beyond the stock of public information which accrues in the context of normal banking relationships.

---

9 The survey was conducted in early 1997 at five German banks: Bayrische Vereinsbank, DG-Bank, Deutsche Bank, Dresdner Bank, West LB. On the data set used, see Elsas et.al. (1998).

3.2.3 Modelling long-term debt contracts

Although empirical inquiry into the existence and significance of relationship lending has only just begun,[10] the general question of the conditions for the co-existence of long-term finance supplied by intermediaries (private debt) and finance obtained directly in the market (public debt) appears to pose a challenge to the theory of finance. Closely linked to this question is not only the question of a permanent line of separation between direct market relationships and indirect, intermediated relationships, but also the theoretically significant question of the general modelling of long-term contractual relationships. As well as providing an explanation of relationship lending, other possible applications of such models include the more general issue of how reputation is accumulated. These models need to take account of the risks and opportunities created by the possibility that the preferences of the participants may change (for opportunistic reasons) over time in the sense of time-consistent behaviour.

Whether the possibility of renegotiation is to be seen as something positive or something negative - as a welfare-reducing risk or as a welfare-enhancing opportunity - is by no means clear *a priori*, but depends on the design of the model. An initial examination reveals that the models differ from one another in terms of their informational assumptions. The modelling tradition that goes back to the principal-agent model (Stiglitz/Weiss 1981, Diamond 1991, Ewert/Wagenhofer 1997: Chapter 10, Kürsten 1997) imposes a limit on the quantity of possible contract designs by assuming permanently asymmetric information between the parties to the contract. Therefore, as a matter of principle, contracts can never be made conditional on factors that are only observable to one of the parties, e.g. investment decisions, labour input, and accordingly renegotiation must be precluded.

In contrast, models aimed at explaining incomplete contracts (Aghion/Bolton 1992, Hart 1995, Dickhut/Hartmann-Wendels 1997) assume that the relevant decision or result variables (returns on investment, labour input) are non-verifiable. As the distribution of information is at the same time symmetrical, these models leave room for renegotiation between the parties to the contract as a potentially useful possibility.

---

10 The reader is referred to the conference on "Credit Risk Management and Relationship Banking" organised recently by the Center for Financial Studies at the University of Frankfurt (Main) and the Salomon Center of Stern School of Business (NYU), where the findings of empirical research into relationship lending in the United States, Norway, Germany and Italy were presented (see also the forthcoming symposium in the 1998 Journal of Banking and Finance).

The annex (see below) presents one formulation of each of these two modelling traditions. Both are designed to model the negotiations between a lender ("bank") and a borrower ("entrepreneur") in examples that are as simple, and as similar, as possible. In both formulations, the objective is to compare a long-term contract with a sequence of short-term contracts.

Although the assumptions on which these two types of model are based differ with respect to information and preferences, the outcome in the two cases is the same. The explanation of the superiority of short-term financing in the model with asymmetric information is based on the incentive effect of the right of termination,[11] combined with the inability of the owner-manager to obtain alternative finance elsewhere. In the model with incomplete contracts the superiority of short-term financing follows from the possibility that control will shift from the owner-manager to the lender, combined with the ability of the lender itself to manage the firm without loss of efficiency. The results in both modelling traditions are highly sensitive to small variations in the assumptions, in particular regarding the chronological sequence of access to information and opportunities for action (see Sutton 1990 and Schauenberg 1995).

Where I see an important difference between the two types of model is therefore not so much in the results that can be (or are) derived from them, but rather in the hypothetical situations that are typically described. Whereas most models with asymmetric information focus on the conflict between equity and debt capital (with the owner simultaneously performing management functions), in models with incomplete contracts, the lenders deal with a management that is seen as an autonomous group of actors, i.e. as distinct from the owners. Although both types of model are perfectly capable of being used to inquire into this issue, in today's theory of finance it is the incomplete-contract models which have a virtual monopoly of the corporate control theme.

3.3 Internal finance and corporate control

The market for corporate control is to equity capital what relationship banking is to debt capital. In both cases, the description of the fundamental situation is dominated by the conflict between the goals of investors and those of management. In both cases, explicit and implicit institutional precautions in financing contracts are interpreted as means of reconciling these conflicts and the loss of utility associated with their application is derived.

---

11 Indeed, Stiglitz/Weiss examine a similar case to that addressed by Hart (1995): after all, the effect of the self-financing condition in Stiglitz/Weiss's equation (9c) is not so much that it influences the incentives but rather that it exploits the budget condition. See Krahnen 1987.

At this point I would like to draw attention to what is perhaps a remarkable fact and which for about the last 10 years has caused a growing sense of irritation among observers.

It has been observed in many industrialised countries that internal financing volumes (depreciation, retained earnings, reserves) as a fraction of the sizes of aggregate spending on fixed assets are quite large. External financing volumes (share issues less capital reductions and/or repurchases of shares; bank loans), in contrast, account for only a minor share of fixed asset investments. Thus, for countries like the US, the UK, Italy, Germany or Japan, the vastly dominant role is played by internal finance (see also Taggart 1985, Mayer 1988, Hellwig 1991). Typically, fixed asset spending can be financed entirely with internal funds. To the extent that the aggregates can be applied to individual firms, these observations call into question the ability of investors to exercise influence aimed at securing corporate control. For Germany, recent research by Harhoff finds a positive correlation between cash flow and real investment at the corporate level, supporting the view that investment decisions are largely determined by the availability of internally generated funds (see Harhoff 1997).

However, consideration must be given to an objection, the validity of which can only be tested on the basis of more extensive empirical research. It is perfectly conceivable that, while the preponderance of internal finance may well be true in aggregate, there may also be substantial variation between individual firms, especially when one considers that financial investments, which by no means consist solely of liquid portfolio investments, are totally ignored[12]. If this is so, it means that some firms continue to be obliged to obtain additional finance from external sources, in which case the issue of control also remains relevant. Furthermore, even if financing requirements can largely be covered by internal finance, the remainder that cannot be internally financed may then acquire pivotal significance.

This much can be said: in the aggregate, external finance appears to play a quantitatively subordinate role in the mobilisation of investment capital, and therefore we must assume, until otherwise proven, that in a qualitative sense too, external finance can have little impact on corporate investment and financial policy. In the study by Hellwig cited above, given the observations described above, the primary function assigned to the financial system is that of mediating between the members of the corporate sector, whereas the function of mediating between enterprises and investors is seen as being of only secondary importance. Mediation between enterprises implies the transfer from firms with surplus liquidity to those with "surplus" investment projects (see Hellwig 1997, p. 237).

---

12 This possibility is also discussed in Hellwig 1997, paragraph 49.

In this context, doubts concerning the relevance of the control issue apply both to the market for corporate control and to external finance via relationship lending. In the following section the central question considered is: what is the significance of a high proportion of internal finance – the financial autonomy of the management, so to speak –for a theory of corporate finance?

3.3.1 Free cash flow or Commitment – Two positions on internal finance

The central theme of the modern theory of finance, that of corporate control, also touches on the way in which internal finance is utilised. Since the contribution by Jensen 1986, the necessity of control over the management of firms has been identified with their presumed inclination to reinvest free cash flow (see also Hart 1995, Chapter 6). In these models, the asymmetric distribution of information between management and investors leads to a hidden-action problem: investors cannot monitor whether funds are utilised in a manner that will maximise the market value of their investment. Jensen defines free cash flow as those funds of a company which, if re-invested in the best available investment projects, would produce a negative net present value. Adherence to the corporate objective of maximising market value implies that such funds should be distributed to owners in order to be channelled into more attractive investment projects via the capital market. This was an idea already expressed by Gutenberg when he concluded: "... that high dividend payouts and retransfers of profits from the capital markets to companies lead to fewer unprofitable investments and fewer instances of misdirected capital spending than lower dividend payouts." (Gutenberg 1980, p. 271, own translation).

This allocation according to the efficiency criteria of the capital market does not occur if the managements of firms not only aim for market value maximisation but are also able to derive additional benefit from, say, the sheer size of the invested capital base. The benefits of this kind of "empire-building" can manifest themselves in extra-monetary values, such as power and social recognition, but also in monetary values, such as a stabilisation of cash flow and, concomitantly, greater job security.[13] Note, incidentally, that the benefits of empire-building correspond to the "private benefits of control" I mentioned earlier.

No systematic evidence has yet been found to confirm the existence of a tendency to retain free cash flow (not least, because it is virtually impossible for outsiders to observe the capital value of new investment projects), yet there are a number of

13 This type of cash flow stabilisation in the sense of a diversification of the firm's operations is not in the interests of the shareholders, since diversified security portfolios are is a perfect substitute for it. See, for example, Berger/Ofek 1995, Denis/Denis/Sarin 1997.

indirect pointers in this direction. For example, Jensen (1986, 1993) refers in his essay to the uneconomic exploratory activity of large oil companies that were able to realise substantial windfall profits in the wake of the oil price shock.

Jensen's influential free cash flow hypothesis leads to the appeal for more intensive use to be made of the superior allocational qualities of the capital market and accordingly – not just in "mature" industries – for more cash flow to be distributed to shareholders. If this is done, the management teams of all companies compete for the available capital, making inefficient investment strategies, such as empire-building, more difficult to implement.

However, it is also possible to imagine situations in which the allocation of finance via a capital market is less efficient than quasi-automatic internal financing. This is the case if, for example, an informationally efficient capital market implies a negative externality for the competitive situation in the product market. This is a hidden-information problem; conflicts of interest between management and the capital market are disregarded here.

The claimed externality of the informationally efficient capital market can be illustrated by means of an example (on the following, see Krahnen 1994; see also Yosha 1995). The starting point is the competition between two (or among several) enterprises in the product market. Competition in this market reduces potential earnings to a "normal" level. Extra profits can only be earned if a supplier, through product innovation, gains a first mover advantage over his competitors which affords him temporary monopolistic scope. Within a certain period, imitation will erode this lead. In this model, therefore, earnings expectations are driven by innovations that the competitors are not expecting. The possibility of realising a first mover advantage in the subsequent period is a precondition for innovative efforts in the preceding period.

Innovations can be placed at risk if the firm is obliged to obtain the necessary finance on an ad hoc basis in the capital market. If the firm has to mobilise external funds, it is forced to disclose information to the capital market. This in turn means that the intention to innovate has to be publicised earlier than planned, which shortens the firm's lead over competitors. In Krahnen (1994) this disclosure of information leads to the total eradication of the lead effect. The only type of finance which can offer protection against premature imitation is one in which the funds are made available quasi-automatically, or at least without the need to declare specific investment plans and thus without disclosure of information.

This condition is satisfied by internal finance through depreciation, reserves and retained earnings, as these forms are governed by rules and are therefore non-informative. Against this background, it would be in the interests of even equity investors to approve of rule-governed financing with the cash flow of the enterprise, i.e. financing that does not have to be explained each time. Internal finance in this case is an instrument for internalising the external effects of an informationally efficient capital market on the competitive situation in the product market. An alternative method of procuring additional investment capital without having to disclose information publicly is to rely on relationship lending (see Bhattacharya/Chiesa 1995).

Another situation in which the temporary provision of liquidity on the basis of private information functions via relationships, but not via the market, can be constructed for real options. The term real option denotes an investment project which, on account of time-dependent valuation under uncertainty, contains an (implicit) option component (see Myers 1977, Ross 1995). A simple example is the value of a deferred investment (option to wait). For every project whose realisation can be postponed there is a possibility of an increase in value relative to what its value would be if it were executed at once. By way of illustration, consider the net present value of a project with a steady cash flow given a stochastic interest rate structure. Postponing the start of the project until a date in the future has a positive value because there is no risk of loss but there is indeed a chance of a gain (namely, if there is a downward shift in the term structure of interest rates). Furthermore, we can state that the more volatile interest rates are, the greater will be the value of this postponement. Accordingly, the break-even point for a decision to invest immediately must be raised by the value of the option to wait.

Another argument in favour of rule-governed internal finance is offered by Allen/Gale 1997. Here the desire to strengthen its autonomy vis-à-vis the owners is assumed to be an essential element of the management's motivation. Excessive control on the part of the shareholders ultimately means interference in the day-to-day operations. Internal finance, including the deployment of free cash flow, gives firms the opportunity to grow, which at the same time is a precondition for recruiting good staff. In Allen/Gale's model, the attendant incentive gains outweigh the possible efficiency losses due to the retention of free cash flow.

An explicit modelling of enterprises' decisions to use internal finance taking the existence of alternative sources of finance (capital market and intermediaries) into account has played hardly any role at all in the literature to date, even though this issue is obviously of great empirical significance.

4. Some thoughts in conclusion

At this point, the strands of sections 2, 3 and 4 of this essay converge. The "control puzzle" at the level of the individual enterprise given a predominance of internal finance is strikingly similar to the basic situation found by Gutenberg and described in his works – a finding which, as Gutenberg himself repeatedly stated, was shaped more by his own observations than by microeconomic theory (see Albach 1989, Chapters 1-3). Of course, this similarity does not prove how modern Gutenberg's analysis was – but it does reinforce the previously offered diagnosis of the control puzzle.

The derivation of an autonomous management interest, as demonstrated in exemplary fashion by Allen/Gale 1997b, can nonetheless go hand in hand with the long-term safeguarding of owners' interests. A precondition for this is the (expected) infinite prolongation of the existence of the firm, thereby avoiding the problem of the last period.[14] This precondition also demands that a supplementary condition be met, namely an arrangement accepted by all of the parties involved which largely corresponds to Gutenberg's notion of financial equilibrium.

Of course, one should not overemphasise this similarity between the Guternbergian postulate and Allen/Gale's result. To avoid misunderstandings, I would stress that the interest in actual corporate decisions, and their possible connection with the market valuation of companies and with possible monitoring activities on the part of intermediaries and active (large-scale) shareholders, is by no means intended as an argument against taking a shareholder-value orientation. If anything, it is the opposite. Certainly, a normative analysis should take place in an intensive dialogue with observable phenomena, in the sense of continually improved hypothesis tests. So far, this has hardly happened at all – especially in Germany; debates on shareholder value therefore often seem to consist of professions of faith, taking place in what one might call a near vacuum.

This observation can also be applied to other areas of financial research. In the German-speaking world there is a mismatch between theoretical and empirical research. The only exceptions are in the area of market microstructure, where price discovery in share and bond markets has been a dominant issue for quite some time. The un-empirical orientation of financial studies in Germany is also striking when compared with the corresponding discipline in other countries. To

---

14 If a final period were foreseeable, by backward induction the reciprocal control of managers could not function, and indeed, it would already fail to function in the very first period.

my mind, there is good reason to subject this orientation, and also its manifestation in course content and doctoral training, to a critical review.

For the continuation of financial market research beyond the control vacuum described above, the following scenario is conceivable: corporate control comprises two components, one continuous, the other discretionary. For the continuous component an autonomous management develops the self-regulating system of peer monitoring, which is in tune with the long-term existential interests of the firm. Here the main role of intermediaries consists in the necessary smoothing of cash flows over time. The control functions performed by banks, even relationship banks, are marginal at best. External intervention, by contrast, remains discretionary, and confined to just a few events in the life of a company. Here intermediaries, who may be in possession of early information, assume in particular the role of market makers (for voting majorities), and thus the role of brokers of control. Capital markets can, under certain circumstances (not given in mainland Europe), take on a similar function by means of tender offers.

References

Aghion, Philipp/Bolton, Patrick (1992): "An incomplete contracts approach to financial contracting", *Review of Economic Studies*, Vol. 59, pp. 473-494.

Albach, Horst (Hrsg., 1989): *Zur Theorie der Unternehmung*, Schriften und Reden von Erich Gutenberg (Aus dem Nachlaß), Springer-Verlag, Berlin/Heidelberg/New York.

Allen, Franklin/Gale, Douglas (1995): "A welfare comparison of intermediaries and financial markets in Germany and the U.S.", *European Economic Review*, Vol. 39, pp. 179-209.

Allen, Franklin/Gale, Douglas (1997): "Financial markets, intermediaries, and intertemporal smoothing", *Journal of Political Economy*, Vol. 105, pp. 523-546.

Allen, Franklin/Gale, Douglas (1997): *Comparative Financial Systems: Competition versus Insurance*, Mimeo.

Berger, Allen N./Udell, Gregory F. (1995): "Relationship Lending and Lines of Credit in Small Firm Finance", *Journal of Business*, Vol. 68, No. 3, pp. 351-381.

Berger, Philip/Ofek, Eli (1995): "Diversification's effect on firm value", *Journal of Financial Economics*, Vol. 37, pp. 39-65.

Berlin, Mitchell (1996): "For Better and For Worse: Three Lending Relationships", *Federal Reserve Bank of Philadelphia Business Review*, Nov./Dec. 1996, pp. 3-12.

Berlin, Mitchell/Mester, Loretta J. (1997): "Why is the Banking Sector shrinking? Core deposits and relationship lending", *Working Paper No. 96-18/R, The Wharton School*, University of Pennsylvania, April 1997.

Bhattacharya, Supdito/Thakor, Anjan V. (1993): "Contemporary Banking Theory", *Journal of Financial Intermediation*, Vol. 3, pp. 2-50.

Boot, Arnoud W. A./Thakor, Anjan V. (1997): "Financial system architecture", *Review of Financial Studies*, Vol. 10, pp. 693-733.

Brennan, Michael J. (1995): "Corporate finance over the past 25 years", *Financial Management*, Vol. 24, No. 2, Summer 1995, pp. 9-22.

Breuer, Wolfgang (1994): "Finanzintermediation und Wiederverhandlungen", in: *Kredit und Kapital*, pp. 291-309.

Dennis, David J./Dennis, Diane K./Sarin, Atulya (1997): "Agency Problems, Equity Ownership, and Corporate Diversification", *Journal of Finance*, Vol. 52, pp. 135-160.

Dewatripont, Mathias/Maskin, Eric (1995): "Credit and efficiency in centralized and decentralized economies", *Review of Economic Studies*, Vol. 62, pp. 541-55.

Diamond, Douglas (1984): "Financial intermediation and delegated monitoring", *Review of Economic Studies*,Vol. 51, pp. 393-414.

Diamond, Douglas (1991): "Monitoring and reputation: The choice between bank loans and directly placed debt", *Journal of Political Economy*, Vol. 99, pp. 689-721.

Dickhut, Stefanie/Hartmann-Wendels, Thomas (1997): "Die Delegation von Kontrollaufgaben an den Aufsichtsrat", *Working Paper*, RWTH Aachen.

Domanski, Dietrich (1997): "Disintermediationstendenzen im deutschen Finanzsystem und ihre Auswirkungen auf die Rolle der Kreditinstitute – Eine Bewertung aus geldpolitischer Sicht", in: Gahlen, Bernhard/Hesse, Helmut/Ramser, Hans Jürgen (eds.): *Finanzmärkte*, Tübingen, Mohr Siebeck, pp. 271-290.

Drukarczyk, Jochen (1993): *Theorie und Politik der Finanzierung*, 2nd edition, Munich.

Edwards, J.S.S/Mishkin, F.S. (1995): "The Decline of Traditional Banking: Implications for Financial Stability and Regulatory Policy", *Economic Policy Review*, Federal Reserve Bank of New York, Vol. 1, No. 2, July, pp. 27-45.

Elsas, Ralf/Krahnen, Jan Pieter (1998): "Is Relationship Lending Special? Evidence from Credit-File Data in Germany", Working Paper, Institut für Kapitalmarktforschung/ Center for Financial Studies, Frankfurt a.M..

Elsas, Ralf/Henke, Sabine/Machauer, Achim/Rott, Roland/Schenk, Gerald (1998): "Empirical Analysis of Credit Relationships in Small Firms Financing: Sampling Design and Descriptive Statistics", *Working Paper*, Instititut für Kapitalmarktforschung/ Center for Financial Studies, Frankfurt a.M..

Ewert, Ralf/Ernst, Christian (1997): "Strategic Management Accounting, Coordination and long-term Cost Structure", Working Paper, July 1997, Johann Wolfgang Goethe-Universität, Frankfurt a.M..

Ewert, Ralf/Wagenhofer, Alfred (1997): *Interne Unternehmensrechnung*, Berlin et al.: Springer Verlag.

Fama, Eugene (1991): "Efficient capital markets II", *Journal of Finance*, Vol. 46, pp. 1575-1617.

Franke, Günter (1993): "Neuere Entwicklungen auf dem Gebiet der Finanzmarkttheorie", in: *WiSt,* Vol. 8, pp. 389-398.

Gorton, Gary/Schmid, Frank A. (1996): "Universal banking and the performance of German firms", *National Bureau of Economic Research Working Paper 5453,* Cambridge (MA).

Grossmann, Sanford/Hart, Oliver (1988): "One share-one vote and the market for corporate control," *Journal of Financial Economics*, Vol. 20, pp. 175-202.

Grossmann, Sanford/Hart, Oliver/Moore, John (1988): "Incomplete contracts and renegotiation," *Econometria* [heißt die Zeitschrift nicht *Econometrica* mit *c* ??], Vol. 56, pp. 755-785.

Grossmann, Sanford/Stiglitz, Joseph (1980): "On the impossibility of informationally efficient markets", *American Economic Review*, Vol. 70, pp. 393-408.

Gutenberg, Erich (1927): "Die Kreditquellen in der Finanzierung", in: *Zeitschrift für Betriebswirtschaft*, Vol. 9, pp. 683-692.

Gutenberg, Erich (1929): "Die Unternehmung als Gegenstand betriebswirtschaftlicher Theorie", *Betriebs- und Finanzwissenschaftliche Forschung*, Series II, No. 40, Berlin-Wien, Spaeth&Linde, pp. 53-63.

Gutenberg, Erich (1937/38): "Finanzierung und Sanierung", in: Nicklisch, H. (ed.): *Handwörterbuch der Betriebswirtschaft,* 2nd edition, Stuttgart, C.E. Poeschel Verlag, pp. 1739-1786.

Gutenberg, Erich (1951): *Grundlagen der Betriebswirtschaftslehre, Vol. 1: Die Produktion, 1st edition (Enzyklopädie der Rechts- und Staatswissenschaft, Abteilung Staatswissenschaft)*, Berlin/Heidelberg/New York (Springer).

Gutenberg, Erich (1957): "Betriebswirtschaftslehre als Wissenschaft", Academic address delivered on 22 May 1957 at the celebrations to mark the founding of the university, reprinted in excerpts in: *Zeitschrift für Betriebswirtschaft*, Vol. 27, pp. 606-612.

Gutenberg, Erich (1959): *Untersuchungen über die Investitionsentscheidungen industrieller Unternehmen*, Westdeutscher Verlag, Köln, pp. 216-225.

Gutenberg, Erich (1960): "Die gegenwärtige Situation der Betriebswirtschaftslehre", in: *Zeitschrift für handelswissenschaftliche Beiträge*, Vol. 12, pp. 118-129.

Gutenberg, Erich (1961): "Die Investitionspolitik industrieller Unternehmungen", in: *Management International*, Vol. 1, pp. 31-42.

Gutenberg, Erich (1980): *Grundlagen der Betriebswirtschaftslehre, Vol. 3: Die Finanzen, 8th enlarged edition (Enzyklopädie der Rechts- und Staatswissenschaft, Abteilung Staatswissenschaft)*, Berlin/Heidelberg/New York (Springer).

Harhoff, Dietmar (1997): "Are there Financing Constraints for R&D and Investment in German Manufacturing Firms" *Annals d'Économie et de Statistique*, forthcoming.

Harris, Milton/Raviv, Artur (1988): "Corporate Governance: Voting Rights and Majority Rules", *Journal of Financial Economics*, Vol. 20, pp. 203-235.

Hart, Oliver (1980): "Takeover bids, the free-rider problem, and the theory of the corporation," *Bell Journal of Economics*, Vol. 11, pp. 42-64.

Hart, Oliver (1995): *Firms, contracts and financial structure*, Clarendon Press, Oxford.

Haugen, Robert A. (1996): "Finance from a new perspective", in: *Financial Management,* Vol. 25, No. 1, Spring 1996, pp. 86-97.

Hax, Herbert (1982): "Finanzierungs- und Investitionstheorie", in: Koch, Helmut (ed.): *Neuere Entwicklungen in der Unternehmenstheorie, Erich Gutenberg zum 85. Geburtstag*, Wiesbaden, Gabler, pp. 49-68.

Hellwig, Martin (1989): "Asymmetrical Information, financial markets and financial institutions: Where are we currently going?", *European Economic Review*, Vol. 33, p. 277.

Hellwig, Martin (1991): "Banking, financial intermediation and corporate finance", in: Giovannini, Alberto/Mayer, Colin (eds.): *European Financial Integration,* Cambridge, New York, and Melbourne, Cambridge University Press, pp. 35-63.

Hellwig, Martin (1995): "Comment on Julian Franks and Colin Mayer, 'Ownership and Control'", in: Siebert, Horst (ed.): *Trends in Business Organization: Do Participation and Cooperation Increase Competitiveness?,* Tübingen, J.C.B. Mohr (Paul Siebeck), pp. 196-200.

Hellwig, Martin (1997): "Unternehmensfinanzierung, Unternehmenskontrolle und Resourcenallokation: Was leistet das Finanzsystem?", in: Gahlen, Bernhard/Hesse, Helmut/Ramser, Hans Jürgen (eds.): *Finanzmärkte*, Tübingen, Mohr Siebeck.

Hellwig, Martin/Staub, Markus (1996): "Capital requirement for market risks based on inhouse models - aspects of quality assessment", in: *Swiss Journal of Economics and Statistics*, Vol. 132 (4/2), 755-776.

Holmström, Bengt R./Tirole, Jean (1996): "Private and public supply of liquidity", *Working Paper No. 5817, National Bureau of Economic Research*, November 1996.

Jensen, Michael (1986): "Agency costs of free cash flow, corporate finance, and takeovers," *American Economic Review*, Vol. 76, pp. 323-29.

Jensen, Michael (1989): "The eclipse of the public corporation," *Harvard Business Review*, Vol. 67, pp. 60-70.

Jensen, Michael C. (1991): "Corporate control and the politics of finance", *Journal of Applied Corporate Finance*, Vol. 4, pp. 13-33.

Jensen, Michael C. (1993): "The modern industrial revolution, exit, and the failure of the internal control system", *Journal of Finance*, Vol. 48, pp. 831-880.

Jensen, Michael C./Ruback, R.S. (1983): "The market for corporate control: The scientific evidence", *Journal of Financial Economics*, Vol. 11, pp. 5-50.

Krahnen, Jan Pieter (1987): Incentive effects of terminations: A comment on Stiglitz and Weiss, mimeo.

Krahnen, Jan Pieter (1991): *Sunk costs und Unternehmensfinanzierung*, Wiesbaden, Gabler Verlag.

Krahnen, Jan Pieter (1993): "Investitionsmodelle, integrierte", in: Wittmann/Waldemar (eds.): *Handwörterbuch der Betriebswirtschaft*, Stuttgart, Schäffer-Poeschel, pp. 1952-1964.

Krahnen, Jan Pieter (1993a): "Finanzwirtschaftslehre zwischen Markt und Institution", *Die Betriebswirtschaft*, Vol. 53, No. 6, pp. 793-805.

Krahnen, Jan Pieter (1994): "Überlegungen zu einer Theorie der Innenfinanzierung", in: Gerke, Wolfgang (ed.): *Planwirtschaft am Ende - Marktwirtschaft in der Krise?*, Stuttgart, Schäffer-Poeschel.

Krahnen, Jan Pieter/Weber, Martin (1997): "Marketmaking in the laboratory: Does competition matter?", *Finance Working Paper Series*, No. 4/97, University of Frankfurt.

Kürsten, Wolfgang (1997): "Zur Anreizinkompatibilität von Kreditsicherheiten, oder: Insuffizienz des Stiglitz/Weiss-Modells der Agency-Theorie", *Zeitschrift für betriebswirtschaftliche Forschung*, Vol. 49, pp. 819-857.

Laux, Christian (1996): *Kapitalstruktur und Verhaltenssteuerung: Finanzierungsverträge als Bindungs- und Anreizinstrumente*, Wiesbaden, Gabler.

Mayer, Colin (1988): "New issues in corporate finance", *European Economic Review*, Vol. 32, pp. 1167-1188.

Miller, Geoffrey P. (1997): "On the Obsolescence of Commercial Banking", *Discussion Paper*, NY University Law School.

Myers, Stewart (1977): "Determinants of corporate borrowing," *Journal of Financial Economics*, Vol. 5, pp. 147-175.

Myers, S. C./Majluf, N. S. (1984): "Corporate finance and investment decisions when firms have information that investors do not have", *Journal of Financial Economics*, Vol. 13, June 1984, pp. 187-222.

Petersen, Mitchell/Rajan, Raghuram (1994): "The benefits of lending relationships: Evidence from small business data", *Journal of Finance*, Vol. 49, pp. 3-37.

Rajan, Raghuram (1992): "Insiders and outsiders: The choice between informed and arm's length debt," *Journal of Finance*, Vol. 47, pp. 1367-1400.

Rajan, Raghuram (1996): "Why Banks Have A Future: An Economic Rationale", *Banca d'Italia Temi di discussione del Servizio Studi*, No. 280, October 1996.

Ross, Stephen A. (1995): "Uses, Abuses, and Alternatives to the Net-Present-Value Rule", *Financial Management*, Vol. 24, No. 3, pp. 96-102.

Schauenberg, Bernd (1995): "Unternehmerfunktionen, Marktprozesse und Spieltheorie", in: Elschen, Rainer/Siegel, Theodor/Wagner, Franz W. (eds.): *Unternehmenstheorie und Besteuerung*, Wiesbaden, Gabler Verlag, pp. 515-548.

Schauenberg, Bernd/Schmidt, Reinhard H. (1983): "Vorarbeiten zu einer Theorie der Unternehmung", in: Kappler, E. (ed.): *Rekonstruktion der Betriebswirtschaftslehre als ökonomische Theorie*, Spardorf, pp. 247-276.

Shleifer, Andrei/Vishny, Robert W. (1997): "A survey of corporate governance", *Journal of Finance*, Vol. 52, pp. 737-783.

Schmid, F.A. (1997): "Eigentümerstruktur, Agency-Kosten und Unternehmenserfolg: Empirische Evidenz für österreichische Genossenschaftsbanken", *Working Paper, The Wharton School*, University of Philadelphia.

Schmidt, Reinhard H./Spindler, Gerald (1997): "Shareholder Value zwischen Ökonomie und Recht", in: *Wirtschafts- und Medienrecht in der offenen Demokratie, Freundesgabe für Friedrich Kübler zum 65. Geburtstag*, pp. 514-555.

Schmidt, Reinhard H./Tyrell, Marcell (1997): "Financial Systems, corporate finance and corporate governance", *European Financial Management*, Vol. 3, pp. 333-361.

Schmidt, Reinhard H. (1981): "Grundformen der Finanzierung: Eine Anwendung des neo-institutionalistischen Ansatzes der Finanzierungstheorie", *Kredit und Kapital*,
Vol. 14, pp. 186-221.

Schmidt, Reinhard H. (1997): "Erich Gutenberg und die Theorie der Unternehmung", paper presented on the occasion of the centenary of Erich Gutenberg's birth on 12 and 13 December 1997 in Cologne. [Neue Bezugnahme auf den Nachdruck in Englisch ??]

Shanken, Jay/Smith, Clifford W. (1996): "Implications of capital markets research for corporate finance", in: *Financial Management*, Vol. 25, No. 1, Spring 1996, pp. 98-104.

Sharpe, Steven A. (1990): "Asymmetric Information, bank lending and implicit contracts: A stylized model of customer relationship", *Journal of Finance*, Vol. 45, pp. 1069-1087.

Spulber, Daniel F. (1996): "Market microstructure and intermediation", Journal of Economic Perspectives, Vol. 10, No. 3, Summer 1996, pp. 135-152.

Stiglitz, Joseph E. (1972): "Some aspects of the pure theory of corporate finance: bankruptcies and take-overs", *Bell Journal of Economics*, Fall 1972, Vol. 3, No. 2, pp. 458-482.

Stiglitz, Joseph/Weiss, Andrew (1983): "Incentive effects of terminations: Applications to the credit and labor markets", *American Economic Review*, Vol. 73, pp. 912-27.

Summers, L. (1986): "Does the stock market rationally reflect values?", *Journal of Finance*, Vol. 41, S 591-601.

Sutton, J. (1990): "Explaining everything, explaining nothing? Game theoretic models in industrial economics", *European Economic Review*, Vol. 34, pp. 505-512.

Taggart, Robert (1985): "Secular patterns in the financing of U.S. corporations", in: Friedman, Benjamin (ed.): *Corporate Capital Structure in the United States*, Chicago, University of Chicago Press.

von Thadden, E.L. (1995): "Long term contracts, short-term investments, and monitoring", *Review of Economic Studies*, Vol. 62, pp. 557-575.

Wagner, Franz W. (1987): "Ausschüttungszwang und Kapitalentzugsrechte als Instrumente marktgelenkter Unternehmenskontrolle?", in: Schneider, Dieter (ed.): *Kapitalmarkt und Finanzierung*, Berlin, pp. 409-425.

Wagner, Franz W. (1997): "Shareholder Value: Eine neue Runde im Konflikt zwischen Kapitalmarkt und Unternehmensinteresse", *Betriebswirtschaftliche Forschung und Praxis*, pp. 473-498

Weingartner, H.M. (1977): "Capital rationing: n authors in search of a plot", *Journal of Finance*, pp. 1403-1431.

Wenger, Ekkehard (1989): "Allgemeine Betriebswirtschaftslehre und ökonomische Theorie", in: Kirsch, W/Picot, A. (eds.): *Die Betriebswirtschaftslehre im Spannungsfeld zwischen Generalisierung und Spezialisierung*, Wiesbaden, pp. 155-181.

Wenger, Ekkehard (1996): "Institutionelle Defizite am deutschen Kapitalmarkt", *mimeo*, Universität Würzburg.

Worms, Andreas (1997): "Bankkredite an Unternehmen und ihre Rolle in der geldpolitischen Transmission in Deutschland", *Wirtschaftswissenschaftliche Dissertation,* Universität Frankfurt am Main.

Yosha, Oved (1995): "Information disclosure costs and the choice of financing source", *Journal of Financial Intermediation* 4, pp. 3-20.

Zingales, Luigi (1994): "The value of the voting right: A study of the Milan stock exchange", *The Review of Financial Studies*, Vol. 7, pp. 125-148.

Zingales, Luigi (1997): "Corporate Governance", in: *The New Palgrave Dictionary of Economics and the Law.*

Summary

This selective overview of recent developments in the theory of finance began by asserting that relationships are currently the focus of particular interest. Behind this lies the conviction that only a profound understanding of long-term contractual relationships, taking informational and "hold-up" problems into account such as may arise between an investor and an enterprise, can enable us to draw a distinction between market-mediated and bank-intermediated finance. The current issues of concern to theorists of finance focus on the conflicts between equity investors, lenders and management. Whereas earlier studies focused upon the lenders versus investors conflict (see Krahnen 1991, Kürsten 1996), in the past few years attention has shifted to the conflict between lenders and/or investors on the one hand and management on the other. This applies not only to investigations into credit relationships but also to the analysis of corporate governance structures and structural problems of the market for corporate control (see, for example, Hart 1995, Laux 1996).

However, there are growing doubts as to the empirical significance of manager-monitoring through the systematic activities of banks, the stock markets and corporate governing bodies (shareholders' meetings, supervisory boards). In this context, the observation that the markets for equity and debt capital play such a small role in the financing of fixed asset investments in the leading industrialised countries is just one argument among several. In addition, there are fundamental doubts as to the ability of the aforementioned control institutions to perform that function, be they house banks (Hellwig 1997), be they representatives of shareholders (Jensen 1993, Wenger 1997), or be it the market for corporate control (Grossman/Hart 1980, Shleifer/Vishny 1997). Besides, there are theoretical lines of argument which suggest that efficiency gains may be achieved by creating a domain of management autonomy that lies outside the tight control exercised by outsiders, i.e. owners or creditors. In other words, the proponents of these views regard the possibilities for, and instruments of, internal finance not, or not only as signs of opportunistic behaviour, but as signs of decision-making autonomy in the context of a separation of ownership and control.[15]

The emerging consensus is that the managers of big companies, despite several elements of peer-monitoring,[16] enjoy a large degree of decision-making autonomy from the instruments of control of all groups of lenders and investors (Hellwig 1997). What does this mean for the theory of finance? For the time being I see two consequences:

First, to date we have acquired no more than rudimentary empirical knowledge about corporate control issues. Although a great many theoretical works have been written on the basis of models with asymmetric information or incomplete contracts, there have been virtually no serious empirical tests of the hypotheses they contain, especially outside the United States. The lack of available data is, in my view, not so much a cause as a manifestation of the almost complete absence of empirical interest in issues raised by the modern theory of finance, at least as far as corporate control is concerned.[17] It is perfectly conceivable that, while the large proportion of internal finance may well be true on aggregate, there may also be substantial variation between individual firms, especially when one considers that financial investments, which by no means consist solely of liquid portfolio investments, are totally ignored. If this is so, it means that some firms continue to be obliged to obtain additional finance from external sources, in which case the issue of control also remains relevant. Furthermore, even if financing requirements can largely be covered by internal finance, the remainder that cannot be internally financed may then acquire pivotal significance. Not until the appropriate empirical studies have been carried out will it be possible to gauge conclusively the validity of the hypothesis of far-reaching manager autonomy.

---

15 It may be noted en passant that the original explanation for a separation between ownership and control was that it represented the delegation of decision-making authority to specialised actors who were thus comparatively more efficient than the owners. On this point, see also Schmidt 1997.

16 See Hellwig 1995 for the concept of reciprocal (peer) monitoring, relating to cross-holdings between corporations.

17 This diagnosis does not apply to all those issues and model verifications which relate to the organisation of stock and bond markets and their relative valuations.

Furthermore, not enough empirical research has been carried out into the extent of corporate control through intermediaries, such as is supposed to be typical of bank-dominated systems, to substantiate what we think we know about this area (but see Gorton/Schmid 1998). The evidence to support the view that house banks perform insurance functions is an indication that intermediaries may play a significant role in qualitative terms too – yet it is not proof that they perform a control function.

Second, doubts regarding the financial market-related control instruments obviously raise the question: Who really does set the goals in manager-led enterprises? One cannot rule out the possibility that research programs focusing on shareholders' interests, based on the fundamental structure of the principal-agent model, do not sufficiently sharpen our awareness of the empirical connections. In a recent OLG model[18] presented by Allen/Gale 1997b, enterprises develop a long-term survival interest by virtue of their potential long-lasting existence and the constant renewal process in the management team (managers are hired young, do not become highly productive until they have grown older, and eventually go into retirement; at any given point in time, members of *both* generations are employed). Thus, the authors paint a picture of an enterprise that perpetuates itself primarily on the basis of internal finance and whose objective function is defined in the context of a multi-agent model subject to the approval of a principal (equity investor). The possibility in principle that each generation of management will "cheat" (appropriate a non-recurrent rent) is suppressed in the OLG model by the simultaneous presence and monitoring activity of the younger generation (which in turn would like to remain part of the firm in the next generation too, this time as older managers, without being punished by the owners). Under these conditions, the resultant management decisions prove to be efficient, even without an active market for corporate control.

The models that predominate in today's theory of finance do not take long-term OLG scenarios of this kind into account – not least because the typical model design is based on a static two-person situation. The existence of a collective management interest surely has significant implications for the corporate control issue – how they might be connected to the valuation of enterprises in the capital market appears to me to be a completely open question at present.

---

18 Allen/Gale 1997, Chapter 12. "OLG" stands for OverLapping Generations. Models of this type render it possible to observe the dynamics of developments over long time horizons; each of the actors lives for only a limited number of periods, and during their lifetime they pass through various phases. Typically, there will be a phase of employment and a phase of retirement.

Specification, Estimation, and Empirical Corroboration of Gutenberg's Kinked Demand Curve

H. Hruschka[1]

Overview

- After first introducing Gutenberg's demand curve, its nature is clarified by reference to switching costs and preference distributions of buyers. Various model specifications, related approaches in the US literature and available empirical results are also presented.
- In our empirical study we compare specifications used hitherto, as well as piecewise linear and semi-parametric specifications of Gutenberg's demand curve, with competing functional forms, i.e. linear, logistic, exponential.
- For seven out of the eleven brands studied, flexible estimation methods indicate a medium price range characterized by weak price sensitivities. On the other hand large, as well as small, price differences lead to strong responses. These results are in agreement with Gutenberg's demand curve.

Keywords. Demand Curves, Kinked Demand Curve, Attraction Models, Semi-Parametric Estimation

1 Theoretical Foundations

A plot of Gutenberg's demand curve showing sales of a brand, given constant prices of competitive brands, consists of three sections, namely for low, medium and high prices of the brand, respectively. The medium price range is characterized by low price sensitivities, whereas both low and high prices are accompanied by high price sensitivities. The size of the medium price range increases with customers' loyalities, it decreases with substitutability of brands and customers' knowledge (Gutenberg, 1955; Gutenberg, 1984).

---

1 Professor Dr. Harald Hruschka, University of Regensburg, Universitätsstrasse 31, 93053 Regensburg, Germany, email: harald.hruschka@wiwi.uni-regenburg.de.

The medium price range is also called autonomous range because the firm can change prices within this range without competitors reacting. This contrasts with changes in the low, or high, price ranges which lead to reactions from competitors. Therefore Gutenberg's demand curve assumes partial interdependence of competitors with regard to pricing.

Price reductions lower buyers' loyalities in respect of competing brands. This effect becomes especially strong if the price reducing brand leaves its price tier. This brand now attracts buyers of other brands belonging to a lower price tier, who now choose the higher quality brand, as well as buyers of other brands belonging to its former price tier.

On the other hand, a brand loses buyers if its price increases are made outside the medium price range. Buyers now choose similar competing brands because they rate their prices to be significantly lower. In this case preferences no longer prevent brand switching.

These considerations show that the shape of Gutenberg's demand curve is caused by buyers' responses. Albach (1973) starts from the linear function:

$$Q_A = a - b \quad p_A - c \quad (p_A - p_B) \tag{1}$$

Q_A denotes sales volume of brand A, p_A its price and p_B the price of brand B. An infinitesimal change in p_A given a constant p_B leads to a constant change in sales volume $-b-c$. Therefore Albach (1973) calls the linear function the demand function with constant mobility of demand. $-b$ measures the response of latent demand for brand A and $-c$ the response of demand loyal to competing brands. Latent demand refers to potential customers of brand A who do not buy any of the competing brands. Demand loyal to competing brands refers to buyers of competing brands, who may switch to brand A.

Gutenberg's demand curve is characterized by variable mobility of demand loyal to competing brands. In contrast to the linear function, c is not constant. c becomes zero if the price of brand A lies in the autonomous range and increases the further the price of brand A is moved outside this range. Graphically this relationship manifests itself in the two kinks of Gutenberg's demand curve.

Only higher price differences between brands cause brand switching. Albach (1973) explains this effect with buyers' switching costs. According to Klemperer (1995) low compatibility of investments, transactions, learning, quality uncertainty, loss of economic benefits (from e.g. loyalty programs) or psychological brand loyalty can lead to switching costs.

Other possible explanations of Gutenberg's demand curve may be derived from preference distributions. Gabszewicz/Thisse (1986) start from a unidimensional ideal point model. Every buyer chooses the brand with the lowest distance to her ideal point. The authors moreover assume that ideal points follow a uniform distribution and every customer buys, one or none, of the brands.

A buyer's utility u results from a basic utility v, reduced by price p and the disutility due to the distance of a brand with position x from the ideal point x^*:

$$u = v - p - e_1|x - x^*| - e_2(x - x^*)^2 \text{ with } e_1, e_2 > 0 \tag{2}$$

Disutility is a quadratic function of absolute distance (absolute difference between a brand's position and the ideal point). One may interpret the difference in disutilities between two brands as switching costs.

For a duopoly of two brands, and constant price of the competing brand, one obtains a doubly kinked demand curve with three piecewise linear sections. Piecewise linearity results from the uniform distribution of ideal points. Just like Gutenberg's demand curve the medium section has the lowest slope. But this section depends on the price of the competing brand and therefore may be called non-monopolistic. The slopes of all sections increase with e_2. The medium section becomes larger with a higher disutility due to brand switching. Disutility is related to e_1, e_2 and the distance between the two brands. Slopes decrease with higher e_1.

If disutility is linear with regard to distance from ideal points ($e_2 = 0$) one obtains a constellation studied by Kilger (1962) for Gutenberg's demand curve. This constellation leads to a piecewise linear, doubly kinked function whose extreme sections are parallel to the sales volume axis.

For $e_1 = 0$ one finally gets the linear function.

The autonomous price range without the influence of prices of a competing brand emerges if there exists an empty space without demand between two brands. Such an empty space causes small price changes not to lead to brand switching (Willeke, 1967; Piekenbrock, 1980).

2 Model Specifications

Albach (1973) specifies Gutenberg's demand curve as a continuous function in the following way:

$$Q_A = a - b \quad p_A - c \quad \sinh(p_A - p_B) \tag{3}$$

Mobility of demand caused by price changes of brand A for this specification is:

$$\frac{\partial Q_A}{\partial p_A} = -b - c \quad \cosh(p_A - p_B) \tag{4}$$

Mobility of demand loyal to competing brands $(-c \quad \cosh(p_A - p_B))$ increases with the price difference and c. It is symmetric for price increases and decreases of the same amount. Figure 1 shows sales volume according to this specification for variable p_A and constant p_B.

Figure 1: Gutenberg's Demand Curve Specified by Albach (1973)

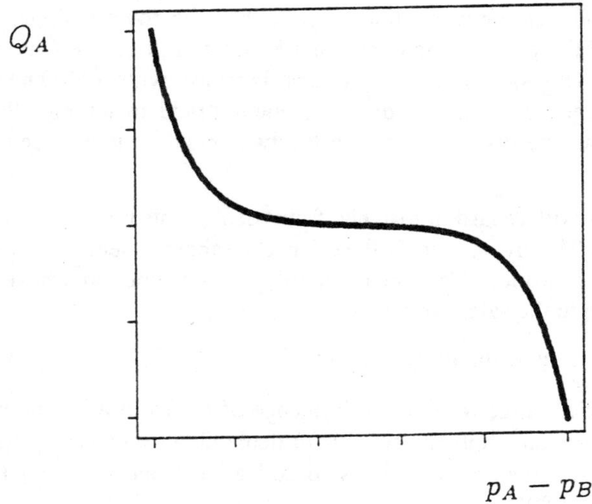

Albach (1979) extends this specification by adding a coefficient d which multiplies the ratio of brand's A price and an average price $\overline{p}$ before plugging it into the hyperbolic sine:

$$Q_A = a - c \quad \sinh(d \quad p_A / \overline{p}) \tag{5}$$

A higher d makes the function more non-linear, low values lead to a quasi-linear shape (Simon, 1979).

Another extension consists in considering price differences with regard to several competing brands (Albach, 1979):

$$Q_A = a - b \quad p_A - c_1 \sinh\left(d_1\left(p_A - p_B\right)\right) - c_2 \sinh\left(d_2\left(p_A - p_C\right)\right)$$

Simon (1979) introduces a dynamic specification comprising a relative price difference whose effect is proportional to the previous period's sales:

$$Q_A(t) = a - b \quad p_A(t) - c_1 \sinh\left(d\left(p_A(t) - \overline{p}(t)\right) / \left(\overline{p}(t)\right)\right) \quad Q_A(t-1) \qquad (7)$$

Brockhoff (1988) considers asymmetric effects with regard to a reference price $\overline{p}$:

$$Q_A = \begin{cases} a - b \quad p_A - c_1 \sinh\left(p_A - \overline{p}\right) & \text{for } p_A > \overline{p} \\ a - b \quad p_A - c_2 \sinh\left(p_A - \overline{p}\right) & \text{else} \end{cases} \qquad (8)$$

Brand A gains more sales because of low prices compared to the sales it loses because of high prices if c_2 is greater than c_1. Such effects may be caused by asymmetric switching costs, e.g. higher costs for acquiring information when switching from a well known to a lesser known brand than vice versa.

Hruschka (1997) introduces the following specification which plugs the price difference to a weighted average price of several competing brands into the hyperbolic sine:

$$Q_A = a - \quad b \quad p_A - c \quad \sinh\left(d_1 p_A - d_2 p_B - d_3 p_C\right) \qquad (9)$$

Sabel (1976) specifies Gutenberg's demand curve as a piecewise linear function:

$$Q_A = \begin{cases} a_A + \left(d_A - b_A\right) p_{AU} - d_A p_A & \text{for } p_A < p_{AU} \\ a_A - b_A p_A & \text{for } p_{AU} <= p_A <= p_{AO} \\ a_A + \left(c_A - b_A\right) p_{AO} - c_A p_A & \text{for } p_A > p_{AO} \end{cases} \qquad (10)$$

p_{AU}, p_{AO} denote the minimum and maximum price of the medium price range, respectively. Sales are independent of the prices of the competing brand if the price of the brand lies in the medium range, i.e. this function has a true monopolistic price range.

The following additive model with smooth functions f_1 and f_2 generalizes the specification of Albach (1979):

$$Q_A = a - b \quad p_A - c_1 f_1\left(p_A - p_B\right) - c_2 f_2\left(p_A - p_C\right) \qquad (11)$$

One advantage of this model is that it may be readily interpreted because it adds up nonlinear effects of price differences. By setting $f_1 = f_2 = \sinh$ one obtains the specification of Albach. The extension of Brockhoff, which allows asymmetric effects, may be subsumed as well. The linear function is another special case, of course.

A semi-parametric approach avoids the necessity of assuming a strict dependence of sales on price differences. To determine smooth functions of price differences we use cubic smoothing splines. Cubic smoothing splines minimize the following expression for all functions with continuous first and second order derivatives (Buja et al., 1989):

$$\sum_{i}(y_i - f_i)^2 + \lambda\int(f''(t))^2 dt \tag{12}$$

y_i observation value of the dependent variable

f_i estimation value of the dependent variable

This expression consists of the error sum of squares and a penalty term. The smoothing parameter λ weights the smoothness of the function. For an infinite λ the penalty terms dominates, which implies the condition $f'' = 0$ for second order derivatives and the fitting of a linear function.

A cubic spline is a function defined for a real value range which is a cubic polynomial for any partial interval bounded by points (knots). A cubic spline and its first and second order derivatives are continuous everywhere (De Boor, 1978).

Partial residuals are helpful for the estimation and interpretation of the effect of any predictor. They result from eliminating the effect of all other predictors (Buja et al., 1989). For the price difference $p_A - p_B$ in equation 11 for example, they are given by:

$$Q_A - a + b \quad p_A + c_2 f_2(p_A - p_c) \tag{13}$$

Standard errors are approximated by the square roots of the diagonal elements of RR' (with $f = Ry$), degrees of freedom by the trace of the matrix SS' (with $f_i = Sy$).

Analogous to the specification of Sabel (1976) we may write the following parametric piecewise linear model:

$$Q_A = a - b \quad p_A - c_1 BS_1(p_A - p_B) - c_2 BS_2(p_A - p_c) \tag{14}$$

BS_1, BS_2 are vectors of B-splines for price differences (De Boor, 1978). B-splines are piecewise polynomials (here: piecewise linear functions). For given knots we obtain a linear regression problem so that degrees of freedom and standard errors may be computed explicitly.

The B-spline for a price difference possesses three sections and two knots if it orresponds to the specification of Sabel. Its knots denote the upper and lower prices of the medium price range, respectively. The medium range has a slope (a regression coefficient) of zero as competing brands' prices have no effect there. The other sections have greater slopes (regression coefficients). If the slopes of the two outward sections are different, price effects are asymmetric between high and low prices.

3 Related Approaches

Attraction models assume that the market share corresponds to the ratio of the respective brand's attraction (numerator) to the sum of the attractions of all brands of a market (denominator). The market share of brand A for an oligopoly is written as follows:

$$M_A = A_A / (A_A + A_B) \tag{15}$$

M_A denotes market share of brand A. A_A represents attraction of brand A. A_B stands for attraction of brand B.

As a rule, multiplicative or exponential functional forms are assumed for attractions:

$$A_A = a \quad p_A^{-b}$$

or

$$A_A = a \quad \exp(-b \quad p_A) \tag{16}$$

Like Gutenberg's demand curve, attraction models possess three sections given a constant competitive price p_B. But the medium price range of attraction models has the steepest slope and the outward sections have lower slopes. Small price differences in the medium range lead to large changes in market share. Figure 2 shows the shape of an attraction model given a constant p_B.

This feature of attraction models may be changed by replacing raw prices by zeta-transformed prices as suggested by Cooper/Nakanishi (1983). After this transformation the medium range has the smallest price effects. Figure 3 represents the shape of an MNL function with zeta-transformed prices for the respective brand. The similarity to Gutenberg's demand curve is obvious.

Figure 2: Attraction Model

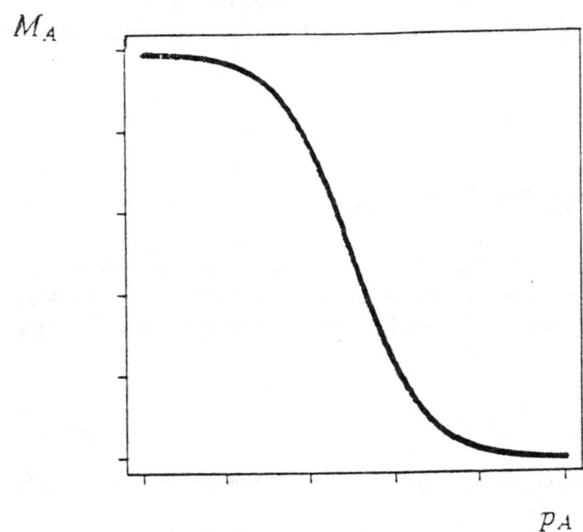

An average price $\overline{p}$ serves as standard of comparison. Using the standard deviation s, z-transformed values are computed as first step:

$$z(p) = (p - \overline{p}) / s \tag{17}$$

On the basis of these z values the zeta values are derived in the following manner:

$$\text{zeta}(p) = \begin{cases} \left(1 + z(p)^2\right)^{1/2} & \text{for } z(p) >= 0 \\ 1 / \left(\left(1 + z(p)^2\right)^{1/2}\right) & \text{else} \end{cases} \tag{18}$$

The zeta values are positive. They are equal to one for the average price, are less than one for prices below, and greater than one, for prices above the average price.

Kalyanaram/Little (1989 and 1994) expect low sensitivities for a medium price range, but strong effects for more extreme prices, according to the assimilation-contrast theory. Prospect theory postulates that responses to high prices (losses) should be greater than responses to low prices (gains). Kalyanaram/Little use scanner panel data and analyse household purchase data by means of a multinomial logit model. The authors determine reference prices on the basis of adaptive expectations, i.e. by exponential smoothing. Differences of observed prices from the reference price are divided by standard deviations. The medium price range is symmetric with regard to the reference price.

Figure 3: Attraction Model with Zeta-transformed Prices

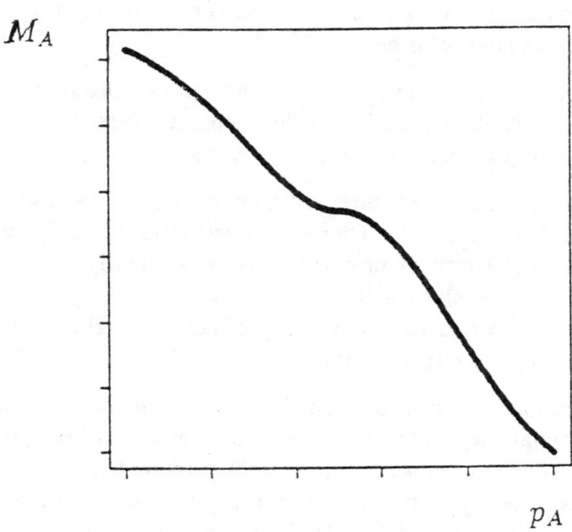

4 Published Empirical Results

We first present an overview of econometric studies. In the paper by Albach (1967) Gutenberg's demand curve attains goodness-of-fit values comparable to linear functions.

In the paper mentioned above, Simon (1979) analyzed 35 brands of categories like pharmaceuticals, detergents and household cleaners. For 83% of the brands Gutenberg's demand curve provides coefficients of determination greater than 60%. These results are not compared to those of other functional forms.

Brockhoff (1988) estimates multiplicative functions only as observed prices are always less than the reference price. Therefore only one half of Gutenberg's demand curve is relevant. Coefficients of determination are rather high, especially if hold-over terms are included.

In a study mentioned above based on scanner data, Hruschka (1997) obtains worse goodness-of-fit measures for Gutenberg's demand curve compared to a piecewise nonlinear function with two regimes of mobility of demand (high mobility for low prices, low mobility for high prices). As a rule, a logistic function fares better than Gutenberg's demand curve.

Kalyanaram/Little (1989 and 1994) significantly improve the fit of multinomial logit models by introducing a medium price range for different brands of coffee and sweet soft drinks. The effect of price differences from the reference price in the medium price range is not significant. Moreover, asymmetric effects of price increases and decreases are confirmed.

Econometric studies may face the problem of low price variation. According to Simon (1992) prices outside the medium price range are rare. More experimental studies are needed that guarantee greater price variations.

Totten/Block (1994) maintain that most products sold by food retailers are characterized by kinked demand curves. They cite Wiesniewski and Blattberg (1988), who, in an experimental study of price reductions, generally discovered kinked functions. Tooten/Block emphasize the example of bleachers with no effects of price reductions between 5 and 10%, but strong effects for higher and lower prices (see Simon, 1992 for a price experiment for oranges).

Another series of studies is based on surveys of decision makers. Their external validity is controversial, however. According to a study of Fog (1960) of 139 Danish firms, many decision makers believe that price changes pass a threshold before they are perceived by customers. According to a survey of Austrian firms by Nowotny/Walther (1978a and b), 71% of the respondents assume that an autonomous price range exists and that it is more probable for heterogeneous products.

5 Empirical Study

5.1 Data and Variables

The empirical study presented here is based on weekly scanner panel data of one retail outlet. It covers brands with higher market shares in three categories, namely orange juice, canned tuna, margarine, i.e. 4, 4 and 3 brands, respectively. Only the package size purchased most often is considered. For each category we have 104, 120 and 115 observations, respectively.

Besides the dependent variable sales volume we analyse the following independent variables for each brand:

- price differences in respect of each competing brand
- price
- previous period's sales volume
- previous period's price
- sales promotion relative to each competing brand
- seasonal dummy variables

5.2 Functional Forms

The following functional forms are used:

- semi-parametric additive model with cubic smoothing splines
- piecewise linear function with B-splines
- logistic function

$$Q_A = Q_{max} / \left(1 + \exp\left(-\left(a - bp_A - c\left(p_A - p_B\right)\right)\right)\right) \tag{19}$$

For low prices p_A or high prices of the competing brand p_B, sales volume approaches the maximum value Q_{max}. The shape of this function is similar to that of attraction models (see Hruschka, 1997).

- logistic function with zeta-transformed price differences
- exponential function

$$Q_A = \exp\left(-\left(a - bp_A - c\left(p_A - p_B\right)\right)\right) \tag{20}$$

- linear function
- Gutenberg's demand curve according to Albach (1979)
- the asymmetric version of Gutenberg's demand curve according to Brockhoff (1988)

5.3 Estimation und Model Selection

A search over interior parameters $d_1, d_2, \cdots$, followed by ordinary least squares estimation proved better for both parametric specifications of Gutenberg's demand curve than nonlinear least squares estimation by means of a Gauss-Newton algorithm. This corresponds to the experiences of Simon (1979). Exponential and logistic functions are estimated by nonlinear least squares, linear functions by ordinary least squares.

The knots needed for the B-splines of piecewise linear functions are optimized by a procedure of Friedman/Silverman (1989) which encompasses a recursive linear least squares estimation as subproblem.

Table 1: AIC Values for Response Functions

						Gutenberg's Demand Curve	
	semipara-metric	piecewise linear	logistic	exponen-tial	linear	Albach (1979)	Brockhoff (1988)
Orange Juice							
1	**-1.900**	-1.825	**-1.911**	-1.851	-1.810	-1.791	**-1.892**
2	**-2.170**	**-2.156**	-2.095	-1.173	-2.007	-2.005	-2.056
3	-1.686	**-1.733**	-1.694	**-1.797**	-1.705	-1.708	-1.694
4	**-1.986**	**-1.968**	**-1.972**	-1.797	**-1.970**	-1.948	-1.952
Canned Tuna							
1	**-2.161**	-2.102	**-2.161**	-2.026	-2.001	-1.984	-2.130
2	**-2.365**	-2.316	-2.351	-2.266	**-2.379**	**-2.362**	-2.345
3	-1.904	-1.895	**-1.914**	-1.835	**-1.925**	**-1.908**	-1.654
4	**-1.847**	-1.817	**-1.860**	-1.546	**-1.850**	-1.833	-1.822
Margarine							
1	**-2.291**	-2.213	**-2.283**	-2.169	-2.244	-2.226	-2.226
2	**-2.271**	-2.239	**-2.288**	-1.548	-2.241	-2.230	-2.230
3	**-2.127**	**-2.129**	-2.080	-1.934	-2.081	-2.063	-2.049

Estimation of the semi-parametric models is done by means of the backfitting algorithm, which determines effects for a predictor holding all other predictors' effects constant. The algorithm iterates as long as any of the effects changes significantly (Buja et al., 1989). The smoothing parameter λ is determined by cross validation.

Predictors are selected by means of a stepwise forward and backward model search on the basis of the semi-parametric model trying to minimize AIC (Akaike, 1974):

$$\mathrm{AIC} = \ln\left(s^2(e)\right) + 2p / n \tag{21}$$

AIC starts from the residual variance $s^2(e)$ and penalizes a high number of parameters p relative to the number of observation n.

Model search considers linear effects for sales promotion and saisonal dummies, cubic splines or linear effects for metric variables (i.e. price differences, price, previous period's sales and price).

Figure 4: Effect of the Difference $p_1 - p_2$ (Orange Juices)

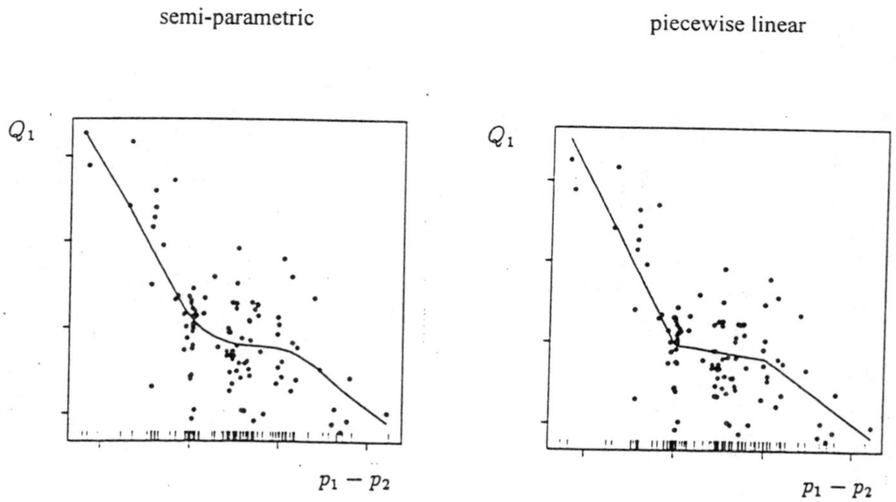

semi-parametric

piecewise linear

Q_1

$p_1 - p_2$

Q_1

$p_1 - p_2$

5.4 Results

Table 1 contains values of the AIC-criterion for the functional forms studied. For any brand the best values of variance accounted for lie between 53 and 95%. The unsatisfactory AIC values that the logistic function with zeta-transformed price difference achieved – maybe because of its restrictive shape – are not given.

Both the semi-parametric model and the logistic function attain the best AIC values in four cases. Therefore they excel all other functional forms. Nine times the semi-parametric model attains AIC values, whose difference from the best AIC value is less than or equal to 0.02. The same thing applies to the logistic function for seven brands, to the piecewise linear function for three brands, to the linear function for four brands and to both parametric specifications of Gutenberg's demand curve for three brands. The exponential function attains the best AIC value in one case.

Figure 5: Effect of Price Differences (semi-parametric)

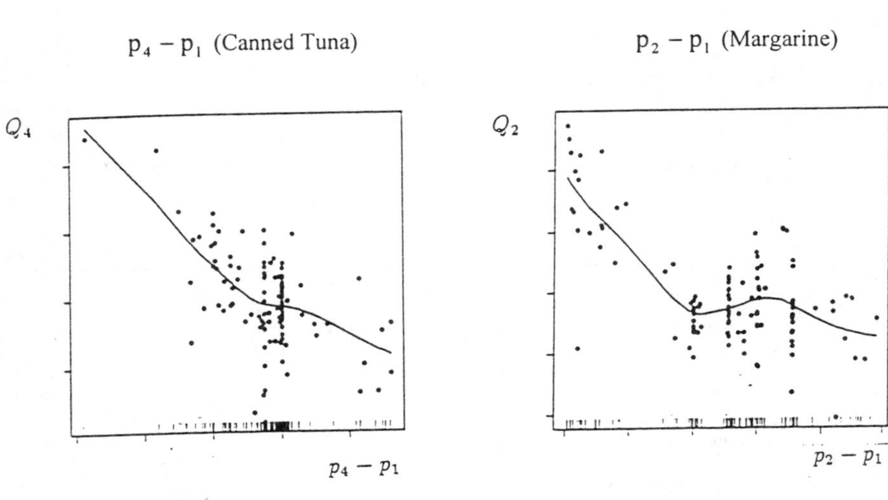

For seven out of nine brands for which the semi-parametric model achieves good AIC-values, it identifies effects of price differences which are in accordance with Gutenberg's demand curve. In other words, in the medium range, price effects on sales volume are rather weak, whereas high or low prices are accompanied by strong effects. As a rule these relationships are asymmetric with stronger effects for lower prices.

Figures 4 and 5 showing nonlinear or piecewise linear effects and partial residuals of selected price differences illustrate these results.

References

Akaike, H. (1974): A New Look at the Statistical Model. Identification. In: IEEE Transactions on Automatic Control, 716–723.

Albach, H. (1973): Das Gutenberg-Oligopol. In: Koch, H. (ed.): Zur Theorie des Absatzes. Festschrift zum 75. Geburtstag von Erich Gutenberg. Wiesbaden, 9–34.

Albach, H. (1979): Market Organization and Pricing Behavior of Oligopolistic Firms in the Ethical Drugs Industry. In: Kyklos, 523–540.

Brockhoff, K. (1988): Die Bewährung von Gutenbergs Preis-Absatz-Funktion im Zigarettenmarkt. In: Zeitschrift für Betriebswirtschaft, 828–838.

Buja, A., Hastie, T., Tibshirani, R. (1989): Linear Smoothers and Additive Models (with discussion). In: The Annals of Statistics, 453–555.

Cooper, L.G., Nakanishi, M. (1983): Standardizing Variables in Multiplicative Choice Models. In: Journal of Consumer Research, 96–108.

De Boor, C. (1978): A Practical Guide to Splines. New York.

Fog, B. (1960): Industrial Pricing Policies: An Analysis of Pricing Behaviour of Danish Manufacturers. Amsterdam.

Friedman, J.H., Silverman, B.W. (1989): Flexible Parsimonious Smoothing and Additive Modelling (with discussion). In: Technometrics, 3–39.

Gabszewicz, J.J., Thisse, J.-F. (1986): On the Nature of Competition with Differentiated Products. In: Economic Journal, 160–172.

Gutenberg, E. (1955): Grundlagen der Betriebswirtschaftslehre, Der Absatz. 1st Edition, Berlin.

Gutenberg, E. (1984): Grundlagen der Betriebswirtschaftslehre, Der Absatz. 17th Edition, Berlin.

Hruschka, H. (1997): Schätzung und normative Analyse ausgewählter Preis-Absatz-Funktionen. In: Zeitschrift für Betriebswirtschaft, 845–864.

Kalyanaram, G., Little, J.D.C. (1989): A Price Response Model Developed from Perceptual Theories. Sloan School Working Paper, MIT, Cambridge, MA.

Kalyanaram, G., Little, J.D.C. (1994): An Empirical Analysis of Latitude of Price Acceptance in Consumer Package Goods. In: Journal of Consumer Research, 408–418.

Kilger, H. (1962): Die quantitative Ableitung polypolistischer Preisabsatzfunktionen aus den Heterogenitätsbedingungen atomistischer Märkte. In: Koch, H. (ed.): Zur Theorie der Unternehmung. Festschrift zum 65. Geburstag von Erich Gutenberg. Wiesbaden, 271–309.

Klemperer, P. (1995): Competition when Consumers have Switching Costs: An Overview with Applications to Industrial Organization, Macroeconomics, and International Trade. In: Review of Economic Studies, 515–539.

Nowotny, E., Walther, H. (1978a): Die Wettbewerbsintensität in Österreich: Ergebnisse der Befragungen und Interviews. Wien.

Nowotny, E., Walther, H. (1978b): The Kinked Demand Curve - Some Empirical Observations. In: Kyklos, 53–67.

Piekenbrock, D. (1980): Zur Entwicklung der Theorie autonomer Preisintervalle. In: Jahrbücher für Nationalökonomie und Statistik, 19–51.

Sabel, H. (1976): Zur Diskussion des Gutenberg-Oligopols. In: Zeitschrift für Betriebswirtschaft, 205–224.

Simon, H. (1979): Dynamics of Price Elasticity and Brand Life Cycles. An Empirical Study. In: Journal of Marketing Research, 439–452.

Simon, H. (1992): Preismanagement. 2nd Edition, Wiesbaden.

Totten, J.C., Block, M.P. (1994): Analysing Sales Promotion. 2nd Edition, Chicago, IL.

Willeke, F.-U. (1967): Autonome Preisintervalle im heterogenen Dyopol. In: Jahrbücher für Nationalökonomie und Statistik, 373–396.

Wisniewski, K.J., Blattberg, R.C. (1988): Analysis of Consumer Response to Retail Price Dealing Strategies. Report, University of Chicago, Chicago, IL.

Summary

After first introducing the concept of Gutenberg's kinked demand curve its nature is clarified by reference to buyers' switching costs or preference distributions. Various model specifications, related approaches from the US literature and empirical results are also elaborated. In addition to well-known specifications of Gutenberg's demand curve, piecewise linear and semi-parametric models are used in an empirical study. These specifications, as well as rival functional forms (linear, logistic, exponential), are evaluated by means of the AIC-criterion. The more flexible semi-parametric models fare best. For 7 of a total of 11 brands these models indicate a range of medium prices where price response is low. High and low prices cause strong sales volume effects. These results are in accordance with Gutenberg's demand curve. As a rule, price effects are asymmetric, i.e. low prices lead to stronger responses compared to high prices.

The Choice between Employed Salespersons and Independent Manufacturer Representatives

S. Albers[1]

Overview

- In his book "Der Absatz (Marketing)" published in 1955 Gutenberg introduced the well-known formula for the critical sales volume beyond which it is profitable to work with employed salespersons rather than with independent manufacturer representatives. Gutenberg was later criticized for neglecting important factors in his formula. We show that this criticism is erroneous. Already in his first edition, Gutenberg discussed many additional considerations that have subsequently been elaborated in the context of transaction cost analysis.
- We implement Gutenberg's reasoning, namely, that sales also depend on the number of salespersons, in a formalized decision model.
- Gutenberg omitted the risk considerations which now play an important role in principal-agent theory. The incorporation of risk facilitates decision models that help determine the optimal compensation contract. An appropriate type of salesforce organization can be inferred from the structure of this contract.
- Principal-agent models can suggest optimal contracts with a negative fixed salary. This is interpreted here as a sales-franchise contract, i.e. a hybrid salesforce organization that combines the advantages of a better control of employed salespersons with the advantages of a better motivation of independent manufacturer representatives.[2]

Keywords: Salesforce management, Salesforce organization, Principal-agent theory, Independent manufacturer representatives, franchising

---

[1] Prof. Dr. Sönke Albers, Professor of Marketing and Management Science, Christian-Albrechts-University at Kiel, D-24098 Kiel, Germany, email: albers@bwl.uni-kiel.de

[2] I would like to thank Manfred Krafft, Bernd Skiera, and especially Karen Gedenk for many valuable suggestions.

A. Introduction

In 1955 Gutenberg published his very influential book "Der Absatz" which discusses the many decision problems related to the marketing and selling of a product. It is also the first book in Germany to apply microeconomic analyses to this problem-area. An important part of the book is devoted to the choice of an adequate type of salesforce organization. The question is whether it is better to work with employed salespersons or with independent manufacturer representatives (ind. reps). Gutenberg suggested the, now well-known, formula for the critical sales volume beyond which it is more profitable to work with employed salespersons rather than with ind. reps. This formula is based on a qualitative discussion of the topic in the book by Hennig (1928). Later researchers have asserted that this formula offers a readily applicable, well-grounded decision support. Other authors (Dichtl/Raffée/Niedetzki, 1981) have criticized the formula because it only considers costs of compensation while, in practice, selling may incur many other costs. They conclude that additional factors have to be incorporated into the formula even if they are hard to quantify. We first investigate here the types of costs and influences Gutenberg took into account and also those elements of the now well-developed transaction cost analysis and principal-agent theory which he anticipated well before the emergence of these theories. Next, we investigate those elements of the new institutional economics that were not taken into account by Gutenberg and how their recognition would alter his conclusions. In particular, this includes selling-risk. The allocation of this risk between a firm and its salespersons is a central component in the derivation of optimal contracts, or compensations plans, in principal-agent theory. The result is that optimal compensation plans may consist of a negative fixed salary. This solution may be interpreted as an alternative type of salesforce organization, other than employed salespersons or ind. reps, that was not discussed by Gutenberg at the time.

B. Derivation of the critical sales volume and its importance

Gutenberg investigated the case of a firm that can choose between selling its products through employed salespersons or ind. reps (1955, pp. 114 ff.). He assumed that employed salespersons receive a higher fixed salary but a lower commission rate on sales volume as compared to ind. reps. Relevant variables are denoted as follows:

F_S, F_R: fixed salary of an employed salesperson (S) and an independent manufacturer representative (R),

c_S, c_R: commission rate based on sales volume of an employed salesperson (S) and an independent manufacturer representative (R),

S_k: critical sales volume.

The critical sales volume S_k is determined by equating the two expressions for the compensation costs for employed salespersons (S) and ind. reps (R):

(1) $$F_S + c_S \cdot S_k = F_R + c_R \cdot S_k$$

(2) $$S_k = \frac{F_R - F_S}{c_S - c_R}$$

If the planned sales volume is higher (lower) than the critical sales volume S_k, this approach implies that it is more profitable to work with employed salespersons (ind. reps). This is illustrated by Figure 1.

Figure 1: Choice of type of salesforce organization depending on the critical sales volume

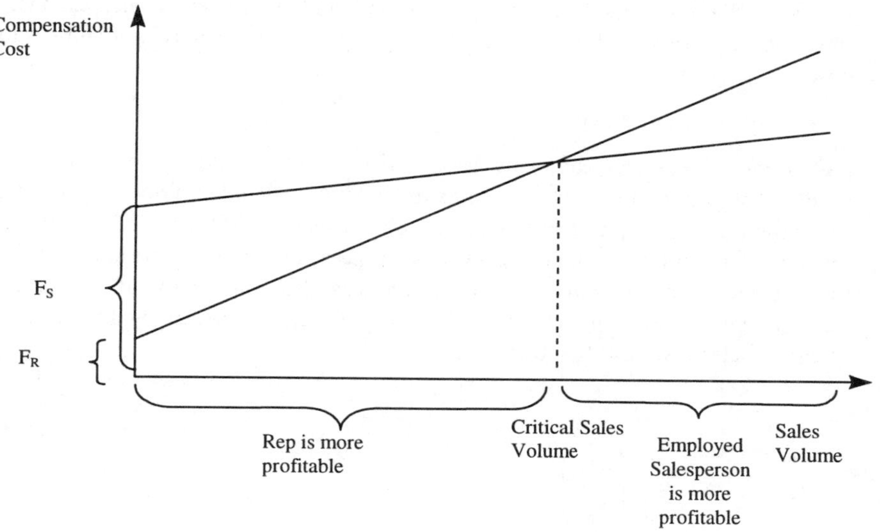

Gutenberg suggested his formula (2) as a means of supporting the salesforce organization decision. Already in the first edition of his book, Gutenberg (1955, p. 115 et seq.) considered more complex situations with nonlinear compensation cost curves, differing commission rates for different products and even prices expressed as a function of sales volume. However, in his equation he intentionally dealt only with compensation cost and did not provide a comprehensive cost comparison as proposed by Dichtl/Raffée/Niedetzki (1981). In this way, Gutenberg wanted to make it clear that his solution mainly depends on the acceptance of the type of salesforce organization by the chosen type of salesperson. However, things may be different in the U.S.A. due to legal differences between Germany and U.S.A. which are described in Albers/Krafft/Bielert (1998).

In practice, the sales volume achieved by a salesperson does not represent an exogenous event but depends on the number of employed salespersons. Therefore, before describing the derivation of his formula, Gutenberg (1955, p. 111 et seq.) argues, that a firm should choose ind. reps for its salesforce as long as the intended compensation is not sufficient to provide an employed salesperson with a satisfactory income. He emphasizes that it is not possible to guarantee a minimum income by employing only a few salespersons with large sales territories because individual sales volumes would not increase proportionally with territorial size due to greater travelling times. However, a firm may engage ind. reps because they have the opportunity to work for more than one company (if not restricted by contract) and, thus, can operate in any sales territory irrespective of its size. The choices of the type of salesforce organization, and the number of salespersons, are thus interdependent and can only be realized by focussing solely on compensation cost.

Gutenberg's ideas can obviously be quantified and incorporated into a decision model. The problem may be solved as in COSTA, a detailed model of sales territory alignment, with alternative numbers of salespersons (Skiera/Albers, 1998). In this paper we follow another path. It is also based on the assumption of a number m of sales coverage units (SCU) but reduces the complexity of the problem through the assumption that all SCU's may be characterized by the following identical sales response function:

$$(3) \qquad S = S_o \cdot \left(\frac{t}{t_o} \right)^{\beta}$$

In this response function the achieved sales volume (S) in a SCU depends on the calling-time (t) of a salesperson in relation to the calling-time norm (t_0) per SCU. β represents the elasticity of sales with respect to changes in the calling-time. If the calling-time is equal to the norm t_0 ($t = t_0$), the salesperson achieves exactly the norm value for the sales volume (S_0). A similar response function has proved to be advantageous in the model CAPPLAN which provides the optimal allocation of calling-time and the optimal price schedule for different account groups (Albers, 1996a). In the case of employed salespersons, the average calling-time in a SCU can be determined by the product of the number of salespersons (n), the average calling-time (T) of a salesperson and the achievable rate of calling-time (h) with respect to the total working time divided by the number of SCU's:

$$(4) \qquad t = \frac{n \cdot T \cdot h}{m}$$

The calling-time rate (h) in turn depends on the number of salespersons (n). It takes on its lowest value when only one salesperson serves all SCU's because then the travel times are at their highest values. These travel times decrease when more salespersons are employed relative to the number of SCU's (n/m). This can be modeled through the following logistic function:

$$(5) \qquad h = \frac{1}{1 + e^{-(a + bn/m)}}$$

Replacing h in equation (4) with its value according to equation (5), inserting the resulting calling-time in (4) into equation (3), and assuming equal conditions in each SCU, results in the following optimization problem for the profit maximizing firm:

$$(6) \qquad PC = m \cdot (g - c) \cdot S_o \cdot \left(\frac{t}{t_o}\right) - n \cdot F \Rightarrow Max!$$

$$PC = m \cdot (g - c) \cdot S_o \cdot \left[\frac{\dfrac{\frac{n}{m} \cdot T}{1 + e^{-(a + bn/m)}}}{t_o}\right]^{\beta} - n \cdot F \Rightarrow Max!$$

$$(7) \qquad F + c \cdot \frac{m}{n} \cdot S_0 \cdot \left[\frac{\dfrac{\dfrac{n}{m} \cdot T}{1 + e^{-(a + bn/m)}}}{t_0} \right]^{\beta} \geq I$$

Equation (6) represents the objective function as given by the profit contribution of sales (with g as gross margin) from which the compensation cost consisting of a fixed salary (F) and the commissions c on sales (S) are subtracted. The constraint (7) ensures that each salesperson achieves a sufficient income (I). This can be enforced through the choice of a sufficiently low n or through the adjustment of the fixed salary F. However, such a restriction is only necessary for the optimal number of employed salespersons because ind. reps are able to adjust themselves to any size of territory by choosing contracts with several other firms. Therefore, the firm only has to offer a certain commission rate c_R. To choose between employed salespersons and ind. reps it is first necessary to determine the optimal number of employed salespersons and the resulting sales per salesperson S_S. It is then necessary to ascertain whether this sales volume of an employed salesperson can be generated through ind. reps with lower compensation cost $c_R \cdot S_S$.

The optimization problem (6) - (7) cannot be solved analytically. However, using the now available nonlinear optimization software, as implemented in the Add-In-Program Solver in the spreadsheet program EXCEL, the problem can easily be solved numerically. Such a possibility did not exist at the time of Gutenberg. This is generally assumed to be the reason why Gutenberg did not propose more complex model formulations. His exposition is thus intended to provide the basic logic of the problem rather than to deliver concrete solutions.

The relevance of Gutenberg's focus on aspects of compensation cost is underlined by the development of the market share of ind. reps over time. According to Batzer/Lachner/Meyerhöfer (1991) their share has decreased constantly over the last 40 years. These authors argue that the size of firms has increased to the point that, for many of them, it ultimately became profitable to switch from ind. reps to employed salespersons (see Figure 1). This is confirmed by Krafft (1996, p. 769 et seq.) who uses logistic regression to explain the choice of the type of salesforce organization depending on the salesforce's size. In summary, it can be concluded, that, in practice, it is mainly the logic developed by Gutenberg that is depicted in Figure 1, which explains the changes in the market shares of salesforce organizations.

C. Additional factors considered by Gutenberg

Simplified versions of the formula for the critical sales volume with respect to the choice of the salesforce organization type appeared later. These versions have created the impression that Gutenberg incorporated only quantifiable costs and, therefore, provided a procedure that is too mechanistic (Dichtl/Raffée/Niedetzki, 1981). However, in his first edition, Gutenberg (1955) already points to further considerations. In particular, he discusses the opportunity of accessing an existing set of customers by working with multi-agent ind. reps. In addition, he mentions that ind. reps very often have a better knowledge of their customers, the market situation and competitors than do employed salespeople (p. 111). Finally, he draws attention to costs of control that are typically higher with ind. reps. Ind. reps are harder to control because, according to German law, a company cannot require them to engage in certain activities (p. 112). These have become classical arguments of the transaction cost theory that found empirical support in tests conducted by Anderson (1985) and Krafft (1996). Gutenberg himself subsequently realized that his discussion about the critical sales volume had been too narrow. In a revised version of the 6th edition of his book he writes in response, "When comparing the two different types of salesforce organization it is advisable to apply calculations as long as the required data are available. However, the result of this first phase of calculations does not provide a sufficient basis for the decision as to the type of salesforce organization that should be chosen. This is because there are a number of other factors that are not quantifiable but which may be of importance to the ultimate decision." (Gutenberg, 6th ed., 1963, p. 146, translated by the author). Indeed a very modern point of view at that time!

D. Factors of the New Institutional Economics not considered by Gutenberg

As discussed above, Gutenberg anticipated in his monograph many arguments that are now subsumed under transaction cost theory. However, he did not discuss the major factors implicit in principal-agent theory. This theory provides a framework for deriving the optimal contract between a principal (the firm) and an agent (the salesperson). It assumes that the salesperson has to be motivated by means of financial incentives to devote effort, operationalized here as calling and travel time, in the best interest of the firm. In addition, the contract has to be attractive enough for the agent to accept it. This is modeled as a constraint requiring that the utility from compensation minus the disutility from effort is greater than a certain minimum utility that can be achieved with other contracts offered on the labor market (Albers, 1995). This constraint was already recognized by Gutenberg when he indicated that sales territories must be designed with respect to size and income opportunities such that skilled ind. reps can be attracted (Gutenberg, 1955, p. 111).

By applying principal-agent theory to the problem of compensating salespersons, optimal compensation plans, which were considered exogenous by Gutenberg, can be derived endogenously. This theory helps determine the optimal commission rate and whether it should increase under- or overproportionally with sales (Albers, 1986). Much more important for the problem considered here, however, are approaches for determining the optimal level of the fixed salary, relative to the total income of the salesperson, and thus, implicitly, the variable proportion of the income. This is important because the optimal percentage of the fixed proportion of the income provides information as to whether it is more advantageous to work with employed salespersons or with ind. reps. Contracts with a rather high fixed income percentage can be implemented only by employing salespersons, while low fixed income percentages imply working with ind. reps. In addition, the issue of risk sharing between principal and agent, which represents one of the most important components of principal-agent theory, has to be resolved. Although Gutenberg discusses different types of risks, e.g. the ind. rep bearing the whole risk of operations (Gutenberg, 1955, p. 105), he did not analyze the effect of these risks on the choice of the type of salesforce organization.

The optimal fixed salary can be determined with a model proposed by Basu/Lal/Srinivasan/Staelin (1985). In a simplified model, Albers (1995) restricts the compensation plans to linear functions. He operationalizes the utility function of the salesperson as the utility of the expected commission income, minus the disutility of effort $\mu \cdot t^{\eta}$ (with η as elasticity of disutility with respect to changes in working time), minus the standard deviation of the commission income weighted with a risk aversion factor (k). The latter represents the uncertainty equivalent. Linear compensation plans are efficient with regard to intertemporal considerations because they cannot be misused by shifting sales from one period into another (Holmström/Milgrom, 1987). The model formulated by Albers incorporates explicitly stated sales response functions of the form $S = \alpha t^{\beta}$. In this case the expected sales is S while the standard deviation in case of gamma distributed sales is $q \cdot S$ where q is a parameter of the gamma distribution. Thus, the standard deviation is proportional to the sales volume and the salesperson maximizes the following risk utility function:

$$(8) \qquad F + c \cdot \alpha \cdot t^{\beta} - k \cdot q \cdot c \cdot \alpha \cdot t^{\beta} - \mu \cdot t^{\eta} \Rightarrow \text{Max!}$$

In this objective function, utility is given by the expected income minus the uncertainty equivalent and the overproportionally increasing disutility of effort. Taking the derivative of (8) with respect to t provides the utility-maximizing working time:

$$(9) \qquad t^{*}=\left(\frac{c\cdot(1-k\cdot q)\cdot\alpha\cdot\beta}{\mu\cdot\eta}\right)^{\frac{1}{\eta\cdot\beta}}$$

If the firm knows this utility-maximizing working time t* of the salesperson it can maximize its profit contribution as in (10):

$$(10) \qquad PC=(g-c)\cdot\alpha\cdot(t^{*})^{\beta}-F \quad \Rightarrow Max!$$

There is a restriction that the compensation must be chosen such that the resulting utility for the salesperson is equal to, or greater than, the minimum utility (M), i.e. the utility which the salesperson can achieve with an alternative contract on the labor market:

$$(11) \qquad F+c\cdot(1-k\cdot q)\cdot\alpha(t^{*})^{\beta}-\mu\cdot t^{\eta} \geq M$$

Since the fixed salary (F) only represents a residual value as long as the commission rate c and the optimal working time t* have been determined, constraint (11) is always fulfilled as an equation. Thus, the firm can solve this optimization problem by setting up the respective LaGrangean function and taking the derivatives with respect to F, c and the LaGrangean multiplier. If the derivatives are set equal to 0, and solved with respect to F and c, we get the following optimal values (Albers, 1995):

$$(12) \qquad c^* = \frac{g \cdot \beta}{k \cdot q \cdot \eta + (1 - k \cdot q) \cdot \beta}$$

$$(13) \qquad F^* = M - c^* (1 - k \cdot q) \cdot \alpha \cdot (t^*)^\beta + \mu \cdot (t^*)^\eta$$

The structure of this optimal solution shows that the optimal fixed salary increases with increasing uncertainty, and risk aversion of the salesperson, while the commission rate increases with decreasing uncertainty. This happens because the risk premium in the form of a fixed salary incurs less costs than in the form of a higher commission rate when facing high uncertainty and a rather small effort by the salesperson. A high fixed salary also indicates that it is advantageous to work with employed salespersons. Thus, we can conclude that it is advisable to work with employed salespersons in markets with high uncertainty. However, if the salespersons can diversify the risk across many different customers and across several firms by working as multi-agents, it is then more profitable for the firm to offer a rather low fixed salary, i.e. to work with ind. reps (Albers/Krafft, 1996). This is empirically supported by Krafft (1996) who finds a significant positive relationship between the diversification of risk (as measured by the inverse number of customers per salesperson) and the likelihood of choosing employed salespeople rather than ind. reps. In summary, we conclude that the results of Gutenberg's approach in respect of the critical sales volume can change radically when risk is taken into account.

E. Alternative salesforce organizations

A closer look at the optimal solution for the commission rate c* (12) and the fixed salary F* (13) in the model formulated by Albers (1995) reveals another particularity. In the special case of no selling risk, the optimal commission rate is equal to the profit contribution rate (c* = g). This implies that the fixed salary F* must be negative, otherwise the firm would not make a profit. The same result also holds for the more general model with nonlinear compensation rate functions (Albers, 1996b). The proportion of fixed income plotted as a function of the degree of uncertainty is depicted in Figure 2.

Figure 2: Optimal fixed salary proportion as a function of uncertainty

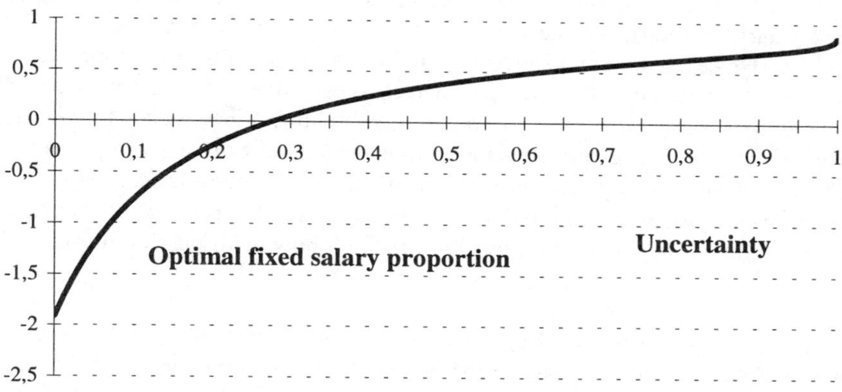

Figure 2 shows that a low degree of risk requires the distinctive type of salesforce organization whereby the firm offers a contract with a negative fixed salary. In the case of employed salespersons, the firm carries the selling risk as well as the compensation cost risk. In case of ind. reps, the firm has transferred the compensation cost risk to the ind. reps but still bears the selling risk. In the case of a negative fixed salary, the firm has even transferred the selling risk to an independent salesforce organization. It is therefore necessary to distinguish the three different types of salesforce organization that are illustrated by the respective compensation cost curves in Figure 3.

Figure 3: Compensation cost curves of different types of salesforce organization

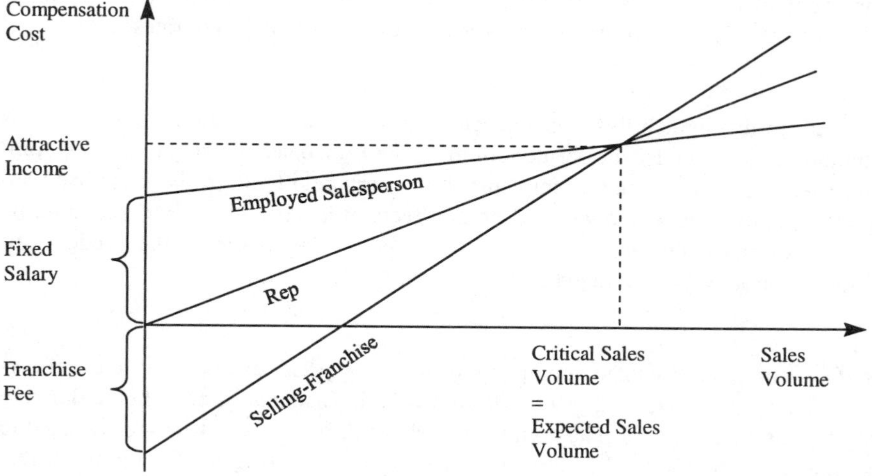

The compensation plan with a negative fixed salary and a commission rate as high as the profit contribution rate (c = d) may be interpreted as the firm's owner leasing his firm to a salesperson, who has to pay a leasing fee equal to the negative fixed salary in return for the entire profit contribution from the selling of the products. However, Figure 3 shows that under certain circumstances compensation plans can be optimal if the firm's owner charges a fixed leasing fee along with some kind of commission rate (1-c) on the sales volume. Since such solutions seem very unusual, the interesting question is whether they already exist in practice. In fact, such contracts can be observed in the form of selling-franchises (Albers, 1996b). Selling-franchises should not be confused with the better known contracts of service franchise firms (Skaupy, 1997), as the following discussion illustrates.

If a company sells successful products, any sales territory which is offered to a salesperson represents an asset to the company. This asset consists of the set of customers to which the products of the firm can be sold. Taking this point of view, it is quite logical for the firm to charge a fee to the salespersons for the use of this asset. This does not imply that the entire risk has been transferred to the salespersons. Rather, it means that the franchisee is forced to invest effort and money beforehand and is only repaid if he devotes enough effort to reach the critical sales volume beyond which he earns money. This creates a completely different motivational situation compared to that of an ind. rep who does not risk losses but only the opportunity costs of profits forgone if he does not devote enough effort to his task. It is exactly for this reason that, from a company's standpoint, ind. reps have been judged to be an unattractive salesforce organization. A company has no instrument with which to motivate its ind. reps sufficiently to penetrate the assigned sales territory and thereby achieve specific sales volume quotas. This is a particular problem if ind. reps work as multi-agents for several different firms whose product lines differ with respect to attractiveness and commission rates.

In order to distinguish this franchise contract from more traditional contracts it is emphasized that, under the former contract, the franchisee has to pay a fixed franchise fee annually and not a lump sum at the very beginning of the franchise contract. The latter fee would have different effects. It is normally considered as some kind of entrance fee that is intended to cover the legal title of the predecessor whose contract was terminated by the company.

In Germany, the Eismann company provides a good example of the selling-franchise contract (Hanser, 1993) discussed here. Eismann offers a home delivery service for frozen goods. The company works with franchisees who are assigned to certain sales territories. The franchisee has to pay a leasing fee for the truck that the company provides for delivering the goods. He also has to pay a monthly rent for the sales territory. In exchange he is offered a rather high commission rate on the sales volume. However, the compensation plan is constructed in a way which ensures that the salesperson can only achieve a satisfactory income if he really penetrates his sales territory to the firm's satisfaction.

Besides creating an even stronger entrepreneurial motivation than in the case of ind. reps, this kind of selling-franchise also offers the advantage that the company can make the franchisee sell the products exactly as desired by the company (Kloyer, 1995). For instance, the firm can require the salesperson to sell its products according to a specified marketing mix. Such a franchise contract can, therefore, make marketing and selling fit together. In addition, the firm gains more control over its salespersons. On the basis of the contract, the firm can control whether the franchisee really does his selling according to the negotiated rules, and whether his selling approach is profitable enough. In some contracts, the firm may also have the right to direct the franchisee according to predetermined instructions. Finally, the firm can require sales training activities to ensure that the franchisee always has adequate product, market, and company know-how, which otherwise is superior in the case of employed salespersons compared with ind. reps (Meffert/-Kimmeskamp/Becker, 1982).

In conclusion, it can be said that a selling franchise represents a hybrid salesforce organization which combines the advantage of employed salespersons, i.e. better control, with the advantage of ind. reps, i.e. stronger entrepreneurial motivation. Under such a franchise contract the franchisee can be expected to have an even higher motivation for high performance than may be expected from an ind. rep. The franchisee has to invest and must therefore devote sufficient effort to selling in order to obtain a commensmate return on his investment.

F. Conclusion

A prevailing impression given by the literature is that Gutenberg's method of calculating the critical sales volume as a basis for choosing between employed salespersons and ind. reps is not relevant for practical decisions because he neglected a variety of costs and focused excessively on quantifiable factors. However, we have shown here that Gutenberg had already considered many other influences, in the first edition of his book.

Gutenberg pointed out that the sales volume is not an exogenous variable and that it depends on the number of salespersons. The latter, in turn, determines the income opportunities of the salespersons. This paper therefore presents a new approach for determining the optimal number of salespersons for a given commission rate subject to the constraint that each salesperson achieves an income that is competitive relative to the market situation. Given this optimal salesforce size and the resulting sales volume per salesperson, it can then be determined which type of salesforce organization leads to lower compensation costs.

Gutenberg discussed other factors influencing the choice of the salesforce organization. Some of these anticipated aspects of transaction cost analysis were developed later. Focussing on compensation costs Gutenberg was successful in drawing attention to the paramount motivational considerations in the design of contracts. Recognising the current popularity of transaction cost analysis, which was unknown in 1955, the avant garde character of Gutenberg's approach becomes readily apparent. Gutenberg's focus on compensation cost is empirically supported by the large number of companies which, following expansion, switched from ind. reps to employed salespersons. Thus, his contention that the critical sales volume explains the choice of type of salesforce organization has been empirically corroborated.

However, one important factor was not analyzed by Gutenberg, namely, risk. Although he mentions this factor in his book, he dispenses with an analysis because he regards the compensation system as an exogenous variable. Principal-agent theory was developed later to endogenously determine the optimal compensation contract. In determining the optimal proportion of the fixed salary relative to total income, risk considerations cannot be ignored. Having derived the optimal solution, the fixed salary proportion indicates which kind of salesforce organization is suitable, namely employed salespersons and ind. reps in the cases of high and low fixed salary proportions respectively.

The analysis in this paper has also shown that there are situations of low uncertainty in which it is profitable to offer a negative fixed salary. This unusual solution can be implemented as a selling-franchise. We show that this represents a hybrid salesforce organization which combines the advantages of an efficient control of employed salespersons with the higher entrepreneurial motivation and lower compensation cost risk in the case of ind. reps.

References

Albers, S. (1986): Controlling Independent Manufacturer Representatives by Using Commission Rate Functions Depending on Achieved Sales Volume, in: K. Backhaus, D.T. Wilson (ed.): Industrial Marketing, A German-American Perspective, Springer-Verlag, Berlin - Heidelberg - New York - Tokyo 1986, 88-112.

Albers, S. (1995): Optimales Verhältnis zwischen Festgehalt und erfolgsabhängiger Entlohnung bei Verkaufsaußendienstmitarbeitern, in: Zeitschrift für betriebswirtschaftliche Forschung, 47. Jg., 124-142.

Albers, S. (1996a): CAPPLAN: A Decision Support System for Planning the Pricing and Sales Effort Policy of a Salesforce, European Journal of Marketing, Vol. 30 (1996), No. 7, 68-82.

Albers, S. (1996b): Optimization Models for Salesforce Compensation, in: European Journal of Operational Research, Vol. 89, 1-17.

Albers, S./Krafft, M. (1996): Zur relativen Aussagekraft und Eignung von Ansätzen der neuen Institutionenlehre bei der Absatzformwahl sowie der Entlohnung von Verkaufsaußendienstmitarbeitern, in: Zeitschrift für Betriebswirtschaft, 66. Jg., 1383-1407.

Albers, S./Krafft, M./Bielert, W.: Global Salesforce Management: A Comparison of German and U.S. Practices, in: G.J. Bauer, M.S. Baunchalk, Th.N. Ingram, R.W. LaForge (eds.): Emerging Trends in Sales Thought and Practice, Quorum Books: 1998.

Anderson, E. (1985): The Salesperson as Outside Agent or Employee: A Transaction Cost Analysis, in: Marketing Science, Vol. 4, 234-254.

Basu, A. K./Lal, R./Srinivasan, V./Staelin, R. (1985): Salesforce Compensation Plans, An Agency Theoretic Perspective, in: Marketing Science, Vol. 4, 267-291.

Batzer, E./Lachner, J./Meyerhöfer, W. (1991): Die Handelsvermittlung in der Bundesrepublik Deutschland: Strukturelle Entwicklungstrends, Köln: Forschungsverband für den Handelsvertreter- und Handelsmaklerberuf.

Dichtl, E./Raffée, H./Niedetzki, H.-M. (1981): Reisende oder Handelsvertreter: Eine Anleitung zur Lösung eines Entscheidungsproblems mit praktischen Vorschlägen, München: Beck Verlag.

Gutenberg, E. (1955): Grundlagen der Betriebswirtschaftslehre, Band 2: Der Absatz, 1. Auflage, Berlin/Göttingen/Heidelberg: Springer-Verlag.

Gutenberg, E. (1963): Grundlagen der Betriebswirtschaftslehre, Band 2: Der Absatz, 6. Auflage, Berlin/Göttingen/Heidelberg: Springer-Verlag.

Hanser, P. (1993): Turbolader für die Eismann-Reform des Eismann-Franchise-Systems, in: Absatzwirtschaft, Heft 4, 86-88.

Hennig, K. W. (1928): Betriebswirtschaftslehre der Industrie, Berlin: Verlag von Julius Springer.

Holmström, B./Milgrom, P. (1987): Aggregation and Linearity in the Provision of Intertemporal Incentives, in: Econometrica, Vol. 55, 303-328.

Kloyer, M. (1995): Management von Franchisenetzwerken - Eine Resource-Dependence-Perspektive, Wiesbaden: Deutscher Universitäts Verlag.

Krafft, M. (1996): Neue Einsichten in ein klassisches Wahlproblem? - Eine Überprüfung von Hypothesen der Neuen Institutionenlehre zur Frage "Handelsvertreter oder Reisende", in: Die Betriebswirtschaft, 56. Jg., 759 - 776.

Meffert, H./Kimmeskamp, G./Becker, R. (1983): Die Handelsvertretung im Meinungsbild ihrer Marktpartner: Ansatzpunkte für das Handelsvertreter-Marketing, Stuttgart et al.: Kohlhammer Verlag.

Skaupy, W. (1987): Franchising - Handbuch für die Betriebs- und Rechtspraxis, München: Verlag Franz Vahlen.

Skiera, B./Albers, S. (1998): COSTA: Contribution Optimizing Sales Territory Alignment, in: Marketing Science, Vol. 17, 196-213

Summary

Gutenberg's formula for determining the critical revenue, above which employee salespeople constitute a superior alternative to independent sales representatives, has become well-known. It is shown that, not withstanding later criticism, he anticipated many other relevant criteria, including some from transaction cost analysis, for the choice of the salesforce organization. We extend his view that revenue depends on the number of salespersons by developing an appropriate optimization model. However, Gutenberg did not deal with risk as in principal-agent theory which facilitates the formulation of optimal incentive contracts, the structure of which implies the institutional form of salesforce organization. The solution also shows that in situations of low uncertainty, a negative optimal fixed salary may be implemented via a sales-franchise which combines the advantages of better controllable employed salespersons with the stronger motivation of independent sales representatives.

Dynamics of Technological Competencies

K. Brockhoff[1]

Overview

- It is frequently suggested that companies should adopt specific paradigms to secure their success. This is also suggested with respect to the use of new technological knowledge.
- In reality it can be observed that even successful companies have adopted quite different paradigms. While some cooperate in respect of R&D cooperations, others cover a broad range of technologies.
- In this paper we suggest that specific aspects of technological knowledge should be organised within a spectrum of knowledge. Four specific positions in the spectrum are considered in particular.
- The benefits and costs of choosing particular positions within the spectrum of knowledge are discussed. It is shown that each position is contestable.
- As a general result it is concluded that R&D activities should not be limited to the same core competencies as those favored with respect to production activities.

Keywords. Technological Competencies, Knowledge Management, Firm Dynamics, Cooperation

1 Introduction

Integrating technological progress into the theory of the firm is a difficult problem. While Erich Gutenberg saw clearly the necessity of this integration, as well as the dynamics of technological progress influencing the production functions of firms, he could not include these phenomena as endogenous factors into his theory[2]. Even today, no fully developed theory of technological progress

---

1 Prof. Dr. Klaus Brockhoff, WHU Koblenz, Otto-Beisheim-Hochschule, Burgplatz 2, 56179 Vallendar, email: brockh@whu-koblenz.de

2 Gutenberg, E., Einführung in die Betriebswirtschaftslehre, Wiesbaden 1958, p. 9; Gutenberg, E., Grundlagen der Betriebswirtschaftslehre, vol. 1: Produktion, 7th ed., Berlin et al. 1962, pp. 221 et seq.

is available. It is necessary to develop further views of the firm that integrate technological progress.

It has also become clear that technological progress is not restricted to shaping production functions of firms. Many other company activities are affected as well, and research and development produces new technological knowledge. An even broader view reveals that the firm is no longer clearly separated from its surrounding markets. Hybrid forms of cooperation have been established between legal entities that we continue to call firms, although the interrelatedness of their relations has partially undermined a major constituent characteristic of firms, namely their economic independence. *When Kiekert, a manufacturer and the sole supplier of locks for the Ford Motor Corp. in Germany recently failed to supply his products for a few hours due to "software problems", Ford had to stop its production and suffered substantial losses. This raises the question of the degree to which Ford is independent of Kiekert and vice versa, as some of Kiekert's investments have been financed by Ford.*

Different forms in which companies integrate technological knowledge into their production and transform it into marketable products can evidently exist successfully alongside each other. Economic explanations for this observation must therefore be sought in which a general failure of competition, and permanent survival by defending monopolistic niches, are not relevant in the long run. We suggest that economically relevant explanations arise from characteristics of technological progress which can be used to explain the wide variety of observations that can be made as companies adjust to such external conditions. Nevertheless, the explanatory model that is developed here is only a partial model. Gutenberg discussed how the economic environment could impact managerial decisions[3]. Adopting this idea, we explore how certain characteristics of new technological knowledge co-determine the way in which "companies" produce outputs.

2 Cost theory as a basis of explanation

The economic effects of technological progress vary widely and occur on various levels. A theoretical review can only be given in very brief form.

On a first level, costs of knowledge generation within one organization can be considered. The competitive effects of these can be devalued by radically new knowledge. On a second level, transaction costs become relevant[4]. These result from asymmetric information and their possible opportunistic exploitation, which each partner in a process that is based on the division of labor strives to preserve.

---

3 Gutenberg, E., Einführung in die Betriebswirtschaftslehre, op. cit., p. 10.

4 Cf. in summary: Picot, A., Transaktionskostenansatz, Handwörterbuch der Betriebswirtschaft, 5th ed., 3rd vol., Stuttgart: Poeschel 1993, columns 4194-4204.

This causes the transaction costs which are a result of "frictions" that arise from the coordination between the companies participating in the generation of an output of goods or services. The level of these frictions, and therefore also the amount of the costs, is determined by cultural influences or value systems which are not specific to the transaction, as well as by the form of the information and communications systems. Transaction-specific influences depend on the specificity, the variability or uncertainty, and the frequency of the transactions[5]. These influencing factors[6] which can be affected not least by technological developments, are examined in more detail later.

In principle, it is assumed that transaction costs increase with increasing specificity, and that high specificity can less expensively be controlled through hierarchical coordination than through market-based exchanges. The transaction costs per transaction decrease with increased transaction frequency and thereby promote coordination via markets. Where specificity is low, increasing uncertainty will encourage coordination via markets, whereas high specificity will incline more towards hierarchical coordination.

On a third level, we might observe opportunity costs. These arise, for instance, if binding relationships with particular partners inhibit more profitable relations with others. Within networks of companies, such as suppliers and users of jointly developed new technologies, such opportunity costs are of special importance.

What now needs to be clarified is: how does new technological knowledge affect these costs, and thereby favor different types of organization for its use in new products? For this purpose we need first of all to refer to some specific characteristics of knowledge.

Knowledge can be used any number of times without being exhausted. This explains the interest in its dissemination from the point of view of every other potential user of the knowledge, because dissemination helps to reduce specificity. The specificity can be maintained through non-dissemination and thereby becomes a basis for the attainment of "rents".

Knowledge can be combined with other knowledge, thus creating new technologies that help to satisfy a wider range of needs. This reduces uncertainty about the exploitation of the original knowledge base. It leads to "architectural innovations": "Existing technologies are applied or combined to create novel products or services, or new applications. Competition is based on serving specific market niches and on close relations with customers"[7]. *Two examples will*

---

5 Op. cit., columns 4198 et seq.

6 Cf. the diagrammatic model in: Brockhoff, K., R&D Co-operation between Firms - A Perceived Transaction Cost Perspective, Management Science, vol. 38, 1992, pages 514-524.

7 Tidd, J., J. Bessant, K. Pavitt, Managing Innovation. Integrating Technological, Market and Organizational Change, Chichester et al.: Wiley 1997, page 165.

demonstrate this. The garden tool manufacturer Gardena views knowledge as a condition for a high level of innovativeness and combines it with high vertical integration to ensure delivery capability in the case of high seasonal fluctuations, or uncertainty of demand[8]*. Henkel developed its core competence in the adhesives industry from the packaging needs that were not adequately met by its suppliers in the 1920s*[9].

Where there is cumulative technological progress, knowledge owners can achieve synergism from a technological point of view from the integration of new elements of knowledge. Whether these can be exploited in the market is a different question, which depends, in particular, on whether this market remains homogenous, or will itself be heterogenized with the increase in offerings based on the new technologies. This can lead to excessively high costs if all needs are satisfied from a single source.

These characteristics of technological knowledge are important for the reasons enumerated below.

3 Developing a "knowledge spectrum"

3.1 Dissemination of knowledge

At one extreme, technological knowledge can be monopolized by one person or institution. Alternatively, it might be disseminated throughout a very large number of people or institutions. The owner of monopolized knowledge will rarely have an interest in its dissemination (network products could form an exception to this); however, s/he can hardly effectively resist it in the long-term. It can be demonstrated that the monopolization of knowledge stimulates "technology races", whilst, when knowledge is disseminated ("technical parity competition"), other variables determine the competitive position of companies[10]. This suggests the instability of a position on an axis depicting dissemination of knowledge. The transition from monopolized to disseminated knowledge appears to be influenced by the type of technological progress, amongst other things. Empirical technological progress is more likely to facilitate monopolized knowledge, whilst cumulative technological progress makes wide dissemination easier through the use of the underlying theory. This character of technological progress can change in the course of time as theories are developed to explain, and forecast, the effects

---

8 Gardena Aktien zwischen 34 und 38 DM, Frankfurter Allgemeine, 18. September 1996, page 26.

9 Henkel klebt seit 75 Jahren, Frankfurter Allgemeine Zeitung, Jan. 9, 1998.

10 Cf. Miller, R., The new agenda for R&D: strategy and integration, International Journal of Technology Management, vol. 10, 1995, pages 511-524; also, a distinction is drawn between the situation of "market contest" and "learning in technology systems".

of new knowledge. *For example, two consecutive phases are described during the development of the radio in the history of technology: "the emergence of a pre-technical system, characterized by a high degree of empiricism and the concentration of innovators on solving operational problems arising from the incapacity of the dominant technical system to support further development of new services. When these tensions decreased, and when scientific knowledge was able to follow, and even precede technical evolution, the pre-technical system was able to generate by itself new services or products"*[11].

3.2 Complexity of output

Knowledge can be employed in the form of very simple products or very complex products. The combinatorial properties of technological knowledge can support a development towards more complexity. The transition from one level of complexity to another is influenced by the latent, or manifest, demands of buyers on the one hand. On the other hand, technologically complex products, in particular, place high demands on learning within companies[12]. It is not certain that all competitors in an industry can meet these demands as they tend to increase costs of production. *Griset argues that the rise of electronics in the "radio industry" required the mastery of very complex technological systems with elements of hardware and software, which RCA mastered, whilst the "classical" companies within the industry, such as Marconi, Telefunken, or CSF, did not*[13].

Let us now examine complexity somewhat closer. The creation of complex means to satisfy needs is not one-dimensional. On the one hand, complexity can arise through the integration of more parts in one product[14]. On the other hand, however, it can also arise through the delivery of an increasing number of product functions, which can only occur as a result of a change in the range of performance of the same number of product components. These complexity dimensions are in principle independent of one another[15], so that they can appear

---

11 Griset, P., Innovation and Radio Industry in Europe during the Interwar Period, in: Caron, F., Erker, P., Fischer, W., Innovations in the European Economy between the Wars, Berlin, New York: de Gruyter 1995, pages 37-64, here page 47.

12 Griset, P., Innovation and Radio Industry in Europe during the Interwar Period, op. cit.

13 Griset, P., Innovation and Radio Industry in Europe during the Interwar Period, op. cit., pages 54ff. The failure of the European firms is also attributed to a mistaken concentration on "professional and military equipment markets".

14 This was called "architectural innovation" by: Henderson, R., Clark, K.B., Architectural innovation: the reconfiguration of existing product technologies and the failure of established firms, Administrative Science Quaterly, vol. 35, 1990, pages 9-30.

15 Another viewpoint is expressed in: Singh, K., The concept and implications of technological complexity for organisations, Proceedings of the Academy of Management Meeting, Michigan: School of Business, here quoted from: Tidd, J.,

in every possible combination. Similar ideas on complexity have been expressed many times. Sometimes these ideas have been empirically substantiated[16].

The ability to generate synergism from the combinatory use of knowledge could lead to a tendency to develop ever more complex products, unless it is balanced by a cost factor such as the learning mentioned above. This indicates another instability on the complexity spectrum.

3.3 Knowledge spectrum

Dissemination and complexity represent scales which span what we call a knowledge spectrum. Each scale can be divided into any desired level of fineness. Only four particularly prominent points on the scales are considered here. This makes it possible to keep the representation within manageable limits. The four positions shown by combining selected points on the two scales are dealt with in succession. These positions are illustrated in Figure 1.

Figure 1: The knowledge spectrum

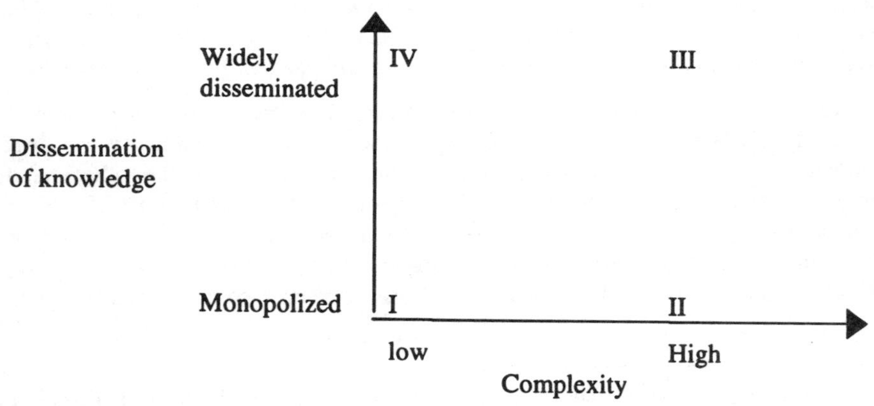

Complexity, Networks & Learning: Integrative Themes for Research on Innovation Management, International Journal of Innovation Management, vol. 1, 1997, pages 1-21, here page 6. The author adds a third characteristic "non-decomposable - cannot be separated into its components without degrading performance". Later it is argued that this does not represent a necessary criterion, but characterizes just one of several possible situations.

16 Henderson, R.M., Clark, K.B., Architectural Innovation: The Reconfiguration of Existing Product Technologies and the Failure of Established Firms, op. cit., pages 9-30; Fujimoto, T., Comparing Performance and Organization of Product Development Across Firms, in: Eto, H., Ed., R&D Strategies in Japan, Amsterdam 1993, pages 165 et seq.

Often, only one of the quadrants of this diagram is dealt with. This creates the impression that only this position secures corporate competitiveness. The theory that such particular positions represent absorbing states, towards which all successful companies must develop carries this idea further. As stated elsewhere, "Industry will gravitate toward the concept of core competencies, or strategic technologies, to focus its efforts"[17]. This seems to imply that when this state is reached no further changes will follow. Such theories overlook the dependence of successful management on adjustments to economic or technological constraints which, in turn, may be subject to radical change. It is therefore not justifiable to recommend particular positions to all companies, as has recently occurred when concentration on core competencies, or R&D cooperation as its consequence, or the use of system suppliers, have been suggested as particularly successful strategies.

4 Four quadrants in the knowledge spectrum

4.1 Monopolized knowledge in non-complex products (I)

At the extreme, one individual can create or possess new knowledge which can be exploited economically, even if it is in the form of a product which is not complex initially. This product can be a radical innovation. The owner of the new knowledge simultaneously creates information asymmetries vis-a-vis other people. *The Benz motor car, for which petrol had to be bought at the pharmacy and which was driven on traditional dirt roads, the crystal receiver with the headphones for listening to radio transmissions, or the first Apple PCs, are examples of this.* At this stage, the products do not require complementary products for their performance. They appear as "stand alone products". The specificity is high, as is the uncertainty of their future success, and only a few transactions are expected at first. Production takes place through hierarchical coordination.

The technological progress which makes such products possible can be "radical", in that it facilitates considerable increases in performance compared to traditional products. This makes the new products potentially desirable to customers. However, this technological progress can also be "disruptive": i.e., an innovation which opens up previously undeveloped market segments, and enables value to be added there, even if a majority of customers detects underperformance with

---

17 Bridenbaugh, P.R., The Future of Industrial R&D, or, Postcards from the Edge of the Abyss, in: Rosenbloom, R.S., Spencer, W.J., Ed., Engines of innovation. U.S. Industrial Research at the End of an Era, Cambridge, MA: MIT Press, 1996, pages 155-163, here page 162.

respect to characteristics presently held in high esteem[18]. Established market players can easily overlook this kind of technological progress, because it only appeals to a small customer group, possibly allows only for lower margins at first and does not (yet) meet the expectations of the mainstream customers. Should the major suppliers recognize this type of technological progress, they might choose to push ahead the further development of the old technology because by doing so they can protect their sunk cost from the pending devaluation of the technological potentials tied up in it. The "sailing ship effect" describes this response. It is bound to fail when the performance potential of the new technology is significantly higher than that of the old technology.

The hierarchical coordination in the first quadrant of the knowledge spectrum does not remain stable. There are various reasons for this. Firstly, the integration of knowledge in a product does, as assumed here, lead to a "feasible" solution, but there may be superior technologies which can fulfill the same purposes. In the case of a more or less simultaneous perception of needs, in particular, this can trigger demand pull technical progress, which is characterized by the fact that the same outputs can be achieved by very different factor inputs. As a rule, different factor inputs cause different costs; the most cost-effective combination of factors will be superior, all other things being equal. This is indicated by a multitude of parallel inventions documented in the history of technology[19] as well as the attempts to secure specificity through the comprehensive fencing of important patents by their applicants[20]. Both of these are indications of the technical races referred to above. The existing specificity can, therefore, get lost. *An interesting indication of this problem occurs in the computing industry: "When Apple had been the only game in town, the engineering team could design a machine to please themselves. But competition, and the need for larger sales volumes, raised the stakes and restricted design freedom"*[21].

Secondly, a monopolistic technological position cannot necessarily justify economic specificity, if it is in a firm's best interest to give it up. The technological knowledge is made generally accessible in order to gain an economically more advantageous position through the initiation of complementary products (e.g., software for a particular hardware), the coverage of markets which

18 Cf. Christensen, C.M., The Innovator's Dilemma. When New Technologies Cause Great Firms to Fail, Boston, MA: Harvard Business School Press, 1997, pages XV and passim.

19 Cf. Lamb, D., Easton, S.M., Multiple Discovery. The pattern of scientific progress, Avebury Publ. Co., 1984, pages 47ff. The authors state on page 59: "Given a common problem it is not unusual to find independent discoveries in different laboratories, often in different countries, by researchers unaware of each other's work."

20 Spero, D.M., Patent Protection or Piracy - A CEO Views Japan, Harvard Business Review, vol. 68, 1990, 5, pages 58-67.

21 Penzias, A., Ideas and Information. Managing in a High-Tech World. New York, London 1989, page 185.

cannot be easily accessed by the firm itself (e.g., through licensing), to secure future participation in a cumulative technological advance, or to obtain network effects.

Thirdly, a legally protected unique technological position with specificity cannot usually be maintained in the long run, because the period of legal protection is limited. Specificity can be lost through the appearance of imitators who are attracted by the rents created by that specificity. *The rise of generics manufacturers on the ethical pharmaceutical markets is a good example of this.*

Even when the period of protection is not limited, technological progress and the differentiation of demand can mean that the monopoly must be surrendered. *In telecommunications, it has been observed that technological progress "...enables a wide variety of outputs and therefore leads to a diversification of the markets which can no longer be managed by a state administration. Here, therefore, a causality is formulated which posits technological development as an action component, and the economic opening of the market as its consequence"*[22]. This "causality" is also supported empirically[23]. The monopoly cannot prevent the appearance of technologically related outputs, which in the subsequent period develop into technological alternatives to the core output. This suggests that market heterogeneity makes the exploitation of technological synergies by one market player seem uneconomic.

Fourthly, radically new knowledge, in particular, makes its owner into an interesting acquisition target or into a highly esteemed cooperation partner. If this occurs, however, knowledge is transferred to others. Acquisition of the whole firm is more expensive than the acquisition only of the desired technology, or cooperation, for two reasons: firstly, a higher degree of control is obtained, in particular over the owners of the knowledge, and this has to be paid for; secondly, it is not always possible to avoid the acquisition of assets that cannot be used optimally by the acquirer along with the acquired firm.

In the case of cooperation, the hard-to-come-by knowledge can be so well protected that its owner can put a visible and economically valuable stamp on the cooperation. *The reference to the label "Intel inside" on many PCs produced by different manufacturers documents this. But it is not an entirely new phenomenon. Around 1920, L'Hohlwein cigarettes were sold. The designer of the boxes, Ludwig Hohlwein, granted a license to the manufacturer, the Menes cigarette factory in Wiesbaden, to use his name as a trademark*[24].

---

22 Witte, E., Der Zusammenhang zwischen nachrichtentechnischen Innovationen und Veränderungen der Marktordnung, Sitzungsberichte der Bayerischen Akademie der Wissenschaften, vol. 5, 1997, page 4.

23 Op. cit., page 13.

24 From the exhibition catalog of the Altona Museum, Hamburg, on: Frühe Formen der Werbung, 1996, catalog numbers 11.36 to 11.38.

Thus, the first position in the knowledge spectrum is not stable. A firm which takes this position may either leave it for self-interest or will find itself confronted by attacks on ist position from others.

4.2 Monopolized knowledge in complex products (II)

Knowledge can be "combined" with other knowledge without being exhausted. This creates new opportunities for the satisfaction of needs. These combinations increase the complexity of the product which is to satisfy the wants of potential buyers. The possibility that the demands of the customer may be exceeded, and that undesirably complex products could be created as a result, will only be mentioned in passing here. It is a result of incomplete information. This "overengineering" is a first indication of the instability of the economic position adopted.

There are many examples describing the second position in the knowledge spectrum discussed here. We are told that: "for years, Eastman Kodak was the only company that did all three: cameras, film, and developing"[25], thus offering a very complex product. In another case "plain old telephone services (pots)" became over time "progressively combined forms of communication..., which include speech, text, data, stills, and eventually also moving pictures"[26]. Initially these opportunities were bundled by a monopoly, however, they then broke the bounds of this market regime with their increasing breadth and complexity. Another case: The Meissen china manufacturer is, even today, proud of excavating its own clay, developing and mixing its own colors etc. All of these are made into complex works of art.

The treatment of knowledge that leads to complex products is an important part of the training of engineers and scientists. *Pavitt points out that research is carried out "precisely to train technological problem-solvers to integrate knowledge from a variety of disciplines in the development and use of complex systems"[27]. Kesselring devised a "theory of design (composition)", which was intended to support the creative activities of an engineer in the interaction of invention, design, and formation with regard to economic, ethical and other goals[28]. The principle of variants, that is, the search for similar solutions to meet a need which is formulated as a task, and the principle of generation, that is, searching for existing and re-combinable assemblies, or the development of new assemblies and*

---

25 Design Management Institute, Polaroid Corporation: Camera Design and Development 1984, Case 9-993-023, Boston, MA 1993, page 5.

26 Cf. Witte, E., Der Zusammenhang zwischen nachrichtentechnischen Inventionen und Veränderungen der Marktordnung, loc. cit., page 8.

27 Pavitt, K., Basic Sciences and Innovation, UNESCO World Science Report 1993, London 1993, page 133.

28 Kesselring, F., Technische Kompositionslehre, Berlin et al.: Springer Verlag, 1954.

components, are nowadays taught as elements of technical problem-solving[29]. *It is important also to mention various creativity techniques, in particular morphological analysis, which Hauschildt describes as "structuring concepts for the generation of alternatives"*[30]. *In the above sense, these therefore support the principle of generation.*

Because of the multi-dimensionality of "complexity" referred to above, sustaining competitiveness requires the pursuit of both the technological development of the "product architecture" and the performance of the individual elements, or modules, of a product which are connected in the architecture of the product.

In particular, when the interfaces between the components or the causes of the improvement in their performance are difficult to ascertain from the outside, this again forms a basis for specificity. In so far as the increase in complexity also entails coverage of shrinking market segments, down to one-piece production, the number of transactions decreases[31]. So does the number of possible transactions where external sourcing of components is attempted. For both these reasons, it is therefore to be expected that, with growing complexity, an increasing share of the value added of a product will be generated within the firm.

The resulting coordination costs are seen as one of the main obstacles to economic efficiency. For single product firms, Gutenberg did not consider coordination costs[32] as being a factor limiting the size of the firm "under any conditions and in any magnitudes likely to occur in practice"[33]. However, such an effect cannot entirely be ruled out and - which appears more crucial here - the argument does not take into account the case of variable complexity or multiple types of products. *An example of the shift of cost levels is the success factor for book clubs. In 1948 it consisted of a close link to a printer, which could deliver the desired titles on time and promised additional incremental profits. Forty years later printing has become a commodity which is offered on a competitive basis. Thus, efficient book clubs no longer operate their own print shops. Another example: "As Apple grew ... so did the 'team'. Specialization became necessary, and with it a need for more*

---

29 Eversheim, W., Technische Problemlösung, in: Eversheim, W., Schuh, G., Produktion und Management "Betriebshütte", part 1, 7. A., Berlin et al.: Springer Verlag, 1996, pages 7-20 et seq.

30 Hauschildt, J., Innovationsmanagement, 2nd edition, Munich: Vahlen-Verlag, 1997, pages 311 et seq.

31 Tidd, J., Complexity, Networks & Learning: Integrative Themes for Research on Innovation Management, loc. cit., pages 6 et seq., even assumes a connection between "technical complexity" and "market complexity" in the sense of a multitude of segments.

32 These costs were referred to by Robinson, E.A.G., Betriebsgröße und Produktionskosten, Vienna: Springer Verlag, 1936, page 87.

33 Gutenberg, E., Der Einfluss der Betriebsgrösse auf die Kostengestaltung in Fertigungsbetrieben, Schweizerische Zeitschrift für Kaufmännisches Bildungswesen, vol. 50, 1956, pages 1-10, 28-37, here page 35.

coordination. Now teams split off ... and some tasks ... got done twice while others ... went neglected"[34].

Tidd suggests that firms which find themselves in the situation described above gear their communication and information relationships too much to the performance of the modules and assume that the traditional architectural knowledge will persist[35]; they can then be forced out of their competitive position by new architectural ideas. Research and development activities in successful firms will therefore extend to both aspects of complexity. However, the appearance of disruptive technologies and the manufacturer's disregard for them (on the grounds already stated with respect to the first quadrant and in the field of technology, in particular, because of the existence of the well-known "not invented here syndrome"[36]) attack the position achieved. A necessary condition for recognizing radical and disruptive innovations can be met by investment in research, if this is used to create the potentials for identifying and absorbing external knowledge[37].

The creation of a special organizational unit for the development of new technology and its later exploitation is advisable[38], in order not to lose the opportunity of innovation by being too strongly bound to the past. This unit will tend to move the firm back towards quadrant I, but on a different technological level from that at which the firm was originally located.

A second reason for instability again lies in the fact that knowledge cannot generally be completely protected in the long term. In particular, knowledge about the technical interfaces between modules (and therefore the basis for architectural innovations) would, as manufacturing becomes increasingly standardized (thus creating market entry barriers through economies of scale and scope), have to be documented or passed on to many owners of knowledge. This increases the chances of an unintentional leakage of this knowledge, especially since, in the case of successful activity, systematic efforts will be directed at the absorption of this knowledge by external competitors[39].

---

34 Penzias, A., Ideas and Information. Managing in a High-Tech World, op. cit., page 183.

35 Tidd, J., Complexity, Networks & Learning: Integrative Themes for Research on Innovation Management, loc. cit., page 7.

36 Katz, R., Allen, T.J., Investigating the Not Invented Here (NIH) Syndrome: A Look at the Performance Tenure and Communication Patterns of 50 R&D Project Groups, R&D Management, vol. 12, 1982, pages 7-19.

37 Cf. Brockhoff, K., Industrial Research for Future Competitiveness, Berlin et al.: Springer Verlag, 1997.

38 Christensen, C.M., The Innovator's Dilemma. When New Technologies Cause Great Firms to Fail, loc. cit., pages XX, 101ff., 197ff.

39 For a summary see: Lange, V., Technologische Konkurrenzanalyse, Wiesbaden: DUV, 1994.

A third reason for the instability of the situation described here could be that, despite the fact that the knowledge components to be combined can be identified unambiguously and cost-effectively, their in-house development for productive exploitation is associated with higher costs than development or delivery from outside the firm[40]. *An example can be cited here too: The search for a supplier for sodium perborate, which Henkel needs for the production of its leading brand detergent Persil, led to Degussa AG. In order to secure the supply, Henkel held an indirect share in Degussa AG until 1997*[41].

This shows in a particularly striking way that firms have difficulties in staying in position II of the knowledge spectrum. Moving towards position III they will aim to secure relationships as long as the knowledge has to become common and shared by many. If a precise description of the object of a transfer is not possible, as in the case of necessary research and development, then instead of a contractual obligation it is advisable to attempt to build trust-based relationships[42]. This is especially true in the development of complex systems which have parts which interact with each other, and therefore do not allow an exact prior formulation of the final technical interfaces or their characteristics. Trust is "produced through interpersonal interactions that lead to social-psychological bonds of mutual norms, sentiments, and friendships" and is supported by the motivation "to seek both equity and efficiency outcomes because of the desire to preserve a reputation for fair dealing that will enable ... to continue to exchange transaction-specific investments under conditions of high uncertainty"[43]. These descriptive statements have, however, only rarely been analyzed in time-series studies of development for real situations which are characterized by partners changing their employers quickly, where there is a high level of environmental variability and where inflexibilities in the labor market exist, etc. Perhaps the securing of stability among partners through trust-building is not quite as effective as supposed (i.e., it causes relatively high costs), because one observes that when discontinuous technological change occurs, contractually secured forms of cooperation (joint ventures, technology licensing agreements, and various forms of R&D consortia)

---

40 On the differentiation of identifying and absorbing knowledge cf.: Brockhoff, K., Industrial Research for Future Competitiveness, op. cit.; also: Steuerung der Forschung durch abgestimmten Potentialaufbau, Zeitschrift für Betriebswirtschaft, vol. 67. 1997, pages 453-470, here page 459.

41 The GFC Gesellschaft für Chemiewerte mbH holds more than 25% of Degussa AG; Henkel KGaA had a holding of 46 % in GFCmbH, the remaining shares were held by Dresdner Bank AG and the Münchner Rückversicherungs-Gesellschaft.

42 Ring, P.S., van de Ven, A., Development Processes of Cooperative Interorganizational Relationships, Academy of Management Review, vol. 19, 1994, pages 90-118, here page 93.

43 Op. cit. pages 93, 94.

are preferred to generate knowledge[44]. Trust-building might need to be supplemented by formal legal agreements (which could then be interpreted as a cost-saving measure). *This is shown by the ABS case. In 1965, Daimler-Benz AG hinted to Robert Bosch GmbH that it should address itself to the development of an anti-locking system*[45]. *It also supported Bosch's acquisition of Teldix in 1973, where corresponding developments were already well advanced*[46]. *Intensive discussions took place between Daimler-Benz and Bosch in "weekly meetings", but without the conclusion of a binding development contract or marketing contract. Although Bosch had agreed to an - undefined - lead time for the use of ABS by Daimler-Benz, in 1977 Bosch offered the development to other auto manufacturers as well at a stage when it was practically functional and ready for mass production. One week before the planned press presentation by Daimler-Benz, Bayerische Motorenwerke (BMW), aware of Daimler-Benz's timing, launched a press release with its own announcement of ABS. "The breach of the decades-old 'good faith' process led to a substantial loss of trust in Robert Bosch GmbH on the part of Daimler-Benz, which was still being referred to as 'ABS-Trauma' in 1988"*[47]. *It seems that Bosch gambled its trust capital because by that time competitors were hot on its heels with their own developments; and, rapid establishment of its own development in the market to amortize the development expenses could not be guaranteed if it only supplied one firm.*

Assuming that Bosch's behavior was rational, it can be explained by considering opportunity costs. Obviously, the sum of future transaction costs between Bosch and Daimler-Benz, as well as the opportunity costs of delayed information and supply to other automotive manufacturers if the company had been committed to this partnership for a certain period, were higher than the comparative costs. The latter comprise the (higher) transaction costs arising from supplying several auto manufacturers as well as the opportunity costs for lost follow-up business. The situation is represented in Figure 2.

Assuming that transaction costs are a decreasing function of the length of a relationship (because of the reduction in uncertainty as well as the larger number of transactions), then cooperating firms would have to continue their commitment or replace it with even more favorable market conditions. The departure from the

---

44 Lambe, C.J., Spekman, R.E., Alliances, External Technology Acquisition, and Discontinuous Technological Change, Journal of Product Innovation Management, vol. 14, 1997, pages 102-116. The authors give six examples in their table 1.

45 Cf. Bingmann, H., Antiblockiersystem und Benzineinspritzung, in: Albach, H., Culture and Technical Innovation. A Cross Cultural Analysis and Policy Recommendations, Berlin, New York: de Gruyter, 1994, pages 736-821, here page 780.

46 Op. cit. pages 786f.

47 Op. cit. pages 789, 790.

Figure 2: The cost situation

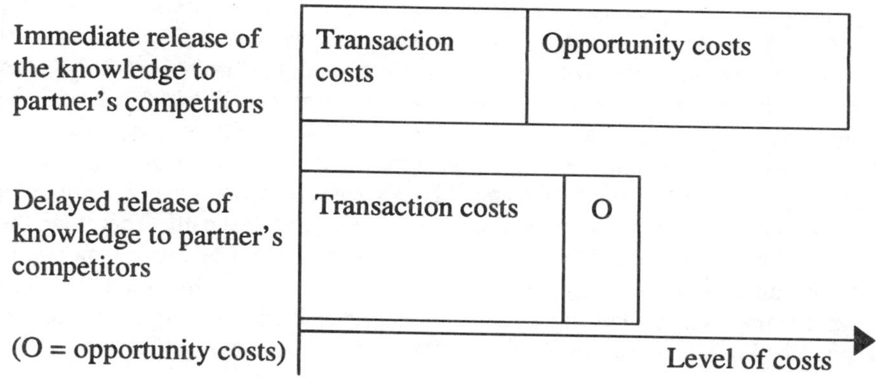

adopted development direction can be explained by taking opportunity costs into account in addition to transaction costs. In conclusion we find that a position in quadrant II is not stable either. It is technologically vulnerable and changeable. The economic consequences can then force the abandonment of the position.

4.3 Disseminated knowledge in complex products (III)

Digression from position II, we posit that the knowledge required for manufacturing product modules is no longer monopolized. If we assume that efficiently designing and bridging interfaces between modules of complex products can be a special technological competence, then in the case of low product-sales volumes, which may even be constructed according to the individual wishes of the purchaser, a collaboration between several firms in production may be cost-efficient. Tidd has formulated the thesis: "Technological and market complexity is positively associated with network participation"[48]. In such a case, the most economic solution for satisfying the customer can be, for example, the formation of a working group, or a network, of firms with a lead firm. Depending on the design of the relationships, different forms of hybrid organizations of networks of firms are created.

Network organizations exploit specialization and thus information assymetries. In particular for the lead firm, one assurance against the opportunistic exploitation of information asymmetry in such organizations could be the selection of a broader range of research and development activities than what is required by production. In addition to the knowledge which is necessary for internal activities, at least as much additional knowledge should be provided in research and development as is

---

48 Tidd, J., Complexity, Networks & Learning: Integrative Themes for Research on Innovation Management, loc. cit., page 4.

necessary for the identification of technological alternatives for the externally produced modules. *High transaction costs were incurred by Hoechst AG until 1925, when it tried to rely on external knowledge and cooperation. These costs resulted from profit sharing agreements with the external possessors of knowledge, and they were greater than the costs of internal personnel. This led to the establishing of Hoechst's own R&D laboratory. When some of the competencies later had to be transferred to the IG Farben laboratory in Leverkusen this was again seen as a disadvantage*[49]. In other words: at least a partial reduction in information asymmetry is viewed as economically sensible, in order to limit the temptation of partners to behave opportunistically. Therefore, the degree of specialization in research and development should be lower than that in manufacturing. Different degrees of specialization are not uncommon as between the marketing departments and production departments of system manufacturers. The same idea is here transferred on to a further functional area.

The situation described here may not be stable either. On the one hand, deviations are to be expected because, as a result of increasing sales volumes, standardization of the modules and their interfaces becomes possible and necessary. As a result, special skills in interface structuring might get lost. On the other hand, such standardization may also facilitate an increase in sales. It is to be expected that for both these reasons the transaction costs will decline, so that the situation described in quadrant IV may arise.

It is also noteworthy that the function of the lead firm can be lost through particular efforts by the supplier in the innovation process. Direct suppliers and system suppliers in the automotive industry can be differentiated by, amongst other things, the fact that the latter show higher product innovation skills, patentability, and readiness for know-how transfer in the research and development processes. At the same time, however, they are subject to less intervention by the car manufacturers in their research and development and their process innovations[50]. They therefore try to counter the dissemination of knowledge by monopolizing their own knowledge. If we take into consideration that the system suppliers earn higher returns than the direct suppliers[51], then this is indicative of a stronger position vis-à-vis auto manufacturers. The originally leading role of the auto manufacturer is, correspondingly, weakened in relative terms. This, in turn, can be an incentive to standardize the interfaces, in order to place suppliers under competitive pressure.

---

49 Wimmer, W., Wir haben fast immer etwas Neues, Berlin: Duncker & Humblot 1994, pp. 149 et seq.

50 Cf. Gaitanides, M., Integrierte Belieferung - Eine ressourcenorientierte Erklärung der Entstehung von Systemlieferanten in der Automobilzulieferindustrie, Zeitschrift für Betriebswirtschaft, vol. 67., 1997, pages 717-757, here page 750.

51 Op. cit. page 741: These statements are valid from the viewpoint of the supplier.

4.4 Disseminated knowledge in non-complex products (IV)

As a consequence of standardized interfaces in particular, several firms will offer modules in competition as the knowledge required for each module is increasingly disseminated. The definition of the interfaces makes division of labor in invention easier. If so, it will no longer only be a case of the system leader combining the modules for its customers: the customers themselves will put the modules together from complementary parts. In comparison to the resultant total bundle of outputs, each module is less complex. *Examples are tuner, receiver, tape drive and speakers instead of a "radio" or a truck with different tires, units and chassis all made by different manufacturers at the customer's order. In the computer industry, it was found that: "After thirty years of progress at a rate of 25 percent per year and after internationalization of the know-how required, many of the hardware technologies in computing and telecommunications are available as commodities. Therefore, these technologies in themselves are no longer the source of comparative advantage that they once were"*[52]. *Elsewhere it is stated: "Rather than every computer company in the world designing and building its own proprietary parts, independent suppliers provided standard building blocks. As a consequence, a wide array of companies could build machines that performed across a broad spectrum of price and performance features"*[53]. If the technological interface problems cannot be resolved by a manufacturer which assembles the elements, this can result in serious competitive disadvantages from the customer's point of view[54]. If the problems are solved in a way which is visible to the outside world, however, competitors are given the opportunity to imitate the output, *e.g., in the computer market, the "IBM clones"*. If standardization occurs, competitive advantages can no longer be derived from technology developed in-house, but must be obtained from other outputs (e.g., services, consultancy, reliability, upwards compatibility). The exploitation of technologically based advantages might be shifted to the suppliers of the modules (*"Intel inside" is then put on the computers*), who will take a position within their markets in accordance with quadrants I or II as described above. In such a situation, it appears extraordinarily difficult to regain the position of the technology-developing lead firm once the role of "assembler" has been accepted. *The example of the failure of the development of the Apple Lisa computer demonstrates this. In contrast to immediately preceding developments (but not Macintoshes), Apple itself wanted in this case to be involved again in the*

---

52 Armstrong, J., Reinventing Research at IBM, in: Rosenbloom, R.S., Spencer, W.J., Engines of Innovation. U.S. Industrial Research at the End of an Era, op. cit., pages 151-154, here page 152.

53 Yoffie, D.B., Pearson, A.E., The Transformation of IBM, Harvard Business School, Case 9-391-073, 1991, page 4.

54 Op. cit. page 6.

programming of the operating system[55]. If a supplier cannot be quickly changed, its problems in maintaining, or advancing, a desired state of the art are naturally also problems for its customer, the "assembler". *Delays in the supply of Motorola Chips in 1990 obviously did significant damage to Apple's image as the performance leader in PCs*[56]. *IBM, in contrast, kept on its own microchip production for internal use and secured its supplies from Intel by investing in the company*[57]. *Beyschlag produces 5 billion resistors per year for the automotive and electronics industries. It relies on proprietary production processes, reliability and product quality, and engagement in problem solving together with their customers.* An alternative for the powerful customer in securing its competitive position is the condition that the supplier must ensure that its products are interchangeable with others[58].

The manufacturers of the individual modules which are standardized at their interfaces will only aim for performance improvements in the modules if the customer can thereby improve the total performance of its system and wishes to do so. Otherwise, the realization of competitive advantages will focus on cost reductions prepared by process development, which as far as necessary will be passed on in the form of lower prices. Similar considerations also apply to the case where a dominant design has become established[59].

The stability of a situation shown in quadrant IV can also be disturbed by radical innovations, which in turn can lead to quadrants I or III, but at a new technological level and therefore, probably, with new market players.

Profit-maximizing module manufacturers, or system suppliers, may perceive that their own situation offers room for improvement and may act accordingly. *When the planned establishment of a development laboratory in Germany by an American automotive industry system supplier was announced, whereby the "required closeness to the auto manufacturers" was to be achieved, acquisitions were also promised. Two reasons were given for this: firstly, obtaining more customers; secondly, reducing the dependence on individual customers*[60]. If this strategy makes the module supplier stronger, that is, makes it possible for the supplier to assert higher prices because control by competition is reduced, a firm

55 Swanger, C.C., Maidique, M.A., Apple Computer: The First Ten Years, Case, S-BP-245, Stanford CA 1985, page 18.

56 Yoffie, D.B., Cohn, J., Levy, D., Apple Computer 1992, Harvard Business School, Case 9-792-081, 1992, page 10.

57 Coleman, J.J., The Semiconductor Industry Association and the Trade Dispute with Japan, Harvard Business School, Case, 9-387-191, 1987, page 1.

58 Cf. Bingmann, H., Antiblockiersystem und Benzineinspritzung, loc. cit., page 800.

59 Utterback, J. M., Mastering the Dynamics of Innovation, Boston, MA: Harvard Business School Press, 1994.

60 hap., Technologiekonzern TRW baut Forschungszentrum in Deutschland, Frankfurter Allgemeine Zeitung, July 19, 1997, page 16.

may arrive once more at the point of technological backward integration of subcontracted parts. Such a firm would be aiming to change its position from IV to II or even to I for economic reasons.

5. Summary and further considerations

(1) It has been demonstrated that the situations considered in the four quadrants of the knowledge spectrum are not stable, but are vulnerable to technological innovations, amongst other things. They represent ideal types at prominent points on a continuum of changes of knowledge dissemination and product complexity. Some of the transitions between III and IV have already been described in more detail[61]. Because of the technology-related vulnerability of every situation described, it cannot be expected that all firms or even business units will develop towards a single position, as is sometimes maintained. An overview of the destabilizing influences discussed here is given in Figure 3.

(2) Broad knowledge dissemination and high complexity, as considered here, do not represent "natural" extremes of the respective scales. The dissemination of knowledge could in theory be extended to every person. This, however, is not practicable on economic grounds amongst others. The maximum level of dissemination is determined by learning costs, storage costs of the knowledge, and the value of knowledge. Complexity could also increase further from any attained level. From an economic point of view, this is chiefly to be expected when the costs of coordination of the complexity-inducing elements of a product decrease. The development of electronic communications media could, in this sense, offer an opportunity for an increase in complexity. Whether this condition is then exploited in one firm or whether it leads to new forms of cooperation between firms is partly determined, in turn, by the dissemination of knowledge.

(3) Furthermore, it is interesting to observe that the direction and scope of research and development are neither confined to the range of activities of other functional areas of the firm, nor are they the same for all ideal types considered. This is significant for the technology management of this function and for general management. In reality, the more diversified a firm is, the harder it is to perceive this significance.

(4) Each business unit of a firm can find itself in one or another of the four quadrants and be attacked more or less strongly. Different research and development policies should be chosen accordingly. The considerations expressed here may also help to explain the trend, observed in the last few years, towards the

61 Cf. Meyer, M., Ökonomische Organisation der Industrie. Netzwerkarrangements zwischen Markt und Unternehmung, Wiesbaden: Gabler, 1994, pages 102ff., 164.

Figure 3: Destabilizing influences on the positions in the spectrum of knowledge

I:	Lower costs because of competing technology (parallel invention) Loss of specificity in the case of network effects High costs through differentiated technological progress and differentiated demand Being overtaken by radically new knowledge
II:	High coordination costs and neglect of innovations in the case of "architectural knowledge" No ability to protect knowledge permanently High costs of internal generation of knowledge High opportunity costs in the case of trust-based commitments to particular customers as development partners
III:	Opportunistic exploitation of information asymmetry High cost of securing "minimum knowledge" outside the range of core products Standardization of technological interfaces
IV:	Costs of securing a "minimum knowledge" for the "assemblers" of the parts Being overtaken by radically new knowledge Monopolization by the module manufacturers

formation of independently operating business units or the spin-off of independent companies from a firm.

(5) Finally, it is apparent that the transition between the situations described does not take place according to a mechanistic, sequential pattern. The advantageous transitions are rather determined by economic conditions which are, in part, technology-based and which can be formulated using the concepts of transaction costs and opportunity costs. If we posit that knowledge is not lost (which, however, can occur in individual cases, as shown by, e.g., the repeated reinvention of the process for manufacturing ruby glass), then transitions from III or IV to I and II with the same knowledge are not primarily explained by technology, but by economics. All other transitions can have both technological and economic grounds.

(6) To date, no studies are known which empirically describe the dynamics of these transition processes in terms of the influences considered here.

A study of firms which offer complex systems (e.g., radar systems), that is, firms which could be positioned either in situations II or III as described above, or - for individual modules - in situation IV, offers initial indications[62]. *The authors consider four "structuring alternatives"*[63]. *However, only four of the 16 possible transitions between these (observing two different points in time) are considered*[64]. *Particular attention is paid here on the one hand to development capacities and their ability to deliver the necessary level of technological progress cost-effectively (in particular to pioneer or be a follower in radical innovations). On the other hand, the production capacities for modules are considered, as well as the capability of realizing economies of scale (which does not promise crucial advantages in markets with a very small demand), of avoiding supply bottlenecks for critical resources or of keeping the relative factor costs low, and defining the technological interfaces between modules.* One of the important conclusions drawn from the observation of the transitions is that an "appropriate level of control over each technology" is necessary. This means, therefore, that even in the case of cooperation, or the procurement of modules from outside a firm, the firm should maintain in-house the capability to judge technological progress competently as well as access to its results. This agrees with the idea considered above which posits that the breadth of the development tasks does not necessarily have to match the breadth of the production tasks. It appears that this necessity has not been considered in every one of the core competency-based reorganizations of the past years. Disadvantages arising from this are not immediately visible, but only after a time lag. They can, however, only be corrected at that stage by internal efforts which also have a delayed effect, or by the expensive acquisition of external knowledge, e.g., by acquiring a company. This is one of the dangers of neglecting the dynamics of technological competencies.

In our presentation, information drawn from reports and case studies has been used to support the reasoning. There has been no comprehensive empirical test of the main question: how do economically relevant characteristics of technological progress interact with a form of corporate organization designed to secure competitiveness and with markets? This question offers opportunities for further research.

---

62 Paganetto et al., The System Company, draft, in: Danielmeyer, H.G., Ed., Company of the Future, Berlin et al.: Springer Verlag, to appear.

63 These are: (a) development internal, production internal; (b) development internal, production external, assembly internal; (c) development external, production external, some in-house development capacity; (d) development external, production external, no in-house development capacity.

64 The description is not quite clear. As far as can be ascertained, the following cases are considered: "persistence of vertical integration" from (a) to (a), whereby the structural alternatives in the footnote above are called by the corresponding letters; "de-verticalization" from (a) to (b), (c) or (d); "partial de-verticalization" from (b) to (c) or (d); "vertical integration" from (c) or (d) to (a) or (b); "re-verticalization", which corresponds to the last case, but refers back to a different case history.

References

Armstrong, J., Reinventing Research at IBM, in: Rosenbloom, R.S., Spencer, W.J., Engines of Innovation. U.S. Industrial Research at the End of an Era, Cambridge, MA: MIT Press, 1996, pages 151-154.

Bingmann, H., Antiblockiersystem und Benzineinspritzung, in: Albach, H., Culture and Technical Innovation. A Cross-Cultural Analysis and Policy Recommendations, Berlin, New York: de Gruyter, 1994, pages 736-821.

Bridenbaugh, P.R., The Future of Industrial R&D, or, Postcards from the Edge of the Abyss, in: Rosenbloom, R.S., Spencer, W.J., Ed., Engines of innovation. U.S. Industrial Research at the End of an Era, Cambridge, MA: MIT Press, 1996, pages 155-163.

Brockhoff, K., Steuerung der Forschung durch abgestimmten Potentialaufbau, Zeitschrift für Betriebswirtschaft, vol. 67, 1997, pages 453-470.

Brockhoff, K., Industrial Research for Future Competitiveness, Berlin et al.: Springer Verlag, 1997.

Brockhoff, K., R&D Co-operation between Firms - A Perceived Transaction Cost Perspective, Management Science, vol. 38, 1992, pages 514-524.

Christensen, C.M., The Innovator's Dilemma. When New Technologies Cause Great Firms to Fail, Boston, MA: Harvard Business School Press, 1997.

Coleman, J.J., The Semiconductor Industry Association and the Trade Dispute with Japan, Harvard Business School, Case, 9-387-191, 1987.

Design Management Institute, Polaroid Corporation: Camera Design and Development 1984, Case 9-993-023, Boston, MA 1993.

Eversheim, W., Technische Problemlösung, in: Eversheim, W., Schuh, G., Produktion und Management "Betriebshütte", part 1, 7. A., Berlin et al.: Springer Verlag, 1996.

Exhibition catalog of the Altona Museum, Hamburg, on: Frühe Formen der Werbung, 1996, catalog numbers 11.36 to 11.38.

Frankfurter Allgemeine Zeitung, Gardena Aktien zwischen 34 und 38 DM, 18. September 1996, page 26.

Frankfurter Allgemeine Zeitung, Technologiekonzern TRW baut Forschungszentrum in Deutschland, July 19, 1997, page 16.

Frankfurter Allgemeine Zeitung, Henkel klebt seit 75 Jahren, Jan. 9, 1998.

Fujimoto, T., Comparing Performance and Organization of Product Development Across Firms, in: Eto, H., Ed., R&D Strategies in Japan, Amsterdam 1993, pages 165 et seq.

Gaitanides, M., Integrierte Belieferung - Eine ressourcenorientierte Erklärung der Entstehung von Systemlieferanten in der Automobilzulieferindustrie, Zeitschrift für Betriebswirtschaft, vol. 67., 1997, pages 717-757.

Griset, P., Innovation and Radio Industry in Europe during the Interwar Period, in: Caron, F., Erker, P., Fischer, W., Innovations in the European Economy between the Wars, Berlin, New York: de Gruyter 1995, pages 37-64.

Gutenberg, E., Der Einfluss der Betriebsgrösse auf die Kostengestaltung in Fertigungsbetrieben, Schweizerische Zeitschrift für Kaufmännisches Bildungswesen, vol. 50, 1956, pages 1-10, 28-37.

Gutenberg, E., Einführung in die Betriebswirtschaftslehre, Wiesbaden 1958.

Gutenberg, E., Grundlagen der Betriebswirtschaftslehre, vol. 1: Produktion, 7th ed., Berlin et al. 1962.

Hauschildt, J., Innovationsmanagement, 2nd edition, Munich: Vahlen-Verlag, 1997.

Henderson, R., Clark, K.B., Architectural innovation: the reconfiguration of existing product technologies and the failure of established firms, Administrative Science Quaterly, vol. 35, 1990, pages 9-30.

Katz, R., Allen, T.J., Investigating the Not Invented Here (NIH) Syndrome: A Look at the Performance Tenure and Communication Patterns of 50 R&D Project Groups, R&D Management, vol. 12, 1982, pages 7-19.

Kesselring, F., Technische Kompositionslehre, Berlin et al.: Springer Verlag, 1954.

Lamb, D., Easton, S.M., Multiple Discovery. The pattern of scientific progress, Avebury Publ. Co., 1984.

Lambe, C.J., Spekman, R.E., Alliances, External Technology Acquisition, and Discontinuous Technological Change, Journal of Product Innovation Management, vol. 14, 1997, pages 102-116.

Lange, V., Technologische Konkurrenzanalyse, Wiesbaden: DUV, 1994.

Meyer, M., Ökonomische Organisation der Industrie. Netzwerkarrangements zwischen Markt und Unternehmung, Wiesbaden: Gabler, 1994.

Miller, R., The new agenda for R&D: strategy and integration, International Journal of Technology Management, vol. 10, 1995, pages 511-524.

Paganetto et al., The System Company, draft, in: Danielmeyer, H.G., Ed., Company of the Future, Berlin et al.: Springer Verlag, to appear.

Pavitt, K., Basic Sciences and Innovation, UNESCO World Science Report 1993, London 1993.

Penzias, A., Ideas and Information. Managing in a High-Tech World. New York, London 1989.

Picot, A., Transaktionskostenansatz, Handwörterbuch der Betriebswirtschaft, 5th ed., 3rd vol., Stuttgart: Poeschel 1993, columns 4194-4204.

Ring, P.S., van de Ven, A., Development Processes of Cooperative Interorganizational Relationships, Academy of Management Review, vol. 19, 1994, pages 90-118.

Robinson, E.A.G., Betriebsgröße und Produktionskosten, Vienna: Springer Verlag, 1936.

Singh, K., The concept and implications of technological complexity for organisations, Proceedings of the Academy of Management Meeting, Michigan: School of Business.

Spero, D.M., Patent Protection or Piracy - A CEO Views Japan, Harvard Business Review, vol. 68, 1990, 5, pages 58-67.

Swanger, C.C., Maidique, M.A., Apple Computer: The First Ten Years, Case, S-BP-245, Stanford CA 1985.

Utterback, J. M., Mastering the Dynamics of Innovation, Boston, MA: Harvard Business School Press, 1994.

Tidd, J., Complexity, Networks & Learning: Integrative Themes for Research on Innovation Management, International Journal of Innovation Management, vol. 1, 1997, pages 1-21.

Tidd, J., J. Bessant, K. Pavitt, Managing Innovation. Integrating Technological, Market and Organizational Change, Chichester et al.: Wiley 1997.

Wimmer, W., Wir haben fast immer etwas Neues, Berlin: Duncker & Humblot 1994.

Witte, E., Der Zusammenhang zwischen nachrichtentechnischen Innovationen und Veränderungen der Marktordnung, Sitzungsberichte der Bayerischen Akademie der Wissenschaften, vol. 5, 1997.

Yoffie, D.B., Pearson, A.E., The Transformation of IBM, Harvard Business School, Case 9-391-073, 1991.

Yoffie, D.B., Cohn, J., Levy, D., Apple Computer 1992, Harvard Business School, Case 9-792-081, 1992.

Summary

It is often suggested that companies should adopt strategic positions that have proven successful in other industries, business sectors or companies. Some authors even go so far as to suggest that there exist absorptive states towards which all firms will gravitate. In this paper we argue that distribution of technological knowledge and complexity of products span a knowledge spectrum, in which firms can take particular positions. None of the positions is undisputed. Therefore, careful analysis of the technological conditions and the economic reasons that call for a change of positions is necessary to be successful in competition.

The Dispositive Factor in a System of Inventory-Controlled Production

J. Reese[1]

Overview

- The subject of research in this paper is to analyze how the role of the "dispositive factor" in Erich Gutenberg's theory of the firm should be interpreted in inventory-controlled production systems.
- The new institutional economics approach is applied to reveal interrelations and differences regarding the "dispositive" tasks in the neoclassical and in the modern production system design.
- The results show that Gutenberg's theory is still valid to some extent but that there is also need for some extensions following fundamental economic developments.

Keywords. Production System, Dispositive Factor, Organization, New Institutional Economics

1 Object and Legitimation of the Study

Erich GUTENBERG's neoclassical theory of the firm (1929, 1951) has proved to be very efficient over many decades. A central element of this theory is the "dispositive factor". It is defined as all those management inputs which organize, plan and control the other elemental inputs in a production process (GUTENBERG 1951, p. 6). The dispositive factor consists of rational and irrational components. Though it aims at optimizing the production process, there still remains some kind of intuition within the dispositive factor which cannot be rationally explained

[1] Professor Dr. Joachim Reese, University of Lüneburg, Chair of Production Economics, D-21332 Lüneburg, Germany, email: reese@uni-lueneburg.de

(GUTENBERG 1951, pp. 104). In GUTENBERG's theory of the firm, the dispositive factor is decisive for the firm's success or failure.

GUTENBERG's production system design, which is closely connected with the role of the dispositive factor, has undergone a drastic change in many industries. Following the classification of competitive strategies (PORTER 1980), production and logistic concepts have been developed which can be specified as inventory-controlled or inventory-driven (ZÄPFEL and MISSBAUER 1988). Those concepts, especially JIT production and lean production, promote a concentration of control activities on the (unproductive) stocks of current assets. Some components of the new concepts were already part of GUTENBERG's system, e.g., the close cooperation between supplier and customer (GUTENBERG 1951, p. 154), the establishment of production teams (GUTENBERG 1951, p. 25), and the decentralization of planning efforts (GUTENBERG 1962, pp. 60), but the question now is whether GUTENBERG's theory of the firm is also able to explain the inventory-controlled system as a whole.

The subject of interest in an inventory-controlled system reaches far beyond what is explained by GUTENBERG's theory of the firm. In order to maximize the advantages of an inventory-controlled system, the "institutions" involved in such a system must be fully recognized and identified.[2] Although institutional behavior was not really important in the context of the neoclassical production system, it seems worth considering whether GUTENBERG's theory of the firm can be enlarged by aspects of the new institutional economics (ALBACH 1989b, pp. 234) in order to explain the inventory-controlled production system and, in particular, the importance of the dispositive factor in this system.[3]

---

2 There is no doubt that GUTENBERG recognized the influence of organization and human behavior on firms' outputs. But, in order to obtain clear results, he ignores this influence in his theory of the firm (ALBACH 1982, pp. 20).

3 This corresponds with a basic attitude of the theory of the firm. It is regarded as a transitorial state (GUTENBERG 1989, p. 107) which has to be developed further and complemented by other theories if necessary (ALBACH 1989a, p. VII).

2 The Dispositive Factor in GUTENBERG's Theory of the Firm

To the extent that the dispositive factor is taken to explain efficient production processes[4], rational behavior on the part of economic agents is assumed. The agents have to plan the optimal use of resources in order to maximize the firm's productivity.[5] The competitive situation is completely known so that competitive advantages result first and foremost from increasing productivity and decreasing production costs. On these assumptions, the optimization of material and information inputs, lot sizes, and other parameters of the production process seems uncomplicated (GUTENBERG 1951, 1957, 1962). Classical contracts guarantee that supply risks are minimized. Labor contracts are signed which allow payment according to the production output (GUTENBERG 1951, pp. 47).[6] In summary, the production process can be planned and controlled by a central authority.

Regarding the overall capacity of a production system, GUTENBERG (1951, p. 126) formulated the law of balancing organizational plans. In the short run, bottlenecks in the production process have to be accepted, while in the long run the capacities of the system elements in question are enlarged. In the case of permanently growing firms, this law can be readily accepted. But if the market situation changes, GUTENBERG's law may cause considerable surplus capacity, because additional profits tend to be realized immediately even if they are not sustainable (SIMON 1988).

---

4 GUTENBERG interpreted the dispositive factor as a psychophysical subject which may also disturb the smooth relation between man's ratio and the result ("material") (GUTENBERG 1929, pp. 39). For example, the psychophysical subject suffers from a limited capability of reducing complexity and processing information. The psychological elements of economic actions reflect a good eye for business situations, energy to overcome difficulties, and the determination to make decisions. It is true that, theoretically, there exists only one optimal solution for each problem, but the psychophysical subject and the organizational component of the dispositive factor ("irrational factor") will then be eliminated as a reason for the problem (GUTENBERG 1929, p. 26; cf. also ALBACH 1982, p. 8). Deviations from the theoretical optimum may therefore also be explained by the complexity of the decision problem, for example.

5 Compared with this internal function of the dispositive factor, the external function of coordinating production and market demand, which was also recognized in the theory of the firm (HERMANN 1994, pp. 64), was not analyzed with the same effort because of its minor importance in seller's markets.

6 This does not mean that there is an original equivalence between payment and incentive systems. The connection between both systems was only considered later (ALBACH 1982, p. 7).

In GUTENBERG's theory of the firm, production process inefficiency is mainly due to technical and environmental causes. For example, important production problems result from machine breakdowns, unbalanced capacities of the different system elements, and delays in material procurement. Considering the market and the organization, all these defects can only by avoided at additional production costs. To avoid shortages of material, inventories can be increased. If inventory costs then become too high, it can be determined whether there exist suppliers with whom a permanent close cooperation can be agreed upon so that excess inventory costs can be obviated or inventories can even be eliminated.[7]

As can be seen from this discussion of the theory of the firm, the inventory level is not the starting point, but the result of a cost optimization procedure. Inventories are increased or reduced depending on cost considerations. On the one hand, a JIT supply system will be installed as soon as the customer can oblige his suppliers to accept all the costs which arise from frequent deliveries. In addition, multiple sourcing can further decrease costs by using market competition. Adopting this skimming strategy, profits are maximized (WILDEMANN 1988). On the other hand, JIT production can hardly be explained by GUTENBERG's theory. Although the theory explains flexible adaptations in respect of both machine intensities and the daily production period as a reaction to short-term disturbances of the production process, every deviation from the optimal process parameters causes costs which are not acceptable in the long run. It is notable that the narrow fields of application for a JIT system, as demarcated by GUTENBERG's theory of the firm, are still representative for many industries.[8]

---

7 However, as long as a decrease in current assets always results in an increase of fixed assets, this situation is not realized in the theory of the firm, which means that there still exists a systematic inventory (KISTNER 1994).

8 A comprehensive study of different German industries has shown that the JIT concept is still applied, and misinterpreted, as a simple instrument of rationalization for reducing production costs. The strategic orientation of the JIT concept is often ignored (REESE and GEISEL 1997).

3 The Inventory-Controlled Production System

3.1 The View of Institutional Economics

3.1.1 The Firm as Institution

Social and economic developments in the past decades have created a new situation in which the irrationality of the dispositive factor has receded step by step. Some milestones of these developments are manager enterprises with short-term labor contracts, high rates of innovation but short life-cycles of new products, and the dissemination of information and communication technologies inducing global competition.

The dispositive factor ran out of balance when meeting these developments. Growing task complexities revealed a lack of information and coordination both within and outside the firm. The centralization of management tasks caused an overload at the top management level. The incentive systems proved unspecific and not well suited for the emerging complex tasks. Altogether, a considerable unorganized complexity became established which planning efforts were hardly sufficient to resolve. Instead, a reorganization of the firm proved necessary in order to control the production process and management attitudes (ZÄPFEL 1991, p. 220).[9] Thus, comparing the main components of the dispositive factor and recalling the "artificial" character of the firm as compared with "natural" market coordination, institutionalization, i.e., organization, became the prominent component. While in GUTENGERG's theory of the firm the instrumental character of organization was stressed, it now became a precondition for every increase in the efficiency of a production process.

3.1.2 An Extended Definition of Costs

In order to establish, i.e. organize, a production system there is need for specific investment which can be interpreted as sunk costs. These costs comprise first, the costs of fixed and current assets which are necessary for production. These costs are obvious production costs. Additionally, the firm qua institution incurs the costs of institutionalizing and monitoring transactions, the so called transaction costs.[10]

---

9 The development of production concepts which are centered upon the firm's organizational structure (ZÄPFEL 1996, p. 256) became the basic idea.

10 Institutionalization usually means a network of contracts which cause contractual costs as well as pre-contractual and post-contractual costs (WILLIAMSON 1985, p. 20). An enumeration of these costs and problems of their measurability are given by ALBACH (1989c) and others. The important cost determinants can be found in THEUVSEN (1997).

Transactions are characterized by a certain degree of asset specifity for both customer and supplier (WILLIAMSON 1979, JOSKOW 1988) which is the decisive determinant of the level of these costs. Production costs are also influenced by these dependencies because there is a general trade-off between production and transaction costs. The less inputs are required for the production system, and therefore the lower the level of production costs, the higher the level of transaction costs that must be taken into account in order to maintain the relationships between supplier and customer. The dominance of an inventory-controlled production system can be observed if the savings in production costs are not overcompensated by additional transaction costs - provided the transactional conditions are constant.

3.1.3 The New Concept of Productivity

Following the new institutional economics, the firm's productivity is not only determined by classical input-output relations but is also influenced by other parameters. Less productivity can also be attributed to human behavior which violates the classical rationality principle insofar as there exist asymmetric information (GROSSMAN and HART 1983) and individual property rights to select uses of the resources (ALCHIAN and DEMSETZ 1972). Under these circumstances, the self-interest of economic agents becomes visible so that any lack of organization leads to reduced human efforts and may prevent the firm from reaching Pareto-optimal solutions. Adequate incentive and control schemes to prevent these tendencies are characterized as the management of no-confidence (HERMANN 1994, p. 89). A controversial issue is whether these additional measures are really necessary if the coalition of heterogeneous attitudes and interests is intended to be long-lasting and not to be readily terminable.[11] This controversy is also a feature of assessments of an inventory-controlled production system. On the one hand, teamwork is a constitutive element of this system in order to maximize system productivity. Mutual confidence between the team members is therefore absolutely necessary. On the other hand, there is some empirical evidence of resolute self-control within each team. Not only are external monitoring activities minimized by this control, but there emerges also growing pressure on the team members to perform well which limits the membership to a certain period.

The insights provided by the new institutional economics show that the productivity of a firm is also influenced by property rights. A concentration of property rights serves to internalize external effects and thus to prevent disturbances in the production process. Conversely, economic institutions can be scaled down

---

[11] In this connection, the hypotheses of individualism and opportunism are opposed to each other (PICOT, DIETL, and FRANCK 1997, pp. 39). Individualism is based on a fair safeguarding of one's own interests, whereas opportunism means that advantages are also realized with a great deal of cunning and without bearing the costs.

by selling property rights and concentrating on core activities. These decisions are based on a comparison between the advantages of an internalization of external effects and the transaction costs of property rights (ORDELHEIDE 1993, p. 1842). Adopting this result for the inventory-controlled system, for example, unfinished products, which are less specific, should be procured from an external supplier because the transaction costs are overcompensated by an increase in productivity.

Every smooth procurement of goods is closely related to a perfect information system. Information asymmetries interfere with an efficient exchange of goods.[12] Transaction costs increase and do not permit the realization of economies of scale. Furthermore, inventories remain at a higher level, because incomplete information may cause shortages and thus reduce productivity. For example, shortages may occur due to hidden quality defects or suppliers' contracts with other customers. Such behavior uncertainties can be minimized if long-term single sourcing agreements are reached and the information systems of both parties are interconnected.

In an inventory-controlled production system, the definition of productivity must also be extended in respect of the time-dimension. While flexibility and short-term productivity usually conflict, flexibility should be interpreted in an inventory-controlled system as a form of long-term productivity (CORSTEN 1996, p. 3, PICOT, DIETL and FRANCK 1997, p. 285).[13]

The new dimensions of productivity facilitate a better treatment of internal and external uncertainties (REESE 1991, p. 370). The flexibility of the production system obviates high transaction costs of information procurement without increasing the risk of efficiency losses.[14] As regards a KANBAN-controlled production system, these consequences of flexibility become immediately obvious.

---

12 To the extent that opportunistic behavior cannot be excluded from the analysis, three risks of information asymmetries have to be distinguished: hidden characteristics, hidden intention ("holdup") and hidden action ("moral hazard") (SPREMANN 1990, p. 566).

13 Further objectives of an inventory-controlled system, as e.g. zero defects and minimal flowtimes of the products, can be expressed by productivity and flexibility measures.

14 On the other hand, flexibility usually causes additional production and transaction costs. The optimal degree of flexibility is therefore a matter of a long-term cost calculation.

3.2 General Principles of an Inventory-Controlled Production System

Every inventory-controlled production system is based on the wider definitions of cost and productivity. The uncertainty[15] and specifity[16] of transactions, as well as the organizational behavior which can be manipulated by the "dispositive" factor, are thereby explicitly taken into account.

Inventories become directly controlled parameters, because they are symptoms of uncertainty and specifity in the supplier-customer relations:

- Uncertainty in the form of stochastic demands and unforeseeable economic developments requires (safety) stocks which hide planning defects.

- Specifity because specific products generally require longer order times so that inventories obviously point to a lack of coordination between supplier and customer.

To uncover the causes of these problems, it is necessary to look far beyond their symptoms. In reality, human behavior is rationally bounded and opportunistic (WILLIAMSON 1991). Controlling and decreasing inventories therefore means revealing and getting rid of behavioral defects by reorganization and complexity reduction.[17]

Uncertainty as well as specifity are pre-eminently descriptions of the firm with its given organization and environment. In order to control both parameters, some general principles have been developed as a foundation for an inventory-controlled production system:[18]

- Decentralization of inventory control. By reunifying competences and responsibilities in operating units, system flexibility can be increased.

---

15 Due to the new institutional economics, uncertainty results from a coincidence of system dynamics and complexity.

16 The different forms of specifity are given in WILLIAMSON (1989, p. 143).

17 Defects of the coordination, information, and incentive systems are, at the same time, symptoms of a suboptimal productivity.

18 Even if the system characteristics can hardly be completely specified there seems a broad agreement on these principles (cf. ZÄPFEL 1996, p. 216, and CORSTEN 1996, p. 6).

- Teamwork. Self-coordination and self-organization allow a better use of productivity and flexibility potentials. Organizational learning can be optimized.[19] The existence of semi-autonomous teams leads to an efficient use of inputs so that procurement and production times are reduced and inventories can be lowered.

- Modularization (PICOT and REICHWALD 1994, p. 555). Asset specifity is reduced by the standardization and multiple use of system components. The consequential positive effects on inventories are especially apparent when the interfaces between modules are clearly and completely defined.[20]

- Pull Strategy. The vertical integration of modules allows every customer module to express his demand as late as possible. This is why a certain degree of flexibility is required for the supplier modules.[21]

- Integration of material and information flows. The information and material flows have to be linked together to facilitate prompt reactions. If one considers the KANBAN principle, it is evident that both the relevant information and the materials are delivered just in time. The two integration principles are closely connected with each other.

These general principles are primarily intended to improve the control of current assets. The consequences for the firm's performance depend on how the parameters specifity and uncertainty are affected by an appropriate development of the "dispositive" factor.

---

19 Undoubtedly, the process of continuous improvement in the working groups ("Kaizen") is most important for every inventory-controlled production system.

20 The principle of modularization can be extended to the principle of segmentation. Building production segments causes a specialization of operating units so that the portion of productive times can be considerably increased. As in the case of assembly-line production, inventories are dropped and transaction costs are also reduced (WILDEMANN 1995).

21 Generally, the pull principle can be combined with the push principle without risking the efficiency of an inventory-controlled production system. Nevertheless, the pull principle belongs to the constitutive characteristics, because it can never be given up totally and under general assumptions.

4 The Role of the "Dispositive" Factor

4.1 Main Activity Areas

As can be concluded from the preceding sections, the dispositive factor in an inventory-controlled production system has first of all to deal with organizational decisions.[22] The "irrational" layer of the dispositive factor is not excluded from these considerations but is explicitly taken into account by allowing for human bounded rationality (SIMON 1979), the unorganized complexity of decision problems[23], and the resultant behavioral and informational uncertainties. A prominent dispositive task in an inventory-controlled production system is the diminishing of the influence of the "irrational" layer by organizing the decision problems according to human abilities.

The subjects of dispositive tasks are both internal and external transactions (REESE 1991, p. 370, THEUVSEN 1997, p. 976). Internal transactions, especially the realization of optimal input combinations within the firm's sphere of activity, are not merely undertaken in pursuit of maximum short-term productivity, but also have to fulfil high flexibility criteria. In this manner, the bounded rationality of the firm's agents is accommodated in a double way: first of all by simple task modules with definite input-output relations, and second by exogeneously given requirements of system flexibility (REESE 1991, p. 385). Both preconditions have to be set by the dispositive factor. By establishing appropriate mechanisms, the distribution of further dispositive tasks between the firm's owner and his agents is rearranged. The production process can then be rationally planned to a greater extent. The origin of innovation processes switches from internal sources to market demands. The ideal of SCHUMPETER's entrepreneur and visionary leader of the firm becomes less important. The dispositive factor is now oriented towards continuously improving the production system, although certain basic system innovations are still possible.

---

22 From the standpoint of decision theory, organizational decisions have to be distinguished from market decisions (LAUX and LIERMANN 1997, p. 13, REESE 1994, p. 17). This distinction is important, because organization is a result of a special decision process with no immediate influence on the firm's market position. After the organization has been established it serves as a limiting factor for future market decisions.

23 Whenever unorganized complexity arises, there still remains the chance of more organization. As a rule, unorganized complexity is therefore concentrated on decision problems within the firm (REESE 1994, p. 11), but strategic cooperation with suppliers may also permit measures of complexity reduction beyond the firm's scope.

As far as external transactions are concerned, the dispositive factor continues to play the role of a mediator between market and hierarchy. The extended cost definition may cause revised decisions on firm size[24] and market relations[25]. It is again most important to define strategies which have to be taken into account in the planning activities of the operating units of the firm. Prominent examples of these strategic decisions are the implementation of JIT cooperation, global sourcing, and total quality management. As compared with the internal transactions, complexity cannot be totally eliminated in case of the external transactions so that there always remains some residual uncertainty. This means that an essential task of the dispositive factor is to concentrate the remaining uncertainty by further extending the system's flexibility.

4.2 Design of the Incentive System

The rights of residual control[26], that is, the authority to use resources, are transferred to the organizational units as soon as an inventory-controlled production system is installed. As these modules are usually non-hierarchically organized, the result is team decisions on how to spend the resources. Whenever property rights are split between several persons, opportunistic and bounded rational behavior involve the danger of inefficient uses of resources (PICOT, REICHWALD, and WIGAND 1996, p. 39). Incentives and monitoring become inevitable in order to sustain the owner's rights to the residual returns.

On the one hand, it becomes obvious that the dispositive factor - as it was already derived in GUTENBERG's theory of the firm (1951) - cannot be assigned to a certain group of organization members, because planning and organizing activities were executed from the top to the bottom of the firm over all hierarchical levels.[27] On the other hand, the corporate control tasks of the dispositive factor grow and become more complex in order to maximize the firm's productivity. The two aspects come together in the requirements of hierarchical integration. An incentive system which is based merely on production output fails, because production times and production outputs are largely fixed and cannot be significantly improved in an inventory-controlled system. This is why those efforts, which are expressed by human flexibility and willingness to work, have to be adequately rewarded as well. This component of an incentive system is far more important in

---

24 For example, concerning economies of scope and outsourcing of production stages.

25 For example, considering the type of contracting.

26 The rights of residual control have to be distinguished from the owner's rights to decide upon the residual returns which remain with the firm's owners (HART 1995, p. 63).

27 Overcoming the traditional division of labor in this way may be interpreted as a fresh attempt at the "detaylorization" of labor (PICOT and REICHWALD 1994, p. 553).

the case of an inventory-controlled production system than in classical flow shop or job shop production (REESE 1993).

In a turbulent environment, efforts cannot be supervised easily so that the costs of monitoring are considerable. Though the method of building modules can counteract this tendency to some degree, the result will usually be second best solutions, which means that efforts are stimulated in advance and are not rewarded on the basis of observation and control.[28] In other words, team incentives have not yet reached the practical relevance that their importance deserves (GROB 1993).

Moral hazard risks are reduced if the dispositive factor practises the management of confidence instead of the management of no-confidence. The resulting positive transaction atmosphere (OUCHI 1980) provokes intrinsic incentives which can, together with the type of payment and other extrinsic incentives, ameliorate the productivity of the production process. The final stage of this development is a modified corporate culture. The way there is actually not very concretely traced, though there are several confidence-building elements among the general principles of an inventory-controlled system which still have to be activated. It seems necessary to compare the transaction costs of building confidence with the agency costs which otherwise arise.

Within the semi-autonomous operating teams, the dispositive factor has first and foremost to implement all the functions of planning, coordination, and control. In many cases, several boundary conditions[29] limit these functions to simple routine measures. In the extreme case, a mechanism of self-control may not require any further disposition provided that the production process is not subject to heavy disturbances. Uncertainty which is caused by a fluctuating demand or unreliable machines is accommodated by system flexibility.

Shifting the rights of residual control to a team leads to another attenuation of property rights. As the responsible agent does not have to bear the full consequences of any action or decision, the operating team has to manage a further problem of moral hazard, namely that of shirking (ALCHIAN and DEMSETZ 1972, p. 780). This is a serious problem, because cooperative behavior can no longer be manipulated by incentives from outside the team (HERMANN 1994, p. 94). This is why there exists just one solution, namely, social control. This control is practised non-hierarchically if the external conditions restrict the property rights.

---

[28] Second best solutions differ from first best solutions in that moral hazard cannot be excluded in advance (JENNERGREN 1980). Welfare losses and monitoring costs, which are caused by moral hazard, belong to agency costs (JENSEN and MECKLING 1976, p. 308).

[29] Among these conditions are the needs for immediate order processing and maximum utilization of the given "lean" assets.

These conditions are called property surrogates. As already shown, some of these surrogates are established in an inventory-controlled production system. The pull strategy, as well as the integrated information processing, limit the rights of residual control so far that production delays are discovered immediately and lead to benefit losses for each team member. This is why shirking by a single team member will never be accepted. If sufficient surrogates do not exist, any hierarchical self-organization would, by means of monitoring, produce the same effect but system flexibility would, to a considerable extent, disappear (PICOT, DIETL and FRANCK 1997, p. 307).

4.3 Design of the Information and Communication System

In a dynamic world, the tasks of the dispositive factor are grouped around the procurement and processing of information. Therefore, the construction of an information system is an essential task of the dispositive factor. In a decentralized production system, the amount of information supplied will strictly correspond to the responsibilities of its recipient. In accordance with the general principles of an inventory-controlled system, the information should be procured as late as possible by means of KANBANs as information media, for example. This "lean" procurement of information causes considerable system instability and losses of efficiency when only slight disturbances occur. To mitigate this dilemma, the dispositive factor can choose between two alternatives. Thus, the system characteristics can either be modified in order to further reduce the costs of information; or, information may be substituted by additional flexibility if it should still remain too expensive.

The information flow can be easily standardized in an inventory-controlled system due to the application of the principle of modularization and a complete specification of the module interfaces. As a consequence, information requirements can be precisely fixed by the information processing units.[30] Furthermore, transaction costs can be significantly reduced by choosing simplified order policies and similar measures. Finally, there remains the task of establishing the working units in the information system. Their relevant costs are fixed, and represent an investment, because they do not depend on the number of transactions.[31] In summary, the cost minimization solution is optimal. From this it can be deduced that electronic data processing should be restricted to those areas in which standardization leads to permanent transaction cost savings. This applies, e.g., to close cooperation with first-layer suppliers.

---

30 In a KANBAN-controlled system this information is fully contained on the KANBANS.

31 These costs belong to the set-up costs of the organizational design (WINDSPERGER 1996, p. 29).

Information systems, which support mere administrative or simple dispositive tasks, reduce the flexibility of the whole production system. This is why the information system should be less standardized the greater the degree of flexibility that is required, either because of market conditions, or as a result of the production structure. Exceptional, specific transactions call for measures which have no lasting effect on the organizational design. They arise first and foremost from the customer orientation of the system and have to be accommodated by the existing organizational flexibility (REESE 1991, p. 379).

Summarizing, as it is conceived in an inventory-controlled production system, information represents an additional input that is similar to material inputs.[32] In contrast to its treatment in a centralized production planning and control system, information is not stored over a long period in a global data base, but is volatile and has to be immediately processed. Hence, in accordance with GUTENBERG's theory of the firm, the dispositive task is extended to an overall combination of all elemental input components, with special attention to the information input. The production process itself, of course, has to be evaluated anew under the perspective of transaction costs of which the information system is the crucial determinant.

4.4 Vertical Coordination

The realization of the decentralization and pull principles ensures that the vast majority of transactions takes place between operating units. In general, transactions can be controlled by signing contracts.[33] Assuming that uncertainty will never completely disappear, but has to be parried by system flexibility, the form of contractual relations is basically influenced by the specifity and number of transactions (WILLIAMSON 1985, p. 79). It follows that the "dispositive" factor is not confronted with a significant planning problem in vertically coordinating different modules but, in selecting an efficient type of contract, does meet a challenge. Vertical coordination may take the form of either internal or external transactions. Internally, each operating unit receives a task from its successor due to the pull principle. Usually, those transactions are highly specific, often recurring, and part of the firm's core business.[34] Under these circumstances, a relational contract has to be concluded which does not specify details, for example exact supply quantities,

---

[32] In this context, the relevant difference between material and information is that information can be used many times. This is particularly important in the case of all technical production data.

[33] The new institutional economics distinguishes between classical, neoclassical, and relational contracts (MACNEIL 1978, WILLIAMSON 1985).

[34] In these operating units, which are close to the customer, the limits of modularization are obvious (PICOT, DIETL, and FRANCK 1997, p. 282).

but is merely a declaration of intent to cooperate on a permanent basis. As continuous transactions are involved, the supplying modules in an inventory-controlled system provide an adequate capacity. Therefore, serious supply problems should not be expected. If they occur, they are indicative of temporary internal problems in a single supply module and signal a suboptimal use of the rights of residual control.

A decision in favor of external transactions means that services, or materials, have to be bought from external suppliers. Such an outsourcing is not only a question of the optimal firm size (PICOT 1991) but has to be considered together with another strategic decision:[35] Any external vertical coordination can be managed as an investment in long-term cooperation or as a skimming procedure. In principle, external transactions are restricted to those situations in which low or medium specifity can be assumed.

In the case of medium transaction specifity, permanent supply relations are worth considering. They can be developed into extensive supply networks (WILDEMANN 1997). Assuming a reasonable number of transactions, relational contracting is again applicable. But as the customer is not fully informed about all technical and economic details known to suppliers, it becomes a fundamental task of the dispositive factor to invest in measures of confidence-building and to compensate for information asymmetries before a contract is entered. The intended long-term cooperation usually offers good chances of amortizing these transaction costs.

In order to avoid the risks of ex ante information asymmetries, the dispositive factor can choose between two procedures, screening and signalling. Screening requires the firm to take measures to improve the informational situation, e.g. by inspecting suppliers' sites and studying documents and records. Conversely, signalling is initiated by the other party. For example, quality certificates according to ISO 9000ff are presented to demonstrate the suppliers' capability and reduce information asymmetries (WEISENFELD-SCHENK 1997). Which solution is to be preferred depends again on the level of transaction costs.

Even if a contract is agreed upon, the possibility of opportunistic behavior cannot be precluded. Permanent investment activities may result in a situation of bilateral monopoly[36] with an extremely high asset specifity on both sides (DIETL 1993, p. 111, MÜHLENKAMP 1997, p. 105) which may be turned to advantage

---

35 Here, that part of the dispositive factor is used which can be identified as top management.

36 The transition from a low specifity state to a high specifity state is also described as fundamental transformation (WILLIAMSON 1985, p. 61). The final state symbolizes a lock-in-effect (HART and HOLMSTRÖM 1987, p. 72).

by renegotiating. Therefore, two further dispositive tasks arise. On the one hand, it is necessary to analyze whether the firm itself can improve its benefits. Skimming the suppliers' quasi rents may lead, of course, to a loss of reputation and adverse selection[37] so that the use of this strategy[38] will definitely depend on market competition.

On the other hand, the second party to the contract may react to the monopoly situation by making new demands.[39] To avert such a danger, preventive measures have to be taken by the dispositive factor. Though guarantees, securities and other "economic equivalents of hostages" have proved to be effective (MÜHLENKAMP 1997, pp. 130), these measures are hardly compatible with relational contracts and cannot be imposed. As a consequence, there still remains the alternative of establishing additional flexibility by, e.g., resorting to dual sourcing or the stimulation of competition in the supply markets.

The application of the principle of modularization in an inventory-controlled production system causes asset specifity to decrease from module to module along the production stages. The advantages of building modules are initially revealed at the early stages of component assembly. As soon as asset specifity has reached an advanced level, cooperation with external suppliers needs to be seriously re-evaluated. The case of low specifity within the internal area of an inventory-controlled system is therefore not very realistic as long as an efficient organization is assumed. Nevertheless, should this case arise, dispositive tasks analogous to those which are a feature of the neoclassical theory have to be added to the task manual of the dispositive factor.

5 Some Perspectives on Production Strategies

Inventory-controlled production has been developed as an answer to the growing complexity of management in dynamic and global markets. It now represents a strong challenge to the dispositive factor. Certainly, the problems of operations

37 Strong pressure on the suppliers eventually leads to a situation in which the market is controlled by those suppliers who produce low quality products. This corresponds to an adverse selection (AKERLOF 1970).

38 This strategy must not be mistaken for a skimming strategy. A skimming strategy requires contracts which are based on the classical law of contract.

39 Here, in contrast to the preceding results, measures of confidence-building obviously cause increases of transaction costs.

management have greatly decreased. The partitioning of large decision problems by delegating decision responsibilities, less optimization, and a tendency towards the self-control of the production system exemplify simplifications of the planning process. But, simultaneously, new organizational problems have arisen which first of all concern the control of human resources within and outside the firm.

Productivity gains may result from specialization and time efficient procurement, but at additional transaction costs. The cost minimization task of production management is therefore extended to production and transaction costs. In following that direction, the design of an efficient incentive system is of paramount importance. As in the case of a supply contract, an incentive system has to take into account that the use of resources is, to a great extent, stochastic. Therefore, the transaction specifity determines the type of contract which should be entered. In the case of low specifity, classical contracts will be efficient. All details can be embodied in those contracts and there is no need for any management of confidence. Transaction costs can be neglected so that the efficiency of an inventory-controlled production system solely depends on production costs. The relevant markets are systematically skimmed.

The realization of an inventory-controlled production system is more probable in the case of medium or high transaction specifity. Here, relational contracts are appropriate. The resulting transaction costs reflect a management of confidence by the dispositive factor. As soon as the behavioral uncertainties of the contractual parties have disappeared, the production system once installed should prove stable due to the asset specifity. Nevertheless, it is worth mentioning that confidence-building measures do not relieve a firm from the maintaining of permanent relations with suppliers and other agents. It remains to be seen whether developments beyond the self-control and simplification of planning as, e.g., any self-organization of the system (WARNECKE 1993), will contribute to a further dissemination of inventory-controlled production.

References:

Akerlof, G.A., The Market for "Lemons": Qualitative Uncertainty and the Market Mechanism, in: Quarterly Journal of Economics 84, 1970, pp. 488-500

Albach, H., Organisations- und Personaltheorie, in: H. Koch, ed., Neuere Entwicklungen in der Unternehmenstheorie, Wiesbaden 1982, pp. 1-22

Albach, H., ed., Zur Theorie der Unternehmung. Schriften und Reden von E. Gutenberg. Aus dem Nachlaß, Berlin et al. 1989a

Albach, H., Die Betriebswirtschaftslehre: Eine Wissenschaft, in: H. Albach, ed., Zur Theorie der Unternehmung, Berlin et al. 1989b, pp. 213-266

Albach, H., Kosten, Transaktionen und externe Effekte im betrieblichen Rechnungswesen, in: H. Albach, ed., Organisation. Mikroökonomische Theorie und ihre Anwendungen, Wiesbaden 1989c, pp. 27-42

Alchian, A.A., Demsetz, H., Production, Information Costs, and Economic Organization, in: American Economic Review 62, 1972, pp. 777-795

Corsten, H., Neuere Organisationsformen der Produktion - Ansätze und konzeptionelle Gemeinsamkeiten, Discussion paper, Kaiserslautern 1996

Dietl, H., Institutionen und Zeit, Tübingen 1993

Grob, R., Betriebliche Leistungs-Anreizsysteme für Arbeitsgruppen, in: H. Corsten, Th. Will, eds., Lean Production, Stuttgart et al. 1993, pp. 158-175

Grossman, S.J., Hart, O.D., An Analysis of the Principal-Agent Problem, in: Econometrica 51, 1983, pp. 7-45

Gutenberg, E., Die Unternehmung als Gegenstand betriebswirtschaftlicher Theorie, Berlin and Wien 1929

Gutenberg, E., Grundlagen der Betriebswirtschaftslehre, vol. 1, Die Produktion, Berlin et al. 1951

Gutenberg, E., Sortenproblem und Losgröße, in: H. Seischab, K. Schwantag, eds., Handwörterbuch der Betriebswirtschaft, 3rd ed., Stuttgart 1957, pp. 4897-4906

Gutenberg, E., Unternehmensführung - Organisation und Entscheidungen, Wiesbaden 1962

Gutenberg, E., Rückblicke, in: H. Albach, ed., Zur Theorie der Unternehmung, Berlin et al. 1989, pp. 1-109

Hart, O., Firms, Contracts, and Financial Structure, Oxford et al. 1995

Hart, O., Holmström, B., The Theory of Contracts, in: T. Bewley, ed., Advances in Economic Theory, Cambridge 1987, pp. 71-155

Hermann, Th., Zur Theoriegeschichte des dispositiven Faktors, Stuttgart 1994

Jennergren, L.P., On the Design of Incentives in Business Firms - A Survey of Some Research, in: Management Science 26, 1980, pp. 180-201

Jensen, M.C., Meckling, W.H., Theory of the Firm: Managerial Behavior, Agency Costs, and Ownership Structure, in: Journal of Financial Economics 3, 1976, pp. 305-360

Joskow, P.L., Asset Specifity and the Structure of Vertical Relationships: Empirical Evidence, in: Journal of Law, Economics, and Organization 31, 1988, pp. 95-117

Kistner, K.-P., Die Substitution von Umlaufvermögen durch Anlagevermögen im Rahmen der Produktion auf Abruf, in: Operations Research-Spektrum 16, 1994, pp. 125-134

Laux, H., Liermann, F., Grundlagen der Organisation, 4th ed., Berlin et al. 1997

Macneil, I.R., Contracts - Adjustments of Long-Term Economic Relations under Classical, Neoclassical, and Relational Contract Law, in: Northwestern University Law Review 72, 1978, pp. 854-906

Mühlenkamp, H., Eine ökonomische Analyse ausgewählter institutioneller Arrangements zur Erfüllung öffentlicher Aufgaben, Habilitation thesis, Lüneburg 1997

Ordelheide, D., Institutionelle Theorie und Unternehmung, in: W. Wittmann et al., eds., Handwörterbuch der Betriebswirtschaft, 5th ed., Stuttgart 1993, pp.1838-1855

Ouchi, W.G., Markets, Bureaucracies and Clans, in: Administrative Science Quarterly 25, 1980, pp. 129-141

Picot, A., Ein neuer Ansatz zur Gestaltung der Leistungstiefe, in: Zeitschrift für betriebswirtschaftliche Forschung 43, 1991, pp. 336-357

Picot, A., Dietl, H., Franck, E., Organisation - Eine ökonomische Perspektive, Stuttgart 1997

Picot, A., Reichwald, R., Auflösung der Unternehmung?, in: Zeitschrift für Betriebswirtschaft 64, 1994, pp. 547-570

Picot, A., Reichwald, R., Wigand, R.T., Die grenzenlose Unternehmung, Wiesbaden 1996

Porter, M., Competitive Strategy, New York 1980

Reese, J., Unternehmensflexibilität, in: K.-P. Kistner, R. Schmidt, eds., Unternehmensdynamik, Wiesbaden 1991, pp. 361-387
Reese, J., Is Lean Production Really Lean?, in: G. Fandel, Th. Gulledge, A. Jones, eds., Operations Research in Production Plannung and Control, Berlin et al. 1993, pp. 49-70
Reese, J., Theorie der Organisationsbewertung, 2nd ed., München and Wien 1994
Reese, J., Geisel, R., JIT Procurement. A Comparison of Current Practices in German Manufacturing Industries, in: European Journal of Purchasing & Supply Management 3, 1997, pp. 147-154
Simon, H., Management strategischer Wettbewerbsvorteile, in: Zeitschrift für Betriebswirtschaft 58, 1988, pp. 461-480
Simon, H.A., Rational Decision Making in Business Organizations, in: American Economic Review 69, 1979, pp. 493-513
Spremann, K., Asymmetrische Information, in: Zeitschrift für Betriebswirtschaft 60, 1990, pp. 561-586
Theuvsen, L., Interne Organisation und Transaktionskostenansatz, in: Zeitschrift für Betriebswirtschaft 67, 1997, pp. 971-996
Warnecke, H.-J., Revolution der Unternehmenskultur: Das fraktale Unternehmen, 2nd ed., Berlin et al. 1993
Weisenfeld-Schenk, U., Die Nutzung von Zertifikaten als Signal für Produktqualität. Eine informationsökonomische Betrachtung, in: Zeitschrift für Betriebswirtschaft 67, 1997, pp. 21-39
Wildemann, H., Produktionssynchrone Beschaffung, München 1988
Wildemann, H., Transaktionskostenreduzierung durch Fertigungssegmentierung, in: Die Betriebswirtschaft 55, 1995, pp. 783-795
Wildemann, H., Koordination von Unternehmensnetzwerken, in: Zeitschrift für Betriebswirtschaft 67, 1997, pp. 417-439
Williamson, O.E., Transaction-Cost Economics: The Governance of Contractual Relations, in: Journal of Law and Economics 22, 1979, pp. 233-261
Williamson, O.E., The Economic Institutions of Capitalism. Firms, Markets, Relational Contracting, New York 1985
Williamson, O.E., Transaction Cost Economics, in: R. Schmalensee, R. Willig, eds., Handbook of Industrial Organization, vol. I, Amsterdam 1989, pp. 135-182
Williamson, O.E., Comparative Economic Organization: The Analysis of Discrete Structural Alternatives, in: Administrative Science Quarterly 36, 1991, pp. 269-291
Windsperger, J., Transaktionskostenansatz der Entstehung der Unternehmensorganisation, Heidelberg 1996
Zäpfel, G., Produktionslogistik, in: Zeitschrift für Betriebswirtschaft 61, 1991, pp. 209-235
Zäpfel, G., Grundzüge des Produktions- und Logistikmanagement, Berlin 1996
Zäpfel, G., Missbauer, H., Neuere Konzepte der Produktionsplanung und -steuerung in der Fertigungsindustrie, in: Wirtschaftswissenschaftliches Studium 17, 1988, pp. 127-131

Summary

Global competition in many industries has led to new production and management concepts. As regards the applicability of an inventory-controlled production system, there is still considerable uncertainty in both theory and practice. The main problem is to identify the role of planning and organization in such a system and to redefine the task of the "dispositive factor" as compared with traditional production management. By using the new institutional economics approach, this article shows that Erich GUTENBERG's theory of the firm can explain inventory-controlled production, though the main areas of management have to be shifted towards such organizational tasks as, for example, constructing incentive and information systems. A generalized productivity oriented view of the firm remains relevant if basic premises of GUTENBERG's theory of the firm, which were formulated for reasons of simplification, are modified according to the complexity of current economic developments.

Dynamic Models Based on Erich Gutenberg's Approach to Production Theory

A. Luhmer[1]

Overview

- In 1951, Erich Gutenberg proposed an approach to production modelling that is especially suitable for managerial purposes.
- Gutenberg's concept assumes input and output explicitly to depend on the current condition of production equipment. Gutenberg production models can easily be dynamised by supplementing a formulation of the dynamic laws of change of equipment condition.
- The present paper gives a short exposition of Gutenberg's approach, and its dynamic extension, and considers two applications in some detail: machining processes and aircraft fueling.
- It is shown how to construct a neoclassical substitutive production function from the dynamic extension of a Gutenberg production model of machining processes under steady state conditions.
- Constructing Gutenberg type production models is highly dependent on the specific application and opens up a field of joint interdisciplinary research by engineers and management scientists.

Keywords: Production Theory, Dynamic Models, Machining Processes, Aircraft Fueling.

---

1 Professor Dr. Alfred Luhmer, Otto-von-Guericke-University Magdeburg, Faculty of Economics and Management, Universitätsplatz 2, D-39106 Magdeburg, e-mail: luhmer@ww.uni-magdeburg.de

1 Introduction

In 1951, *Erich Gutenberg* published the first volume of his magnum opus "Grundlagen der Betriebswirtschaftslehre" (Foundations of Managerial Economics). In his view a business enterprise is essentially a productive system embedded in markets for inputs and outputs. Inputs require cash outflows and outputs yield cash inflows. But cash inflows from a productive activity occur only after a time lag and are subject to risk. Therefore, capital is needed to bridge this lag and to bear the risk. Consequently, the system is viable only if it earns what is needed to remunerate capital for these services after having covered the outlays for the other inputs. From this point of view business management is composed of the following three key functional areas: 1. production (along with procurement of input), 2. marketing output, and 3. financing this process. To each of them *Gutenberg* devoted one volume of his "Grundlagen".

The characteristic which distinguishes *Gutenberg*'s approach from standard economics texts is its systematic managerial orientation. The result of productive activity has first to be explained from independent influences either determined exogeneously or by management's decisions. Based on such an explanation it is then possible to enquire into the principles of economic choice of values for the variables under management's control.

For *Gutenberg*'s purpose a classical production function

$$x = f(r_1, ..., r_n)$$

(where x denotes output and the r_i input quantities) is not a satisfactory model of manufacturing production, because it does not capture management's control variables at all. Manufacturing inputs are decision consequences rather than decision variables. Therefore *Gutenberg* offers an alternative approach. He proceeds from a required output quantity x determined on a hierarchical level superior to production management. Production management then has to adapt its control variables such that the output target x is met at a minimal cost. Output usually requires processing at several workplaces each of which may be chosen from among several alternatives. Several types m of workplaces may be appropriate for each processing function required. Therefore, for each task and each workplace type m, one has to decide on: 1. the number n_m of workplaces (and equipment) to be used, 2. the working time τ_m per week, and 3. the output rate d_m per busy time. The decision variables are chosen to meet the output target x. This requires an *output target condition*

$$x \leqq \sum_m n_m \cdot \tau_m \cdot d_m \tag{1}$$

for each processing task necessary to complete the kind of product under consideration.

In order to explain the input quantities required for production, *Gutenberg* focuses on the individual workplaces. For each workplace and each kind of input i he defines an *input function*

$$r_i = f_i(z_1, z_2, ..., z_v; d)$$

to determine the quantity r_i of input i which is needed per hour of busy time at the workplace considered. This quantity is a function of the output rate d per unit of busy time and the *state of the equipment* in use at the workplace. (See *Gutenberg* 1971, p. 330). The state of equipment is captured by the variables $\mathbf{z}{:=}(z_1, z_2, ..., z_v)$. According to *Gutenberg* the z-variables can be adapted within certain limits determined by the design of the equipment. He mentions the coating of melting furnaces, the quality of the cutting tool and the gears used on a lathe. In these instances the z-variables are decided upon before deciding on utilization. In his exposition *Gutenberg* takes the values of the z-variables as given. Based on this assumption he derives production cost as a function of the control variables only. For every output target x one can set up and solve the problem of minimising production cost. By solving this problem for parametrically varying x production management is able to report a cost function $C(x)$ to the marketing department where it may serve as a basis for optimal decisions on output selling price and quantity. It is in this way that *Gutenberg*'s approach supports decentralised decision making. Marketing management gets the cost function and need not worry about details of production control. Production management, in turn, is only charged with the problem of how to produce given product quantities at minimal cost. This decomposition of the overall management task works without loss of optimality.

In general, however, the state of equipment is not discretionary as originally conceived by *Gutenberg*. On the contrary, it is subject to continual change from wear and tear. The performance of a machine tool, for example, depends on past utilisation. Wear and tear may result in an increase of the fraction defective, trigger rework, and require more frequent tuning and setup. Consequently, the production process itself governs the change in the z-variables. Only an explicit formulation of the laws of wear and tear or, in other words, the dynamics of the z-variables is needed to turn *Gutenberg*'s theory of production into a full-fledged dynamic production model. In fact, this approach leads quite naturally to an optimal control formulation of industrial production problems (as noted in Luhmer 1975).

The purpose of the present paper is to describe the general structure of a dynamic version of *Gutenberg*'s production model conceived along these lines and to mention possible measures of the z-variables (section 2). Some very simple examples of application are also presented (section 3). For the sake of mathematical simplicity they are restricted to a variety that is solvable without variational methods and the theory of optimal control.

2 The General Model

2.1 Structure

A general and concise formulation of *Gutenberg*'s production model treats both input and output as resulting from the performance of the productive system. Both are considered to depend on management's decisions on the control variables. A vector $\mathbf{y}$ is composed of input and output components. Positive and negative components represent outputs and inputs respectively. For each workplace m an activity vector $\mathbf{a}_m$ is defined. The components of this vector are functions of the state $\mathbf{z}_m$ of the equipment and its utilisation rate d_m. They represent input or output rates of the workplace per hour of working time. Therefore the vector of input and output quantities per week can be written as $\tau_m \cdot \mathbf{a}_m(\mathbf{z}_m, d_m)$. *Gutenberg*'s production model can therefore be interpreted as a generalised activity analysis model in which working hours per week play the rôle of activity levels, while input and output

Figure 1: Static *Gutenberg* production model

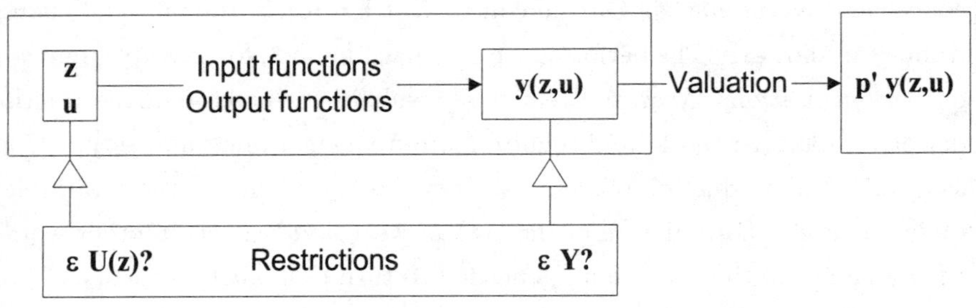

coefficients are functions of the condition $\mathbf{z}_m$ of the equipment and of the production rate d_m per working hour (see *Albach* 1962 and *Kloock* 1969). Let $\mathbf{z}$ denote a matrix of z-variables for all workplaces and

$$\mathbf{u} := \left\{ \begin{pmatrix} \tau_1 \\ d_1 \end{pmatrix}, \ldots, \begin{pmatrix} \tau_m \\ d_m \end{pmatrix}, \ldots \begin{pmatrix} \tau_M \\ d_M \end{pmatrix} \right\}$$

the production control decision. The production vector of the entire shop can then be written as

$$\mathbf{y}(\mathbf{z}, \mathbf{u}) = \sum_m \tau_m \cdot \mathbf{a}_m(\mathbf{z}_m, d_m).$$

Premultiplying by an appropriate price vector $\mathbf{p}$ yields the objective function of an optimisation model. Feasibility constraints for the production vectors ($\mathbf{y} \in \mathbf{Y}$) and the control variables ($\mathbf{u} \in \mathbf{U}(\mathbf{z})$) may be added. The set $\mathbf{Y}$ may restrict the components for goods which cannot be sold, or disposed of externally, to be nonpositive, while components for goods which cannot be purchased externally have to be nonnegative. In this way the model also captures pollutants which are sold, or bought, at a negative price. The components of items which can neither be bought, nor sold externally, have to be restricted to zero in $\mathbf{Y}$. The amounts produced and consumed by all workplaces must balance out. The structure of the complete model is illustrated in Figure 1.

Gutenberg's original model is a special case in which all production vectors in $\mathbf{Y}$ meet a given output target (1) while output prices may be set to zero. This means cost minimisation for a given output.

If the dynamics of the z-variables is added to the static model, it is transformed into a dynamic production model as shown in Figure 2.

Figure 2: *Gutenberg* production model, dynamic extension

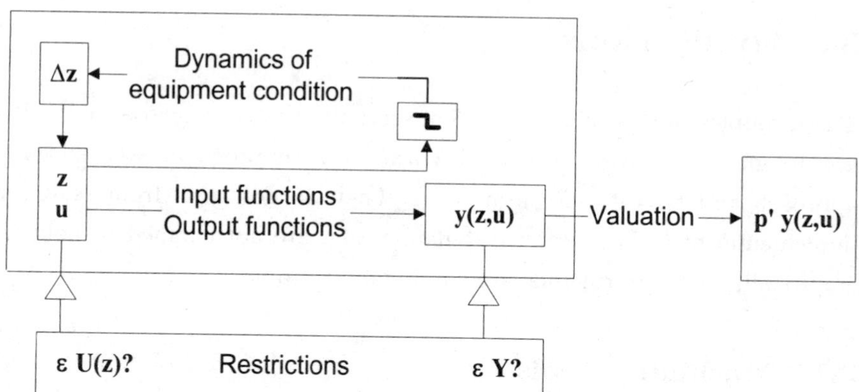

2.2 Specifying z-Variables

Applying the theory calls for the measurement of the z-variables. On the one hand, these measures must be sufficient statistics in respect of the impact of the previous history on the future performance of the equipment or, more generally, of the subsystem under consideration. On the other hand, information gathering and processing must not be too expensive. Recent developments in CIM allow for automatic production data acquisition which has reduced these costs considerably. A classical measure of the equipment condition, cumulative energy consumption, was proposed by *Vernon L. Smith* (1961 p. 303–306). Motor management systems in cars use it as a measure of the condition of motor oil and determine oil change intervals accordingly. Another measure, cumulative output since installation, is fundamental to the concept of the experience curve. More recent contributions to the theory of cost dynamics, however, seem to prefer cumulative defects as a statistic for equipment condition. They consider failures as an opportunity to detect and remove a source of trouble (see e.g. *Fine* 1986, *Marcellus & Dada* 1991). Also the failure rate itself, which represents the quality performance of a productive system, can be used as a measure of z. Each individual application requires a specific dynamic model to explain the change in the z-measures resulting from influencing factors.

3 Applications

The examples in the following section serve illustrative purposes only. They are designed to convey an idea of typical analysis procedures based on the approach and how it can be applied. They do not stem from real world implementations. The assumed dynamics of z are not claimed to hold true empirically, but, in principle, are empirically testable.

3.1 Machining Tools

Machining tools such as drill bits, saw blades and other cutting tools are blunted by utilisation. This means that the output rate for given values of the control variables such as pressure and r.p.m. declines gradually with the wear and tear of the tool. As a concrete example, consider a circular saw for cutting steel rods in a farm equipment factory.

Let T denote the capacity of the saw in work hours during the planning period. The output target is derived from a set of jobs j. Job j requires T_j work hours to fix work pieces on the saw. Machining time required for job j depends on the condition of the blade, on the sectional area and on the hardness of the material to be sawn. The latter two factors also determine the output components y_j of the production vector. There are three essential inputs: setup work proportional to $\sum_j T_j$, machining time r_1, and the number r_2 of blades used up. (Blades will be dressed and reused a number of times. So the cost of one replacement blade consists of the dressing costs and an appropriate portion of the purchase cost.) The setup work requirement cannot be influenced by the production manager. It is fixed for the given set of jobs and neglected in what follows. Input r_1 is followed by motive power and by auxiliary material for lubrication and cooling as shadow factors in the sense of *Danφ* 1966. Setup time for changing blades is a shadow of r_2. Changing a blade requires T_w work hours. The condition of equipment is, in this case, the sharpness of the incumbent saw blade. It can be measured by past cumulative workload. Let the saw blades be numbered consecutively by an index ℓ and let z_ℓ denote the workload assigned to blade ℓ. The z_ℓ are the decision variables under management's control. The increase in z due to one unit of sectional area sawed for job j is

$$\mathrm{d}z = \alpha_j \cdot \mathrm{d}y_j. \tag{2}$$

The constant α_j depends on the hardness of the material used for job j. (2) captures the dynamics of the equipment condition subject to the initial conditions

$$z\left(y_1 + y_2 + \ldots + y_{\ell-1}\right) = 0 \text{ for each } \ell.$$

These conditions mean that z is set back to zero whenever a blade is replaced. The input function for machining time can be written as

$$\mathrm{d}r_1 = \varphi(z)\mathrm{d}z$$

with a positive, strictly convex, increasing function φ. Accordingly, the amount of machining time required for the marginal unit of workload is an increasing function of blade bluntness. The input function for saw blades is

$$r_2 = \sum_{\ell} \operatorname{sgn}(z_\ell)$$

where $z_{\ell+k} = 0$ holds for all positive integers k if $z_\ell = 0$. (The function $\operatorname{sgn}(z)$ returns 1 for $z > 0$ and 0 for $z = 0$.) Furthermore capacity is restricted according to

$$\sum_{\ell=1}^{r_2} \left[\int_0^{z_\ell} \varphi(z)\mathrm{d}z + T_w \right] \leqq T - \sum_j T_j. \tag{3}$$

This condition states that the sum of working hours for machining time, for the replacement of saw blades, and for setup times of jobs must not exceed the working hours available in the planning period.

The optimal cost for a given set of jobs is defined as

$$C = \min_{r_2,\{z_\ell\}} \left\{ \sum_{\ell=1}^{r_2} \left[p_1 \cdot \int_0^{z_\ell} \varphi(z)\mathrm{d}z + p_2 \right] - V(z_{r_2}) \right\}$$

subject to (3). The function V accounts for the fact that the saw blade incumbent at the end of the planning period can in general be further used in the next period. Its z-condition is $z_{r_2} = \left(\sum_j y_j - \sum_{\ell=1}^{r_2-1} z_\ell\right)$.

For any given number r_2 of saw blades to be used, the Kuhn-Tucker necessary optimality conditions for cost minimisation require that there exist $\lambda \geqq 0$ such that

$$\begin{aligned}(p_1 + \lambda)\varphi(z_\ell) - V'(z_{r_2})\frac{\partial z_{r_2}}{\partial z_\ell} &= 0 \text{ for } \ell \in \{1, ..., r_2 - 1\} \\ \lambda &= 0 \text{ if there is slack in (3).}\end{aligned} \tag{4}$$

From these conditions it follows that the z_ℓ are all equal for $\ell = 1, ..., r_2 - 1$, since $\dfrac{\partial z_{r_2}}{\partial z_\ell} = -1$ for $\ell \in \{1, ..., r_2 - 1\}$. Consequently, a stationary replacement policy is optimal.

The function V can be estimated on the assumption that the machine will be used after the end of the planning period for an infinite future without capacity becoming scarce. Because of the optimality of a stationary replacement policy it is then optimal to repeat the same replacement cycle indefinitely over the entire post-planning period. Each cycle ends when the saw blade reaches the state at which the average cost attains its minimum

$$c^\circ = \min_z \frac{p_1 \cdot \int_0^z \varphi(\zeta)\mathrm{d}\zeta + p_2}{z}.$$

Using the incumbent blade in the post-planning period saves the difference between the average and marginal cost for each unit of workload for which it is then used. The blade will be replaced when it reaches the condition z^∞ at which further use would drive the marginal cost to a level above the post-planning period's average cost. If the state of the blade is worse than z^∞, at the end of the planning period, it is worthless for the post-planning period. Consequently, the function V may be defined by

$$V(z) = \max\left\{0, \int_z^{z^\infty} [c^\circ - p_1\varphi(\zeta)]\,\mathrm{d}\zeta\right\}$$

where z^∞ is determined by the condition $p_1 \cdot \varphi(z^\infty) = c^\circ$.

There are two cases to consider. In case 1, $r_2 \leqq z^\infty \cdot \sum_j y_j$, it is optimal to replace blades with $z_\ell = \dfrac{1}{r_2} \cdot \sum_j y_j$ for $\ell = 1, ..., r_2$ so that $V(z_{r_2}) = 0$. Clearly, reducing the number of blades r_2 below $z^\infty \cdot \sum_j y_j$ increases cost and machining time but saves setup time. So case 1 can be optimal only if the increase in machining time is more than offset by the savings in setup time. If it is at all possible to achieve feasibility by **de**creasing the number of setups then the optimal level of r_2 will be the largest number of setups meeting the capacity constraint.

For case 2, $r_2 > z^\infty \cdot \sum_j y_j$, the cost minimization problem can be rewritten as:

$$
\begin{aligned}
C &= \min_{r_2, z} \Bigg\{ (r_2 - 1) \left[p_1 \cdot \int_0^z \varphi(\zeta) \mathrm{d}\zeta + p_2 \right] + \int_0^{z^\infty} p_1 \varphi(\zeta) \mathrm{d}\zeta + p_2 \\
&\quad - \left(z^\infty + (r_2 - 1)\, z - \sum_j y_j \right) c^\circ \Bigg\}
\end{aligned}
$$

subject to (3). The optimality condition (4)then becomes

$$
(p_1 + \lambda)\varphi(z_\ell) = c^\circ \text{ for } \ell = 1, ..., r_2 - 1. \tag{5}
$$

In this case, $\lambda > 0$ can only hold if capacity can be gained by **in**creasing the number of setups. The optimal number r^* of setups is then the smallest r_2 meeting the capacity constraint. The optimal replacement point is $\frac{\sum_j y_j}{r^*}$ for the first r^* replacements. The last blade, however, is replaced only in the post-planning period at a state of z^∞.

So the optimum can be found by trying $r_2 = \left\lceil \frac{\sum_j y_j}{z^\infty} \right\rceil$ first. If this is feasible it is optimal. If not, it should be checked whether reducing (case 1) or raising (case 2) the number of setups yields a gain in capacity; r_2 should be moved stepwise in the direction in which capacity is gained until feasibility is reached. When such a step in r_2 no longer results in a capacity gain before feasibility is reached, the work cannot be completed during the planning period.

When capacity restrictions are not binding, a steady state replacement rule for the saw blades is optimal. In this case a classical production function with factor substitution is in fact an appropriate model of the process. Let $\bar{z}$ denote the replacement point of saw blades which is defined as the cumulative output processed with each blade. If $\bar{y}$ units of output are produced during a time period, then an average number of $\bar{r}_2 = \frac{\bar{y}}{\bar{z}}$ saw blades is needed. Average machine time is then $\bar{r}_1 = \bar{r}_2 \cdot \int_0^{\bar{z}} \varphi(z)\mathrm{d}z$. For given values of $\bar{r}_1, \bar{r}_2$ this equation can be uniquely solved for $\bar{z}$. The solution depends only on the proportion $\frac{\bar{r}_1}{\bar{r}_2}$. So let $\bar{z}(\bar{r}_1/\bar{r}_2)$ denote the solution. Clearly $\bar{z}' = \frac{1}{\varphi(\bar{z})} > 0$

and $\bar{z}'' = -\frac{\varphi'(\bar{z}) \cdot \bar{z}'^2}{\varphi(\bar{z})} < 0$. The production function

$$\bar{y}(\bar{r}_1, \bar{r}_2) = \bar{r}_2 \cdot \bar{z}(\bar{r}_1/\bar{r}_2)$$

has the neoclassical properties:

1. It is clearly linear homogeneous.

2. The production elasticity of $\bar{r}_1$ can be written as

$$\frac{\partial \bar{y}}{\partial \bar{r}_1} \frac{\bar{r}_1}{\bar{y}} = \frac{\int_0^{\bar{z}} \varphi(z)dz}{\bar{z} \cdot \varphi(\bar{z})}$$

   which is positive but < 1 because of the strict convexity of φ. Consequently, according to the well-known Wicksell-Johnson theorem, the production elasticity of $\bar{r}_2$ must also be positive and smaller than one. Therefore the marginal productivities are both positive.

3. Marginal returns are decreasing because of

$$\frac{\partial^2 \bar{y}}{\partial \bar{r}_1^2} = \frac{\bar{z}''}{\bar{r}_2} < 0,$$

$$\text{and } \frac{\partial^2 \bar{y}}{\partial \bar{r}_2^2} = \frac{\bar{z}''}{\bar{r}_2} \cdot \frac{\bar{r}_1^2}{\bar{r}_2^2} < 0.$$

4. The marginal rate of substitution (MRS) can be written as

$$-\frac{\mathrm{d}r_2}{\mathrm{d}r_1} = \frac{1}{\bar{z} \cdot \varphi(\bar{z}) - \int_0^{\bar{z}} \varphi(z)dz}.$$

   Note that the denominator of this fraction increases with $\bar{z}$, so that the MRS is decreasing in $\bar{z}$; $\bar{z}$, however, is increasing in $\bar{r}_1$. Therefore the production function has the property of decreasing MRS[2].

For the specification $\varphi(z) \equiv \frac{1}{\beta} z^{1/\beta}$ the production function would be of the Cobb-Douglas type $\bar{y}(\bar{r}_1, \bar{r}_2) = \bar{r}_1^{\beta} \cdot \bar{r}_2^{(1-\beta)}$. The specification $\varphi(z) \equiv (1-\alpha) + \alpha \cdot (1-z)^{-\beta}$, however, seems more realistic because it initially rises more slowly and more sharply for larger z. This function is displayed in Figure 3 for the parameter values $\alpha = 0.8$ and $\beta = 0.2$.

---

2 In a sense, this contradicts *Gutenberg*'s statement, that the "type A" production function is not representative for industrial manufacturing processes. *Gutenberg* 1971, chapter 8, last sentence, p. 325.

Figure 3: Required machine time as a function of wear and tear

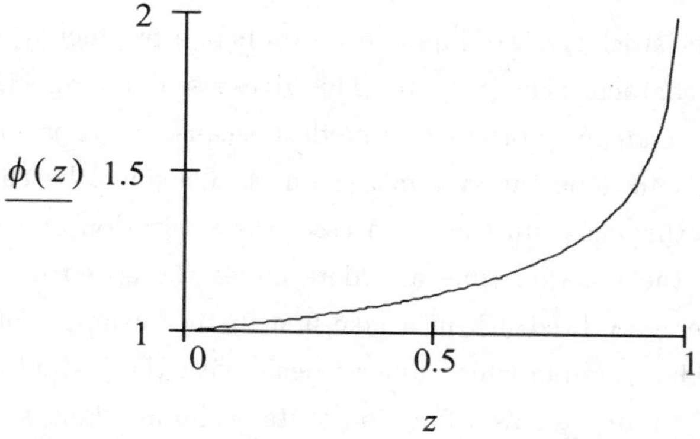

The optimal $\bar{z}$ is located at the intersection of marginal and average cost curves (w.r.t. z):

$$\frac{p_1 \cdot \int_0^{\bar{z}} \varphi(z)dz + p_2}{\bar{z}} = p_1 \varphi(\bar{z}). \tag{6}$$

For a price relation of $p_2/p_1 = 0.08$ both sides of the equation are displayed in Figure 4. The solid line represents the left and the dotted line the right hand side of equation (6).

Figure 4: Intersection between marginal and average cost

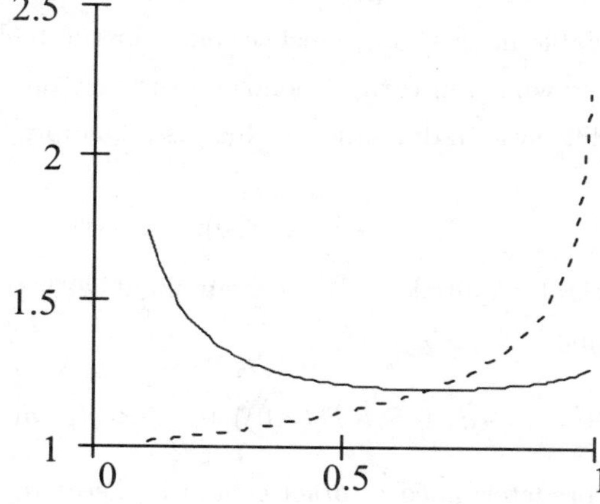

3.2 Stocks of Input or Output as State Variables

In some cases the stock levels of inputs or outputs of a productive system are appropriate for characterising its state. This gives rise to an especially simple class of dynamic *Gutenberg* production models because input or output functions suffice to determine the system dynamics. Chemical batch processes often belong to this class. In these processes the saturation of a compound changes during the reaction time and determines the speed of further reaction. Commercially bred fish in a lake is a further example of this kind of dynamics. The example which follows deals with the instantaneous fuel consumption of an airplane as a function of its declining flight weight.

The instantaneous rate of fuel consumption of a plane is a function of its weight $z(t)$ and its speed $d(t)$, each at time t :

$$\dot{r}(t) := \frac{\mathrm{d}r}{\mathrm{d}t} = \varphi(z(t), d(t)).$$

The purpose of the production model is to determine the fuel consumption required for a T-hour flight with given payload x and a fuel reserve of R at the time of landing. R can be used to save cost when fuel prices are much higher at the destination than at the origin of the flight. Let g_0 denote the dead weight (inclusive of the weight of the crew) and $F_0(z(0))$ the amount of fuel needed to reach the standard flying altitude. This amount of fuel is a function of take-off weight. Consequently, the take-off weight $z(0)$, which is the decision variable in this case, must account for the fuel consumption for the whole journey which, in turn, depends on the take-off weight inclusive of the reserve R. The system dynamics in this case is simply the input function for fuel:

$$-\dot{z} = \varphi(z, d). \tag{7}$$

The take-off weight required for the T-hour flight with payload x and fuel reserve R is defined by

$$z(0) = x + g_0 + R + F_0(z(0)) + \int_0^T \varphi(z(t), d(t))\mathrm{d}t. \tag{8}$$

The speed d is predetermined in practice and is therefore irrelevant in what follows. Substituting linear approximations of the fuel consumption functions

$$F_0(\zeta) \;\; : \;\; = \alpha + \beta\zeta$$

$$\varphi(\zeta) \quad : \quad = a + b\zeta$$

in (8) yields

$$(1-\beta)\cdot z(0) = x + g_0 + R + \alpha + \int_0^T [a + b\cdot z(t)]\,\mathrm{d}t. \tag{9a}$$

From (7) it follows that

$$a + b\cdot z(t) = (a + b\cdot z(0))\cdot e^{-bt}.$$

Substituting this in (9a) and simplifying determines the fuel consumption for the flight:

$$z(0) - (x + g_0 + R) = \frac{\frac{a}{b}(1 - e^{-bT}) + x + g_0 + R + \alpha}{e^{-bT} - \beta} - (x + g_0 + R)\,.$$

The additional fuel consumption due to the reserve R is then

$$\Delta\Phi(R) = R\cdot\left[\frac{1}{e^{-bT} - \beta} - 1\right].$$

Let p_0 and p_T denote the fuel prices at the origin and at the destination respectively. Then money can be saved by stocking up with fuel at the origin if the absolute price difference between destination and origin on the reserve R is greater than the fuel cost $p_0 \cdot \Delta\Phi(R)$ for the additional weight. That is to say, R should be chosen to maximise

$$(p_T - p_0)\cdot R - p_0 \cdot \Delta\Phi(R).$$

In the general case, when $\Delta\Phi(R)$ is strictly convex, one has to solve the necessary optimality condition

$$\frac{\mathrm{d}\Delta\Phi(R)}{\mathrm{d}R} = \frac{p_T}{p_0} - 1.$$

If the solution is admissible, it is also optimal; otherwise the nearest admissible value for R is an optimum. For the linearly approximated input functions the maximisation yields the following *Golden Rule of Aircraft Fueling*:

> If $\dfrac{p_T}{p_0} > \dfrac{1}{e^{-bT} - \beta}$ then fill up to the maximum
> otherwise take only the minimum R permissible.

References

Albach, Horst (1962): Produktionsplanung auf der Grundlage technischer Verbrauchsfunktionen, Arbeitsgemeinschaft für Forschung des Landes Nordrhein-Westfalen, Heft 105, Köln und Opladen (Westdeutscher Verlag).

Danϕ, Sven (1966): Industrial Production Models: A Theoretical Study, Wien (Springer).

Fine, C.H. (1988): A Quality Control Model with Learning Effects, Operations Research 36, 437–444.

Gutenberg, Erich (1971): Grundlagen der Betriebswirtschaftslehre, Erster Band, Die Produktion, 1. Aufl. 1951, 18. Aufl., Berlin/Heidelberg (Springer).

Kloock, Josef (1969): Betriebswirtschaftliche Input-Output-Modelle, Wiesbaden (Gabler).

Luhmer, Alfred (1975): Maschinelle Produktionsprozesse, Köln und Opladen (Westdeutscher Verlag)

Marcellus, R.L.; M. Dada (1991): Interactive Process Quality Improvement, Management Science 17, 1365–1376.

Smith, Vernon L. (1961): Investment and Production, Cambridge (Mass.), (Harvard University Press).

Summary

In 1951, Erich *Gutenberg* proposed an innovative approach to production modelling for managerial purposes. His formulation does not conceive of input quantities as independent variables of a production function. Rather, both input and output are assumed to depend on the rate of utilisation of production equipment which is determined by managerial decisions. Moreover, the current condition of equipment plays an important role. *Gutenberg*'s approach lends itself to a natural dynamic extension. To this end no more than a model of the dynamics of equipment condition, or, more generally speaking, of the productive system's condition, is needed to supplement his original concept. The present paper analyses two simple applications of the dynamic extension of *Gutenberg*'s approach, namely, machining processes and aircraft fueling respectively.

Gutenberg's Concept of Production Control, Uncertainty, and the Implications for Modelling Production and Cost

H. Jahnke[1]

Overview

In his contribution to production theory, Gutenberg assumes that there is no direct relationship between input and output at the level of the individual firm. Instead the firm chooses optimal values for several control parameters, e.g., production speed, operating time, lot sizes, priority numbers, inventory levels etc., which, in turn, induce the consumption of input factors and the production of a prespecified number of output goods. It is reasonable to assume for the deterministic case that the choice of the optimal parameter values is carried out automatically. Hence, in the single product case, the firm's, or a work centre's, production function can be defined by combinations of input factors and the corresponding maximal output. Therefore, output volume is the central cost driver in this theory. Things are different under uncertainty. Arguments similar to those brought forward by Alchian (1950) show that there is no conventional single period production function if the production process itself is stochastic. Moreover, in the case of stochastic demand, production planning techniques like MRP systems can be interpreted as adaptive planning systems. Here, the firm selects values for the control parameters on the basis of which the system adjusts the production volume to the actual level of demand when it becomes known. Consequently, the control parameters are the decision variables and, therefore, the main cost drivers under uncertainty, while the production volume no longer plays this role.

Keywords. Production, uncertainty, cost accounting, production management, adaptive planning

1 Manufacturing control parameters and the theory of production functions

One of the main purposes of microeconomic theory is the analysis of general equilibria in markets for goods and services, i.e., the determination of the prevailing

[1] Prof. Dr. Hermann Jahnke, Universität Bielefeld, Postfach 10 01 31, D-33501 Bielefeld, email: hjahnke@wiwi.uni-bielefeld.de, URL: http://www.wiwi.uni-bielefeld.de/~jahnke.

prices and the quantities of commodities traded in equilibrium. Due to its role in this context, it is admissible for the neoclassical theory of production, or more specifically the theory of production functions, to exclude details about the production process and to restrict attention to the quantitative relationship between the factors put into the transformation and the products yielded by it. However, for a successful application of production theory in production management, production planning, or the theory of cost, it is essential that the decisions on the efficient organization of the firm's input-output relations are taken into account in detail. Although this optimization problem underlying the production function appears in the microeconomic literature[2], Erich Gutenberg's *Grundlagen der Betriebswirtschaftslehre* (first published in 1951) contributed significantly to the development of a theory of industrial production that is relevant for the individual firm's decision-making [3].

Gutenberg assumes that the transformation of input factors into product units takes time. Instead of eliminating time from his analysis, he therefore explicitly models manufacturing processes as taking place in a time period of positive length T. The definition of a basic period gives rise to the partitioning of the input factors into two categories. On the one hand, *secondary input factors* like raw materials, components, energy or fuel, lubricating oil etc. are consumed and completely transformed into the product units as a result of the manufacturing process[4], whilst, on the other, such fixed equipment as machines, or the plant itself, typically lasts for more than one period. The fixed equipment is physically indivisible but the volume of services it can provide during a period may be variable. As an input factor labour should be regarded in the same way if the work force is employed on a long term basis. Hereafter, the term *primary input factors* is used to denote these factors[5]. Often a number of primary input factors are arranged into the work centres or production stages in which the fundamental manufacturing operations are carried out[6]. In this way, the transformation of input factors into final products is broken down into a number of processes which are more readily operated, described, and analysed[7]. These work centres are the focal point of Gutenberg's theory, while in some respects the secondary input factors only play a minor role.

Gutenberg characterizes a work centre by its output, the parameters by which the

---

2 For example in the context of the linear activity model proposed by Koopmanns (1951); see Danø (1966, 11 and 29 - 31) or Mas-Colell et al. (1995, 158). For a more general approach to the optimization problem see Magnússon (1969, 249).

3 For Gutenberg's contribution to production theory see Gutenberg (1983, esp. 326 - 337) and Fandel (1991). For an overview of a number of industrial production models see for example Danø (1966) or Fandel (1991).

4 Secondary input factors are *Verbrauchsfaktoren* in Gutenberg's terminology.

5 These are *Gebrauchsfaktoren* or *Potentialfaktoren* in Gutenberg's terminology. A more comprehensive introduction into Gutenberg's system of input factors may be found in Fandel (1991, 37 - 41). For the two classes of input factors also see Danø (1966, 7 - 8, 115).

6 This coincides with the common notion of a work centre, see Askin/Standridge (1993, 9). Gutenberg's corresponding term is *Produktionsstelle*.

7 Danø (1966, 148).

centre is controlled, and the relationship between these control parameters and the amount of secondary input factors consumed per output unit. He first assumes that the output of a work centre is homogenous and unidimensional. In general, the elementary service provided by a piece of the equipment like, e.g., the number of revolutions of a drilling machine meets these requirements[8]. In industrial production usually each output unit is associated with a certain amount of service. Since, hereafter we concentrate on the single item case, we may thus also measure the output of a work centre by the number of output units yielded by the process in question. It may be noted that for constant production coefficients the definition of a work centre is easily generalized to the multi-item case if output is measured in terms of units of elementary service. Secondly, Gutenberg assumes that the output level of a work centre and the corresponding amount of input factors are determined completely by a combination of certain control parameters, chiefly the production speed or intensity d, i.e. the number of output units manufactured per time unit, and the operating time of the work centre. A third assumption is that associated with each intensity is a certain consumption of secondary input factors $r = 1, 2,..., R$ per output unit which may be described by an input function[9].

For example, let $\boldsymbol{G}:=\{0<d_1, d_2,..., d_M\}$ be the set of $M \in \mathbb{N}$ alternative production speeds that may be selected for operating a work centre, and $d_i < d_j$ for $i < j \in M$. Given the production speed $d \in \boldsymbol{G}$, processing one output unit takes exactly $1/d$ time units. Entry r of the input function $\boldsymbol{v}$: $\boldsymbol{G} \rightarrow \mathbb{R}_+^R$, where $\boldsymbol{v}(d)=(v_1(d),..., v_R(d))$, is the amount of secondary input factor r required for the production of one unit of the output depending on the production speed. The influence of the intensity on the consumption of input factors is best illustrated by a vehicle's combustion engine. In such a case, the amount of fuel burned per kilometre in a given gear a typically a u-shaped function of speed. The operating time s, $0 \leq s \leq T$, indicates the utilization of the group of primary input factors forming the work centre. Operating the work centre for s time units with production speed $d \in \boldsymbol{G}$ yields ds units of output, while the consumption of input factors $r = 1, 2,..., R$ is given by $\boldsymbol{w}(d):= \boldsymbol{v}(d)d$ or $\boldsymbol{w}(d)s$ per time unit or per period, respectively[10].

More generally, let t_m indicate the number of time units the work centre is operated at speed $d_m \in \boldsymbol{G}$, $m \in \{1,..., M\}$, given that it is possible to switch from one production speed to another during the period. Variable $t_0 := T - \sum_{m=1}^{M} t_m$ is the (planned) idle time, in which no production and hence no consumption of input factors take place. While the total output per period can be expressed again in terms of intensities and

---

8 The elementary service corresponds to Gutenberg's *Leistung*.

9 A more detailed definition of a work centre is found in Gutenberg (1983, 329 - 330 and 335) or Fandel (1991, 124 - 134). Note the similarities between Gutenberg's input function and the concept of the engineering production function, see Fandel (1991, 158 - 180).

10 The case of a finite set of production speeds is found in Albach (1962, S. 154 - 159). Danø (1966, 115 - 122) is among the few economists explicitly including the time dimension in their models of production in a similar way.

operating times by $\sum_{m=1}^{M} d_m t_m$ and the corresponding total amount of input factors is $\sum_{m=1}^{M} w(d_m) t_m$, it is obvious, that the only decision variables in this framework are the operating times t_0, t_1, ..., t_M. In contrast to the neoclassical theory of production, a mere indirect relationship between input factors and output exists, and this relationship depends on the actual choice of values for the decision variables. Nevertheless it is possible to represent the input-output relation by a production function. If the vector of secondary input factor endowments is denoted by $\boldsymbol{b}=(b_1,..., b_R)$, $b_r \geq 0$, the corresponding value of the production function $f(\cdot)$ for the work centre is given by the maximal output that can be made from the inputs over a period of length T[11], i.e.

$$f(\boldsymbol{b}) = \max\left\{\sum_{m=1}^{M} d_m t_m \,\middle|\, \sum_{m=1}^{M} \boldsymbol{w}(d_m) t_m \leq \boldsymbol{b},\ \sum_{m=0}^{M} t_m = T,\ \forall\ m\colon t_m \geq 0,\ d_m \in \boldsymbol{G}\right\}. \quad (1)$$

The capacity restrictions for primary and secondary input factors are treated similarly in the side constraints of (1). This appears unusual for Gutenberg's theory. He focuses his analysis on the primary factors, the number of which is given, and hence upon their capacity; this principle constraint on the production possibilities is represented by the restriction of the total operating time in (1) to a maximum of the capacity T. The selection of the work centre control parameters, on the other hand, determines the wear and tear of the equipment as well as the amount of the secondary inputs required to undertake production. Gutenberg implicitly assumes that the latter input factors can satisfy any choice of control parameters at any time. However, due to the definition of a production function, it is necessary to impose restrictions on all input factors including the secondary inputs.

Formula (1) shows that $f(\cdot)$ can be interpreted as a production function within the framework of the linear activity model[12]. Therefore, the classical theory of cost is applicable to (1). Given an output volume and a set of constant input factor prices, a least-cost combination can be derived from the isoquants of (1). The set of the different possible output levels, and the corresponding cost of the least-cost combination, define the cost function, whereby the variable cost is determined by the cost of the secondary input factors. In this interpretation it is implicitly assumed that the optimization procedure in (1) is carried out automatically, even if the catalogue of control parameters of the work centre is enlarged to include other variables like batch sizes, or if the production speed is a continuous variable, or if the multi-item case is treated, or if the network structure resulting from a multi-stage manufacturing process is contemplated[13]. As in the classical theory of cost, the output volume per

---

[11] See the definition of a production function in Kreps (1990, 238).

[12] For the linear activity model see Danø (1966, 23 - 43) or Mas-Colell et al. (1995, 154 - 160).

[13] See Fandel (1991, 342 - 366) and Kilger (1982), Kloock (1969), and Kistner/Sonntag (1993) for generalizations in the directions mentioned.

period thus remains the main cost driver although the input-output relationship is only indirect due to the role of the control parameters[14].

2 Sources, types, and consequences of uncertainty in production

In order to study the impact of uncertainty on manufacturing it is reasonable to consider a more general production environment than that of section 1, while the monetary sources and consequences of uncertainty may remain excluded from the analysis. Figure 1 illustrates a simple single-item one-unit-at-a-time production process with two serial work centres (nodes 1 and 2), an inventory for the supply of secondary input factors (I), and a final product inventory (IV), where output units emerging from the production process are stored[15]. The two arcs directed towards the inventories symbolize the flow of goods replenishing the stocks of secondary inputs and the demand process. These flows will generally display some uncertainty with respect to quantities and the time of events. For example, the demand instances and the number of output units demanded per customer may both be stochastic (demand uncertainty) whilst the lead time as well as the number of input factor units delivered per order may be random variables (supply uncertainty).

Figure 1: Simple model of a two-stage manufacturing process.

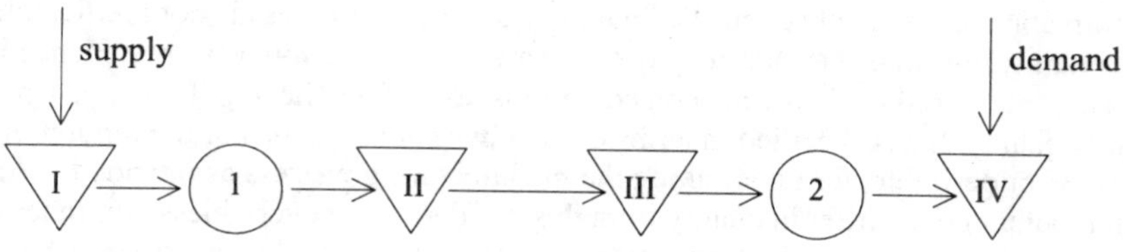

The two corresponding arcs in Figure 1 will therefore generally represent stochastic processes; hence they are external sources of uncertainty for the manufacturing process (see Figure 2).

[14] Jacob (1962, 212); for the role of output volume in classical cost models see Christensen/Demski (1995).

[15] Hackman/Leachman (1989) propose a general network model for the analysis of manufacturing processes. More details on the different sources of uncertainty effecting production and a review of the related literature are given in Jahnke (1995, section 2.2).

Figure 2: Types of uncertainty affecting manufacturing processes (Jahnke 1995, 36).

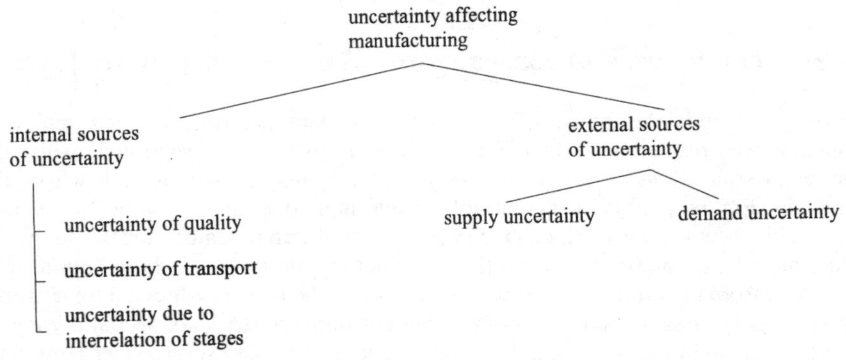

In addition to these external sources of uncertainty, internal circumstances may cause the manufacturing process itself to be non-deterministic. This is analysed best by starting with the most fundamental definition of a production process. Industrial production is the transformation of specified amounts of input factors into certain output products[16]. If this transformation is to be represented by a meaningful model of industrial production, the input has to be quantitatively measurable und controllable; otherwise the model would be useless for the decision maker in charge of a firm's manufacturing. However, if the quantities of commodities put into the transformation are perfectly controlled but the result of the process is not predictable with certainty, this must be caused by quality variations in the input factors. Hence it is reasonable for the following considerations to define the input factors by a standard quality that is specified in terms of the physical properties of the input units necessary, or desirable, for undertaking the manufacturing process as intended[17]. An actual input unit may differ in quality from this standard and nevertheless continue to be a commodity of the specified type. For example, a truck used by a firm remains a truck even if one of its tyres is flat (standard quality: all tyres are intact); an hour of an employee's labour is regarded as an hour of labour despite his poor motivation and therefore low productivity on a certain day (standard quality: an hour of labour of a given productivity); and, although during some chemical reaction in the manufacturing process it is discovered that a kilogram of a substance is contaminated due to unsatisfactory quality management in the inventory, it is a kilogram of that substance (standard quality: the pure substance). Thus, quantitative control of the input factors means that they enter the manufacturing process in a predetermined amount (given by T and the input vector $\boldsymbol{b}$ in (1)), while it is not clear if all input factor units are of the standard quality.

Returning to the production of a single output one unit at a time, the deviation of

---

[16] See, e.g., Gutenberg (1983, 298) and Danø (1966, 5).

[17] This contrasts with the usual definition of commodities as in Debreu (1959, 30) or Danø (1966, 6 - 7, 132 - 133). Already Gutenberg considers the problem of variations in the quality of input factors, see Gutenberg (1983, 300 - 301).

the actual from the standard quality of some input factor units will have one of the three following consequences. First, despite the deviation the output emerges from the process as expected - in which case no internal uncertainty has an impact on manufacturing. Second, due to its physical properties, the resulting output is of no use at all to the subsequent production stages or for demand satisfaction. Third, the poor quality of the output may be raised to an adequate level by expending additional secondary input factor units and manufacturing time. Except in the first case, the deviation in quality affects the time, and possibly the quantity, dimensions of the production model. In contrast to the deterministic situation, the length of the time interval between the completion of two subsequent output units of sufficient quality is not exactly $1/d$ ($d \in \boldsymbol{G}$) time units. It may be longer if a machine, which is part of the work centre, breaks down, or if improving the original product quality is time consuming, or if a unit of useless scrap results from the manufacturing process which is does not constitute a product unit. In the latter case, the next product unit emerges after another $1/d$ time units at the earliest. In this context, manufacturing intervals are random variables if the deviation in quality occurs by chance (uncertainty of input quality)[18]. Note that for a predetermined volume of output units to be manufactured, the stochastic character of individual production intervals means a random utilization of the work centre, which is limited in capacity by T. The special role of the uncertainty of manufacturing intervals here accords with the importance of the primary input factors in Gutenberg's concept of production control.

In a system like that illustrated in Figure 1, stochastic production intervals result in random instances at which the output units of stages 1 or 2 are put into stock in inventories II and IV, respectively. The arc directed towards triangle III represents the transport of stage-1 output to this inventory, where it is stored for later use as an input of stage 2. Transporting an intermediate product and keeping it in stock add to the internal uncertainty, since, e.g., transfer times may be random due to failing vehicles, or stocks may be affected by damage or loss. Moreover, the production stages are interdependent; delayed arrivals of intermediate products at stage 2 due to random production intervals, or random transport lead times, may bring manufacturing at the second stage to a halt. Interruptions of the stage-2 process may, in turn, cause stage-1 production to stop if stocks of the intermediate product reach the capacity limit of inventories II or III. Hence, uncertainty of transport and stock control as well as the interdependence of different production stages contribute to the internal manufacturing uncertainty.

3 Internal uncertainty and the production function

The theory of the production function typically incorporates internal uncertainty into its approaches to stochastic production in a way that neglects the effect of

---

[18] Stochastic manufacturing intervals, e.g. in the form of random production lead times, are well documented in the literature on production and operations management. See Jahnke (1995, 56 - 59) for an overview of some of the relevant literature and, additionally, Nadzeyka/Schnabel (1975) who study empirically the stochastic lead times in German manufacturing.

randomness on the underlying optimization procedure. In a number of models, a deterministic production function is combined with an additive, or multiplicative, stochastic term in order to describe the uncertainty of the production environment[19]. Another common approach is to represent the output, that corresponds to a combination of input factors, as a random variable[20], again without explicitly considering the optimization procedure as expressed in (1). Hence, these models are only of moderate help for the description and analysis of the cost efficient organization and design of a firm's manufacturing process.

To determine the effects, in a situation characterised by internal uncertainty, of including the internal optimization procedure in the production model, we return to the simple case contemplated in section 2., i.e. the manufacturing of a single product in an isolated work centre or, technically, a single node in Figure 1. Again, the work centre is controlled by its operating times. After the corresponding combination $\boldsymbol{t} = (t_1,..., t_M)$ is determined, a set of technical parameters like temperature, pressure, revolutions per minute etc. is chosen to adjust the work centre to the completion of d_m units of output per time unit during an uninterrupted period of length t_m, given all input factors are of standard quality.

Further, suppose that the production process requires just two input factors. Firstly, as in (1) the primary factors that define the work centre are treated as a single factor. The operating times t_m are limited by the corresponding capacity of the T time units the work centre is available for production. Secondly, while the work centre is adjusted to production speed d_m, the consumption of a single secondary input factor, e.g. the power needed to run the work centre, is given by the value of the input function $w(d_m) \in (0, \infty)$.[21] The amount of the secondary input factor available in the period is $b \in (0, \infty)$[22].

Given b, the internal manufacturing uncertainty leads to random manufacturing intervals of the product units, and consequently to a stochastic utilization of the primary input factors. Note that the relationship between the different types of deviation from standard quality on the one hand, and the probability distribution of the manufacturing intervals on the other, will generally be complex. For example, the wear of the tools used for drilling or metal-cutting will be influenced to some degree by the properties of the raw materials handled. Depending on the decreasing tool characteristics, output units completed after a certain critical time instance will be of inadequate quality and require reconditioning. The availability of the maintenance personnel determines, among other things, the point in time at which the tool is renewed. Therefore, the distribution of the renewal instance not only depends on the

---

19 See, e.g., Magnússon (1969, section 4.3), or the overview of the corresponding literature given by Aiginger (1987, ch. 5), or Hasenkamp (1976).

20 See Fandel (1991, 222 - 230) and, for example, Tintner (1941) (random production coefficients) or Diamond (1967) (output as a random variable in an equilibrium model). Henn/Krug (1974) and Krug (1976) define stochastic production correspondences in a similar fashion.

21 The multi-factor case is considered in a linear activity framework in Jahnke (1995, 54 - 64).

22 Note that this implies an assumption on the way the necessary improvement of the initially inadequate output quality leads to an additional consumption of secondary factor units.

distribution of the raw material quality, but also on the efficiency and the work schedules of the personnel. Both the point in time at which the tool no longer holds its tolerances and the renewal instance have an influence on the distribution of the random manufacturing intervals. Moreover, it should also be noted that the manufacturing intervals of the product units are not stochastically independent in this example.

Since, apparently, such aspects as these cannot be readily accommodated in the analysis, we resort to a simpler concept of random manufacturing intervals hereafter. Specifically, let identically distributed, stochastically independent, and almost surely, i.e. with probability one, positive random variables $A_1(d_m)$, $A_2(d_m)$, $A_3(d_m)$, ... represent the manufacturing intervals of the subsequent output units produced at intensity d_m. The distribution of these random variables depends on the production speed only, since we assume that the intensity d_m is the sole technical parameter of the work centre. As in the deterministic case, $E[A_1(d_m)] = 1/d_m$ is the corresponding expected length of the manufacturing interval. If the work centre is operated at intensity d_m for t_m time units, the process yields $N_m(t_m)$ output units; this is a random variable due to the stochastic character of the manufacturing intervals. With this notation (1) may be rewritten as

$$\left\{ N(\boldsymbol{t}) := \sum_{m=1}^{M} N_m(t_m) \,\middle|\, \sum_{m=1}^{M} w(d_m) t_m \le b,\ \sum_{m=0}^{M} t_m = T,\ \forall m\colon t_m \ge 0,\ d_m \in \boldsymbol{G} \right\}. \tag{2}$$

At first sight, (2) resembles the set (1), where the side constraints define feasible constellations of the control parameters $\boldsymbol{t} = (t_1, \ldots, t_M)$ that serve as candidates in the search for operating times maximizing the output. But in contrast to the deterministic case, the output variable $N(\boldsymbol{t})$ associated with $\boldsymbol{t}$ is a random variable. Therefore the choice between two vectors of operating times $\boldsymbol{t}$ and $\boldsymbol{t}'$, with respect to the corresponding output, is equivalent to the choice between two probability distributions. In general there is no direct criterion to indicate whether one probability distribution is larger than (or preferred to) another[23]. Hence, the maximal elements of set (2) are not defined and, consequently, no single period production function as given by (1) exists under internal manufacturing uncertainty.

The mathematical maximization in (1) contributes to the technological and objective character of the resulting production function[24]. The firm's decision processes, the decision maker himself, or the information available to him are not taken into account explicitly. Under uncertainty, however, there is by definition no complete knowledge or foresight and those elements omitted in the deterministic case have to be considered in the production model[25]. The procedure proposed by

---

23 In economic research, Alchian (1950, 212) appears to be the first to make use of this argument.

24 Indeed, production functions are often interpreted as expressing "a purely technical relationship that is void of economic content", Chambers (1988, 7).

25 Mak (1983), e.g., includes aspects of the information structure and the decision process into his microeconomic analysis of the production process. Related considerations may be found in Kreps (1990, ch. 19).

decision theory would be as follows[26]. In a first step, it is assumed that a preference relation exists on the set of probability distributions. This relation describes the preferences of the decision maker with respect to the different random variables *N(t)*. Next, the von-Neumann-Morgenstern theory tells us that, under certain conditions, the preference relation may be represented by a utility function and *N(t)* may be replaced by its von-Neumann-Morgenstern expected utility. This is a real number, and the maximization in (2) can be carried out as usual. The result is a production function similar to (1).

This procedure is followed in parts of the microeconomic literature[27]. However, due to this procedure, the production function, the least-cost combinations, the cost function, and the marginal product cost depend on the subjective preference relation of the individual decision maker and will change (and need to be re-calculated) with the individual in charge of the manufacturing process. Moreover, in practical situations, the set of control parameters in addition to Gutenberg's operating time and production speed will probably include more important parameters like batch sizes, job schedules, stock levels etc. Typically, mathematical models for determining this enlarged catalogue of control parameters will be numerically complex[28]. This is especially true, if the set of states grows rapidly due to the need to represent uncertainty[29]. In order to cope with complexity, companies often partially decentralize decision making to a number of managers on different hierarchical levels. In such a case, the preferences of all decision makers would have to be considered in the production model[30].

A review of the general debate on expected utility theory and the analysis of the problems of risk preference aggregation are beyond the scope of this paper[31]. However, while the above procedure may be useful in the context of equilibrium theory, with its focus on equilibrium prices in markets with many participants, the crucial influence of the subjective risk preferences of a number of individual decision makers on the form of the production function, on the least-cost combinations, the form of the cost function, and the marginal product cost would hardly be acceptable from a company's point of view[32]. Moreover, the application of the procedure is only

---

26 See Kreps (1988, ch. 4 and 5).

27 See, e.g., Tintner (1941), Magnússon (1969, section 5.3) and the papers reviewed in Aiginger (1987, ch. 5).

28 Even simple models of this kind are numerically complex, see Florian et al. (1980).

29 Note that this complexity argument is also valid for the approach of the theory of general equilibrium to uncertainty as it may be found, e.g., in Mas-Colell et al. (1995, ch. 19). See Kreps (1990, 221) for considerations in this direction.

30 Mack (1970) in her contribution to the discussion of a paper by Roy Radner on the theory of equilibrium under uncertainty pointed to the impact these observations have on equilibrium theory.

31 For some arguments suggested in the debate see French (1988, 196 - 204) and Kreps (1988, ch. 14). For the aggregation of risk preferences and group decisions see French (1986, 280 - 320).

32 See Jahnke (1995, 6 - 16). Note that, following the procedure described above, a product unit's marginal cost would depend on the risk preferences of all decision makers involved in the manufacturing of that unit and, hence, would have to be re-calculated whenever one of the individuals leaves the company.

possible if the distribution of the random manufacturing intervals is known, which is unlikely to be the case in practical production planning. Therefore expected utility theory seems to be of little use in solving the problem of choice under uncertainty in the production context developed here.

Besides the additional consumption of secondary input factors required to improve output quality, uncertainty of the manufacturing process primarily affects the length of the manufacturing intervals and hence the utilization of the primary inputs. Consequently it is reasonable to base an alternative approach on a description of the time aspects of the processes within the work centre. In this way, the resulting model would, like Gutenberg's theory, concentrate on the role of the primary input factors. Under the assumptions enumerated above, the sequence $\boldsymbol{D}:=\{(I_i, D_i), i\in\mathfrak{I}\}$ contains all the information relevant for such a description[33]. The set $\mathfrak{I}:=\{1,..., N\}\subset\mathbb{N}$ is the index set of the manufacturing intervals, where N is the total number of intervals during the life cycle of the product. If the end of the product's life cycle lies far ahead in the future, or is unknown, or if the product's successor differs only slightly with respect to manufacturing and demand, $\mathfrak{I} = \mathbb{N}$ (or $N = \infty$) will yield a good approximation to the actual situation. $I_i\in\{0, 1,..., M\}$ indicates the production speed of manufacturing interval i; $D_i = A(d_{I_i})$ is its random length. An idle period of D_i time units precedes the manufacturing interval $(i+1)$, if $I_i = 0$.

The index values I_i serve as the control parameters in this model. In contrast, in (2) the production process is controlled by operating times t_m. Since the manufacturing intervals are random variables under internal uncertainty, it is likely that operations on the last of the product units made during the t_m time units will be preempted before completion. This weakness of model (2) is avoided here. The operating times are no longer used to control manufacturing, but they result from the production speeds determined by control parameters I_i and the random length of the corresponding manufacturing intervals. Hence they are random variables themselves and it is possible to abandon the discretization of time into periods.

The information contained in the sequence $\boldsymbol{D}$ may be aggregated into a number of parameters. For example, let $n(t) := \sum_{n=1}^{N} \mathbf{1}(\sum_{i=1}^{n} D_i \leq t)$ be the total number of output units completed by time t, where for any real x the indicator function $\mathbf{1}(X\leq x) = 1$, if X is not larger than x, and $= 0$ otherwise. Then $N^{(m)}(t) := \sum_{i=1}^{n(t)} \mathbf{1}(I_i = m)$ is the corresponding number of output units produced with intensity d_m by the same time. Under some additional assumptions that include $\mathfrak{I} = \mathbb{N}$, a sufficiently regular structure of the control sequence $\boldsymbol{I}:=(I_i)_{i\in\mathfrak{I}}$, and that the technical equipment is at the end of its life replaced by identical machines, it is possible derive a production function from these aggregates by using the strong law of large numbers for renewal processes[34]. This production function is mathematically equivalent to (1), but has to

---

[33] The idea of describing the operations in a work centre by a sequence of certain parameters is due to Dobson (1987). He defines the well known economic lot scheduling problem (ELSP) in terms of sequences of lot sizes, product indices etc.

[34] For a detailed analysis including considerations of the consequences for the theory of cost see Jahnke (1995, 84 - 100 and section 2.5).

be interpreted differently. It relates the rate of secondary input factors almost surely required per time unit in the long run if control sequence $\boldsymbol{I}$ is applied to the corresponding output rate. Mathematically, the output rate is similar to the output in (1), but it is an average over the complete product life cycle and not the output of a specific period. Because of this interpretation, we will leave the attempt to aggregate the information contained in $\boldsymbol{D}$ into a production function based on averaging[35]. From the viewpoint of decision making a direct analysis of that sequence appears to be more promising.

The deterministic production model is characterized by the possibility of replacing the set of production control parameters with a single equivalent variable, namely, the output volume per period. The preceding analysis shows that this is no longer the case in an environment of internal manufacturing uncertainty, because the basis for the substitution is the existence of a production function. This in turn affects cost theory. In an analysis of the relationship between the classical theory of cost and activity based costing, Christensen and Demski (1995) state that the question of integrating uncertainty into the classical theory is open. However, since the duality of production and cost models is fundamental to this theory, it follows from the considerations presented here that there is probably no way of including uncertainty in the classical framework under the assumptions of this section.

4 External sources of uncertainty, adaptive systems and the choice of the control parameters

The change on the part of control parameters and output volume under uncertainty is even more distinct in production planning. Theoretically, if the sequence $\boldsymbol{D}$ serves for describing the manufacturing process of a certain work centre, production planning would have to determine this sequence up to the end of the product's life cycle. Of course, at least demand, and hence demand uncertainty as one type of external uncertainty, must be taken into account here.

Although different types of market organization are found in the literature, there is empirical evidence that some properties of markets are more important than others in our context. In an empirical study of markets for industrial products under uncertainty, Aiginger (1987, 156 - 157) finds that companies react to random variations in demand, or demand shocks, by adjusting inventory levels, output volumes, or the amount of backlogged demand, while there is little evidence of price adjustments to balance demand and supply. Product prices show a relatively small variance and follow prices on the factor markets. Apparently, many companies accept their product prices as exogenously given, or as cost based parameters that have to be determined for a relatively long period (Aiginger, 1987, 157 and 176). Therefore it is plausible, to represent demand in production planning by a stochastic process as in section 3, where the distribution of this demand process may depend, for example, on the given product price, or a sequence of given product prices. But

---

35 Note that in order to derive such an average production function it is necessary to compute this function's values for the set of all relevant control sequences $\boldsymbol{I}$. The determination of these sequences may itself be a formidable task.

if the demand instances and the amount demanded per customer are not completely anticipated, and if the lead times of production orders are stochastic due to internal manufacturing uncertainty, a sufficient level of demand satisfaction requires adequate inventory levels or a suitably flexible manufacturing system. The degree to which a firm relies on stock keeping in this context will be influenced by holding costs, the cost of manufacturing flexibility, and the lead time preferences of customers.

Due to similarities in respect of demand uncertainty, inventory theory may serve as a guideline in studying the choice of a certain sequence $\boldsymbol{D}$ in production planning. Even if the distribution of the demand process is known, it is common in inventory theory to propose a system of parameters, that generates a flow of replenishment orders adapted to the successively realized demand, instead of coming up with a specified sequence of order instances and sizes. For example, the order point s and the maximal stock level S are the control parameters of the well known (s, S) system. If the inventory position due to the demand realization decreases to level s, an order of, e.g., $(S - s)$ product units is placed. Using this (s, S) rule has at least two advantages over the explicit determination of the whole order sequence. Firstly, given a stationary demand process, only two parameters have to be computed rather than every single element in that sequence; moreover, these two numbers are relatively easily re-calculated as and when new information on the demand process becomes available. Secondly, a pair of parameters (s, S) is amenable to economic judgement based on cost or profit before demand realization, because the profit rate, i.e., the long run profit to be almost surely earned per time unit, can be calculated under this rule[36]. Contrastingly, the decision on the individual order size has to cope with problems similar to those discussed in section 3. The cost effects of the choice of the individual order size will depend on future demand, subsequent order sizes etc. Hence the cost of an order size is a random variable and the determination of the order quantity can only be carried out by comparing probability distributions if these are known[37].

It is reasonable to think of the sequence $\boldsymbol{D}$ as generated in a similar fashion. In a first step, values for a number of suitable manufacturing control parameters have to be selected. In general, (fixed) batch sizes, inventory levels adjusted to a certain degree of customer service, fixed production cycles, the average set-up frequency of the products, priority numbers etc. will be among these parameters. The demand for the final products then triggers manufacturing orders for the different components, for final and intermediate products which are produced in a specified sequence at the work centres. In this way, the sequence $\boldsymbol{D}$, controlled by the system parameters, evolves simultaneously with the demand realization and production is adapted to the demand process via stock levels or lead time, depending on the circumstances prevailing in the markets[38]. Note that in practical production planning, the plans

---

36 See, e.g., Jahnke (1995, 182 - 190) for the profit rate of an inventory system related to the (s, S) system.

37 Note that these arguments also apply to a batching decision in a production environment subject to internal or external uncertainty.

38 Note that these control parameters are *standard operating procedures* in the terminology of the evolutionary theory of economic growth, see Nelson (1995).

proposed by conventional MRP systems with fixed lot sizes can be interpreted as part of the adaptive determination of the sequence $\boldsymbol{D}$[39].

For an adaptive production planning procedure of this type, the important decisions with impact on profits and costs pertain to the production control parameters, while the output volume (of the different periods) results from these parameters and the realized demand. Consequently, under uncertainty, costs are caused by decisions on these parameters, not by the choice of an output volume. It may be noted that this observation is similar to the findings of Banker and Hughes (1994). In their paper, the firm decides on the production capacity to be installed at the beginning of the planning period and therfore on the cost of this capacity. In this way, too, the cost of instantaneous, unrestricted extra capacity is determined, which is required to satisfy demand in excess of the original capacity since no lost sales are allowed. The manufacturing system adapts itself to the realized demand. Once the product price is set, the firm accepts every product order even if it has to buy (expensive) extra capacity in order to manufacture the output units demanded. The model by Banker and Hughes also contains costs that are proportional to output volume. However, these costs are not caused by a decision on output volume, since there is no such decision, but by the determination of the price.

5 Summary and Conclusion

If production is affected by internal manufacturing uncertainty, the conventional production function given by (1) for the deterministic case is non-existent. In contrast to the situation under certainty, it is therefore not possible to replace the manufacturing control parameters with the output volume as the central variable in the production model. Hence, instead of output volume, the control parameters are the main cost drivers under internal uncertainty. This remains valid, if demand uncertainty is included in the analysis. If demand is stochastic, it is reasonable to control manufacturing by an adaptive production planning system, in which output volume is determined by certain system parameters and the realization of demand. Here again, output volume is not a decision variable. Gutenberg's observation that the relationship between input factors and the volume of output emerging from a production process is only indirect, and, that a thorough analysis of production includes a close look at the parameters that control manufacturing, thus seems crucial to an understanding of modern industrial production under uncertainty.

References

Aiginger, K. (1987): Production and Decision Theory under Uncertainty, Oxford.
Albach, H. (1962): Zur Verbindung von Produktionstheorie und Investitionstheorie, in: Koch,

---

[39] The relationship between MRP systems and adaptive production planning is also considered by Lambrecht et al. (1984). Note that the adaptive planning procedure fits well into the picture Aiginger (1987, for example on page 176) draws of industrial manufacturing under uncertainty based on his empirical study.

H.: Zur Theorie der Unternehmung, Wiesbaden, 139 - 203 (in German).

Alchian, A. A. (1950): Uncertainty, Evolution, and Economic Theory, The Journal of Political Economy 58, 211 - 221.

Askin, R. G., C. R. Standridge (1993): Modeling and Analysis of Manufacturing Systems, New York.

Banker, R. D., J. S. Hughes (1994): Product Costing and Pricing, The Accounting Review 69, 479 - 494.

Chambers, R. G. (1988): Applied production analysis, Cambridge.

Christensen, J., J. S. Demski (1995): The classical foundation of 'modern' costing, Management Accounting Research 6, 13 - 32.

Danø, S. (1966): Industrial Production Models, Wien.

Debreu, G. (1959): Theory of value, New Haven.

Diamond, P. A. (1967): The role of a stock market in a general equilibrium model with technological uncertainty, American Economic Review 57, 759 - 776.

Dobson, G. (1987): The Economic Lot-Scheduling Problem: Achieving Feasibility Using Time-Varying Lot Sizes, Operations Research 35, 764 - 771.

Fandel, G. (1991): Theory of Production and Cost, Berlin.

Florian, M., J. K. Lenstra, A. H. G. Rinnooy Kan (1980): Deterministic Production Planning: Algorithms and Complexity, Management Science 26, 669 - 679.

French, S. (1988): Decision Theory, Chichester.

Gutenberg, E. (1983): Grundlagen der Betriebswirtschaftslehre I: Die Produktion, 24. Auflage, Berlin (in German).

Hackman, S. T., R. C. Leachman (1989): A General Framework for Modeling Production, Management Science 35, 478 - 495.

Hasenkamp, G. (1976): Specification and Estimation of Multiple-Output Production Functions, Berlin.

Henn, R., E. Krug (1974): On Efficient Points of a Stochastic Production Correspondence, in: Eichhorn, W., R. Henn, O. Opitz, R. W. Shephard (Eds.): Production Theory, Berlin, 221 - 230.

Jacob, H. (1962): Produktionsplanung und Kostentheorie, in: Koch, H. (Eds.): Zur Theorie der Unternehmung, Wiesbaden, 206 - 268 (in German).

Jahnke, H. (1995): Produktion bei Unsicherheit, Heidelberg (in German).

Kilger, W. (1982): Die Theorie der industriellen Produktion auf der Grundlage dispositiv variierbarer Prozeßparameter, in: Koch, H. (Ed.): Neuere Entwicklungen in der Unternehmenstheorie, Wiesbaden, 99 - 148 (in German).

Kistner, K.-P., S. Sonntag (1993): Ansätze einer Theorie der Gutenberg-Produktionsfunktion, Zeitschrift für Betriebswirtschaft 63, 1297 - 1329 (in German).

Kloock, J. (1969): Betriebswirtschaftliche Input-Output-Modelle, Wiesbaden (in German).

Koopmans, T. C. (1951): Analysis of Production as an Efficient Combination of Activities, in: Koopmans, T. C. (Eds.): Activity Analysis of Production and Allocation, New York, 33 - 97.

Kreps, D. M. (1988): Notes on the Theory of Choice, Boulder.

Kreps, D. M. (1990): A Course in Microeconomic Theory, Princeton, NJ.

Krug, E. (1976): Stochastic Production Correspondences, Meisenheim am Glan.

Lambrecht, M. R., J. A. Muckstadt, R. Luyten (1984): Protective stocks in multistage production systems, International Journal of Production Research 22, 1001 - 1025.

Mack, R. P. (1970): Contribution to the discussion of R. Radner: New Ideas in Pure Theory, Problems in the Theory of Markets under Uncertainty, American Economic Review 60, 461 - 462.

Magnússon, G. (1969): Production under Risk, Uppsala.

Mak, K.-T. (1983): Dynamic Laws of Returns under Uncertainty, in: Eichhorn, W. R. Henn, K. Neumann, R. W. Shephard (Hrsg.): Quantitative Studies on Production and Prices, Würzburg, 27 - 39.

Mas-Colell, A., M. D. Whinston, J. R. Green (1995): Microeconomic Theory, New York.

Nadzeyka, H., B. Schnabel (1975): Untersuchungen über die Fertigungsdurchlaufzeiten in der Maschinenbau-Industrie, REFA-Nachrichten 28, 267 - 271 (in German).

Nelson, R. R. (1995): Recent Evolutionary Theorizing About Economic Change, Journal of Economic Literature 33, 48 - 90.

Tintner, G. (1941): The Pure Theory of Production under Technological Risk and Uncertainty, Econometrica 9, 305 - 312.

The Influence of the Gutenberg Production Theory on Production Planning and Control

M. Steven[1]

Overview

- The production theory formulated by Erich Gutenberg in the early fifties is influential in extensive areas of modern business administration.
- Current developments in the field of production planning and control (PPC) usually ignore their explicit relation to Gutenberg's theoretical system.
- The aim of this article is to investigate the extent to which an implicit influence of Gutenberg on the development of modern PPC-concepts can be shown.
- Evidence is given which shows that Gutenberg's fundamental work has frequently penetrated and stimulated production planning and control.
- Deficits in PPC systems' performance, as often reported in practice, could be reduced, if more consideration was given to Gutenberg's central ideas.

Keywords. PPC-systems, production functions, material requirements planning, strategic / tactical / operative planning, OR-techniques

1 Introduction

Erich Gutenberg's monograph "Grundlagen der Betriebswirtschaftslehre" (fundamentals of business administration), first published in the fifties, is of undisputed relevance to the further development of the discipline and its various special areas. Because of its comprehensive approach, covering all functional areas of the firm, and its orientation towards productivity as the core of a company's combination process, the work is in Germany regarded as "the most

[1] Professor Dr. Marion Steven, Ruhr-Universität Bochum, Fakultät für Wirtschaftswissenschaft, D-44780 Bochum, e-mail: marion.steven@ruhr-uni-bochum.de

significant event in the development of the theory of the firm since World War II".[2]

The further development of Gutenberg's theory of the firm resulted in so much specialization in reported business administration research that the origin of a concept can often hardly be detected. This article therefore attempts to relate production planning and control (PPC), which is an innovative special discipline of business administration with a strong interdisciplinary approach, to Gutenberg's propositions on production management.

The investigation starts from the following thesis: Although most, primarily the newer, literature on production planning and control makes no explicit reference to Gutenberg's arguments,[3] the concepts, models and methods discussed therein are at least implicitly built on the central ideas of the theory of the firm, especially Gutenberg's production theory. The following arguments are intended to provide systematic proof of these relations. Thus, it can be demonstrated that production planning and control is a part of modern business administration that was definitely inspired by the fundamental work of Erich Gutenberg.

The article is structured as follows. Part B outlines the basic elements of Gutenberg's production theory on the one hand and on the other, the development and basic structure of PPC-systems. Part C demonstrates the relations between these two fields in respect of their general conception as well as their various sub-sections. Part D gives a summary of the results.

2 Definitions

The two fields examined below first need to be defined. The Gutenberg production theory is here understood in a wider sense as the totality of statements on production management found in "Grundlagen", and in the publications based on it. Its more usual narrower interpretation would restrict the focus to the type B production function.[4] The field of production planning and control comprises not only PPC-systems, but also all concepts and approaches for organizing and controlling operations in the production area. The subject of this investigation is thus an essential part of production management.

---

2 Cited from Wöhe (1996), p. 75.

3 See representing the abundance of PPC-literature e.g. Glaser/Geiger/Rohde (1992), Hackstein (1989), Helberg (1987), Scheer (1990), Zäpfel (1989). Opposite examples are the work of Scheer (1976) from the beginning of PPC-development and the textbook of Kurbel (1995).

4 See Gutenberg (1983), in particular pp. 326.

2.1 Central propositions of the Gutenberg production theory

In the first volume of his "Grundlagen" (fundamentals), which is centered on production, Gutenberg's research focuses on productivity relations.[5] His aim is to demonstrate "structure and order...in empirically elicited facts".[6] The enterprise is described as a black box, i.e. an input/output system, in which the desired outcome is generated by different transformation processes. This production function, characterized by input, transformation and output, thus represents the basic element of the business process.[7]

Gutenberg transfers these results, which were originally found in the production area, to the enterprise as a whole, emphasizing the interdependence of all its functions. The mutual dependencies of the different functional areas are represented by mathematical methods, e.g. from operations research. The enterprise is thus regarded as a coherent set of variables, whose reactions to changes in external data can be modeled with an analytical approach. Gutenberg recommends a simultaneous description of the functional areas and their relations in order adequately to capture the effects of the existing interdependencies.[8]

An essential element of the Gutenberg production theory is the production factor system he has defined, which is still the basis for further developments in this area.[9] Abandoning the macroeconomic classification of production factors into labor, land and capital, which is a feature of income distribution, he differentiates between the elementary factors material, production facilities, and operative work on the one hand, and the derivative management functions of planning, organization and control on the other.[10]

Starting from microeconomic theory, Gutenberg challenges the validity of the law of diminishing returns in respect of industrial production[11] and replaces it with the type B production function, which is based on technical factor input functions.[12] Characteristic for the theory of adjustments enunciated by Gutenberg is that production factors are not completely substitutable, but have to be combined in predetermined proportions in order to produce a given output efficiently. A production unit can react to a change in demand by resorting to the following forms of adjustment:

- adjustment of time. A change in demand can be accommodated by extending or reducing the running time of the production facilities and thereby also the

---

5 See Albach (1989), p. 79.

6 Gutenberg (1983), p. V.

7 See Albach (1989), p. 160.

8 See Albach (1989), p. 155.

9 See e.g. Beuermann (1996), Sp. 1494 ff., Bloech (1993), Sp. 3405 ff., Corsten (1997), pp.121, Kern/Fallaschinski (1978/79).

10 See Gutenberg (1983), pp. 3.

11 See Gutenberg (1983), pp. 303 - 318.

12 See Gutenberg (1983), pp. 326.

staff's working hours. In this case the production coefficients stay constant and result in a linear cost function.

- adjustment of quantity. Another means of adapting output to demand is employing additional or fewer identical machines. This method permits only discrete output quantities and results in costs, which behave accordingly.
- adjustment of intensity. A variation in production speed, i.e. in output per unit of time, causes consumption rates, especially that of materials, to vary in a specific mode. This type of adjustment typically leads to u-shaped input functions, which imply a similar u-shaped unit cost function, and an S-shaped total cost function for the production unit.

The cost function of the firm is formulated by aggregating the results for the different production units along the flow of material.

In addition to his approach to the production factor system[13], to the production and cost function type B,[14] and to the organizational structure of manufacturing enterprises[15], "Grundlagen", vol. I, contains a detailed analysis of production planning and control problems[16] as they appeared to Gutenberg at the time. This was namely when the development of PPC-systems had just started. He distinguishes between the following three interdependent problems:[17]

- program planning. The task of program planning is the determination of the production program by type, quantity, and time within a given planning horizon.
- requirements planning. Requirements planning has to provide the input factors required by the production program at the appropriate times.
- process planning. The planning and scheduling of production processes includes the coordination of operations and their sequences.

These problems show considerable differences with respect to their planning horizons and hierarchical structure. The following statement expresses their mutual dependence:

> "Planning mistakes in one section of this planning system endanger the performance of production planning in the other sections".[18]

2.2 Structures of PPC-systems

A PPC-system is an integrated, computer-aided information, disposition and control system built upon a central data base. It supports the coordination of

---

13 See Gutenberg (1983), pp. 11 - 146.

14 See Gutenberg (1983), pp. 298 - 456.

15 See Gutenberg (1983), pp. 234 - 297.

16 See Gutenberg (1983), pp. 147 - 233.

17 See Gutenberg (1983), p. 149.

18 ibid.

decisions from medium-range production planning at the tactical level up to short-term production planning and order control at the operative level. The development of PPC-systems can be traced back into the sixties. From stock keeping and bill explosion systems rooted in materials control, successively emerged material requirements planning (MRP), manufacturing resource planning (MRP II), and the general concept of computer integrated manufacturing (CIM), in which the economic PPC-components and the technical CA-components play a central role.[19]

Standard PPC-systems, which are often sold as standard software, are based on a successive, modular planning concept covering all subproblems of production planning and control. Each solution of a subproblem becomes a parameter of the following module. This top-down method runs through the various functions subsequently with an increasing degree of detail and a decreasing planning horizon. Information feedback serves primarily to actualize data for the next run under a rolling planning horizon. Figure 1 gives an overview of the basic structure of a PPC-system.

Figure 1: Basic structure of a PPC-system

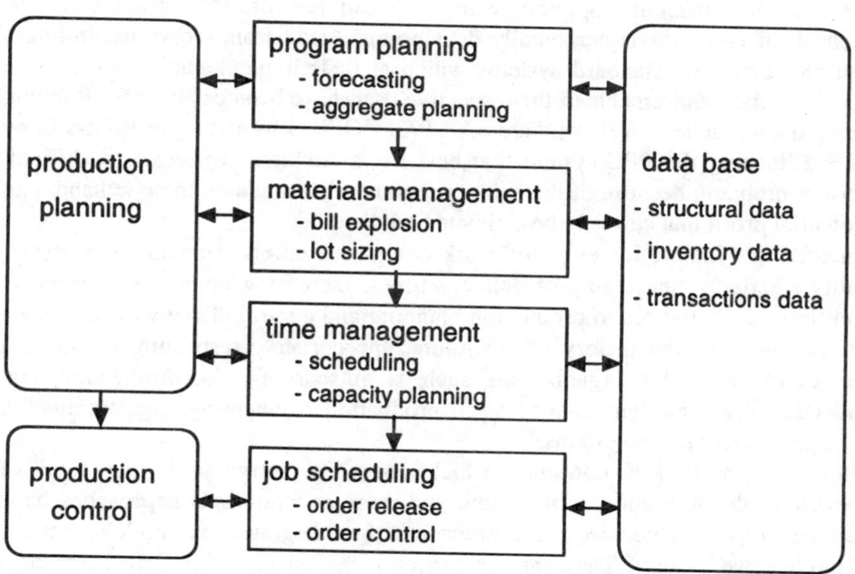

19 See Kistner / Steven (1993), pp. 255.

Production planning usually comprises the following subproblems: production program planning with the aggregate determination of the production program based on orders or on demand forecasts, materials management with the explosion of the bills of material and lot sizing, and time management with a provisional scheduling of orders and capacity balancing. Job sequencing comprises the operative planning of sequences with order release, order control, and quality control.

Via suitable interfaces, all modules access a common data base containing the relevant structural data, inventory data, and transactions data. Therefore the development of appropriate data structures and a continuous actualization of the data base with the aid of production data acquisition are essential conditions for the application of PPC-systems. The design of the modules differs considerably depending on whether production is market driven or order driven.[20]

As the mass of data involved can only be managed with data processing support, the development of PPC-systems was strongly influenced by the possibilities of computer construction on the hardware side and by progress in business data processing on the software side. Due to their predominantly technical field of application, PPC-problems are not only discussed in the literature of business administration, but also in the engineering literature.[21]

Meanwhile different suppliers offer a multitude of PPC-systems whose spectrum of functions is perpetually developing. Aside from individual in-house solutions, primarily standard systems which at their implementation have to be adopted to the requirements of the respective user, have been established. Ranking among the top sellers in Europe are SAP R/3, COPICS by IBM and PIUSS-O by PSI.[22] Choosing the PPC-system that best fits a company's needs is a difficult decision problem, because of the heavy investment it entails on the one hand, and a potential profit that can only be estimated on the other.

Increasing dynamic forces in the markets - globalization, competitive pressure, quality standards, shortening of delivery times, increasing number of variants - result in new challenges to production planning and control. They will be met by PPC-concepts for the factory of the future, appropriately respecting the current changes in production organization, such as outsourcing, decentralization, and production segmentation, as well as in production engineering, e.g. automation and flexible production systems.[23]

Besides general PPC-concepts, which cover all activities in the field of production planning and control, more and more decentralized approaches have been developed, which in some cases can be integrated as modules into a comprehensive system. These newer concepts can be classified into inventory-

---

20 See Kurbel (1995), pp.117 resp. pp.195.

21 See e.g. Hackstein (1989).

22 Market surveys are found e.g. in Geitner/Chen (1990) or in the periodicals Computerwoche and PPS-Management.

23 See e.g. Kistner/Steven (1992), Drexl et al. (1994).

oriented approaches, like the work-load oriented order release and the input/output control, into capacity-oriented approaches, like optimized production technology (OPT) and further developments of MRP II, and into time-oriented approaches such as KANBAN, the method of inverse sequencing and the concept of cumulative timing.[24]

3 Relations between the Gutenberg production theory and production planning and control

Some general relations between Gutenberg's propositions on production management and the concept of production planning and control are outlined below. This is followed by an examination of the extent to which the influence of the Gutenberg production theory can be demonstrated in the various domains of production planning and control that are shown in Figure 1.

3.1 General relations

An initial examination of the two approaches discussed here indicates some common characteristic features. The Gutenberg production theory and the PPC-approaches both make use of mathematical and analytic instruments to map relevant situations and relationships in the field of production. This is to be expected as production control mainly deals with "hard" facts, which are eminently amenable to a quantitative approach.

But their orientation with respect to models is quite different. Gutenberg solved subproblems by resorting to the most progressive methods known in his days, mainly from the field of operations research.[25] However, most PPC-systems lack a theoretical foundation. As empirical investigations have shown[26] and as elaborated in the next section, the tasks of the modules are mostly realized by using simple heuristics with no guarantee of a solution even when readily implementable optimizing procedures are available, and even though ever increasing computer capacity now permits the computing of complex operational research models.

In the operation of PPC-systems, information management plays an important role, i.e. the generation of adequate data structures, data management, and the integration of partial solutions by proper interfaces. Gutenberg also deals with the

---

24 See e.g. Zäpfel/Missbauer (1987), Schröder (1990), Steven/Meyer (1998).

25 So in Gutenberg (1983) network technique is used for time control (pp. 227), linear programming for program planning (p. 170) and personnel allocation (pp. 187), and combinatorial algorithms for job shop scheduling (pp. 217).

26 In the last few years, masters' theses written by some of the author's students have contained analyses of the solution methods of single PPC-modules, e.g. program planning, lot sizing, bill explosion and job shop scheduling.

relevance of information for production planning and control,[27] but he concentrates mainly on the theory of information and communication.

Another difference concerns the main subject of the approaches. Gutenberg enunciates a more comprehensive view embracing long-term and strategic decisions, primarily in the areas of labor supply and production capacity. In contrast, production planning and control concentrates on tactical and operational planning within the framework set by previous strategic decisions.

The two approaches also vary with respect to objective function: Gutenberg adopts a cost minimization approach as a sub-objective that is consistent with the economic efficiency in the production area. In PPC-approaches on the other hand, the handling of the complexity of the planning problem and the issue of a feasible master schedule prevail over an explicit performance orientation. Only in the newer, decentralized PPC-approaches as opposed to standard PPC-systems, partial objectives are accommodated.

Finally, the unequal treatment of interdependencies in the production sector should also be mentioned. While Gutenberg - as already cited above - gives high priority to the adjustment of planning results of different subproblems for a satisfactory solution of the total problem, the necessity of a simultaneous approach is largely ignored in PPC-literature. The successive top-down approach with isolated partial models systematically prevents feedback from downstream planning modules to upstream planning modules. Even though the impossibility of a simultaneous determination of all decisions within the scope of a total model has long been recognized,[28] an extensive coordination of the subproblems of production planning and control by means of proper interfaces and feedback mechanisms is still an aspiration.[29] Moreover, PPC-systems do not contribute to the coordination of strategic production planning and operational production control. This is a further reason for the sub-optimal performance of PPC-systems.

3.2 Influences on single PPC-functions

To demonstrate the influence of Gutenberg on production planning and control, it is perhaps preferable to base a detailed analysis on the succession of PPC-functions, and not to adopt Gutenberg's structure of program planning, requirements planning, and process planning.

3.2.1 Production program planning

The module production program planning - also known as master production scheduling - usually gets the first impulse in the run of a PPC-system. Type, quantity and preliminary completion dates of the final products within the given

---

27 See Gutenberg (1983), pp. 267 - 292.

28 See Bretzke (1980), pp.127.

29 See e.g. the coordination mechanisms at Steven (1994), pp. 180.

planning horizon are determined on the basis of customer orders or demand forecasts.[30] As, in practice, mixed forms of make-to-order and make-to-stock production often occur, many PPC-systems offer individual modules for order administration and for demand forecasting respectively. Common forecasting techniques, like moving averages and first and second order exponential smoothing are usually embodied in the latter module.

These preliminary production requirements lead to the planned output by means of a counter-check against available inventory and by adding any scheduled make-to-stock production quantities. Characteristically, on this planning level, neither an exact capacity balancing nor a strict scheduling of production times is carried out. The production schedule results rather from the data given by customers or by sales planning; capacity planning is, at best, based on estimates of the average aggregated capacity demand of the final products. The resultant production quantities represent the data input for the subsequent modules of the PPC-system. In order to reduce the complexity of the planning problem, which is caused by a wide spectrum of product variants, use may, for example, be made of the standard software package MPSX sold by IBM that offers the possibility of aggregating products into product groups. This software package carries out a rough balancing of production demands and available resources with the aid of simulation techniques.[31]

Gutenberg describes the production planning problem in general by the methods of linear programming, but he does not formulate the program explicitly.[32] He recognizes the interdependencies between production program planning and requirements planning by providing for an adjustment of the production program to the available capacities as well as to the materials in stock. The objective of his approach is the maximization of the profit contribution which is achievable with the planned production program.

From a strategic point of view not only the output volume, but also the product types, i.e. the composition of the production program, are to be determined. Here a typical conflict of interests between production and distribution arises. Further extensions of the program planning problem imply the assumptions of volume-dependent selling prices which make the revenue function non-linear, of variable production coefficients leading to a non-linear cost function, and the connection between program planning and investment planning. As regards the solubility of such a complex program, Gutenberg still believed in the progressive advances of computer science. However, the subsequent findings of complexity theory suggest that such large-scale monolithic simultaneous models[33] are NP-complete and will be permanently insoluble.

---

30 See Kistner/Steven (1993), pp. 261.

31 See Glaser/Geiger/Rohde (1992), pp. 37.

32 See Gutenberg (1983), pp.151.

33 This also applies to the models of Dinkelbach (1964), Adam (1969) and Küpper (1980).

In order to reconcile the ideal requirements of modeling theory formulated by managerial scientists with solutions convertible into practice, an hierarchical integration of decisions and the aggregation of variables is suggested.[34] The model of production program planning is thereby reduced to a size that standard software can readily cope with; appropriate interfaces ensure the integration of the subproblems not yet treated. Several PPC-systems have already adopted the idea of hierarchical planning.

3.2.2 Materials management

Materials management, which follows production program planning, is a core module of each PPC-system. This can be explained by the large amount of data to be handled in this sector; also a major root of the development of commercial production planning and control is found here.[35] The task of materials management is the generation of production orders through all production levels in order to ensure a timely supply of the materials required for the realization of the predetermined production program. The following individual tasks must be carried out:[36]

- bill explosion. Starting from the external demand for final products, which is given by the production plan, the derived requirements of intermediate products and parts are determined for all production levels. Bill explosion is related either to levels of production or to levels of disposition; appropriate bill processors are provided by the PPC-systems.
- netting of demands. The net demand of each part is given by balancing gross demand as established in bill explosion against inventories on hand, quantities expected from earlier orders, quantities backordered, and an intended safety stock. The result is the net demand, which for each part has to be covered by production.
- lot sizing. For each part, the net demand of successive periods is transformed into a sequence of production orders on a cost-efficient basis. Normally simple lot size models are applied here, e.g. the economic lot size formula or dynamic lot size heuristics, whose assumptions are not fulfilled, or which myopically end with a first local cost minimum.
- offsetting of lead times. The lots are placed on the time axis, so that, allowing for the manufacturing time each part requires, the final products can be completed punctually.
- inventory management. An inventory of all articles must be kept in a central data base and must always be up to date. To give instant information about the availability of any particular article, not only have physical receipts and issues

---

34 See Stadtler (1988); Schneeweiß (1994); Steven (1994).

35 See Kistner/Steven (1993), p. 256.

36 See Orlicky (1975).

of material to be considered, but also reservations for a certain order and subsequent deliveries of articles.

Usually this exact but rather expensive method of material requirements planning is employed only for the A-parts and B-parts specified by an ABC-analysis, because they cause the major deployment of capital. The requirements of the less important C-parts are usually determined with the aid of consumption-oriented heuristics.[37] Inaccuracies resulting from this method can be compensated by a higher safety stock level, which, due to the lower share in value of the C-parts, leads to far less additional costs than an exact planning of these parts.

Materials management thus results in punctual production orders or purchasing orders for each article, thus leading to a prompt completion of the final products. But, as lot sizing ignores available capacities, unfeasibilities resulting from the simultaneous claim of several articles on one facility can occur. PPC-systems totally ignore this problem at the level of materials management; aspects of capacity utilization are considered in time management in the subsequent module.

Gutenberg's "Grundlagen" treat the tasks of materials management to a limited extent:[38] Lot sizing is described as a part of requirements planning and solved by resorting to the economic lot size model and its extensions. Aditionally Gutenberg discusses the determination of order points and order times as the critical parameters of demand-driven lot size heuristics. The economic lot size model is also used for the calculation of production lot sizes, assuming the production rate exceeds the demand rate. Here Gutenberg deals additionally with the batch sequence optimizing problem in the multi-product firm in respect of sequence-dependent changing costs, i.e. he takes into consideration the interdependencies of two planning levels. The comparative brevity of his treatment of materials management can be explained as follows: as the steps of the materials demand calculation described above can be exercised mainly by applying simple arithmetic operations, there is no need for economic modeling.

In contrast to the myopic view of PPC-systems, Gutenberg integrates materials management into its planning environment. In connection with make-or-buy decisions he addresses outsourcing problems and other sourcing strategies which are still under discussion. Furthermore, he notes the problem of the location and organization of warehouses, and anticipates the concept of just-in-time production by suggesting the synchronization of the supply of materials and production. In the field of procurement he deals further with the problem of the choice of suppliers.

3.2.2 Time management

The task of the time management module in PPC-systems is, on the one hand, scheduling, i.e. to attribute starting and closing dates to the manufacturing orders

---

37 See Kistner / Steven (1993), pp. 42.

38 See Gutenberg (1983), pp. 189 - 199, pp. 201 - 215.

previously generated at all production levels, and on the other, loading them on the available production equipment in order to ensure a feasible production plan over all levels. Usually these two interdependent subproblems are handled successively, thus leading to further suboptimalities. An additional problem is caused by the fact that the operating times of orders are not known in advance, either on single production facilities or in total. The operating time of an order consists mainly of its waiting time in the production and transportation system, and it is therefore to hand only after the termination of this module. There is a tendency, called the operating time syndrome, to overestimate operating time in order to provide a sufficient buffer.

There are several solutions to the first subproblem of scheduling; e.g. there is backward timing, starting from the given date of delivery; forward timing, starting from the earliest due date at the lowest production level; or combined forward and backward timing, which makes the time buffer of each production order visible. Methods from network techniques are used here.[39] The PPC-concept of inverse sequencing also follows this logic.[40] If the resulting processing times are too long, PPC-systems offer the following measures to reduce them: shortening of waiting times and transition times, overlaying of the operations of an order, simultaneous allocation to several identical machines, and lot division. Attention is paid only to the current order; interdependencies between different products are disregarded.

As production capacities are usually limited, the orders scheduled often exceed the capacity limits in single sub-periods and on certain machines, i.e. the planned starting and termination dates are not yet feasible. An instantly feasible machine load can occur casually, but this is normally an indication of excess capacity. On the other hand, a recurrent unfeasibility that is hard to eliminate can be a sign of capacity shortage.

The task of capacity balancing is first to determine the extent of these unfeasibilities with the aid of capacity surfaces, and subsequently to eliminate them with appropriate measures. Two general methods are possible: an adjustment of capacity requirements to capacity supply can be achieved by either relocating orders from periods of capacity overload to periods of capacity surplus within the limits of existing time buffers; or, by the outside contracting of production stages which impose an extreme load on a period. Conversely, for the adjustment of capacity supply to capacity requirements, the adjustment measures described in the Gutenberg production theory[41] can be used: capacity supply can be increased by the adjustment of time by means of overtime or extra shifts, by the adjustment of quantity by mobilizing standby aggregates, and by the adjustment of intensity as a variation of the production rate within the technical possibilities. It can be shown[42] that the use of pure forms of adjustment is a cost minimizing strategy.

---

39 See Kurbel (1995), pp. 148.

40 See Adam (1988), pp. 90.

41 See Gutenberg (1983), pp. 302.

42 See von Zwehl/Brink (1994), p. 1115; Steven (1994), p. 1500.

After first adjusting time up to its limit, production intensity is then adjusted to the point at which break-even-analysis indicates that the employment of a standby machine leads to lower costs.

The resource-oriented PPC-concept OPT (Optimized Production Technology)[43] integrates the two subproblems of time management (sequencing and loading) and focuses on the facilities that frequently turn out to be bottlenecks. Thus it follows the law of balancing organizational plans,[44] formulated by Gutenberg. Starting from a product network, which maps the resources in the production system on to their delivery relations, and from the planned termination dates of orders, the expected capacity load for all working systems is first determined by backward timing, and thereby the bottlenecks for the current production program are also shown. Subsequently the product network is split into two parts. The critical part contains the bottleneck resources and the production facilities following them in the workflow whilst the non-critical part contains all production facilities preceding the bottlenecks. In order to make the best use of bottleneck resources, they are planned first. These machine loads are then taken as a basis for a forward timing procedure in the critical part of the network, and for backward timing in the non-critical part.

Gutenberg deals with problems of time management mainly within the scope of process planning.[45] He works out the combinatorial complexity of machine loading, especially for job shop operations, which has come to be known as the dilemma of job shop scheduling, i.e. that the minimization of processing times and maximization of capacity utilization are conflicting goals. For job shop scheduling in the form of GANTT-diagrams, he suggests the integer programming model of Manne[46], which, even now, is incalculable because it constitutes an insurmountable computational problem.

For scheduling, he proposes a retrograde method and favors a decentralized location of this planning problem on the shop floor, as the newer PPC-systems offer it. With the description of the relations between aggregate planning and detailed planning of production dates,[47] he lays the foundation for the concept of cumulative timing (Fortschrittszahlenkonzept)[48] mainly used in the automobile industry. To map the schedule situation, and to trace the various orders that have to be processed by the production facilities in different sequences, Gutenberg recommends the network methods, namely CPM for deterministic and PERT for

43 See Goldratt (1988).

44 See Gutenberg (1983), p. 164.

45 See Gutenberg (1983), pp. 215.

46 See Manne (1960).

47 See Gutenberg (1983), pp. 225 - 226.

48 See hereto Corsten (1995), pp. 468; Glaser/Geiger/Rohde (1992), pp. 232, Zäpfel (1994), p. 740.

stochastic processing times.[49] These methods are also used for scheduling in numerous PPC-systems.

It is typical of Gutenberg's comprehensive view that he reconsiders the interdependencies between time management and other planning problems. He therefore underlines the mutual dependency of scheduling and lot sizing, which are linked not only by capacity utilization, but also by the planned inventories. He further emphasizes the necessity of cost orientation in process planning, whereas, at best, PPC-systems aim at time objectives at this level.

3.2.4 Job scheduling

As a result of time management and capacity planning, in this module jobs are released and finally loaded on to the machines. PPC-systems often use simple priority rules to control the queue in front of a machine. But as priority rules only support a single objective and concern one machine only whilst neglecting its integration into the production process, the results of such rules are often unsatisfactory.

There is therefore a tendency to decentralize order release by taking it out of the central planning process and locating it, together with order control, at the foreman's level. Computer-aided production control stations can support production control interactively and quite accurately.[50]

The tasks of job sequencing, i.e. order release and control which are located very close to the operating level of production, are not dealt with explicitly by Gutenberg. The reason is not so much that he regarded them as negligible, but that this domain is not well suited to a model-oriented approach.

III. The influence of Gutenberg on production planning and control

As the preceding discussion has shown, there is an obvious influence of the Gutenberg production theory on substantial parts of production planning and control. Figure 2 depicts the common properties and the differences between the two approaches to the production management considered here.

In some subproblems of production planning and control, i.e. program planning, lot sizing, and sequencing and scheduling, a considerable implicit influence of the Gutenberg production theory is clearly recognizable. To some extent the methods he proposed are still used in practice today.

---

49 See Gutenberg (1983), pp. 227.

50 See Kurbel (1995), pp. 235.

Figure 2: Interdependencies between the Gutenberg production theory and production planning and control

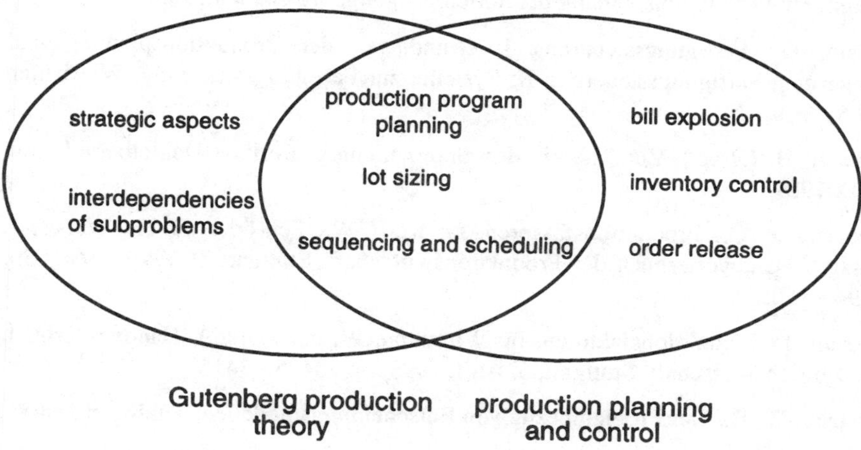

However, some other subproblems which, in Gutenberg's estimation, played an important role, have hitherto not been reflected in the development of production planning and control. This applies primarily to long-term strategic aspects of production management and to the explicit consideration of the interdependencies between the various subproblems. Practitioner dissatisfaction with the suboptimal performance of PPC-systems could be reduced if these important problems were more explicitly taken into account.

But it should also be stated that not all functions of PPC-systems are dealt with by Gutenberg. This refers mainly to administrative functions like the explosion of bills of material, inventory control, and order release that do not require sophisticated theoretical models but rely primarily on a data based technical realization.

4 Final remarks

It is clear that problems in production planning and control constitute an area of business administration that received extensive treatment from Gutenberg. Production planning and control would stand to gain should its further development be more explicitly influenced by the basic findings of Gutenberg, especially in respect of objective functions and interdependencies. Developments in production engineering and data processing technology have undoubtedly reached the stage that permits the direct adoption of the methods proposed by Gutenberg. However, already in the fifties he had reached a conceptual level, which powers above many of today's PPC-concepts.

References

Adam, D.: Produktionsplanung bei Sortenfertigung, Wiesbaden 1969

Adam, D.: Fertigungssteuerung I: Grundlagen der Produktionsplanung und -steuerung; Fertigungssteuerung II: Systeme zur Fertigungssteuerung, Wiesbaden 1988

Albach, H. (Hrsg.): Zur Theorie der Unternehmung, Berlin / Heidelberg / New York 1989

Beuermann, G.: Produktionsfaktoren, in: Kern, W., Schröder, H.-H., Weber, J. (Hrsg.), Handwörterbuch der Produktionswirtschaft, Stuttgart, 2. Aufl. 1996, Sp. 1494 - 1505

Bloech, J.: Produktionsfaktoren, in: Wittmann, W. u.a. (Hrsg.), Handwörterbuch der Betriebswirtschaft, Stuttgart, 5. Aufl. 1993, Sp., 3405 - 3415

Bretzke, W.-R.: Der Problembezug von Entscheidungsmodellen, Tübingen 1980

Corsten, H.: Produktionswirtschaft, München / Wien, 5. Aufl. 1995

Corsten, H.: Dienstleistungsmanagement, München / Wien, 3. Aufl. 1997

Dinkelbach, W.: Ein Problem der Produktionsplanung in Ein- und Mehrproduktunternehmen, Würzburg / Wien 1964

Drexl, A., Fleischmann, B., Günther, H.-O., Stadtler, H., Tempelmeier, H.: Konzeptionelle Grundlagen kapazitätsorientierter PPS-Systeme, in: ZfbF 46, 1994, S. 1022 - 1045

Geitner, U. W., Chen, J.: PPS-Marktübersicht 1990 - 121 Systeme im Vergleich, in: FB/IE 39, 1990, H. 2, S. 52 - 65

Glaser, H., Geiger, W., Rohde, V.: PPS - Produktionsplanung und -steuerung, Wiesbaden, 2. Aufl. 1992

Goldratt, E. M.: Computerized Shop Floor Scheduling, in: International Journal of Production Research 26, 1988, S. 443 - 455

Gutenberg, E.: Grundlagen der Betriebswirtschaftslehre, Band 1: Die Produktion, Berlin / Heidelberg / New York, 1. Aufl. 1951, 24. Aufl. 1983

Gutenberg, E.: Einführung in die Betriebswirtschaftslehre, Wiesbaden 1958

Hackstein, R.: Produktionsplanung und -steuerung (PPS) - Ein Handbuch für die Betriebspraxis, Köln 1989

Helberg, P.: PPS als CIM-Baustein, Berlin 1987

Kern, W., Fallaschinski, K.: Betriebswirtschaftliche Produktionsfaktoren, in: wisu 7/8, 1978/79, S. 580 - 583 u. S. 15 - 18

Kernler, H.: PPS - Stand und Tendenzen, in: HMD Theorie und Praxis der Wirtschaftsinformatik 26, Heft 150, 1989, S. 98 - 109

Kistner, K.-P., Steven, M.: Produktionsplanung, Heidelberg, 2. Aufl. 1993

Knolmayer, G.: Stand und Entwicklungstendenzen der computergestützten Produktionsplanung und -steuerung, in: Kurbel, K., Strunz, H. (Hrsg.), Handbuch Wirtschaftsinformatik, Stuttgart 1990, S.69 - 87

Küpper, H.-U.: Interdependenzen zwischen Produktionstheorie und der Organisation des Produktionsprozesses, Berlin 1980

Kurbel, K.: Produktionsplanung und -steuerung, München / Wien, 2. Aufl. 1995

Manne, A. S.: On the Job Shop Scheduling Problem, in: Operations Research 8, 1960, S. 219 - 223

Orlicky, J.: Material Requirements Planning, New York 1975

Scheer, A.-W.: Produktionsplanung auf der Grundlage einer Datenbank des Fertigungsbereichs, München / Wien 1976

Scheer, A.-W.: CIM - Der computergesteuerte Industriebetrieb, Berlin / Heidelberg / New York, 4. Aufl. 1990

Schneeweiß, Ch.: Elemente einer Theorie hierarchischer Planung, in: OR Spektrum 16, 1994, S. 161 - 168

Stadtler, H.: Hierarchische Produktionsplanung bei losweiser Fertigung, Heidelberg 1988

Steven, M.: Hierarchische Produktionsplanung, Heidelberg, 2. Aufl. 1994a

Steven, M.: Die Einbeziehung des Umweltfaktors in die Gutenberg-Produktionsfunktion, in: ZfB 64, 1994b, S. 1491 - 1512

Steven, M., Meyer, H.: Computergestützte PPS-Systeme - Entwicklung, Stand, Tendenzen, in: WiSt 26, 1997, in Vorbereitung

von Zwehl, W., Brink, A.: Optimale Aggregatanpassung bei begrenzt verfügbaren Einsatzfaktoren, in: ZfB 64, 1994, S. 1109 - 1142

Wöhe, G.: Einführung in die Allgemeine Betriebswirtschaftslehre, München, 19. Aufl. 1996

Zäpfel, G., Missbauer, H.: Produktionsplanung und -steuerung für die Fertigungsindustrie - ein Systemvergleich, in: ZfB 57, 1987, S. 882 - 900

Zäpfel, G.: Strategisches Produktions-Management, Berlin / New York 1989

Zäpfel, G.: Entwicklungsstand und -tendenzen von PPS-Systemen, in: Corsten, H. (Hrsg.), Handbuch Produktionsmanagement, Wiesbaden 1994, S. 719 - 745

Zimmermann, G.: PPS-Methoden auf dem Prüfstand, Landsberg am Lech 1987

Summary

Despite their common field of practical application, systems of production planning and control (PPC-systems) are widely developed without reference to Gutenberg production theory. This paper elucidates the implicit influence of Gutenberg in certain domains of production planning and control. It also shows that the integration of strategic issues and more consideration of interdependencies between the various domains of production planning and control, could lead to considerable improvements in the sub-optimal performance of PPC-systems.

Determination of Intensity Variances for Cost Control

H. Glaser[1]

Overview

- No consensus has yet been reached about the "correct" method for determining information-relevant partial cost variances. As shown below, the problem of choosing a suitable method is complicated by the fact that even optimal planning under certainty cannot preclude actual values from being below standard values. This implies that, in contrast to the conventional view, intensity (production rate) variances resulting from an actual-vs-standard comparison can be negative.
- It is shown that in order to reveal intensity variances caused by inefficient behavior, it is necessary to distinguish between optimum, standard, and actual intensities, and therefore to integrate the theory of adaptation forms developed by Gutenberg into cost control.
- Methods commonly proposed for practical application are analyzed with regard to the extent to which they result in first order partial variances (particularly intensity variances) which comprise concealed, information-distorting variances of higher orders as compensatory amounts.
- In order to avoid the occurrence of compensatory effects, a method based on minimum values is proposed, which, for all data constellations, leads to unambiguous intensity variances indicating possible cost reductions with respect to standard cost.

Keywords. Variance Analysis, Partial Cost Variances, Min-Method

---

1 Professor Dr. Horst Glaser, University of Saarland, Chair for Industrial Management, Im Stadtwald, 66123 Saarbruecken, Germany, email: h.glaser@wiwi.uni-sb.de.

1 Purposes of Cost Control

An essential function of cost control consists in determining cost variances arising from unplanned, or inefficient, behavior and in revealing process-related or implementation-related causes for those variances in order to avoid unnecessary costs in the future. Closely related to this task, cost control should aim at determining cost variances resulting from planning errors. By locating plan-related (or decision-related) causes for variances, the prerequisites are established for the setting of relevant optimum or standard values in the future.

There is general agreement that in order to fulfill the above-mentioned purposes, a comparison of standard and actual costs, differentiated respectively by cost or input factor categories, has to be drawn for each cost center, and that the resulting (total) cost variance has to be split up into partial variances. There are, however, controversial opinions about

- what "inefficient behavior" precisely means, and how such behavior is to be recorded in terms of cost, and
- which of the numerous existing methods of variance analysis[2] should be used.

Some approaches to cost control that is integrated into flexible standard costing introduce a special cost determinant to reflect "operational inefficiency".[3] In this context, the amount traced to the cost determinant "efficiency" (or "inefficiency") exceeding its standard value is said to represent a "genuine usage variance" or an "inefficiency-based (residual) variance." This kind of procedure for determining cost variances resulting from inefficient behavior appears extremely problematic. The control approaches referred to above must, and in fact do, take into account further cost determinants, e.g. intensity (production rate) or intensity-dependent factor usage and yield. Therefore, if all relevant cost determinants are included in the cost control scheme, the partial variance traced to the determinant "efficiency" (or "inefficiency") can only comprise costs arising from theft and/or decay of factor quantities. The misleading introduction of "efficiency" (or "inefficiency") as a separate cost determinant conceals not explicitly recorded, process-related inefficiencies due to other cost determinants unnecessarily exceeding their respective standard values.

Except for theft and/or decay of factor quantities, it seems advisable not to include a distinct cost determinant characterizing "efficiency" (or "inefficiency"). All inefficiencies can then be traced exclusively to differences between the

---

2 A comprehensive and systematic overview and assessment of these methods can be found in Kloock (1994), pp 620ff.

3 Cf. Haberstock (1986), p 260 and p 267; Wimmer (1994), pp 990ff. Haberstock, however, points out that inefficiencies could be attributed to other cost determinants as well.

standard and actual values of those cost determinants governing the usage (in monetary terms) of the respective factor in the work process. In this regard, variance analysis could even result in more than one partial variance indicating inefficient behavior. However, not every partial variance reflecting a cost determinant exceeding its standard value is necessarily caused by inefficiency. In general, it cannot be ruled out that the standard value in question was set too low because of a planning situation characterized by uncertainty and/or a planning error, and that the resulting cost variance was unavoidable. On the other hand, the entire difference between standard and actual cost might be due to inefficiencies which could have been avoided if work had been carried out as prescribed. Attributing a cost variance to inefficiency thus requires careful analysis of the decision situation when the standards were set, as well as of the circumstances in which the decision was implemented.

The controversy about the suitability of the different methods of variance analysis for the purposes of cost control originates from the fact that alternative methods can not only lead to different numbers of partial variances, but also to different values of cost variances with respect to a given standard-vs-actual difference. The latter is also true for intensity variances if they occur in conjunction with other partial variances, which is usually the case in industrial practice.

2 Intensity Variances and Efficiency

In the context of cost control an intensity variance is regarded as a cost variance. Such a variance is ultimately due to the fact that, instead of the optimum or standard intensity of a machine, a different actual intensity is attained. The immediate cause of the intensity-related cost variance is the difference between standard and actual values of input factor usage as a cost determinant depending on production intensity (production rate).

Primarily in flexible standard costing, in the course of "optimal planning", the determination of the so-called "standard cost 1", as minimum cost, is based on the optimum intensity of a machine. The optimum intensity is defined as the intensity at which the variable unit cost of the input factors required for the machine in question attains a minimum.

Let d denote the production intensity of a machine measured in units of output per unit of time, and $r_i(d)$, a usage function, indicate the per-unit usage of input factor i ($i = 1,..., n$) in factor units per unit of output depending on the chosen intensity. Then, with respective input factor prices p_i (> 0), the variable unit cost is given by the expression

$$k_v(d) = \sum_{i=1}^{n} p_i \cdot r_i(d). \tag{1}$$

In particular, given u-shaped usage functions, which are assumed below, the optimum intensity d_{opt} is the (only) intensity for which the first derivative of the unit cost function $k_v(d)$ equals zero:

$$k'_v(d_{opt}) = \sum_{i=1}^{n} p_i \cdot r'_i(d_{opt}) = 0. \tag{2}$$

In the special case of two input factors (n = 2), we have

$$k'_v(d_{opt}) = p_1 \cdot r'_1(d_{opt}) + p_2 \cdot r'_2(d_{opt}) = 0\,, \tag{3}$$

whence the optimality criterion

$$\frac{p_1}{p_2} = -\frac{r'_2(d_{opt})}{r'_1(d_{opt})} \tag{4}$$

is derived. This criterion states that, at optimum intensity, the factor price ratio is equal to the marginal rate of substitution between the two input factors. Contrary to the analogous theorem of neoclassical production and cost theory concerning the minimum cost combination,[4] and according to the production and cost theory developed by Gutenberg,[5] factor substitution ultimately rests on a substitution between production intensity and time.

If the intensities $d_{1,opt}$ and $d_{2,opt}$ at which the usage functions $r_1(d)$ and $r_2(d)$ attain their respective minima are different from each other, the optimum intensity d_{opt} according to (4) assumes a value between $d_{1,opt}$ and $d_{2,opt}$ (cf. Figure 1). This implies that per-unit usage of factor $\tilde{i}$ can definitely fall below the value of $r_{\tilde{i}}(d_{opt})$. If $d_{\tilde{i},opt} > d_{opt}$ (as is the case for $\tilde{i} = 2$ in Figure 1), any intensity d with $d_{opt} < d < d_{\tilde{i},g}$ results in a per-unit usage $r_{\tilde{i}}(d)$ below $r_{\tilde{i}}(d_{opt})$, where $d_{\tilde{i},g}$ denotes the intensity differing from d_{opt} which satisfies the equation $r_{\tilde{i}}(d_{opt}) = r_{\tilde{i}}(d_{\tilde{i},g})$. Given $d_{\tilde{i},opt} < d_{opt}$ (as is true for $\tilde{i} = 1$ in Figure 1), any intensity d with $d_{\tilde{i},g} < d < d_{opt}$ leads to a per-unit usage below the usage at optimum intensity.

---

4 Cf. e.g. Kistner (1993), pp 12ff.

5 Cf. Gutenberg (1983), pp 326ff.

Figure 1: Usage functions

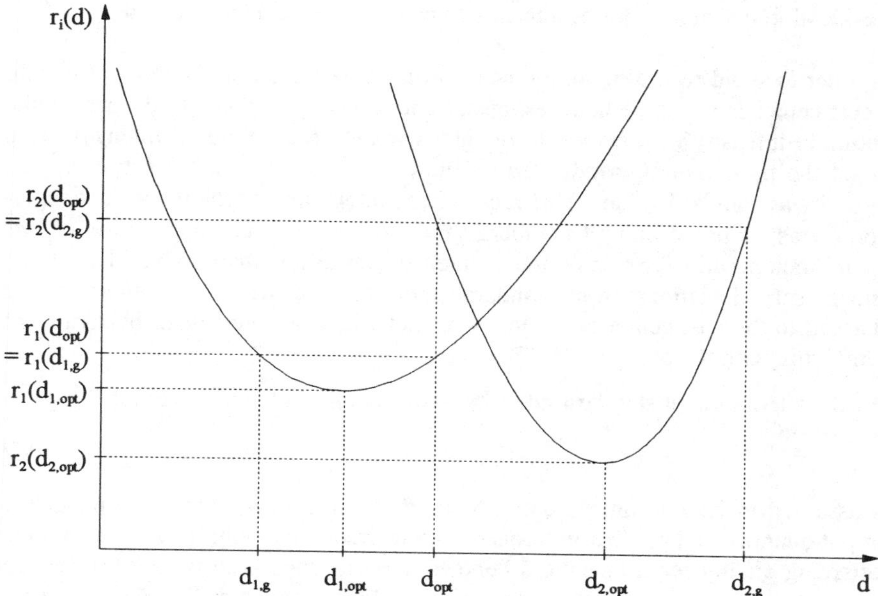

If the per-unit usage of a factor $\tilde{i}$ resulting from optimum intensity is taken as standard value for cost control, a deviation from this intensity can lead to an actual value below its corresponding standard in spite of "optimal planning". As a consequence of this effect of "below-standard usage", and contrary to the prevailing opinion, it cannot be ruled out that an intensity variance resulting from an actual-vs-standard comparison assumes a negative value. The corresponding cost reduction, however, can not be interpreted as evidence of an exceptionally efficient behavior of the worker(s) responsible for carrying out the production process. This cost reduction inevitably takes place if a deviation from optimum intensity d_{opt} is required in order to attain a given output level and the intensity d chosen as adequate to the workload situation is located in the range $d_{opt} < d < d_{\tilde{i},g}$ for $d_{\tilde{i},opt} > d_{opt}$ or $d_{\tilde{i},g} < d < d_{opt}$ for $d_{\tilde{i},opt} < d_{opt}$, respectively.

Conversely, an intensity-related increase of actual cost with respect to standard cost can occur which must, however, by no means be interpreted as an index of inefficiency. This cost increase is inevitable if, e.g. for $d_{\tilde{i},opt} > d_{opt}$, the workload in question requires intensity to be increased to a value $d > d_{\tilde{i},g}$.

In order to avoid recording an intensity variance for which, or for parts of which, a cost center is not to be held responsible, it seems appropriate to determine the optimum intensity with respect to the given workload as standard intensity; and, to set the per-unit usage indicated by the corresponding usage function at that intensity as standard value.[6] This requires the integration of the theory of adaptation forms, as proposed by Gutenberg,[7] into cost control. The application of this theory then permits the calculation of intensity variances, that are based solely on unnecessary deviations from standard intensity, and which can therefore be charged to the cost center as an index of inefficient behavior or of behavior not complying with the plan.

For the stipulation of standard intensity, the general "Gutenberg relation"

$$x = d \cdot b \cdot t \tag{5}$$

is assumed to be relevant.[8] Herein, x, as a measure of workload, signifies the output quantity of a product in terms of usable production volume, i.e. the volume satisfying quality requirements, d denotes intensity measured in units processed (or produced) per unit of time, b represents yield, expressed as the ratio of usable to processed (or produced) units, and t production time.

If the only possible form of adaptation to a given output of $x = x_V$ consists in varying intensity, whereas production time is kept constant at $t = t_V$, then according to (5) intensity d must satisfy the relation

$$d = \frac{x_V}{b \cdot t_V}. \tag{6}$$

Thus, the value of intensity depends on the yield. Substituting the planned, or standard, value of yield, intensity is unambiguously evaluated as

$$d_V = \frac{x_V}{b_S \cdot t_V}. \tag{7}$$

---

6 If unit cost planning is based on optimum intensity and cost control is based on standard intensity, different values of these intensities induce cost variances between per-period cost unit accounting and cost center accounting displayed as intensity variances. Cf. for this Kilger (1993), pp 627ff, particularly pp 641ff.

7 Cf. Gutenberg (1983), pp 354ff.

8 In the sequel, intensity splitting is excluded. For this kind of splitting, cf. e.g. Dellmann/Nastansky (1969), pp 239ff; Schüler (1970); Karrenberg/Scheer (1970), pp 689ff; Bogaschewsky/Roland (1996), pp 49ff.

Whilst taking this value as standard intensity seems plausible at first glance, it can turn out to be problematic. In fact, if the actual yield b_r differs from the standard yield b_s, standard intensity d_s ($\neq d_v$) is given by:

$$d_s = \frac{x_v}{b_r \cdot t_v} \neq d_v . \tag{8}$$

If standard cost is determined on the basis of the intensity value d_v, but the actual intensity attained is d_s, an intensity variance will appear in the course of cost control, the sole cause of which is the deviation from the planned or standard yield. Cost control based on the value d_v implies that any yield variance, in the sense of a yield-related cost variance, no matter whether caused by inefficiency or not, causes an intensity variance to be indicated. In order to prevent this kind of intensity variance from showing up – the amount of which has to be attributed to the yield variance by virtue of the principle of causality – it seems advisable to set d_s equal to the value according to equation (8), which equals the optimum intensity d_{opt} only if output happens to be $x_v = d_{opt} \cdot b_r \cdot t_v$. This means, however, that in contrast to common cost control procedures, the standard value for a particular cost determinant can only be set "ex post", depending on the actual value of another cost determinant.

If the cost center can not only vary intensity, but also production time up to a maximum of t_{max}, then standard intensity can be expressed as

$$d_s = \begin{cases} d_{opt} & \text{for } x_v \leq d_{opt} \cdot b_r \cdot t_{max} \\ \dfrac{x_v}{b_r \cdot t_{max}} & \text{for } x_v > d_{opt} \cdot b_r \cdot t_{max} \end{cases}, \tag{9}$$

based on the optimal combination of these adaptation forms with respect to the actual yield rate.[9]

It should be noted that even with optimal planning subject to restrictions, a limited production time, an actual intensity d_r which is different from standard intensity d_s can lead to a negative intensity variance based on actual-vs-standard comparison. If e.g. $d_{\tilde{i},opt} > d_{opt}$ for $d_{opt} < d_s < d_{2,opt}$ and $d_s < d_r < d_{2,s}$ with $r_{\tilde{i}}(d_s) = r_{\tilde{i}}(d_{2,s})$, then usage of factor $\tilde{i}$ is lower at actual intensity than at standard intensity, and thus, a negative intensity variance occurs. Therefore, the statement that, given an optimal plan (subject to restrictions), "cost variances in the sense of a difference between actual and standard cost ... can, as a conse-

9 It is assumed that any deviation from standard yield is recognized immediately and that it is then possible to adjust intensity to the corresponding standard value without delay.

quence, only take on values greater than or equal to zero"[10], does not generally hold. However, this means that a cost determinant can attain a value below its standard even when planning is free from uncertainty and error. A situation in which actual values are less than standard values leads to particular "compensatory effects" of partial variances that are exhibited by "common" methods of variance analysis.

3 Methods of Variance Determination

Resorting to the general Gutenberg relation, and dropping the index i or $\tilde{i}$, respectively; a cost control differentiated by cost category, or factor category, starts out from the following cost function which pertains to the monetary usage of the input factor in question:

$$K = p_v \cdot x_v \cdot r(d) \cdot \frac{1}{b}. \tag{10}$$

Herein, p_v, as the factor price, and x_v, as the output quantity, represent magnitudes on which the cost center has no influence. Contrastingly, r(d), as the per-unit usage, and 1/b, as the reciprocal value of yield, are (variable) cost determinants.

Setting $y_1 = r(d)$ and $y_2 = 1/b$ for simplicity, and denoting the standard value of cost determinant z (z = 1, 2) by y_z^s and its actual value by y_z^r, standard cost is defined as

$$K^s = p_v \cdot x_v \cdot y_1^s \cdot y_2^s \tag{11}$$

and actual cost as

$$K^r = p_v \cdot x_v \cdot y_1^r \cdot y_2^r, \tag{12}$$

where

$$y_1^s = r(d_s),\ y_1^s = r(d_s) \text{ and } y_1^s = r(d_s),\ y_1^s = r(d_s). \tag{13}$$

Which values will eventually be assigned to the partial variances, when a difference between standard cost K^s and actual cost K^r occurs, depends on the chosen

---

10 Wimmer (1994), p 985 (translated from German).

method of variance analysis. Partial variances resulting from the following classes of methods are derived and critically examined hereafter:

- differentiated-cumulative variance analysis methods,
- min-based differentiated-cumulative variance analysis methods,
- cumulative variance analysis methods.

Within each class, variance analysis can be performed either as a standard-vs-actual comparison based on the difference $K^s - K^r$, or as an actual-vs-standard comparison based on the difference $K^r - K^s$. Depending on the standard or actual values of the cost determinants used as points of reference, two different versions can be distinguished for the first two classes.

3.1 Differentiated-Cumulative Variance Analysis

Differentiated-cumulative variance analysis is generally characterized by the possibility of completely splitting the total variance $K^s - K^r$ or $K^r - K^s$ into the maximum possible number of partial variances that are caused by deviations of individual cost determinants from their respective standards. In the case of a multiplicative relationship between cost determinants, this analysis method formally leads to first order partial variances and partial variances of higher orders. In partial variances of the first order, only one standard-vs-actual difference (only one Δ-quantity) with respect to a cost determinant occurs explicitly (!). Conversely, partial variances of higher orders contain at least two standard-vs-actual differences (at least two Δ-quantities) related to different cost determinants. The number of Δ-quantities appearing in a partial variance thus determines the order.

Performing a standard-vs-actual comparison and choosing actual values as reference basis, furthermore setting

$$y_z^s - y_z^r = \overset{SA}{\Delta} y_z \text{, implying } y_z^s = y_z^r + \overset{SA}{\Delta} y_z \text{;} \tag{14}$$

the total variance $K^s - K^r$ is partitioned into the following partial variances, linked by their respective operators:

$$\begin{aligned} K^s - K^r &= p_v \cdot x_v \cdot y_1^s \cdot y_2^s - p_v \cdot x_v \cdot y_1^r \cdot y_2^r \\ &= p_v \cdot x_v \cdot [(y_1^r + \overset{SA}{\Delta} y_1) \cdot (y_2^r + \overset{SA}{\Delta} y_2) - y_1^r \cdot y_2^r] \\ &= p_v \cdot x_v \cdot \overset{SA}{\Delta} y_1 \cdot y_2^r \end{aligned} \tag{15}$$

(intensity variance as partial variance of the 1st order)

$$+p_v \cdot x_v \cdot y_1^r \cdot \overset{SA}{\Delta} y_2$$

(yield variance as partial variance of the 1st order)

$$+p_v \cdot x_v \cdot \overset{SA}{\Delta} y_1 \cdot \overset{SA}{\Delta} y_2$$

(variance intersection as partial variance of the 2nd order).

With regard to this partitioning method, the following assertion has been made: "In partial variances of higher orders ... with Δ-quantities having different signs, amounts of variances are contained which only fulfill purely compensatory functions, thus canceling out each other, so that they are not required in order to explain the total variance."[11] Firstly, it must be noted that these compensatory effects also occur when Δ-quantities have the same sign, namely, when all Δ-quantities are negative, i.e. in a situation of excess of standards for all cost determinants, which is far from uncommon in business practice. Secondly, analysis must not be limited to compensatory amounts in connection with higher order variances. It is generally true that (at least) one partial variance of the first order (based on actual values) also embraces a compensatory amount if variances of higher orders "fulfill purely compensatory functions". Therefore, it seems inconsistent to classify variances of higher orders as "uninformative" or as "information-distorting" and variances of the first order as generally suitable for control purposes.[12] The problem of information relevance pertains particularly to the latter variances, i. e. in the present context to the intensity variance and the yield variance as established by (15).

With $y_z^r > y_z^s$ (z = 1, 2), the intensity variance and the yield variance, formally classified as partial variances of the first order, in terms of absolute values – and relevant for compensation – each comprise a variance of the second order. This is shown in Figure 2, assuming $p_v \cdot x_v = 1$ without loss of generality.[13] Referring to (14), (15) and Figure 2, the following compensatory effects[14] occur, where signs of, and operators between, variances must be strictly distinguished:

$$K^s - K^r$$

$$= \underbrace{p_v \cdot x_v \cdot \overset{SA}{\Delta} y_1 \cdot (y_2^s - \overset{SA}{\Delta} y_1)}_{(-\mathrm{I}\ \ -\mathrm{III})} + \underbrace{p_v \cdot x_v (y_1^s - \overset{SA}{\Delta} y_1) \overset{SA}{\Delta} y_2}_{(-\mathrm{II}\ \ -\mathrm{III})} + \underbrace{p_v \cdot x_v \cdot \overset{SA}{\Delta} y_1 \cdot \overset{SA}{\Delta} y_2}_{(\mathrm{III})} \qquad (16)$$

---

11 Kloock (1994), p 623 (translated from German).

12 This is the case in Kloock (1994), pp 622ff.

13 The Δ-quantities represent absolute values of the respective standard-vs-actual differences.

14 Wilms emphasises these effects; cf. Wilms (1988), pp 81ff.

$$= \underbrace{p_v \cdot x_v \cdot \overset{SA}{\Delta} y_1 \cdot y_2^s}_{(-\text{I})} + \underbrace{p_v \cdot x_v \cdot y_1^s \cdot \overset{SA}{\Delta} y_2}_{(-\text{II})} - \underbrace{p_v \cdot x_v \cdot \overset{SA}{\Delta} y_1 \cdot \overset{SA}{\Delta} y_2}_{(\text{III})}.$$

Figure 2: Partial variances based on actual values with $y_1^s < y_1^r$; $y_2^s < y_2^r$

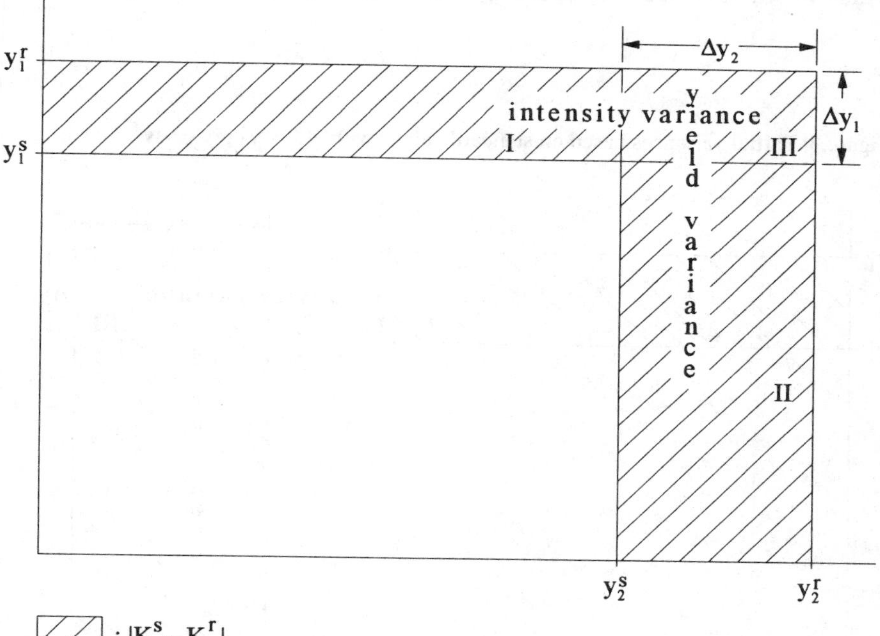

The last amount shown in (16) as intensity variance now exclusively reflects a difference between standard intensity d_s and actual intensity d_r; correspondingly, the yield variance is no longer influenced by deviations from standard intensity.

With $y_z^s < y_z^r$ (z = 1, 2), "compensation-free" partial variances can be obtained directly if standard values instead of actual values are chosen as a reference basis for differentiated-cumulative variance analysis in the form of a standard-vs-actual comparison. In this case we have, in accordance with (16),

$$K^s - K^r = p_v \cdot x_v \cdot [y_1^s \cdot y_2^s - (y_1^s - \Delta y_1^{SA}) \cdot (y_2^s - \Delta y_2^{SA})] \tag{17}$$

$$= p_v \cdot x_v \cdot \Delta y_1^{SA} \cdot y_2^s + p_v \cdot x_v \cdot y_1^s \cdot \Delta y_2^{SA} - p_v \cdot x_v \cdot \Delta y_1^{SA} \cdot \Delta y_2^{SA}.$$

In a situation with $y_z^s > y_z^r$ for all z, however, differentiated-cumulative variance analysis performed as a standard-vs-actual comparison based on standard values, yields partial variances embracing compensatory amounts (also cf. Figure 3), which would be excluded by choosing actual values as a reference basis.

Figure 3: Partial variances based on standard values with $y_1^s > y_1^r$; $y_2^s > y_2^r$

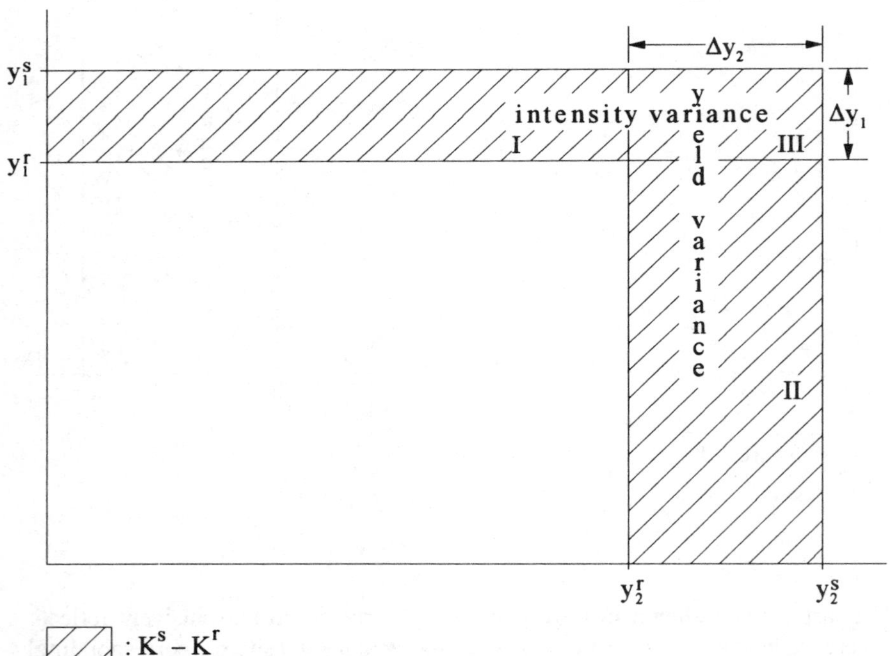

Summing up, we can state that differentiated-cumulative variance analysis carried out as a standard-vs-actual comparison should be based on standard values if $y_z^s < y_z^r$ for all cost determinants and on actual values if $y_z^s > y_z^r$ (for all z).

Special problems arise in case a) $y_1^s > y_1^r$, $y_2^s < y_2^r$ and in case b) $y_1^s < y_1^r$, $y_2^s > y_2^r$. In case a), selecting actual values as reference basis leads to an intensity variance specified as:

$$\overset{SA}{p_v} \cdot x_v \cdot \Delta y_1 \cdot y_2^r = \overset{SA}{p_v} \cdot x_v \cdot \Delta y_1 \cdot y_2^s - \overset{SA}{p_v} \cdot \overset{SA}{x_v} \cdot \Delta y_1 \cdot \Delta y_2 \,, \tag{18}$$

containing an amount which is compensated by the variance of the second order explicitly shown in (15) (also cf. Figure 4). Using the standard reference basis, corresponding observations can be made with respect to the yield variance (also cf. Figure 5). The opposite is true in case b).

Figure 4: Partial variances based on actual values with $y_1^s > y_1^r$; $y_2^s < y_2^r$

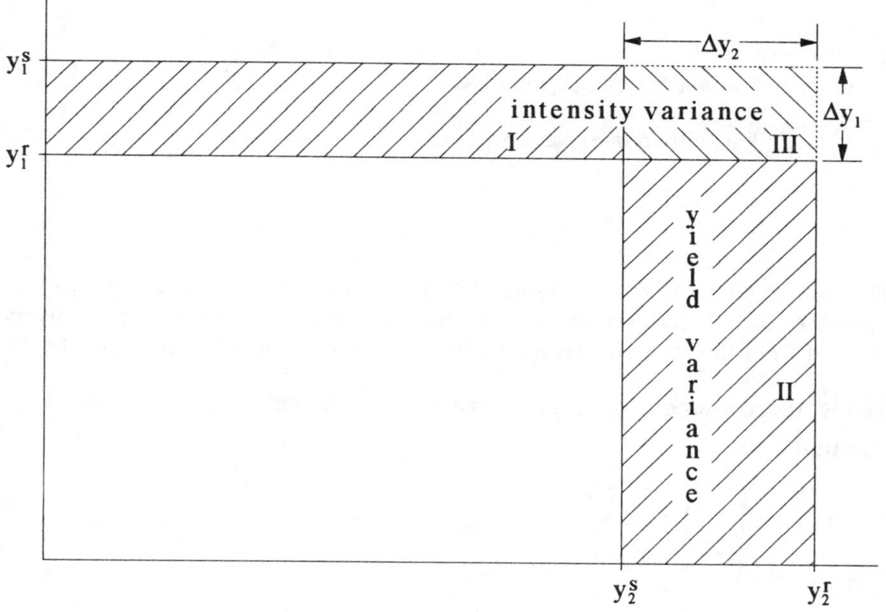

Figure 5: Partial variances based on standard values with $y_1^s > y_1^r$; $y_2^s < y_2^r$

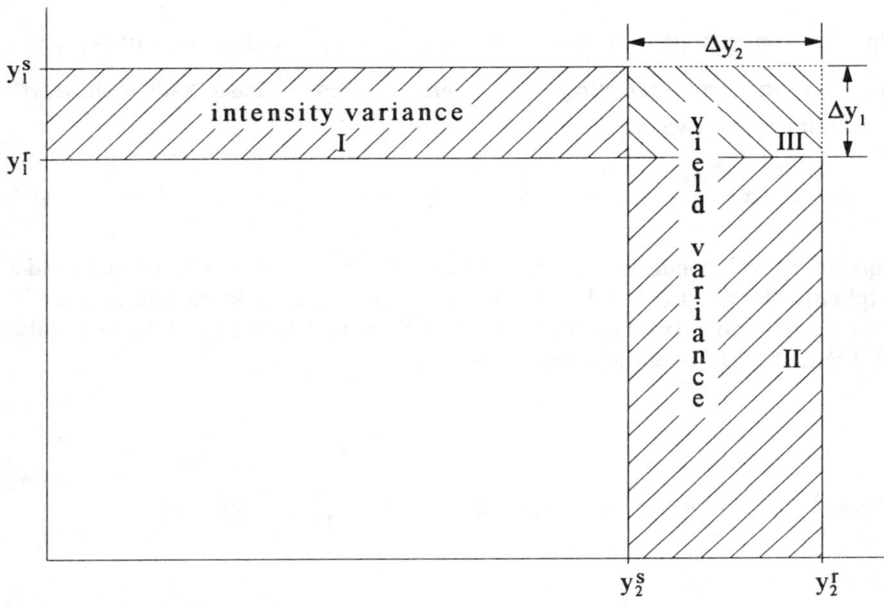

Depending on the reference basis chosen, partial variances and their linking operators, which result from an actual-vs-standard comparison, can easily be derived from the relations developed for standard-vs-actual comparisons. Multiplying the corresponding expressions by −1 and replacing the terms $\overset{SA}{\Delta y_z}$, substitution of

$$\overset{AS}{\Delta y_z} = y_z^r - y_z^s = -\overset{SA}{\Delta y_z} \tag{19}$$

yields

$$K^r - K^s = p_v \cdot x_v \cdot \overset{AS}{\Delta} y_1 \cdot y_2^r + p_v \cdot x_v \cdot y_1^r \cdot \overset{AS}{\Delta} y_2 - p_v \cdot x_v \cdot \overset{AS}{\Delta} y_1 \cdot \overset{AS}{\Delta} y_2 \qquad (20)$$

for actual-vs-standard comparisons based on actual values and

$$K^r - K^s = p_v \cdot x_v \cdot \overset{AS}{\Delta} y_1 \cdot y_2^s + p_v \cdot x_v \cdot y_1^s \cdot \overset{AS}{\Delta} y_2 + p_v \cdot x_v \cdot \overset{AS}{\Delta} y_1 \cdot \overset{AS}{\Delta} y_2 \qquad (21)$$

for actual-vs-standard comparisons based on standard values.

The above statements about compensatory effects in the context of a standard-vs-actual comparison analogously apply here. Thus, if Δ-quantities have alternating signs, these effects can be avoided, neither by a differentiated-cumulative variance analysis based on actual values, nor by the same kind of analysis based on standard values. Only the "min-method" can generally rule out compensatory amounts.

3.2 Min-Based Differentiated-Cumulative Variance Analysis

The min-based differentiated-cumulative variance analysis developed by Wilms implies "weighting" the Δ-quantities with the respective minima of the standard and actual values of the remaining cost determinants.[15] Partial variances calculated in this manner, which attain the lowest possible values, do not comprise any amounts canceling each other out with other partial variances. Following this method, only partial variances of higher orders related to Δ-quantities with matching signs are exhibited. Corresponding to their respective signs, these variances unequivocally indicate either a cost reduction or an increase in cost and thus, like partial variances of the first order, are either part of the total standard cost or of the total actual cost. Variances of higher orders which, due to alternating signs of the corresponding Δ-quantities, are neither a subset of standard cost nor a subset of actual cost, are not recorded at all, being "factually non-existent" variances.

Carried out as a standard-vs-actual comparison (actual-vs-standard comparison), with $y_z^s < y_z^r$ (for all z), the min-method yields the same result as the differentiated-cumulative standard-vs-actual analysis based on standard values (actual-vs-standard analysis based on standard values). If $y_z^s > y_z^r$ (for all z), the respective results of the min-method, and of the corresponding differentiated-cumulative variance analysis based on actual values, coincide. With Δ-quantities having different signs, however, the results of the min-method differ from those of the differentiated-cumulative variance analysis based on standard or actual

15 Cf. Wilms (1988), pp 96ff.

values. Eliminating the "factually non-existent" variance of the second order, a standard-vs-actual comparison based on minimum values for $y_1^s > y_1^r, y_2^s < y_2^r$ yields the "compensation-free" partial variances

$$K^s - K^r = p_v \cdot x_v \cdot \Delta y_1 \overset{SA}{\cdot} y_2^s + p_v \cdot x_v \cdot y_1^r \overset{SA}{\cdot} \Delta y_2 \tag{22}$$

and for $y_1^s < y_1^r, y_2^s > y_2^r$ results in the partial variances

$$K^s - K^r = p_v \cdot x_v \cdot \Delta y_1 \overset{SA}{\cdot} y_2^r + p_v \cdot x_v \cdot y_1^s \overset{SA}{\cdot} \Delta y_2 \tag{23}$$

with their linking operators as shown. An actual-vs-standard comparison in case a) leads to

$$K^r - K^s = p_v \cdot x_v \cdot \Delta y_1 \overset{AS}{\cdot} y_2^s + p_v \cdot x_v \cdot y_1^r \overset{AS}{\cdot} \Delta y_2 \tag{24}$$

and in case b) yields

$$K^r - K^s = p_v \cdot x_v \cdot \Delta y_1 \overset{AS}{\cdot} y_2^r + p_v \cdot x_v \cdot y_1^s \overset{AS}{\cdot} \Delta y_2 \,. \tag{25}$$

The above results can also arise from the cumulative variance analysis method outlined below. Therefore, the hitherto unchallenged assumption, that the latter method always implies partial variances containing higher order variances, should be revised.

3.3 Cumulative Variance Analysis

Cumulative variance analysis is primarily implemented in the context of flexible standard costing systems. Pursuant to this method of analysis, the total variance is partitioned either by successively substituting actual values for standard values (adjustment of standard values to actual values), which implies that the partial variance determined last is based on actual values; or, by successively replacing actual values with standard values (adjustment of actual values to standard values). In the latter case, the last partial variance is thus based on standard values. For each direction of adjustment, the value of a partial variance depends on its position in the partitioning sequence.

If the intensity variance is split off before the yield variance, a cumulative variance analysis in the form of a standard-vs-actual comparison on an "actual reference basis" leads to

$$\begin{aligned}K^s - K^r &= p_v \cdot x_v \cdot y_1^s \cdot y_2^s - p_v \cdot x_v \cdot y_1^r \cdot y_2^r \\ &= p_v \cdot x_v \cdot y_1^s \cdot y_2^s - p_v \cdot x_v \cdot y_1^r \cdot y_2^s \\ &+ p_v \cdot x_v \cdot y_1^r \cdot y_2^s - p_v \cdot x_v \cdot y_1^r \cdot y_2^r \\ &= p_v \cdot x_v \cdot \overset{SA}{\Delta y_1} \cdot y_2^s + p_v \cdot x_v \cdot y_1^r \cdot \overset{SA}{\Delta y_2}\,,\end{aligned} \tag{26}$$

and with variances partitioned in the reverse order, ultimately yields

$$K^s - K^r = p_v \cdot x_v \cdot y_1^s \cdot \overset{SA}{\Delta y_2} + p_v \cdot x_v \cdot \overset{SA}{\Delta y_1} \cdot y_2^r. \tag{27}$$

For corresponding partitioning sequences, the variant "based on standard values" results in

$$\begin{aligned}K^s - K^r &= p_v \cdot x_v \cdot y_1^s \cdot y_2^s - p_v \cdot x_v \cdot y_1^r \cdot y_2^r \\ &= p_v \cdot x_v \cdot y_1^s \cdot y_2^r - p_v \cdot x_v \cdot y_1^r \cdot y_2^r \\ &+ p_v \cdot x_v \cdot y_1^s \cdot y_2^s - p_v \cdot x_v \cdot y_1^s \cdot y_2^r \\ &= p_v \cdot x_v \cdot \overset{SA}{\Delta y_1} \cdot y_2^r + p_v \cdot x_v \cdot y_1^s \cdot \overset{SA}{\Delta y_2}\end{aligned} \tag{28}$$

and

$$K^s - K^r = p_v \cdot x_v \cdot y_1^r \cdot \overset{SA}{\Delta y_2} + p_v \cdot x_v \cdot \overset{SA}{\Delta y_1} \cdot y_2^s, \tag{29}$$

respectively. Analogous relations hold for the actual-vs-standard comparison.

Now, on the one hand, the cumulative method is said to exhibit "partial variances of the first order only in the last calculation stage"[16], the other variances being distorted by variances of higher orders which can not be seen immediately. On the other hand, it is asserted – formerly also by this author – that the last partial variance determined in the course of a cumulative variance analysis comprises variances of higher orders.[17] These statements are both contradictory and, in absolute terms, generally erroneous. They illustrate the problems inherent in a "reference-basis-oriented" definition of first order partial variances.[18] For instance, the intensity variance that is split off first by a cumulative variance analysis in accordance with (28) exactly matches the intensity variance resulting

---

16 Kloock (1994), p 638 (translated from German); also cf. Figure 7 on p 634 there.

17 Cf. Glaser (1986), p 147; Wimmer (1994), p 991.

18 This kind of definition seems to be preferred in the "more recent literature"; cf. for this Ossadnik/Maus (1995b), p 1313.

from a differentiated-cumulative variance analysis based on actual values as shown in (15). Thus, it seems inconsistent to classify this same amount as being distorted by the inclusion of higher order variances if it results from a cumulative analysis on the one hand, and to characterize it as an unambiguous, and therefore control-relevant, first order partial variance if it is the outcome of a differentiated-cumulative analysis on the other.[19] Furthermore, it is not obvious why an identical value of a certain intensity variance should simultaneously be assumed both to contain and not to contain variances of higher orders, depending on the splitting order (first partial variance determined in (27), last in (28)). In order to resolve these contradictions, which emphasise a specific aspect of content, it seems advisable to define a variance as a first order partial variance if it embraces only one Δ-quantity a n d does not contain a compensatory amount.

For certain relationships between standard and actual values, cumulative variance analysis can lead to "compensation-free" partial variances, as can be seen, for example, by comparing expression (27) with the result of the min-method (23) for $y_1^s < y_2^r$ and $y_2^s > y_2^r$. However, as the min-method yields undistorted partial variances for any data constellation, it proves to be superior to the other variance analysis procedures.

4 Indication of Cost Reduction Potentials Using Minimum Values

An objection to the min-method is that, with the constellation $y_z^s < y_z^r$ (for all z), which commonly occurs in the case of inefficiencies, the method does not provide direct information about the potential cost reduction attainable by solely adjusting the actual value of one cost determinant to its standard value. Only first order partial variances based on actual values resulting form a corresponding differentiated-cumulative variance analysis are said to convey that information.[20] At the same time, however, the potential cost reductions indicated by first order partial variances based on actual values are apparently "essentially influenced by the actual values to be included, hence by the possible inefficiencies of other workers".[21] However, taking this into account, to assert fundamental shortcomings of the min-method in this context seems questionable. In the situation contemplated, in which actual values are in excess of standards, it is

---

19 This is the case in Kloock (1994), pp 624ff, corresponding to a "reference-basis-oriented" perspective.

20 Cf. Kloock (1994), p 637 in conjunction with p 635.

21 Kloock (1994), p 636.

particularly the min-method which, in accordance with the purposes of cost control, indicates such cost reduction potentials as are unambiguously traceable to individual cost determinants that are not distorted by other causes of variance. For instance, the intensity variance exhibited by the min-method,

$$p_v \cdot x_v \cdot \overset{SA}{\Delta y_1} \cdot y_2^s, \tag{30}$$

indicates the cost reduction towards standard cost which can be attained by adjusting actual intensity to standard intensity, otherwise assuming efficient behavior (or behavior conforming to plan) by the person(s) in charge.

In general, only by the application of the min-method, can partial variances, and hence also intensity variances, be determined which, for all conceivable relations of standard values to actual values, do not contain compensatory amounts. Hence, only the min-method facilitates unequivocal conclusions about cost reduction potentials for the attaining of standard costs in the future, which in the case of $y_z^s > y_z^r$ have to be revised.[22]

References

Albach, H. (1962): Produktionsplanung auf der Grundlage technischer Verbrauchsfunktionen, in: Veröffentlichungen der Arbeitsgemeinschaft für Forschung des Landes Nordrhein-Westfalen, issue 105, Köln, Opladen, pp 45–109.

Bogaschewsky, R./Roland, F. (1996): Anpassungsprozesse mit Intensitätssplitting bei Gutenberg-Produktionsfunktionen, in: Zeitschrift für Betriebswirtschaft, vol. 66, pp 49–75.

Coenenberg, A.G. (1997): Kostenrechnung und Kostenanalyse, 3rd ed., Landsberg a.L.

Dellmann, K./Nastansky, L.: (1969): Kostenminimale Produktionsplanung bei rein-intensitätsmäßiger Anpassung mit differenzierten Intensitätsgraden, in: Zeitschrift für Betriebswirtschaft, vol. 39, pp 239–268.

Dinkelbach, W./Rosenberg, O. (1994): Erfolgs- und umweltorientierte Produktionstheorie, Heidelberg, New York, Tokyo.

Glaser, H. (1986): Zur Erfassung von Teilabweichungen und Abweichungsüberschneidungen bei der Kostenkontrolle, in: Kostenrechnungspraxis, pp 141–148.

Gutenberg, E. (1983): Grundlagen der Betriebswirtschaftslehre, First Volume: Die Produktion, 24th ed., Berlin, Heidelberg, New York.

Haberstock, L. (1986): Kostenrechnung II, 7th ed., Hamburg.

---

22 Cf. also a corresponding remark in Ossadnik/Maus (1995b), p 1316.

Karrenberg, R./Scheer, A.-W. (1970): Ableitung des kostenminimalen Einsatzes von Aggregaten zur Vorbereitung der Optimierung simultaner Planungssysteme, in: Zeitschrift für Betriebswirtschaft, vol. 40, pp 689–706.

Kilger, W. (1993): Flexible Plankostenrechnung und Deckungsbeitragsrechnung, 10th ed., Wiesbaden.

Kistner, K.-P. (1993): Produktions- und Kostentheorie, 2nd ed., Heidelberg.

Kloock, J. (1994): Neuere Entwicklungen des Kostenkontrollmanagements, in: Dellmann, K./Franz, K.P. (eds.): Neuere Entwicklungen im Kostenmanagement, Bern, Stuttgart, Wien, pp 607–644.

Kloock, J./Bommes, W. (1982): Methoden der Kostenabweichungsanalyse, in: Kostenrechnungspraxis, pp 225–237.

Ossadnik, W./Maus, S. (1994): Kostenabweichungsanalyse als Instrument des operativen Controlling, in: Wirtschaftswissenschaftliches Studium, vol. 23, pp 446–459.

Ossadnik, W./Maus, S. (1995a): Kumulative versus differenziert-kumulative Kostenabweichungsanalyse, in: Zeitschrift für Betriebswirtschaft, vol. 65, pp 1285–1297.

Ossadnik, W./Maus, S. (1995b): Kostenabweichungsanalysen zur Quantifizierung der innerbetrieblichen Unwirtschaftlichkeit, in: Zeitschrift für Betriebswirtschaft, vol. 65, pp 1311–1317.

Schüler, W. (1970): Optimaler Anlageneinsatz im Einproduktunternehmen, Bonn.

Wilms, S. (1988): Abweichungsanalysemethoden der Kostenkontrolle, Bergisch Gladbach, Köln.

Wimmer, K. (1994): Kostenabweichungsanalyse und Kostensenkung, in: Zeitschrift für Betriebswirtschaft, vol. 64, pp 981–998.

Wimmer, K. (1995): Innerbetriebliche Unwirtschaftlichkeit und Kostenabweichungsanalyse, in: Zeitschrift für Betriebswirtschaft, vol. 65, pp 1299–1309.

Summary

In order to fulfill the purposes of cost control, cause-related partial cost variances must be determined. For certain data constellations, however, existing variance analysis methods based on actual, or standard, values result in first order partial variances, particularly intensity variances, in which information-distorting variances of higher orders are concealed. A fundamental prerequisite for the determination of control-relevant intensity variances is the setting of standard intensities, which may, or may not, be equal to the optimum intensity. Generalizing Gutenberg's production relations, standard intensity can be seen to depend on the workload, on the possibilities of adaptation of production technology, and on actual yield. Undistorted intensity variances then can be established by a method of analysis based on the respective minima of standard and actual values of each of the remaining cost determinants. Even based on optimal planning under certainty, however, negative intensity variances can be shown to result from an actual-vs-standard cost comparison.

Activity Orientation of Cost Accounting According to GUTENBERG: Fundamental Principles of a Dynamic Activity-based Marginal Costing

M. Rogalski[1]

Overview

- The activity orientation of cost accounting is a relatively new and frequently discussed development. Over time, this has resulted in numerous variants of activity-based costing[2] which, in Germany, are described as „Prozeßkostenrechnung„[3/4]. Most of these systems work on absorption cost basis.
- The activity orientation is not in fact new. GUTENBERG developed an activity orientation for financial analysis many years ago[5]. In this contribution necessary modifications and extensions of GUTENBERG´s system are presented so that, adopting existing structures, an activity-based accounting is developed as a system of marginal costing.
- The basic processes identified by GUTENBERG are integrated as cost objects in cost centre accounting. Decisive for cost allocation are cost determinants. They are categorised according to the time-period in which they can be modified. The resulting effects on cost are shown.
- A decision-oriented system of *dynamic* activity-based *marginal* costing is developed in the last section. It improves the analysis and planning of fixed costs and extends the range of application of cost unit accounting.

Keywords: Cost Accounting, Activity-based Costing, Marginal Costing

1 The concept of basic-processes according to GUTENBERG

GUTENBERG employs a process analysis with the aim of conjoining three components of an enterprise, namely, procurement, production and marketing, with the

---

1 University of Bielefeld, Faculty of Economics,
Post-box 10 01 31, D-33501 Bielefeld, e-mail MRogalski@WiWi.Uni-Bielefeld.DE

2 see e.g. Cooper/ Kaplan, 1988, Horngren, 1992, Bromwich, 1994

3 Even though the literal translation of this word is process costing, it means activity-based costing.

4 see e.g. Glaser, 1992, Horváth/ Kieninger/ Mayer/ Schimank, 1993, Horváth/ Mayer, 1993, Kloock, 1992(1), Kloock, 1992(2), Küting/ Lorson, 1995

5 Gutenberg, 1980, p. 2 nn.

financial sphere, in order to reveal interdependencies between the financial area and the non-monetary process structure of the capital requirements. In this context, a basic process is defined as a sequence of non-monetary and financial activities which produce a given product or service.[6] A non-monetary process starts with the act of purchasing and ends with the act of selling. The payment triggered by the act of purchasing determines the beginning of the financial process and the cash inflow triggered by the act of distribution determines the end of that process. As a consequence of credit transactions, the beginning and the end of non-monetary and financial transactions can diverge considerably.

According to GUTENBERG, the entire operational event consists of a system of basic processes. For cost accounting only the non-monetary basic processes and activities involved are relevant. They are described in the vocabulary of activity-based absorption costing as main activities[7]. Contrastingly, GUTENBERG distinguishes four different types of basic process and this classification is of great importance for the treatment of cost in the context of a decision-oriented system of activity-based marginal costing. GUTENBERG'S term *basic process* is therefore used hereafter to describe process categories. In an enterprise, four types of basic process can be identified[8]:

(1) **Basic productive processes**
The term basic productive process summarises processing operations and services, which are directly performed on products, and consumable goods, or which directly enter the product in a processed or unprocessed form. Individual units of production emerge directly from this type of process. Each production unit triggers a basic productive process.

Analysing capital requirements, Gutenberg defines further categories of basic processes involving the use of potential factors, the storage activities as well as processing operations, services or tangible goods for the support of the actual production process.

(2) **Basic logistical processes**
Basic logistical processes involve the purchasing, handling and storing of material. These *batch level activities* are performed each time a batch of products is processed; they are executed jointly for several basic productive processes. Machine set-up activities also belong to this category. This type of process relates directly to a quantity, e.g., batch size, order quantity etc.

---

6 Gutenberg, 1980, p. 16

7 see e.g. Horváth/ Kieninger/ Mayer/ Schimank, 1993, Horváth/ Mayer, 1993, Küting/ Lorson, 1995

8 Gutenberg, 1980, p. 18, this is similar to the manufacturing cost hierarchy of Horngren/ Forster/ Datar, 1997, p. 151. The basic productive processes trigger output-unit level costs and the basic logistical processes trigger batch-level costs. Cooper/ Kaplan, 1991, use this also to structure their activity hierarchy, p. 131.

(3) **Basic processes involving the utilisation of machines and equipment**
The technical release of individual benefits to the production process from the bundle of benefits provided by a complex of productive assets is described as an asset utilisation process whereby the length of the time-period in which the delivery of benefits is necessary depends on the intensity of asset usage. The basic processes involving the utilising of machines and equipment involve also the consumption of direct and indirect material, the amount of which depends on the rate and intensity of machine usage. Because *production requires the use of machines,* this type of process is indirectly related to individual units of output.

(4) **Basic managerial processes**
Basic managerial processes involve the planning, organisational and control activities of an enterprise which occur at all of its hierarchical levels. This kind of process is neither directly nor indirectly related to a production unit or batch size, but may be directly related to such other cost objects as, for example, a group of customers, a type of product or a product group.

In the following pages we consider how to integrate the basic processes introduced by GUTENBERG into cost accounting and the additional information that is thereby derived.

2 Integration of the basic processes in cost accounting

It is possible to decompose an enterprise horizontally or vertically into different basic processes depending on its structure, or the aim of cost accounting. A *vertical decomposition* reflects the sequence of activities in question (Figure 1).

Figure 1: An example of vertical decomposition

Purchases	Receipt of goods	Inspections of goods received	Storage	(...)

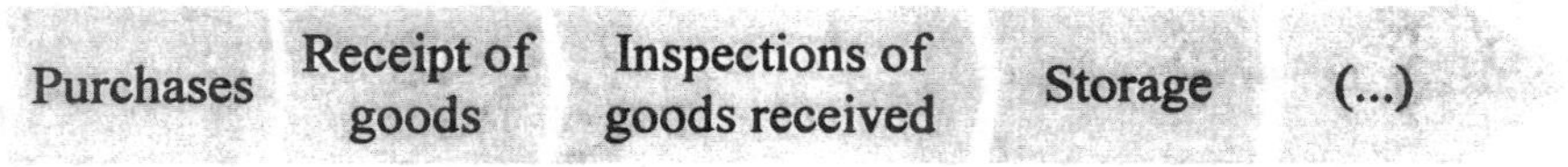

Defining these kinds of activities as (vertical) basic processes is not always meaningful. Vertical decomposition is usually expressed in terms of cost centres, or departments, which means that essential parts of a process are shown as cost centres. That is to say, cost centres in a vertical decomposition are synonymous with processes or activities, or parts of a sequence of the entire business process. The integration of activities in cost accounting is a feature of traditional systems of cost accounting and is not the contribution of activity-based costing.[9]

In a *horizontal decomposition*, the identified processes will frequently cross the functional organisation chart and the activities of the basic processes occur in several cost centres. This is shown in Figure 2 for the basic logistical process

[9] Kilger (1981), p. 313 nn.

"Procurement of materials". A horizontal decomposition is a partial feature of traditional systems because production units are defined as cost units. However, the horizontal decomposition into *overhead departments* is new. The aim is to analyse the cost structure of these departments and to provide more flexible evaluations. Figure 2 illustrates the horizontal decomposition of procurement. With such a decomposition we can analyse whether the costs of procurement correlate with the relevance of purchased material.

Figure 2: An example of horizontal composition

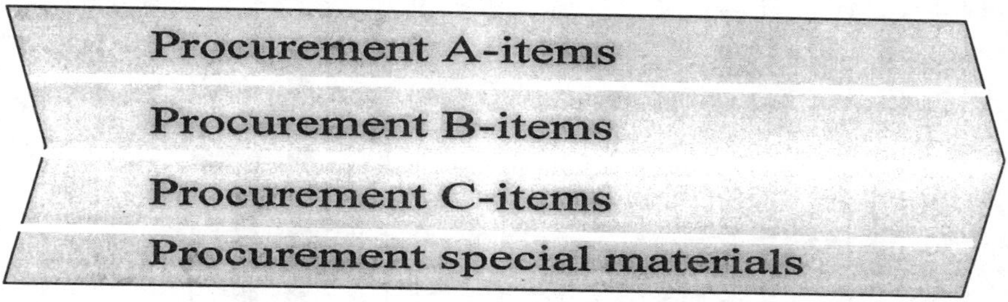

To summarise, we can say that new horizontal cost objects (basic processes and their sub-activities) are integrated into the cost accounting in addition to vertical cost objects (cost centres for example). Vertical and horizontal aggregations of costs, which permit two different views of the cost structure of an enterprise, are now possible.

2.1 Extension of cost centre accounting

In addition to traditional cost objects like products and cost centres, basic processes are integrated into cost accounting as cost objects (Figure 3) The relationship of direct and indirect costs to the various basic process categories is as follows. The numbers in brackets relate to the cost flows in Figure 3.

The cost of the *basic productive processes* can be directly allocated to unit-of-output costing because such processes involve only processing operations and services, which are immediately performed on products and consumption goods and which directly enter products. But to control costs, it is sensible to record them in the cost centres with the corresponding basic productive processes (1). In addition to direct cost, variable indirect cost such as operational materials, indirect material and selling overheads are recorded in cost centres (4, 5, 6). Part of these costs can immediately be traced to the product units via the basic productive processes in the unit-of-output costing (7). Another part of variable overheads results from the logistical processes in the cost centres for purchasing, production or distribution (4, 5, 6). These overheads cannot be allocated in the unit-of-output costing, but only in batch oriented activity accounting (9). This step is necessary if the accounting is to support the planning of economic order quantities or economic lot sizes, because there are cost determinants other than the production output.

Figure 3: Integration of the basic processes in the cost accounting

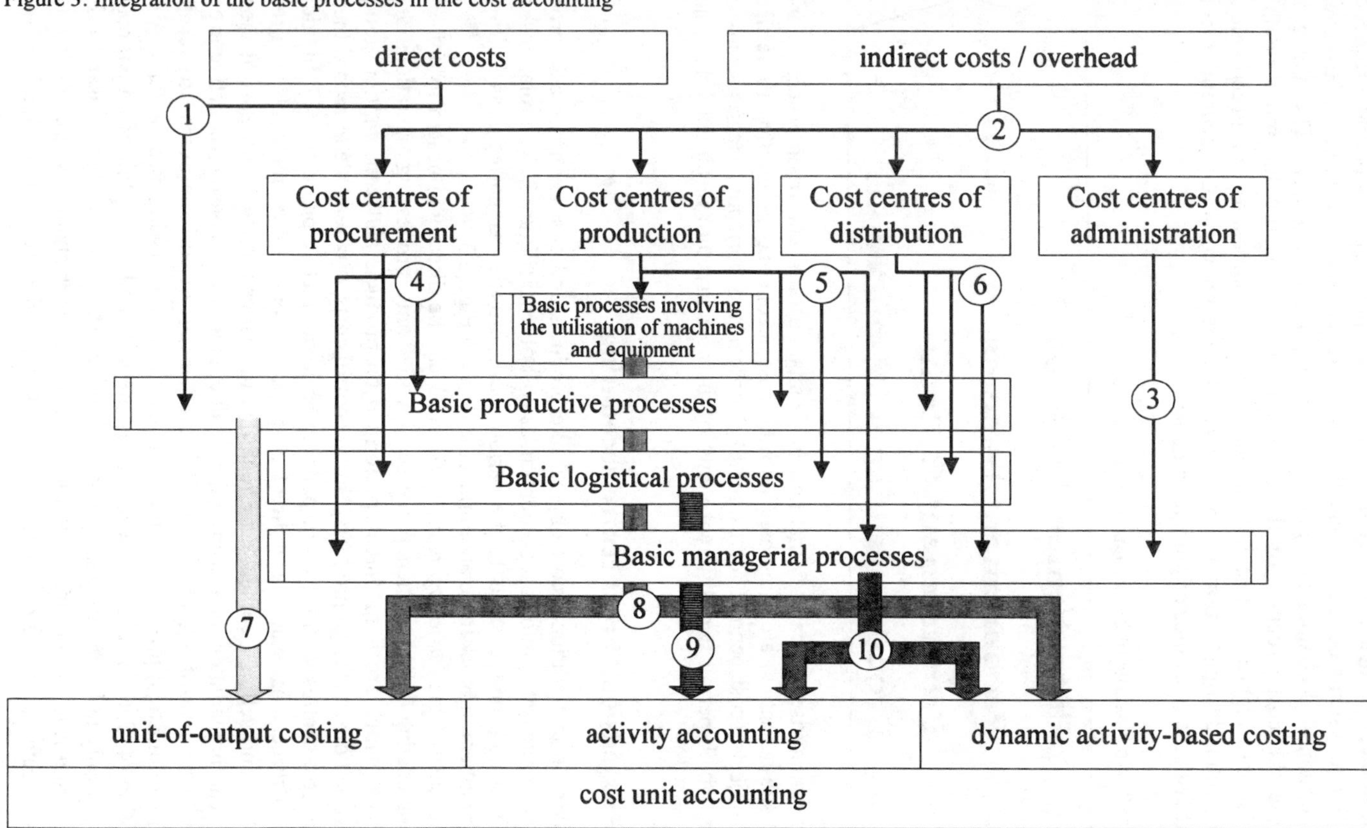

Basic processes involving the utilisation of machines and equipment take place only in production cost centres because they are defined as the technical assignment of time units to production. The costs of these processes are the depreciation of machinery and equipment resulting from use and the effluxion of time. Variable overheads of production are depreciation through use which can be traced in the unit-of-output costing. The allocation of time-dependent depreciation takes place in the *dynamic activity-based costing*[10], which was specially developed for analysing fixed costs (8). Principles of dynamic activity-based costing are described in part C. Additional variable overheads, e.g., indirect material, which vary with the utilisation of machines, are also allocated via the basic processes involving the utilisation machines and equipment.

Depreciation of equipment, which is not used in production, e.g., data processing equipment in administration, cannot be assigned via the basic processes involving machine and equipment utilisation since it has no relationship with production. Hence, these costs are attributed to the basic managerial processes.

A consideration of asset utilisation processes clearly indicates that whilst in cost centre accounting, activity-related cost accounting has always taken place it has been described as *workplace accounting*. But as this was only the case for production cost centres, it is necessary to define further cost points for the indirect departments.

The costs of non-profit-related basic processes occur in all cost centres (4, 5, 6). Only costs of this nature (3) are generally to be found in administrative cost centres. Causalities between the cost function and units of production are not determinable in the case of basic managerial processes. *Repetitive activities* are a part of the activities in the basic managerial processes category. They become periodic and are often carried out, and can be expressed, in functions, e.g. bookkeeping. Hence, we can find cost determinants, e.g., number of records, which allow the planning and allocation of costs in activity accounting (10). But most of the activities in the category of basic managerial processes are *non-repetitive activities*, i.e. they are aperiodic and carried out less frequently. They are more innovative and cannot be formally expressed, e.g. research and development activities as well as management activities. The costs of these non-repetitive processes are not variable with respect to the volume of output of a cost centre, e.g. number of orders. These costs are analysed in dynamic activity-based costing (10).

Figure 3 illustrates the three possible cost allocations in cost unit accounting. Only the unit-of-output costing can be carried out in a conventional manner. Activity costing is new. Here processes and their sub-activities, like transport or setting-up, are integrated as cost objects. The result is information which allows a superior planning of order quantity or batch size. By means of a hierarchical planning model, this information can be integrated in the planning of output.[11] Accounting for period costs is also changed. On the one hand there are activities

---

[10] Developed according to the „Dynamische Grenzplankostenrechnung„ (Kilger 1981).

[11] Kistner /Rogalski, 1996,

which are also integrated as cost objects whilst, on the other, fixed costs will be allocated to successive periods depending on how long they are deployed and their determinants. *Dynamic activity marginal costing* is created in this way.

In what follows it is necessary to consider how to assign the costs of activities. In attempting to define a marginal costing system, the question of how to assign costs also concerns the determinants of costs.

2.2 Structuring and extension of cost determinants

A comparison of an analysis of the determinants of capital requirement[12] with the cost determinants identified in the context of production and cost theory[13] shows that, with one exception, which is important in the context of this work, they largely correspond with each other. In the analysis of the capital requirement Gutenberg explicitly integrates the *process arrangement* (the temporal arrangement) with the *rate of process,* and ignores the cost determinant *state of technical and organisational manufacturing conditions* which is very difficult to quantify (Figure 4). This approach is possible due to the activity orientation of the capital requirement analysis. An activity orientation of cost accounting enables the rate of process to be taken into account as a cost determinant.

Figure 4: Comparison of determinants

Cost determinants		**Determinants of the capital requirement**
- factor prices - activity level - plant size - production and sales mix	⟺	- factor prices - activity level - plant size - production and sales mix
- *state of technical and organisational manufacturing conditions*		- *process arrangement* - *rate of process*

Factor prices are external *determinants on which a firm can only exert* little influence, for example, by making use of quantity discounts. *Activity level* is traditionally measured by the number of units of product to be manufactured[14] but the reference basis (cost driver) depends on the particular cost object[15]. In the traditional cost centre accounting where the different cost centres are the cost objects, many different reference bases are used to measure the activity level of a cost centre, e.g. number of purchases, number of set-ups[16]. In the integration of basic processes in cost accounting, the term activity level is used to denote the volume

---

[12] Gutenberg, 1980, p. 12 nn.
[13] Gutenberg, 1983, p. 344 nn.
[14] Gutenberg, 1958, p. 65, Moriarity/ Allen 1986, p. 26
[15] Moriarity/ Allen, 1986, p. 26
[16] Kilger, 1981, p. 360

of a process or activity (total cost driver level). In the case of basic productive processes, the reference basis is again the number of units of product to be manufactured.

The relevant range of activity, the cost per unit and the shape of cost-functions in the short run, depend on further determinants. One such determinant is the state of technical and organisational manufacturing which involves many different aspects that are difficult to quantify. Cost behaviour is determined by production technology and production methods, but also by the composition and age structure of personnel, or planning and organisation of the enterprise[17]. A new determinant of costs is the rate of process, introduced by GUTENBERG for financial analysis[18]. Rate of process expresses the time necessary for an activity, normally measured in quantity per time unit. The range of possibilities for changing the rate of process is determined by the state of technical and organisational manufacturing conditions. Figure 5 shows examples of different kinds of basic process. There are different ways of changing the rate of process, e.g., stock-keeping can be improved by using more economical methods and a higher rate of stock turnover can be attained. Changes in process engineering or in organisation in the production area or administration may also lead to an increase in the rate of process. The rate of process is also closely related to technical and organisational manufacturing conditions. It is often only possible to change the rate of process by changing the technical and organisational manufacturing conditions. This must be allowed for in integrating the rate of process into the cost accounting.

Figure 5: Examples of reference bases (cost drivers) for rate of process

Category of basic process	**Reference bases for rate of process**
Basic productive processes	assembly time, time for quality inspection
Basic processes involving the utilisation of machines and equipment	degree of utilisation, manufacturing time
Basic logistical processes	number of set-up minutes, rate of stock turnover
Basic managerial processes	time to prepare an offer

Plant size, i.e., *capacity,* is a further cost determinant. For example, a non-linear cost function associated with increasing plant size can be explained by rationalisation measures. In such a case, total cost increases but marginal cost decreases. Progressively increasing costs may also result from a change in plant size, e.g. in distribution departments. Cost dependencies of this nature are difficult to record because they necessitate the quantification of plant size. This is only possible where machines and equipment are exactly similar or in the case of a homogene-

[17] Gutenberg, 1958, p. 65
[18] Gutenberg, 1980, p. 13

ous production programme. In these cases plant size can be measured by the number of machines, number of persons employed or level of output. The final structural cost determinant is the composition of production and sales mix. Some types of cost depend upon the chosen production programme, e.g. changeover costs, which arise if new products are added to the production programme, or set-up costs or inventory costs, which vary if batch sizes are changed.

The foregoing outline indicates that that plant size, production and sales mix, as well as technical and organisational manufacturing conditions, are not determinants which can be measured with a single cost driver and thus necessitate a bundle of cost drivers. For example, the state of technical and organisational manufacturing conditions can be expressed as a number of machines of one type, capacities of machines or number of persons in cost departments. Hence, changes are possible in many ways.

The process arrangement (temporal arrangement) plays an important role in the analysis of the capital requirement. Financial transactions begin either simultaneously or successively or occur in a staggered pattern. This differentiation is irrelevant for cost accounting because it utilises an output-related accruals transformation which makes dates of payment unimportant.

The cost determinants described differ with respect to the periods in which they can be modified and in respect of the effects of the change on the production process and costs. A variation in activity level is possible in the short-term whereas the modification of plant size is a long-term decision. These differences are of the utmost importance for cost accounting which is a short to medium term information instrument that necessitates a differentiation of determinants in accordance with these criteria. Figure 6 illustrates the categorisation of cost determinants in accordance with their variability and the resultant effects on costs.

Plant size, technical and organisational manufacturing conditions and production as well as sales mix programs are only variable in the long-term and therefore influence standby cost. These cost determinants determine the structure of an enterprise and are therefore termed *structural determinants*. The structure of an enterprise determines the *relevant range* of *short-term variable determinants*. For example, the activity level can only be varied within the limits of a given plant size under specific technical and organisational conditions, and is closely related to a given production program and sales mix. Moreover, a reduction in set-up time, or an increase in production rate, is possible only in the context of a given production technology. In general it can be said that the rate of process can only be altered in the short term if the technical equipment in use permits such a change. If this is the case, the resulting effects on costs must be taken into account in activity-based costing. The acceleration of processes which are executed by employees, e.g. preparing an offer, is usually only possible in the context of structural changes in which the process is reorganised.

Short-term variables determine the level of variable costs. Albeit, to extend these beyond the relevant range limits requires a change in structural determinants. This also leads to a change in standby costs, for example, by a reduction in plant size through closure or the elimination of a product from the production mix in favour of another product. *Standby costs* are often *stepped* fixed costs and decisions on them must take account of how long they are deployed. However, a change in structural determinants can also lead to a change in short term marginal costs because different *production and cost functions* then become valid. GUTENBERG illustrates the displacement of cost-functions as a consequence of a change in technical and organisational conditions[19]. He points out that the dependence of costs on the level of activities can only be represented by a *system of cost curves* and not by a single cost curve as in cost theory.

Figure 6: Relationships between determinants and costs

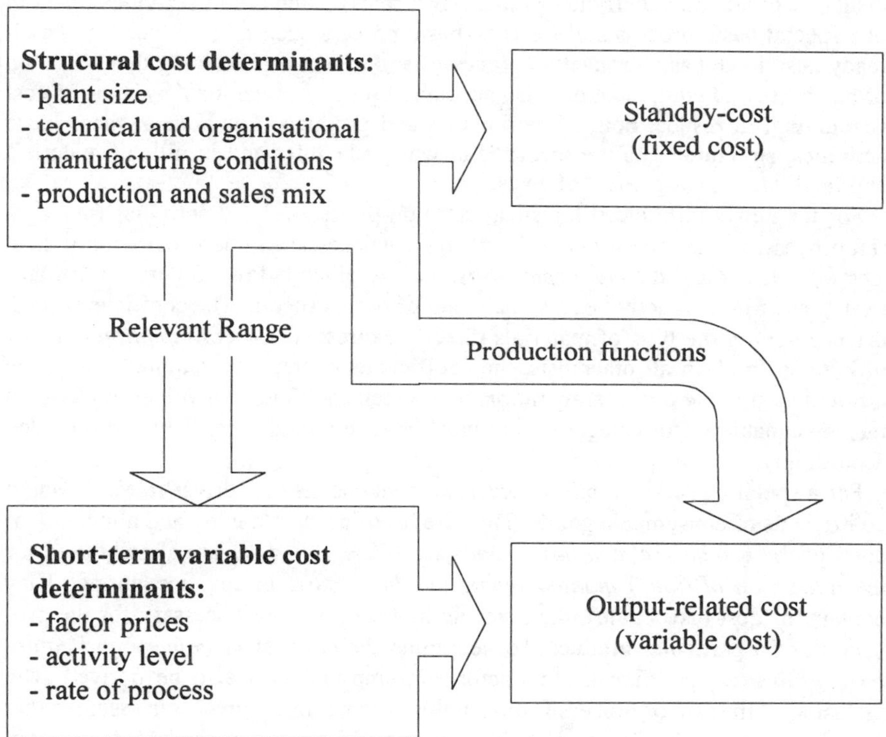

In this way, the cost effects of qualitative changes (interpreted as changes in structural determinants) can be taken into account.[20] This raises the question of whether, and how, these changes can be integrated into the cost accounting. Changes in structural determinants and the resulting effects on the costs of an enterprise are difficult to express in functional form. On the one hand, there exists

---

19 Gutenberg, 1983, p. 401
20 Gutenberg, 1983, p. 389

no uniform scale for quantifying different determinants and, on the other, the effects of changing an individual determinant cannot be isolated because such a change often affects several determinants simultaneously and these can be linked in various ways. Within the framework of activity-based costing it is however possible to capture production and cost functions that result from the structure of an enterprise in order thereby to clarify cost dependencies and reveal possible influences.

2.3 Construction of the dynamic activity-based marginal costing

Bills of activities disclose activities and the accompanying consumption coefficients, or production coefficients (cost driver rates). Each bill of activities refers to one special basic process and for each basic process such a bill is needed. As already described, basic productive processes and processes involving the utilisation of machines and equipment are also accounted for in conventional systems of cost accounting, in respect both of workplaces and products. For both of these basic activities, structural data are recorded in work schedules and in bills of materials and facilitate the assignment of costs.

For the newly introduced logistical and non-product-related activities (managerial processes), *additional bills of activities* are necessary to depict structural data. The *logistic list* and the *management list* are explained below . Figure 7 illustrates examples of bills of activities for each kind of basic process. The coefficients (cost driver rates) in the bills of materials directly express *factor consumption* per *unit* of *activity level.* In all other lists, the coefficients express the required *volume of an activity for one process execution.* The other coefficients involved include all the consumable factor categories and must be determined separately and recorded accordingly.

For a specific product a *bill of materials* contains, as cost driver rates, the input coefficients of consumable goods. They are used for the planning and allocating of costs of the *product-related basic processes*. *Work schedules* are already used for the *allocation of (joint) manufacturing overhead costs* in cost accounting. They contain, as cost driver rates, the machine hours, which are necessary for the production of a particular product. To determine the costs of *machinery and equipment utilisation,* coefficients for factor consumption must also be derived. The inclusion of the rate of process is new in this context. In Figure 7 it is assumed that machine no. 2 can be operated at either of two discrete intensities. All factor consumption which is a function of intensity, e.g., energy, scrap, operating materials, is accounted for accordingly in that factor consumption is defined as a function of intensity.

Logistic lists are used for the planning and allocation of the costs of *logistical processes* and include all activities which are necessary for a batch (order quantities/lot sizes) of a product. The activity cost driver rate (*process coefficient)* indicates either the necessary time for a cost driver unit or the number of process repetitions for one *batch*, depending on whether the resultant factor consumption is time, or quantity, dependent. This depends, in turn, on the base used for factor consumption. If the factor consumption is defined as time dependent, e.g. salaries and wages, a time per unit is needed as a coefficient. However, if factor consumption varies with the volume of activities, quantity units are needed as coefficients.

Figure 7: The recording of structural data in bills of activities

Bill of material

Basic productive process Involved activities are consumption of goods	Process coefficients (units)	Reference base of activity level
R_1	1,0	Output
R_2	0,5	-"-
ZP_1	3,0	-"-
(...)		(...)

noted in traditional systems of cost accounting

Work schedule

Basic process involving the utilisation of machines and equipment Involved activities define usage of a machine by a product	Process coefficients (hours)	Reference base of activity level
Machine_1	1,0	Output
Machine_2 -Level 1	2,0	-"-
Machine_2 - Level 2	1,5	-"-
(...)		(...)

Logistic list

Basic logistical process Activities are defined for a batch of a product or good.	Process coefficients (units)	Reference base of activity level
Purchase material	3	No. of purchases
Set-up machine1	1,0	No. of batches
Set-up machine2	2,0	-"-
Inspections	0,5	-"-
(...)		(...)

new lists in activity-based costing

Management list

Basic managerial process Activities are aggregated to different basic processes	Process coefficients (hours)	Reference base of activity level
Preparing offers	0,5	No. of offers
Serving variants	0,7	No. of variants
Handling complaints	1,0	No. of complaints
(...)		(...)

Management lists refer neither to a single product unit nor to a single product quantum. They are designed for *any cost objects* for which activity-based costs are to be planned and assigned. The management list in Figure 7 can refer, for example, to a particular product group if the factor consumption of the activities of different product groups varies. Non-product-related activities can also be defined for other calculation purposes, e.g. for an administration cost centre. The consumption functions which are defined with the aid of the management lists are not functionally related to a product's output; the cost drivers that are presented relate to *management processes.* The process coefficients in Figure 7 indicate the time required for one process execution. This is meaningful because the costs of management processes are predominantly personnel costs.

The evaluation of the factor consumption of a single activity execution with factor prices yields the activity cost rate. The addition of all activities with the same cost driver results in the *cost per basic process which* must be multiplied by the activity volume to determine the *total costs of an process* within a period. Changes in structural determinants, and therefore in cost functions, e.g., through the introduction of another manufacturing method or reorganisation of the administration, lead to a change in process coefficient, or in the limits thereto, or to the definition of new processes.

3 Features of dynamic activity-based marginal costing

3.1 Short-term activity-based marginal costing

Figure 8 illustrates cost allocation in the context of short-term activity-based marginal costing. The structural determinants are constant in the short-term as are the fixed cost of cost centres and processes (see also Figure 3). *Cost planning* is based upon the previously described cost rates and *estimated values* of the determinants.

Variable *actual costs* in the context of cost centre accounting are *recorded* directly for processes or *allocated* to processes. In the latter case, the activity level and rate of process determinants constitute the allocation basis, or the activity level alone if no technical machines or equipment are used. The rate of process of management and productive activities can only be varied by modifying the structural determinants. The additional factor consumption (scrap) which results from changes in the rate of process is recorded - as described - with machine and equipment usage or with logistical processes. Price variances are eliminated in the accounting by cost type and, for this reason, the factor price cost determinant is redundant.

The *variable costs* of *productive processes* and those of *processes involving the utilisation of machines and equipment* are traced to products, using the bills of materials and work schedules, by reference to *units-of-output. Variable costs* of *logistical processes* are not traced to single output units, but in *activity accounting* are allocated to single activities, which are carried out for a quantum of product, e.g., a batch. The logistic lists are the basis of this allocation. Resorting to the management lists, the *variable costs* of *management processes* which depend on the activity level, for example, telephone call charges and costs of stationery, can now be recorded and planned.

Figure 8: Cost assignment in short-term activity-based marginal costing

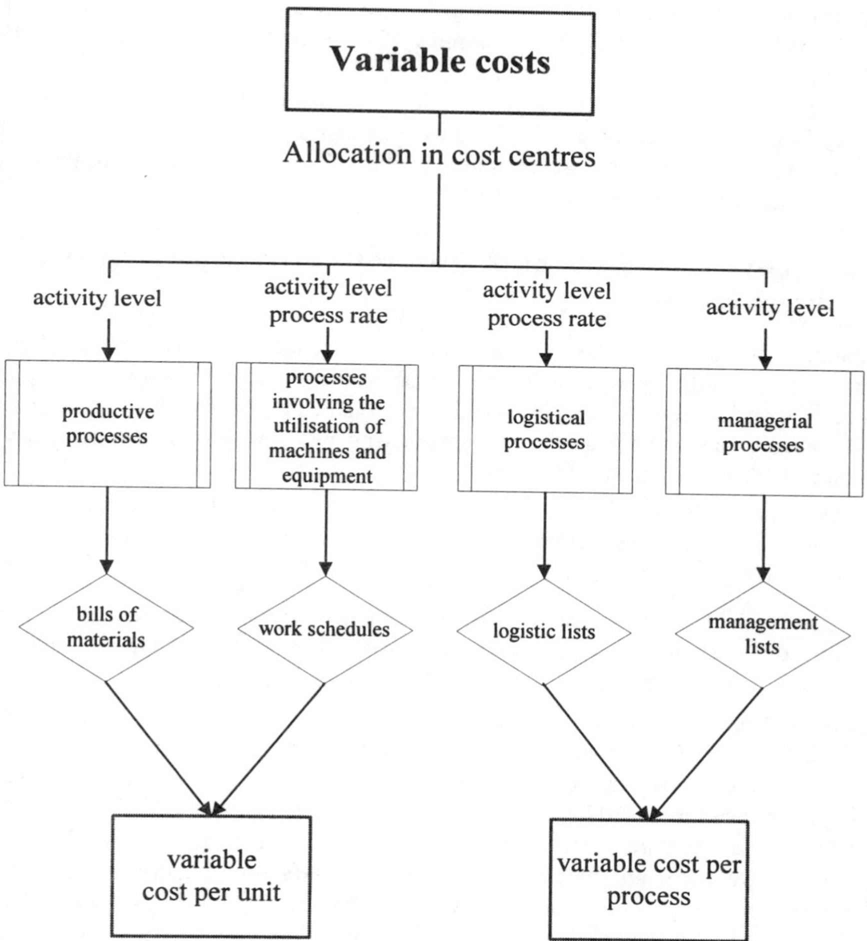

The integration of processes into cost accounting permits a new analysis of the cost structure of an enterprise because possibilities exist for an aggregation of activities across the functional organisation chart. For example, costs of activities in cost centres in the procurement area (purchase, receipt of goods, storage etc.) can be aggregated to give the cost of the process "Procurement A-items".

A consistent marginal cost orientation permits the use of the information received for decision making support because only such costs are assigned to a cost object as vary with decisions on the related determinants. There are no changes in respect of the use of variable costs in the production program planning. In addition, inventory models for planning economic batch sizes, or order quantities, can be supported with activity accounting, because of the (now available) adequate information, e.g., set-up costs, which was hitherto not available in this form. In this way, and only in this way, can economies of scale be taken into account in the planning function.

An objection to the assigning of variable costs alone is that it results in excessively large cost blocks being classified as fixed costs which therefore may not be influenced. This objection is countered in the following section in formulating dynamic activity-based marginal costing.

3.2 Analysis and planning of fixed costs in dynamic activity-based costing

Standby costs are now taken into account. These costs are constant in the short-term but are modified by a decision in respect of operational readiness. The purpose of dynamic activity marginal costing is to indicate how standby costs can be influenced by a change in structural cost determinants. Two essential aspects have to be considered in this regard:

- Only such standby costs can be taken into account as have a deployment duration which is *less than* or *equal* to the *planning horizon*, so that they can be altered in the planning period in question.
- The level of standby costs cannot be influenced by a variation in short-term cost determinants. Changes in standby costs are *only* possible via a *change in structural cost determinants* and usually not in arbitrary steps.

Figure 9 depicts the accounting for structural cost determinants and the treatment of standby costs. Since plant size can be modified only in the long term and decisions about this cost determinant are usually made with the aid of investment analysis, it is not included here.

Changes in structural cost determinants have two direct effects (see also Figure 6). On the one hand, there are changes in the *production functions* which enter the cost accounting in the form of bills of materials, work schedules, logistic lists and management lists as well as the corresponding factor consumption coefficients (cost driver rates (1)). This leads indirectly to a change in variable process costs. On the other hand, a change in the production functions is generally connected with a change in the standby costs, for example, a reduction in personnel or renting of additional storage facilities. These changes affect the total cost of processes (2).

The variable costs can, as shown in the case of short-term activity-based marginal costing, either be adopted in full costing or in activity-based costing for the determination of variable unit or activity costs.

Figure 9: Allocation of standby costs

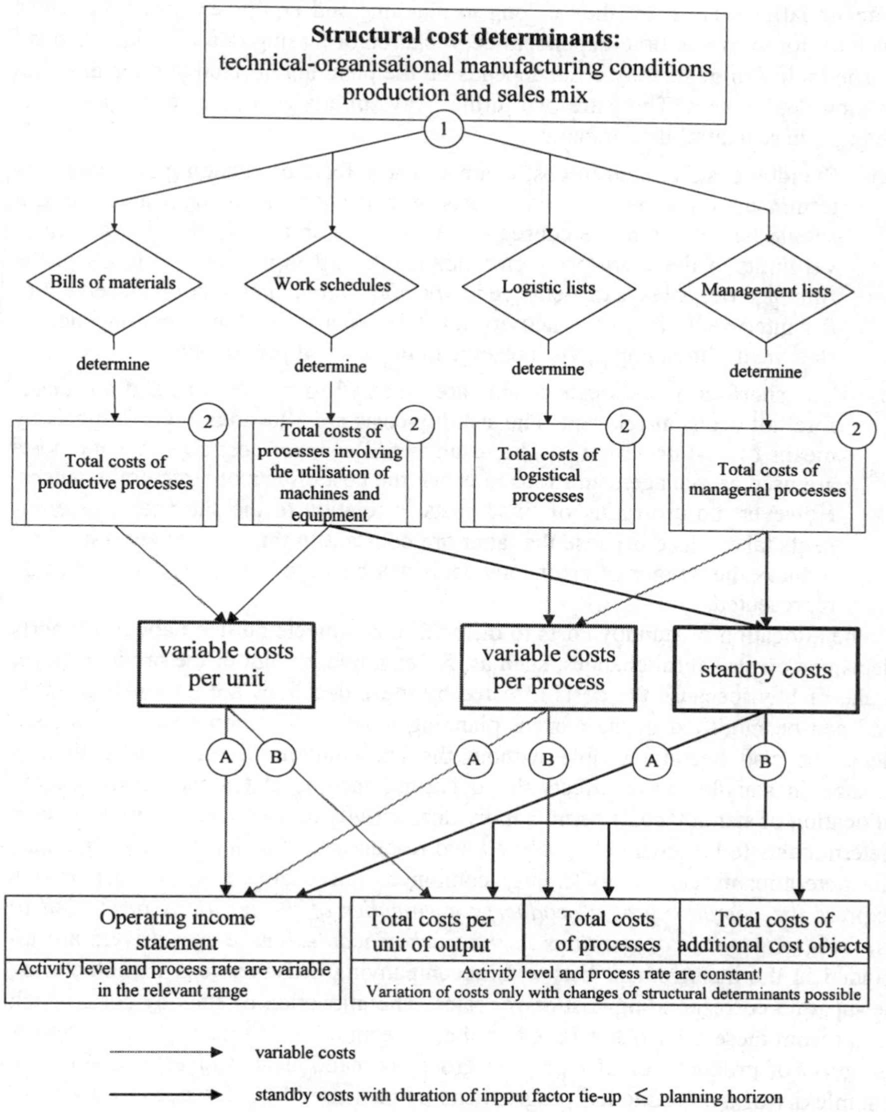

Standby costs are recorded in the corresponding cost centres for *non-repetitive activities*, e.g., the wages of foremen in production, the salaries of administrators or of managers of cost centres. The costs of *repetitive activities* are induced by activity level and are therefore variable.

Non-repetitive activities are related to two kinds of process. They are either managerial processes; or, they belong to machine and equipment usage activities such as, for example, time-dependent depreciation or leasing rates for fixed assets.

The inclusion of standby costs depends on the planning horizon and the duration of their deployment. There are two further ways of analysing the consequences of changes in structural determinants:

A) Standby costs remain in cost centres. The effects of changing structural determinants on variable activity costs or unit costs are recognisable. Here it should be noted that the consequence may be a shifting of the relevant interval limits of the short-term determinants. A shift in the interval limits of the *rate of process* leads to a change in *variable activity costs*. A displacement of the interval limits to the activity level is reflected in the operating income statement, for example, via a change in the level of production.

B) The short-term cost determinants are assumed to be constant and are therefore not decision-relevant. The standby costs are allocated to cost objects by means of cost driver rates. The result is full cost per cost object. Total costs are used as management ratios to check the cost effects of structural changes. However, no pro-rating of fixed costs in relation to the short-term determinants takes place because the latter are constant in this kind of analysis. This reduces the danger of erroneous decisions because cost effects are wrongly represented.

The allocation of standby costs to different cost objects outlined above supports decisions on structural changes, such as, for example, design of the product range, make or buy, because the costs affected by these decisions are now recognisable and can be modified in the current planning horizon. The consequences of such decisions also become visible without the computation of total costs, since a change in standby costs affects the operating income statement. However, the allocation of standby costs permits individual activity cost drivers of structural cost determinants to be separately analysed and re-bundled . For further investigations, the determinants can be differently combined. For example, some cost drivers express the *complexity of a product*, e.g., *number of the positions in the bill of material* or *number of positions in the work schedule*. These cost drivers are included in the management lists with accompanying activities, e.g. manufacturing set-up, and corresponding cost driver rates. The allocation of standby costs which result from these activities is based on these magnitudes. In this way, the *complexity effect* of products, or of a product group, is made clear. Correspondingly, the complexity of the production program can be measured by reference to *number of variants*. Many other aggregations of cost are conceivable. The *quality effect* of a cost object can be identified by selecting, for example, the number of complaints, number of inspections and number of reworked items etc., as an allocation basis.

The objection that, in activity-based costing, excessively large cost blocks are classified as fixed-costs and cannot be influenced is thus countered. Fixed costs and their actual determinants are also taken into account in dynamic activity-based marginal costing. Fixed costs can become assigned to products, activities or other cost objects for different periods without, however, implying that such costs can be changed in the short-term by activity level or rate of process. Only standby costs can be altered whose deployment duration is less than, or equal to, the planning period and whose modification can only be effected through structural determinants. Dynamic activity-based marginal costing is therefore capable of providing decision-oriented information. By means of a problem-relevant bundling of cost drivers can, for example, the complexity of products as cost determinants be revealed accordingly.

No system of cost accounting can allocate overheads to product units according to the principle of causality. And no system is able to transform fixed costs into costs which are related to the volume of an activity. Therefore it is meaningful to integrate structural determinants into cost accounting because costs are a function of *two items* - short-term determinants and structural determinants.

4 Summary

The basic operational processes defined by GUTENBERG for the derivative financing requirement are integrated into the cost accounting. Modifications and extensions are introduced which lead to a decision-orientated activity-based marginal costing. The assignment of costs to the different kinds of processes is decisive because it facilitates propositions about allocation possibilities. The system of cost determinants is extended by introducing rate of process as a cost determinant and by differentiating between structural and short-term cost determinants. Proceeding from this differentiation of cost determinants, it is shown how changes in cost determinants influence costs. Presented finally are the outlines of a dynamic activity-based marginal costing system with which it is possible to structure fixed costs and include them sequentially in the cost planning by reference to the period of their deployment. The complexity effect and economies of scale are clarified by means of an allocation reflecting both the structural and short term cost drivers.

5 References

Bromwich, M. (1994): The economic foundations of activity based costing, in: Dellmann, K./ Franz, K. P. (Eds.) (1994): Neuere Entwicklungen im Kostenmanagement, Bern, Stuttgart, Wien 1994, pp. 167-188

Brimson, J. A. (1991): Activity accounting, New York, Chichester, Brisbane, Toronto, Singapore 1991

Cooper, R./ Kaplan R.S. (1988): Measure costs right: Make the right decisions, in: Harvard Business Review, V. 66, Sep.-Oct. 1988, pp. 96-103

Cooper, R./ Kaplan R.S. (1991): Profit Priorities from activity-based costing, in: Harvard Business Review, V. 66, May.-Jun. 1991, pp. 130-135

Dellmann, K./ Franz, K. P. (Eds.) (1994): Neuere Entwicklungen im Kostenmanagement, Bern, Stuttgart, Wien 1994

Glaser, H. (1992): Prozeßkostenrechnung. Darstellung und Kritik, in: zfbf, 44. Jg. (1992), pp. 275-288

Gutenberg, E. (1958): Einführung in die Betriebswirtschaftslehre. Reprinting with a epilog of H. Albach, Wiesbaden 1990
Gutenberg, E. (1980): Grundlagen der Betriebswirtschaftslehre, Dritter Band: Die Finanzen, 8. Edition, Berlin, Heidelberg, New York 1980
Gutenberg, E. (1983): Grundlagen der Betriebswirtschaftslehre, Erster Band: Die Produktion, 24. Edition, Berlin, Heidelberg, New York 1983
Horngren, Ch. T. (1992): Reflections on Activity Based Accounting in the United States, in: zfbf, 44. Jg. (1992), pp. 289-293
Horngren, Ch. T./ Forster, G./ Datar, S.M. (1997): Cost accounting. A Managerial Emphasis, 9. Edition, New Jersey 1997
Horváth P./ Kieninger, M./ Mayer, R./ Schimank, Ch. (1993): Prozeßkostenrechnung - oder wie die Praxis die Theorie überholt. Kritik und Gegenkritik, in: DBW, 53. Jg. (1993), pp. 609-628
Horváth, P./ Mayer, R. (1993): Konzeptionen und Entwicklungen, in: krp, 37. Jg. (1993), Sonderheft Nr. 2, pp. 15-28, reprinted in: Männel, W. (Ed.), Prozeßkostenrechnung. Bedeutung, Methoden, Branchenerfahrungen, Softwarelösungen, Wiesbaden 1995
Kilger, W. (1981): Flexible Plankostenrechnung und Deckungsbeitragsrechnung, 8. Edition, Wiesbaden 1981
Kistner, K.-P./ Rogalski, M. (1996): Inventory Management in Hierarchical Systems of Production Planing and Control, in: Central European Journal for Operations Research and Economics, V. 4, No. 2-3 (1996), pp. 167-186
Kloock, J. (1992(1)): Prozeßkostenrechnung als Rückschritt und Fortschritt der Kostenrechnung (Teil 1), in: krp, 36. Jg. (1992), pp. 183-193
Kloock, J. (1992(2)): Prozeßkostenrechnung als Rückschritt und Fortschritt der Kostenrechnung (Teil 2), in: krp, 36. Jg. (1992), pp. 237-245
Küting, K./ Lorson, P. (1995): Stand, Entwicklungen und Grenzen der Prozeßkostenrechnung, in: Männel, W. (1995) (Ed.), Prozeßkostenrechnung. Bedeutung, Methoden, Branchenerfahrungen, Softwarelösungen, Wiesbaden 1995, pp. 87-101
Männel, W. (1992) (Ed.): Handbuch der Kostenrechnung, Wiesbaden 1992
Männel, W. (1995) (Ed.): Prozeßkostenrechnung. Bedeutung, Methoden, Branchenerfahrungen, Softwarelösungen, Wiesbaden 1995
Moriarity, Sh./ Allen, C.P. (1986): Cost Accounting, New York, Chichester, Brisbane, Toronto, Singapore, 2. Edition 1986
Rogalski, M. (1996): Prozeßkostenrechnung im Rahmen der Einzelkosten- und Deckungsbeitragsrechnung, in: krp, 40. :Jg. (1996), pp. 91-97

Capacity Planning under Uncertainty in a Gutenberg Production Model

R. F. Göx[1]

Overview

- The paper considers a two stage capacity and production planning model under uncertainty. The optimal second stage production policy falls into three cases: When capacity is slack the firm will produce with the cost minimizing production rate and adjust the production time to meet its output target. When the capacity constraint is binding, the firm will first adjust the production rate and then again produce with a constant production rate but employ overtime to meet the output target.
- The optimal capacity choice of the first stage is determined by the trade off between the sunk costs of slack labor and the expected opportunity costs of adjusting the production rate and employing overtime in the case of a binding capacity constraint.
- The key item determining the firm's labor demand is the overtime premium. The amount of contracted labor strictly increases with the overtime premium and the expected overtime strictly decreases. Since the latter effect dominates the former for small overtime premia, the firm's labor demand is first decreasing and then increasing with the overtime premium.
- A reduction of overtime premia can be Pareto improving because it does not only lead to substantial cost savings but also to an increasing labor demand.

Keywords: Production, Capacity Planning, Uncertainty.

---

1 Dr. Robert F. Göx, Otto-von-Guericke-University Magdeburg, Faculty of Economics and Management, Universitätsplatz 2, 39106 Magdeburg, e-mail: goex@ww.uni-magdeburg.de

1 Introduction

The managerial production model of *Erich Gutenberg* is perhaps one of his most important contributions to the theory of managerial economics. Although the model was already developed in 1951 it still assumes a central place in current German textbooks on production theory[2]. Moreover, empirical studies of German firms in the 'sixties and 'seventies indicate that *Gutenberg*'s production model provides a realistic picture of the production process in the manufacturing industry[3]. *Gutenberg* felt that the black box model of neoclassical production theory was not well designed to capture the specific nature of the manufacturing process mainly because of the straightforward relation between input and output and the assumption of unlimited substitutability of inputs. To circumvent these limitations he based his model on input functions $a_i(u, \mathbf{z})$ defining production coefficients as a function of the production rate u and the vector $\mathbf{z}$ measuring the state of the equipment in use[4]. In the simplest case, the production rate u is measured as the ratio of output x and production time t. According to *Gutenberg* every workplace, or cost center, of the firm can be characterized by the state of its technical equipment, given by $\mathbf{z}$. For a given state vector $\mathbf{z}$, however, each decentralized unit of the firm can meet its output target in the short run by adopting one of the following three types of adjustment policies.

- *Adjustment of production time* for given production rate and production equipment in use.
- *Adjustment of production rate* for given production time and production equipment in use.
- *Adjustment of the production equipment in use* for given production time and production rate.

Thus, unlike the neoclassical production model, the input required to meet a certain output target is not a choice variable per se, rather it is indirectly

2 See e.g. Fandel (1991), pp. 101; Dyckhoff (1994), pp. 249; Dinkelbach/Rosenberg (1994), pp 134 or Kistner (1993), pp. 139.

3 See e.g. Pressmar (1971), pp. 229 or Fandel (1991), pp. 202 for a survey of severel empirical studies.

4 See Gutenberg (1971), pp. 326.

determined by the production rate, the production time and the equipment in use. This paper provides an extension of *Gutenberg*'s production model by incorporating a capacity planning problem into the analysis. In particular, I consider the model of a price-taking single product firm that has to decide about the number of staff for production support activities before the final product demand becomes known. Before production takes place the firm enters identical labor contracts with each worker specifying a fixed salary, an overtime premium and a fixed number of working hours for the period under consideration. After the employment contracts have been signed demand uncertainty is resolved and the firm determines the optimal production policy and the usage of overtime if necessary.

The firm's optimal capacity choice is governed by the trade-off between the sunk costs of slack labor and the expected penalty costs for adjusting the production rate and the use of overtime. The key item determining the firm's labor demand is the overtime premium. However, the relationship between overtime premium and labor demand is far from being trivial because the amount of contracted labor strictly increases with the overtime premium and the expected overtime strictly decreases. Since the latter effect dominates the former for small overtime premia, the firm's labor demand is first decreasing and then increasing with respect to the overtime premium. Thus, a reduction of overtime premia would not only yield cost savings but could also lead to an increasing labor demand. Moreover, an agreement about a reduction of overtime premia could lead to a Pareto improvement, provided that the employees are willing to share some of the firm's risk and the firm is willing to share the cost savings with its workers.

This result not only provides an economic argument for a larger degree of flexibility in collective labor agreements, but also challenges the perpetual claims of German trade unions that a reduction of overtime would increase the demand for labor. Recent evidence from *Volkswagen* suggests that labor agreements containing a lower amount of contracted labor do not necessarily reduce earned income in the long run. In particular, *Volkswagen* had reduced the fixed working time from 36 to 28.8 hours per week in 1994 to avoid mass dismissals in a situation of low demand on the world car market. Meanwhile *Volkswagen*'s employees are regularly working more overtime than the amount of the initial working time reduction. Moreover, the crucial point in recent negotiations between *Volkswagen*'s management and its works committee about producing the *New Beetle* in Germany was the overtime premium to be paid for work on Saturdays.

The remainder of this article is organized as follows. *Section B* explains the model's specification. *Section C* provides the optimal solution of the firm's two-stage optimization problem and some comparative statics in which the overtime premium is identified as the major determinant of the firm's labor demand. *Section D* provides an example, and a discussion, of the impact of the overtime premium on the firm's cost situation and labor demand. By way of conclusion *Section E* contains a short summary and some suggestions for future research.

2 The Model

Consider a single product firm that acts as price taker in the final product market and operates under the conditions of *Gutenberg*'s managerial production model. The production equipment allows a continuous adjustment of the production rate within the interval $\mathcal{U} \equiv [\underline{u}, \overline{u}]$ where the production rate $u = x/t$ is defined as the ratio between production volume x and production time t. Suppose also that the production time t is measured in hours and can assume arbitrary values $t \in \mathcal{T} \equiv [0, \bar{t}\,]$ for the time period under consideration. The production process requires n direct inputs (indexed by $i = 1, \ldots, n$) including raw materials, factory supplies or energy. For each of these direct inputs the required quantity per output unit is determined by an input function $a_i(u)$ defining the production coefficient as a function of the production rate. Denoting the price of input i with q_i, then the general form of the unit cost function for direct inputs is given by

$$k_1(u) = \sum_{i=1}^{n} q_i a_i(u). \tag{1}$$

To provide closed form solutions for the optimal production rate suppose without loss of generality, that the unit cost function (1) can be expressed in the following parameterized form

$$k_1(u) = \frac{\alpha}{u} + \beta u + \gamma, \tag{2}$$

where the parameters α, β and γ are assumed to take on positive values. To introduce the capacity planning problem into the model, suppose that the firm also requires a workforce for supervising and control tasks like maintenance or quality control. To perform these tasks m workers must be simultaneously present during the same production shift. Moreover, to simplify the analysis it will be supposed that the firm does not work more than a single production shift per day. Before production takes place, and the final product demand becomes known, the firm enters identical labor contracts with each worker specifying a fixed salary $W = w\tau$. The salary consists of an exogenously given hourly wage rate w and a fixed number of working hours τ that can take on arbitrary positive values to meet the expected capacity requirements of the firm within the production period. Hence, the costs of contracted labor can be expressed as follows:

$$K_2(\tau) = mw\tau \tag{3}$$

To make things interesting, however, it is assumed that the firm does not know the final product demand at the contracting stage. Rather, from observations of past period's sales the firm can only form a subjective probability distribution $F(x)$ with density $f(x)$ on support $\mathcal{X} \equiv [\underline{x}, \overline{x}]$. Since the firm does not know its output target in advance, the employment contracts must also include an agreement about an hourly overtime payment, designated by θw per hour, for the case in which the firm requires more than the number of contracted working hours to meet the final product demand. It seems natural to assume that the workers will only accept the contract when $\theta \geq 1$. Accordingly, the usage of overtime implies a penalty of $(\theta - 1) > 0$ for the firm that must be balanced against the sunk costs of an excessive workforce when demand turns out to be lower than expected. Hence, the firm's capacity planning problem will be governed by the trade off between the sunk costs of slack labor and the penalties for overtime. If the number of additional working hours per employee be designated h, the total costs of overtime are given by

$$K_3(h) = m\theta wh, \tag{4}$$

where the sum of contracted labor and overtime per worker required to meet the output target is assumed to fall below the production time ceiling for the period under consideration:

$$\tau + h < \bar{t} \tag{5}$$

Summarizing the preceding considerations; the firm's two-stage decision problem is exhibited in *Figure 1.* At the beginning of the period the firm has to decide the amount of labor to be contracted in advance. After the contracts are signed the firm learns the final product demand and determines the production rate together with the required overtime to meet its output target. Finally production takes place and the firm's profits are realized.

Figure 1: Chronological sequence of events

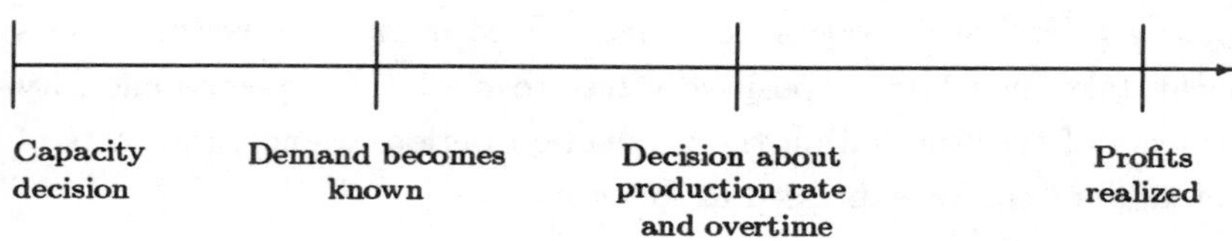

3 Problem Solution

3.1 Optimal Production Policy

The solution of the firm's two stage decision problem is obtained by backward induction starting with *Gutenberg*'s original decision problem, namely, determining the optimal production policy for a given output target x and capacity level τ. Assuming an interior solution for the optimal production rate, the firm's second stage decision problem can be stated as follows:

$$\begin{aligned} \min_{u,h} K &= k_1(u)x + K_2(\tau) + K_3(h) \\ s.t. \quad x &\leq u(\tau + h). \end{aligned} \tag{6}$$

Note that the contracted labor costs $K_2(\tau)$ are fixed at this stage since salaries must be paid regardless of the firm's actual capacity requirement. The optimal solution of the firm's second stage decision problem is found by substituting the expressions from equations (2), (3) and (4) into (6) and minimizing the corresponding Lagrangian

$$L = (\frac{\alpha}{u} + \beta u + \gamma)x + mw(\tau + \theta h) + \lambda(x - u(\tau + h)) \tag{7}$$

with respect to the production rate u and overtime h. From the *Kuhn-Tucker*-conditions

$$\frac{\partial L}{\partial u} = \left(-\frac{\alpha}{u^2} + \beta\right)x - \lambda(\tau + h) = 0 \tag{8}$$

$$\frac{\partial L}{\partial h} = m\theta w - u\lambda \geq 0, \quad h \geq 0, \quad \frac{\partial L}{\partial h}h = 0 \tag{9}$$

$$\frac{\partial L}{\partial \lambda} \leq 0, \quad \lambda \geq 0, \quad \frac{\partial L}{\partial \lambda}\lambda = 0 \tag{10}$$

the firm's optimal policy falls into three cases depending on the level of realized demand:

Case 1: $(\lambda = 0)$ When demand turns out to be relatively low, compared to the workforce capacity contracted in advance, the opportunity costs of capacity usage are zero. Accordingly the firm will choose the constant production rate u_1^* that minimizes the costs of direct inputs given by (2) and *adjust the production time* to meet its output target. This policy is optimal for all demand realizations $x \in [\underline{x}, u_1^*\tau]$ and the optimal solutions for u and h are easily obtained from (8), (9) and the fact that $\lambda = 0$:

$$u_1^* = \sqrt{\frac{\alpha}{\beta}}, \quad h_1^* = 0. \tag{11}$$

Case 2: $(0 < \lambda < \theta mw/u_3^*)$ When realized demand exceeds $u_1^*\tau$, the firm will first *adjust the production rate* u, without utilizing overtime, yielding the solution

$$u_2^* = \frac{x}{\tau}, \quad h_2^* = 0. \tag{12}$$

According to equations (8) and (9) this policy is optimal as long as the marginal value of overtime, $u_2^*\lambda = \beta\,(u_2^*)^2 - \alpha$ does not exceed its marginal cost θmw. Thus, the firm will *adjust the production rate* for production targets from the interval $x \in (u_1^*\tau, u_3^*\tau]$, where $x = u_3^*\tau$ denotes the quantity at which the marginal costs of a further *adjustment of the production rate* equals the constant unit costs of a *production time adjustment* for the case of overtime use[5].

Case 3: $(\lambda = \theta mw/u_3^*)$ Finally, when demand exceeds $u_3^*\tau$, the firm will choose the optimal production rate u_3^* that minimizes the sum of direct input and overtime costs. Hence, all demand realizations from the interval $x \in (u_3^*\tau, \overline{x}]$ will be met by an *adjustment of production time* while the production rate u_3^* remains fixed and the gap between required and contracted capacity is filled up with overtime:

$$u_3^* = \sqrt{\frac{\alpha + \theta mw}{\beta}}, \quad h_3^* = \frac{x}{u_3^*} - \tau. \tag{13}$$

5 See Jacob (1962), pp. 227.

The cost curve resulting from the firm's optimal production policy is exhibited in *Figure 2:*

Figure 2: Cost function

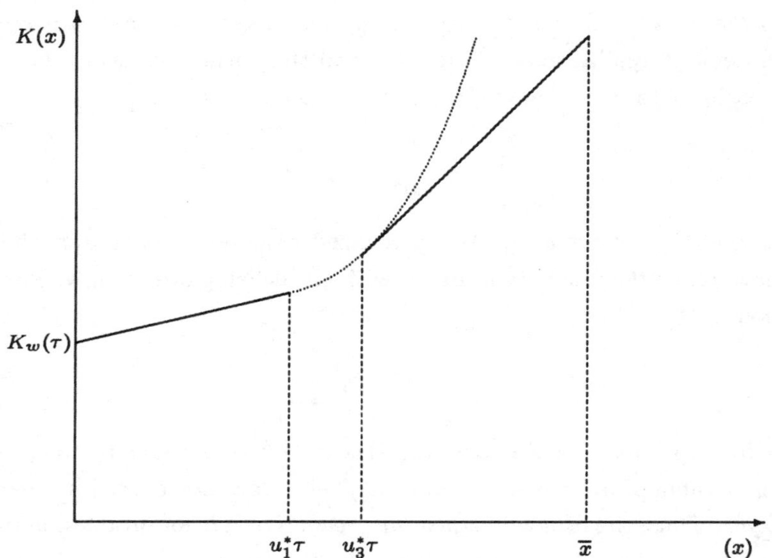

Starting from the fixed costs of the salaries $K_2(\tau)$ that have to be paid regardless of actual capacity usage, the cost function is linear up to the critical demand value of $x = u_1^*\tau$ because the firm produces at the constant production rate u_1^*. Beyond this point, marginal production costs are increasing because the firm *adjusts the production rate* to meet demand with fully utilized capacity. This policy is pursued up to the critical demand $x = u_3^*\tau$ where the marginal costs of a further increase in the production rate equals the unit costs of producing at the constant production rate u_3^*. Obviously, the cost function is again linear beyond this point whilst the unit costs are higher than in the first demand interval since the production rate now reflects the cost of overtime.

3.2 Optimal Capacity Choice

Since the firm anticipates the solution of the second stage decision problem it will already consider the optimal production policy at the capacity planning stage. Substituting the solutions (11), (12) and (13) into the cost function (6) yields the expected production costs at the contracting stage, namely:

$$\begin{aligned}\mathrm{E}\left[K(\tau)\right] &= \int_{\underline{x}}^{u_1^*\tau} K(u_1^*, h_1^*, \tau) f(x) dx + \int_{u_1^*\tau}^{u_3^*\tau} K(u_2^*, h_2^*, \tau) f(x) dx \\ &+ \int_{u_3^*\tau}^{\overline{x}} K(u_3^*, h_3^*, \tau) f(x) dx.\end{aligned} \tag{14}$$

Given the optimal adjustment policies of the second stage, the expected costs are a function of contracted labor τ alone. Utilizing the expressions defined in equations (2), (3), (4) and rearranging terms yields

$$\begin{aligned}\mathrm{E}\left[K(\tau)\right] &= K_2(\tau) + \int_{\underline{x}}^{u_1^*\tau} k_1(u_1^*) x f(x) dx + \int_{u_1^*\tau}^{u_3^*\tau} k_1(u_2^*) x f(x) dx \\ &+ \int_{u_3^*\tau}^{\overline{x}} \left(k_1(u_3^*) x + K_3(h_3^*)\right) f(x) dx.\end{aligned} \tag{15}$$

Finally, substituting the optimal solutions (12) and (13) into (15) results in the following expression for the firm's expected costs:

$$\begin{aligned}\mathrm{E}\left[K(\tau)\right] &= mw\tau + \int_{\underline{x}}^{u_1^*\tau} k_1(u_1^*) x f(x) dx + \int_{u_1^*\tau}^{u_3^*\tau} k_1\left(\frac{x}{\tau}\right) x f(x) dx \\ &+ \int_{u_3^*\tau}^{\overline{x}} \left(k_1(u_3^*) x + m\theta w \left(\frac{x}{u_3^*} - \tau\right)\right) f(x) dx.\end{aligned} \tag{16}$$

Note that the unit costs $k_1(u_1^*)$ and $k_1(u_3^*)$ resulting from the optimal production policies in the first and the third interval are constant and independent of τ. Differentiating equation (16) with respect to τ yield the necessary first order condition for the firm's optimal capacity choice:

$$\frac{d\mathrm{E}\left[K(\tau)\right]}{d\tau} = mw - \int_{u_1^*\tau}^{u_3^*\tau} \frac{k_1'\left(x/\tau\right) x^2}{\tau^2} f(x) dx - m\theta w \int_{u_3^*\tau}^{\overline{x}} f(x) dx = 0. \tag{17}$$

Condition (17) reflects the trade-off between the costs of slack labor and the expected opportunity costs of a binding capacity constraint. The optimal choice of τ requires that the hourly price of contracted labor, given by mw, equals the expected marginal opportunity cost of an additional labor hour in the case of shortage. The latter is given by the last two terms in (17) which measure the marginal increase in production costs in the cases of a *production rate adjustment* and overtime employment respectively. Unfortunately a closed form solution of (17) can only be computed for specific probability distributions. The simplest case, a uniform distribution with density $f(x) = 1/(\overline{x} - \underline{x})$, yields, for example, the solution

$$\tau^* = \frac{mw\left((\theta-1)\,\overline{x} + \underline{x}\right)}{m\theta w u_3^* + (\alpha - \beta z)\,\Delta_u} \tag{18}$$

where

$$\Delta_u = (u_3^* - u_1^*) > 0, \quad z = \frac{(u_3^* + u_1^*)^2 - u_3^* u_1^*}{3} > 0.$$

Since the other parameters of the model are fixed by assumption it is, however, sufficient for the subsequent analysis to note that the optimal solution is in general determined by the value of the overtime premium multiplier θ.

3.3 Comparative Statics

Since the optimal amount of contracted labor per worker $\tau^* := \tau^*(\theta)$ is in general a function of θ, the value function of the firm's cost minimization can be written as $\mathrm{E}[K(\tau^*(\theta), \theta)]$. According to the implicit function theorem, the direction of the effect of a change in θ on the optimal capacity τ^* equals the opposite sign of the mixed partial derivative of the value function with respect to τ and θ[6]:

$$\operatorname{sign}\left(\frac{d\tau^*(\theta)}{d\theta}\right) = -\operatorname{sign}\left(\frac{\partial \mathrm{E}\left[K(\tau^*(\theta), \theta)\right]}{\partial\tau\partial\theta}\right). \tag{19}$$

Thus, from (19) and

$$\frac{\partial \mathrm{E}\left[K(\tau^*(\theta), \theta)\right]}{\partial\tau\partial\theta} = -mw\,(1 - F(u_3^*\tau^*)) < 0 \tag{20}$$

we can conclude that the optimal labor capacity τ^* will increase with the value of the overtime premium multiplier θ. This result is also intuitively

6 See e.g. Chiang (1984), pp. 206 ff.

appealing when we recall the trade-off between the costs of slack labor and the opportunity costs of bottleneck capacity given by condition (17). While the marginal cost of excess capacity mw remains unchanged, the expected opportunity costs of a binding capacity constraint are increasing with θ, not only because overtime becomes more expensive, but also because the firm must cover a larger demand interval by an *adjustment of the production rate.* Thus, as a response to an increasing overtime premium, the firm will contract more labor in advance to balance both effects. In contrast, the firm will keep the capacity level low for small values of θ because the adjustment costs in the case of favorable demand conditions are relatively low.

A complete analysis of the firm's labor demand must not only consider the amount of contracted labor but also the firm's expected overtime demand per worker which is easily obtained by taking the expectation of the optimal solution in (13).

$$\mathrm{E}\,[h^*] = \frac{\mathrm{E}\,[x]}{u_3^*} - \tau^* \geq 0. \tag{21}$$

The firm's expected overtime demand is decreasing with its price, the overtime premium, because both u_3^* and τ^* are increasing as θ becomes larger. Moreover, the decline in overtime obviously exceeds the parallel increase in contracted labor.

Thus, starting from the lowest possible value of θ the firm's total labor demand, $\tau^*+\mathrm{E}[h^*]$, will initially decrease up to a critical value $\widetilde{\theta}$ at which the firm's expected overtime demand equals zero. Beyond this point, the firm's expected labor demand consists only of contracted labor because its capacity is large enough to produce the expected final product demand by *adjusting the production rate.* Accordingly, the firm's labor demand will increase beyond $\widetilde{\theta}$ where the critical value $\widetilde{\theta}$ is determined by solving the condition $\mathrm{E}[x] \leq u_3^*\tau^*$ for θ. The preceding considerations are summarized in *Figure 3.* Starting from a situation where the firm pays no overtime premium ($\theta = 1$), its overtime demand is decreasing up to the critical value of $\widetilde{\theta}$, whereas the optimal capacity τ^* is increasing at a decreasing rate up to a hypothetical value of $\overline{\theta}$. At the latter value the firm would be indifferent between meeting the demand ceiling $\overline{x}$ by an *adjustment of the production rate,* or by the employment of overtime. Finally, the firm's labor demand, given by the dotted line for values of $\theta < \widetilde{\theta}$, is first decreasing but coincides with the increasing optimal capacity curve τ^* for values of $\theta > \widetilde{\theta}$.

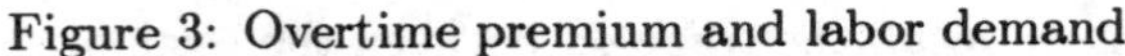

Figure 3: Overtime premium and labor demand

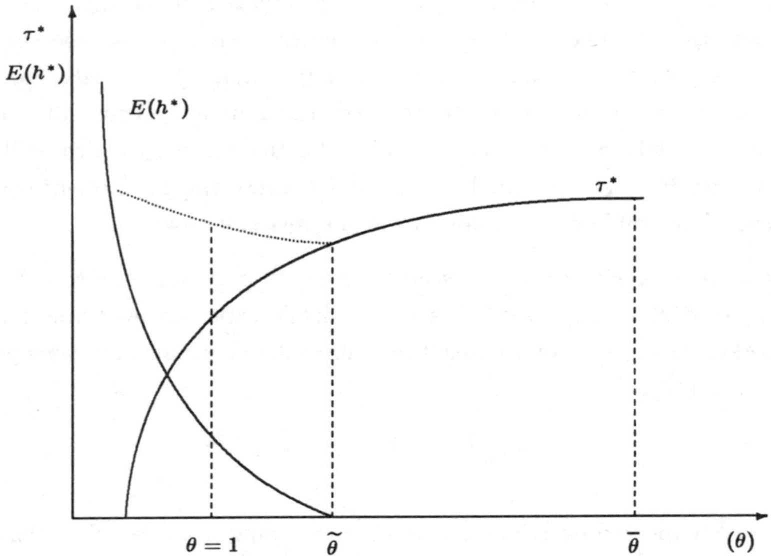

4 Example

The comparative static analysis in the preceding section has demonstrated the crucial role of overtime costs for the firm's labor demand. This section provides an example that not only underlines the importance of overtime arrangements in collective labor agreements for both a firm and its employees, but also facilitates the evaluation of the arguments of both employers and trade unions in the current debate about solutions to the German unemployment problem. In terms of the model, the employers' quest for more flexibility in labor agreements is economically equivalent to a moderate overtime premium because it allows firms to adjust production to changing demand conditions at a lower cost. In contrast, the unions' perpetual demand for a reduction, or even a ban, of overtime is economically equivalent to the pursuit of a prohibitively high overtime premium.

Consider the following example. The final product demand for the next quarter of the year is uniformly distributed random variable with density

$f(x) = 1/200,000$ and support $\mathcal{X} := [100,000, \quad 300,000]$. The production rate is allowed to assume values from the interval $\mathcal{U} \equiv [200, 600]$, the upper bound of the machine time is $\bar{t} = 1,000$ hours for the quarter and the cost function for direct inputs is given by:

$$k_1(u) = \frac{8,000}{u} + 0.1u + 10.$$

Suppose that $m = 150$ workers must be simultaneously present during the production shift and that the hourly wage rate amounts to $w = 40$ (\$). Suppose also that the firm is currently paying an overtime premium of 50 % (or equivalently $\theta = 1.5$). The firm's optimal capacity decision τ^*, expected overtime $\mathrm{E}(h^*)$ and expected labor demand are exhibited in *Table 1* for different values of the overtime multiplier θ.

Table 1: Labor demand and overtime premium[7]

θ	1.00	1.25	1.50	1.75	2.00	(3.22)
τ^*	302	410	474	513	539	574
$\mathrm{E}(h^*)$	232	98	11	0	0	0
$\tau^* + \mathrm{E}(h^*)$	**534**	508	485	513	539	**574**

On the foregoing assumptions the amount of contracted labor per worker in the first row of *Table 1* increases with the overtime premium while the expected overtime per worker in the second row decreases up to the point at which the firm's expected overtime demand becomes zero[8]. Since the second effect dominates the first, the firm's expected labor demand initially decreases from 534 hours to 485 hours and then increases up to the maximum value of 574 hours at $\overline{\theta} = 3.22$ at which the firm is prepared to produce the whole demand interval between $\tau^* u_1^*$ and $\overline{x}$ by *adjusting the production rate.* Under these conditions, the firm's labor demand could be augmented both by a reduction and an increase of the overtime premium. In other words, a more flexible labor agreement and a ban of overtime would lead both to more employment in the short run. The first scheme would lead to a maximum increase of $534 - 485 = 49$ hours per worker while the second scheme would

7 The values in this table are rounded to whole numbers.

8 For the parameter values of the example the critical overtime multiplier $\widetilde{\theta}$ equals 1.54 (rounded).

lead to a maximum increase of $574 - 485 = 89$ hours per worker or $89 \times 150 = 13,350$ hours for the quarter[9]. The resulting cost situation is exhibited in *Table 2:*

Table 2: Overtime premium and expected cost ($ 000s)

θ	1.00	1.25	1.50	2.00	(3.22)
Exp. labor costs	3,204	3,195	2,943	3,234	3,444
Exp. costs	16,970	17,226	17,362	17,478	17,515
Change in costs	–392	–136	–	116	153
Change in costs (%)	–2.26	–0.78	–	0.67	0.88

The cost figures in *Table 2* indicate that only a reduction in overtime premia can lead to Pareto improvement. While halving the original premium would lead to expected savings of $ 136,000 or 0.78 % of the original costs, the most flexible labor agreement with an overtime premium of zero ($\theta = 1$) would lead to net savings of $ 392,000 or 2.26 % of the original costs. Contrastingly, an overtime ban would lead to an increase of $ 153,000 or 0.88 % of the original costs. Thus, the cost gap between the most and least flexible labor agreements is even $ 545,000. These results clearly suggest that the labor unions' perpetual demand for an overtime ban would lead to a considerable decline in the firms' competitiveness and hence encourage investment in labor saving technologies or even the relocation of production in countries with less regulated labor markets. The fact that the overtime premium for work on Saturdays was the critical point in recent negotiations, between *Volkswagen*'s management and its works committee, about producing the *New Beetle* in Germany provides support for the argument.

The problem with a reduction in overtime premia is, that it causes a decrease in contracted labor which makes workers' incomes more risky. However, the resultant cost savings would allow firms to compensate their workers for the increased income risk. Consider, for example, the payment scheme exhibited in *Table 3* whereby the firm shares 50 % of its expected cost savings with its workers.

9 The case of no overtime premium ($\theta = 1$) can only be interpreted as a limiting case because strictly speaking the firm could costlessly avoid any risk by contracting no labor in advance.

Table 3: Expected earnings under profit sharing

Overtime Multiplier (θ)	1.50	1.25	1.00
Fixed salary ($)	18,960	16,400	12,080
Expected overtime payment ($)	660	4,900	9,280
Expected profit share ($)	0	453	1,307
Expected earnings ($)	19,620	21,753	22,667
Expected earnings per hour ($)	40.45	42.82	42.45

The resulting figures indicate that not only expected earnings per employee but also the expected earnings per hour are increasing under the proposed payment scheme. Thus, for risk neutral individuals, the proposed payment scheme leads to a Pareto improvement without raising the wage rate w. Moreover, the firm could also hire additional workers instead of increasing both its current workers' income and working time. However, the example can only serve as a starting point for future research. A comprehensive analysis of the issues raised in this article must not only consider different risk attitudes but also provide a more incisive analysis of the negotiation process.

5 Summary and Conclusions

This paper has analyzed the capacity planning problem of a single product firm which operates under the conditions of *Gutenberg*'s managerial production model. In particular, the firm has to decide about the number of staff for production support activities before the final product demand becomes known. Before production takes place, the firm enters identical labor contracts with each worker specifying a fixed salary, a fixed number of working hours and an overtime premium for the period under consideration. The firm's optimal capacity decision is determined by the trade-off between the sunk costs of slack labor under unfavorable demand conditions and the expected penalty costs for *adjusting the production rate,* or employing overtime under more favorable demand conditions.

Comparative static analysis indicates that the key item governing the firm's demand for labor is the overtime premium. Since the amount of contracted labor strictly increases with the overtime premium and expected overtime strictly decreases, the firm's labor demand is initially decreasing and then increasing with the overtime premium. Thus, starting from a situation with an intermediate overtime premium, both reducing, and raising, the contracted overtime premium would lead to an increasing labor demand. This result provides support for both the employers' quests for a larger degree of flexibility in collective labor agreements and for the unions' demand for a reduction, or a ban, of overtime. Unfortunately, only the first proposal provides a possible solution of the current German unemployment problem. While increasing overtime premia, or equivalently imposing a ban on overtime would raise the firm's costs and provide incentives to relocate production in other countries, a reduction in overtime premia would result in both cost savings and an increasing labor demand. Since the firm would reduce the fixed salaries when overtime becomes cheaper, however, the workers must be willing to share some of the firm's risk. Although a simple profit sharing scheme can solve the problem and lead to improvements for both the firm, and its workforce, provided that the parties are risk neutral, the analysis is only a first step towards a richer theory of flexibility in collective labor agreements. Future research could analyze the robustness of the results for different risk attitudes, and also provide a deeper treatment of the negotiation process between the firm and its works committee and/or trade unions.

References

Chiang, Alpha C. (1984), Fundamental Methods of Mathematical Economics, Third Edition, McGraw-Hill New York.

Dinkelbach, Werner/Rosenberg, Otto (1994), Erfolgs- und umweltorientierte Produktionstheorie, Springer Berlin/Heidelberg.

Dyckhoff, Harald (1994), Betriebliche Produktion, 2. Aufl., Springer Berlin/-Heidelberg.

Fandel, Günther (1991), Produktion I, Produktions- und Kostentheorie, 3. Aufl., Springer Berlin/Heidelberg.

Gutenberg, Erich (1971), Grundlagen der Betriebswirtschaftslehre, Erster Band, Die Produktion, 18. Aufl., Springer Berlin/Heidelberg.

Jacob, Herbert (1962), Produktionsplanung und Kostentheorie, in: Koch, Helmut [Ed.], Zur Theorie der Unternehmung, Festschrift für Erich Gutenberg, S. 205-268, Gabler Wiesbaden.

Kistner, Klaus-Peter (1993), Produktions- und Kostentheorie, 2. Aufl., Physica Heidelberg.

Pressmar, Dieter B. (1971), Kosten- und Leistungsanalyse im Industriebetrieb, Gabler Wiesbaden.

Summary

Gutenberg's production model explains how a firm should optimally adjust its production policy to meet changing demand conditions in the short run. A firm facing an uncertain demand should consider its short run adjustment options in conjunction with its personnel capacity decision. The optimal capacity choice is then governed by the trade-off between the sunk costs of slack labor and the penalty costs in the case of a shortage. The key item determining the firm's labor demand is the overtime premium. While the personnel capacity strictly increases with the overtime premium, the expected overtime strictly decreases. The sum of both effects is strictly negative up to the point at which the firm's expected overtime demand reaches zero. Hence, the firm's expected labor demand first decreases and then increases with the overtime premium. Since a reduction in overtime premia also yields cost savings, it could be beneficial to both the firm and its employees.

Interdependencies Between Network and Activity-analytical Descriptions of Production Relationships in the Implementation of Large-Scale Projects

G. Fandel[1]

Overview

- The paper discusses the respects in which production relationships modelled as networks can also be described through dynamic activity vectors when a large-scale project is implemented.
- The interdependencies between the different focusses of network analysis and of activity analysis are studied by reference to the production of a study letter for teaching purposes.
- Applying dynamic activity analysis allows to evaluate networks in respect of their efficiency in consuming resources.

Keywords: Production Theory, Project Management, Network Analysis, Dynamic Activity Analysis

1 The problem

In production theory, the production of goods and services, i.e. the transformation of inputs into outputs, largely ignores process-organizational issues. This is most clear in the static activity analysis of production relationships (KOOPMANS 1951, FANDEL 1991), in which it is assumed that combinations of resources for the production of goods do not take up time, even if workforce hours and the machine times are found as input variables in the activity vector components. The explicit consideration of the input quantity of coordination is sacrificed here to the theoretical assumption that the combination of inputs takes place at an infinitely

[1] Prof. Dr. Günter Fandel, FernUniversität, Lehrstuhl für Betriebswirtschaft, 58084 Hagen, Germany, email: guenter.fandel@fernuni-hagen.de

high speed; and, that an arbitrarily short production period is therefore sufficient to let this combination generate the desired output quantities. This is the basis of all static production-theoretic approaches and the resultant static production functions, which constitute the greatest part of production theory.

If the assumption of a production process with an infinite velocity lacks practical validity, the explicit inclusion of time and therefore the formulation of dynamic approaches to production theory are necessary. Different methodological paths have been taken in the literature on this subject with the development of transformation functions (KÜPPER 1980, MAY 1992), lead time displacements (TROSSMANN 1986), capital consumption models (KISTNER/LUHMER 1988) and of approaches of dynamic activity analysis (FANDEL 1996). It is usually presupposed that: (i) time can be divided into large equal intervals, towards the end of which the changes in the status of the production process can be read off or analyzed, (ii) one or more final products can be manufactured in large quantity units, (iii) at the same time definable semi-finished products are produced from earlier input combinations, and (iv) the final products can be manufactured from combinations of the latter semi-finished products.

However, these preconditions do not in general govern the management of large-scale projects like, for example, shipbuilding, bridge construction, or just writing study letters on production and cost theory for the students of the German distance-teaching university, the FernUniversität. In production of this nature, in which the logical sequence of operations and the minimal time of completion are modelled and planned by network analysis approaches, normally only one unit of a single product is manufactured. Usually there are hardly any independent or even marketable semi-finished products. Moreover, the different durations of the various operations, and their coordination in time, do not permit the total completion time for the project to be broken down into equidistant partial intervals of production time.

Hence, the scope of this paper is to study (i) the respects in which production relationships modelled as networks can also be described through dynamic activity vectors when a large-scale project is implemented, (ii) the interdependencies subsisting between the process-organizational focus of network analysis and the allocation-theoretic focus of activity analysis, and (iii) the extent to which the set of terminological and selection instruments of the activity-analysis approach require modification. SHEPHARD/AL-AYAT/LEACHMAN (1977) and WITTMANN (1979) investigated similar questions without, however, formulating activities or technologies (as sets of feasible activity vectors) on the basis of processes that do not lead to semi-finished products. Here we attempt to fill the gap left by SHEPHARD et al., taking, as an example, the production of a service, namely, the creation of a study letter.

2 Network and activity-analytical description of the creation of a study letter

2.1 Preliminary remarks

The production process of a large-scale project, which is described here from both the process-organizational viewpoint of network analysis and from the allocation-theoretical perspective of activity analysis, refers to the creation of a study letter to be used at the FernUniversität in Hagen as part of a course in production and cost theory (FANDEL 1995). An explicit examination is undertaken of production alternatives which might be used in this case, and which result from different combinations of resources, depending on whether the study letter is (i) created mainly by a university professor, (ii) together with a faculty assistant as co-author, or (iii) by one or more faculty assistants on the instructions and under the supervision of the professor. Another possibility is to have the study letter created on a contractual basis by an external university professor under the supervision of the faculty. In this case and in contrast to internal production, the faculty's activities take on, to a greater extent, the character of contextual and didactical monitoring of the external author on the one hand and that of the internal coordination of the external creation process on the other. The time saved in the faculty may be contrasted with the period required for creating the study letter externally. In cases of both internal and external creation, our analysis concentrates on the activities of the faculty. Other activities carried out by other departments in the university, which relate to legal and technical issues, are ignored here.

2.2 Network-analytical description

In order to describe the production relationships using network techniques the following steps are carried out:

1. The required operations for the completion of the project "creating a study letter" are systematically recorded, named, numbered and listed in tables.
2. The operations' sequential inter-relationships are determined and depicted in a network diagram showing which operations can be carried out in parallel, or immediately preceding or following one another, and which operations must first be completed before the following operations can be carried out.
3. The actual time requirements are assigned to the respective operations so that the path of the critical operations in the network, and hence in the creation process, is made clear. This allows the ascertainment of those operations which

may need to be accelerated in order to shorten the path of the critical operations, and thus the total completion time of the project.

Since the application of network techniques stresses the procedural aspects of the extent, type, duration and sequence of operations to be carried out to complete a project (BATTERSBY 1977, BHATNAGAR 1986, NEUMANN/MORLOCK 1993, SCHWARZE 1994) in order to serve the time, capacity and cost planning for the process, the description of the production or creation process is itself predetermined by reference to production and cost analysis. What is essential with given operations which, simultaneously co-determine the temporal utilization of inputs, is the minimisation of process time, or the meeting of a binding completion date. Substitutions or efficiencies with respect to the quantities of the resources used, such as those mainly examined in activity analysis, are pushed into the background, again taking up an important place in cost planning, when the question is how to shorten the time for critical operations subsequently by accepting cost increases. This type of post-optimal analysis with all its weaknesses could be dispensed with if the network-analytical description of production operations were supplemented by corresponding activity analysis considerations.

Table 1 shows the operations when the study letter is co-authored by a professor and a member of the faculty staff. Column 1 numbers the operations i $(i = 1,...,10)$ and column 2 shows their contents. Columns 3 and 4 show the logical sequence of operations within the described process and provide information for each operation i on the preceding operations (Prec.) $h \in \{1,...,10\}$, $h \neq i$, which must be completed before the operation can be started, and which are immediately followed by operations, $j \in \{1,...,10\}$, $j \neq i, h$, (Succ.) in the creation process.

Column 5 of Table 1 contains the time-durations d^i, $(i = 1,...,10)$, of the operations in hours, column 6 the personnel qualifications k, $k = 2,3,...,6$, (the component $k = 1$ is reserved for the output) taking part, and column 7 the time spent v_k^i. Because an operation (e.g. No. 6) may in certain circumstances be performed by the interplay of different personnel qualifications, the duration of an activity in column 5 (here $d^6 = 1{,}00\text{ h}$) does not correspond to the sum of time spent for the different work elements (column 7), i.e. $d^6 \neq \sum_{k=2}^{6} v_k^6$, but to its maximum, i.e. $d^6 = \max_{k \in \{2,...,6\}} v_k^6$.

Figure 1 shows an operations-on-node (OoN) network, also known as activity-on-node network, precedence diagram (BHATNAGAR 1986), node diagram (BATTERSBY 1977) or MPM network (NEUMANN/MORLOCK 1993), based on the operations list in Table 1. In this OoN network, the nodes represent the operations and the connecting lines (or in some cases the arrows) the operations' logical inter-relationships in accordance with columns 4 and 5 in Table 1. The network is read in the sequence of its operations from left to right in ascending order of the operation numbers. Operation 1 is the start and operation 10 the end of the project. The critical path through the network, which consists of critical operations for which the total float time is zero, is shown in bold type in the network of Fig. 1. The path determines the shortest project completion time $\underline{t}$ for creating the study letter. This is $\underline{t} = 136$ hours; the critical path consists here of the operation sequence 1,2,6,7,9 and 10.

Tab. 1: List of operations for creating a study letter by means of the co-authorship of a professor and a faculty assistant

No. i	operation description	Prec. h	Succ. j	Duration d^i	Personnel qualifications k	Time spent v_i^k
1	Agreeing the detailed concept		2 3	2.00 h	Professor Faculty assistant	2.00 h 2.00 h
2	Drawing up course objectives and the course text	1	5 6	84.00 h	Professor	84.00 h
3	Drawing up the course text	1	4 6	80.00 h	Faculty assistant	80.00 h
4	Setting the exercises	3	5	16.00 h	Faculty assistant	16.00 h
5	Discussing the exercises, preparing a bibliography and glossary	2 4	7 8	16.00 h	Professor Faculty assistant	4.00 h 16.00 h
6	Word processing the manuscript and preparing the graphics	2 3	7 8	30.00 h	Secretary Student assistant	16.00 h 30.00 h
7	Correcting the graphics	5 6	9	2.00 h	Faculty assistant	2.00 h
8	Word processing the exercises, bibliography and glossary	5 6	10	8.00 h	Secretary	8.00 h
9	Revising the graphics	7	10	16.00 h	Student assistant	16.00 h
10	Integrating the graphics into the text	8 9		2.00 h	Secretary	2.00 h

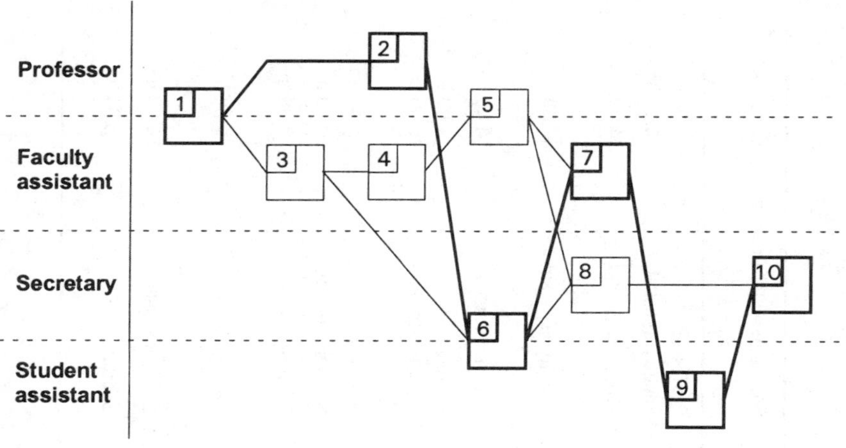

Fig. 1: Network for Table 1

Other tables with figures and networks can now be elaborated for the alternative ways of creating the study letter. Since these are equivalent in their formal representation we first dispense with details and undertake an explicit description of the other variants hereafter in a more rigorous activity analysis presentation.

3 Activity-analytical description

3.1 Formulating dynamic activities

Table 1 and Figure 1 show that four types of input - professor, faculty assistant, secretary and student assistant - take part in creating the study letter and that their input is measured in hours. The fifth type of input, external services, has not yet appeared in the network-analytical description, but now has to be introduced for those cases in which a study letter is created on a contractual basis. For this purpose, the external operations are also recorded in hours and show how long these external operations take for creating the study letter together with the operations carried out in the faculty. The output quantity is here just one single study letter, but for repeatable large projects it can be measured in natural numbers greater than 1.

Additionally, the activity vector has to be extended by a seventh component which indicates the total project completion time for creating the study letter. This total project completion time might be interpreted as (some kind of) input which facilitates an examination of the quality of managerial planning and organization and, at the same time, points to the dynamic interpretation of the activity vector.

Let

v_1 be the output quantity in units,

v_k $(k = 2,3,4,5)$ be the quantities measured in hours of the input types professor $(k = 2)$, faculty assistant $(k = 3)$, secretary $(k = 4)$ and student assistant $(k = 5)$,

v_6 be the external operations expressed in hours of external study letter creation and

v_7 be the total project completion time in hours.

Then the activity vector

$$v = (v_1, \ldots, v_7)'$$

represents, in terms of activity analysis, the study letter creation process described in the previous section. In accordance with the conventions of activity analysis, output and input quantities are shown as positive and negative vector components respectively. The input quantities v_k $(k = 2,\ldots,6)$ result from the summation of the corresponding input quantities v_k^i of type k, which are consumed in the operations $i \in I = \{1,2,\ldots,10\}$ of Table 1. Therefore

$$v_k = -\sum_{i \in I} v_k^i, \quad k = 2,\ldots,6.$$

Employing the data from Table 1 we get the dynamic activity vector

$$v^1 = \begin{pmatrix} 1 \\ -90 \\ -116 \\ -26 \\ -46 \\ 0 \\ -136 \end{pmatrix}$$

The superscript 1 stands for this first kind of creation process described in Table 1 and Figure 1 (professor and faculty assistant as co-authors). The other production alternatives are denoted correspondingly as follows:

v^2 created internally by the professor on his own,

v^3 created internally by a faculty assistant under the instruction of the professor,

v^4 created internally by two faculty assistants under the supervision of the professor,

v^5 created externally with the collaboration of an outside professor with his faculty assistant with support and supervision from the faculty at the FernUniversität,

v^6 created externally by an outside professor with support and supervision from the faculty at the FernUniversität.

As pointed out in the previous section, lists and tables of operations and network diagrams for the other five production alternatives of creating a study letter can be elaborated. This has been done in more detail elsewhere (FANDEL 1995), and we use condensed data from the latter study to get the following dynamic activity vectors:

$$v^2 = \begin{pmatrix} 1 \\ -176 \\ -2 \\ -26 \\ -46 \\ 0 \\ -196 \end{pmatrix}, \quad v^3 = \begin{pmatrix} 1 \\ -6 \\ -232 \\ -26 \\ -46 \\ 0 \\ -252 \end{pmatrix}, \quad v^4 = \begin{pmatrix} 1 \\ -6 \\ -234 \\ -26 \\ -46 \\ 0 \\ -151 \end{pmatrix}, \quad v^5 = \begin{pmatrix} 1 \\ -13 \\ -13 \\ 0 \\ 0 \\ -143 \\ -143 \end{pmatrix}, \quad v^6 = \begin{pmatrix} 1 \\ -13 \\ -13 \\ 0 \\ 0 \\ -203 \\ -203 \end{pmatrix}.$$

3.2 Advantages of an activity-analytical description

The advantages of the activity-analytical description as against the network-analytical description of the project "creating a study letter" are that

1. in its aggregated form of recording input quantities it is shorter and clearer than the corresponding network,
2. it helps to avoid waste for parallel, non-critical operations of the network that do not affect the shortest project completion time (and therefore the time-optimized completion of the project), and
3. through the potential shortening of the project it directly exposes planning and organizational inefficiency which might be caused by a waste of time or by an erroneous logical inter-relationship of the operations.

The disadvantages are essentially that the operations' logical inter-relationships are no longer evident. However, the project completion time v_7, or its minimizing, implicitly provides information that it is a dynamic production process whose realization cannot be assessed without reference to the project completion time.

Just how far the activity analysis's concept and selection instruments are able to highlight the advantages referred to under (2) and (3) is subjected in the following section to a formal examination of the dynamic activities of large-scale projects.

3.3 Describing the production relationships in creating a study letter by means of dynamic technologies

We assume that, for each alternative creation process of the study letter in question, only input types k, $k = 2,\ldots,6$ are involved; or, in other words, that inputs other than those already introduced need not be taken into consideration. Let $v_7 = t$ denote the duration to the completion of the study letter. Furthermore, $v_k \in \mathbb{R}_{-} \cup \{0\}$, $k = 2,\ldots,7$ should apply, i.e. the quantities of these components are measured in non-positive real numbers. For output $k = 1$ let $v_1 \in \{0,1\}$, i.e. either a single unit or no study letter at all is created. Extensions to the form $v_1 \in \mathbb{N} \cup \{0\}$ would not cause problems if there were project outputs which are created by the corresponding re-run of the project. Nonetheless, we shelve this extension for the moment.

Let $\mathfrak{N} = \{N = \langle I, E; d\rangle\} \neq \emptyset$ be the set of all networks (NEUMANN/MORLOCK 1993) considered for the description of the large-scale project of creating a study letter. Let $I = \{i = 0,1,2,\ldots,\bar{i}+1\}$ denote the set of nodes in the network which equals the set of operations in the respective OoN network $N = \langle I, E; d\rangle$. Operation 0 marks the start of the project, whereas operation $\bar{i}+1$ denotes the end of the project. Let $E = \{\langle h, j\rangle, h, j \in I, h \neq j\}$ be the set of arrows or connecting lines in the network with h as the origin node and j as the destination node for the appropriately expressed sequential inter-relationship between operations h and j in the OoN network. The arrow or connecting-line values d of the network N may be defined by

$$d(\langle h, j\rangle) = d^h \quad \text{for all} \quad \langle h, j\rangle \in E.$$

d^h indicates the duration of operation h in network N; $d^0 = d^{\bar{i}+1} = 0$ (i.e. the operations representing the start and the end of the project have zero duration).

A dynamic activity $v = (v_1, v_2, \ldots, v_7)' \in \mathbb{R}^7$ for creating the study letter on the basis of network N is now assigned to this network by the mapping $g : \mathfrak{N} \to \mathbb{R}^7$ in the following way:

$$v_1 = 1,$$

$$v_k = -\sum_{i=1}^{\bar{i}} v_k^i, \qquad k = 2,3,\ldots,6 \;,$$

$$v_7 = -\underline{t}\,,$$

with $\underline{t}$ as the shortest project completion time in network N (NEUMANN/MORLOCK 1993).

This can now be used for defining the set T of the dynamic activities

$$T = \left\{ v \in \mathbb{R}^7 \mid v = g(N),\, N \in \mathfrak{N} \right\}.$$

If the set T meets the following requirements (FANDEL 1991, 1996):

(A1) $v_1 > 0$ implies $v_k < 0$ for at least one $k \in \{2,\ldots,6\}$, i.e. there is no output without an input. Because of the definition of v_k, $v_k < 0$ implies at the same time $v_7 < 0$, i.e. each production requires time;

(A2) $v_1 > 0$ implies $v_7 \le -\underline{t}$, i.e. the output is created as soon as possible after the shortest project completion time;

(A3) $v = (0,0,\ldots,0)' \in T$, i.e. inactivity is possible;

(A4) there exists a $v \in T$ with $v_1 > 0$, i.e. there are networks in which a study letter is created;

(A5) $v \in T$, $w \in \mathbb{R}^7$ and $w \le v$ imply $w \in T$, i.e. waste is possible;

(A6) T is closed and bounded;

then T can be regarded as the dynamic technology of creating a study letter.

The waste defined in (A5) permits the differentiation of sub-cases of performance and of managerial disposition inefficiency. If $v = g(N)$ and $w = g(N')$ with $N' = \langle I', E'; d' \rangle$ and $N = \langle I, E; d \rangle$, $N, N' \in \mathfrak{N}$, $I \subseteq I'$, $E \subseteq E'$, and $d'^i \ge d^i$, $-w_k^i \le -v_k^i$ for all $i \in I$ and all $k \in \{2,\ldots,6\}$, $-w_k^i \ne -v_k^i$ for at least one $i \in I$ and one $k \in \{2,\ldots,6\}$ and $w_7 = -\underline{t}' = -\underline{t} = v_7$, , we may speak of performance inefficiency. In all other cases we can refer to managerial disposition inefficiency.

There may be several reasons for performance or managerial disposition inefficiency. Hence, the case $w_1 < v_1$ is dealt with no further here because it merely indicates output waste. The other cases are more interesting. $w_k < v_k$ for one $k \in \{2,\ldots,6\}$ and $w_7 = v_7$ may have its roots in there being time wasting in resource consumption on the basis of the same graphs $\langle I, E\rangle$ for the non-critical operations which do not yet influence the shortest project completion time $\underline{t}$. Table 1 and Fig. 1 illustrate this performance inefficiency if the faculty assistant takes longer than the required 16 hours, but less than 18 hours, for operation 4 in preparing the exercises. If the assistant requires more than 18 hours for operation 4, the critical path is determined by the activity sequence 1,3,4,5,7,9 and 10, and the shortest project completion time increases. Moreover, performance inefficiency might also be caused by the secretary taking part for 2 hours in operation 1 to coordinate the fine concept without this having an effect on the creation of the study letter. In contrast, managerial disposition inefficiency would occur if unnecessary time buffers were found in the coordination of the operations, or if the creation of the study letter were planned on the basis of other (worse) networks with a greater use of resources and/or longer project completion times. Thus, the activity v^6 described above for creating the study letter is performance inefficient in comparison to activity v^5. On the other hand, if we take the activity list in Table 1 and the activity v^1 assigned to the corresponding network, then other networks, and the respective dynamic activities $v \in T$ representing them, would be managerial disposition inefficient in comparison with v^1, if, for example, operation 8 (word processing the exercises, bibliography and glossary) was not executed in parallel with, but subsequent to operation 7 (correcting the sample graphics), and this lengthened the shortest project completion time by 8 hours. It would also be disposition inefficient in comparison to v^1 if there were two parallel operations 3a and 3b (instead of activity 3), both of which related to the preparation of the course text by a faculty assistant, took 60 hours, but then led to a total of 120 hours instead of 80 hours for the faculty assistant's work in operation 3, without having an effect on the shortest project completion time. Note that the statements on disposition inefficiency assume that the time structure of resource utilization is, apart from capacity restrictions, which are treated later, irrelevant. If this does not hold true (e.g. with regard to subsequent costing on the basis of dynamic factor prices), the requirement (A5) must be restricted to performance inefficiency in order to prevent errors in a subsequent decision.

The previous considerations lead directly to the questions of how the notions of dominance and efficiency should be defined for activities v from dynamic technology T and what characteristics technology T possesses from a practical standpoint.

Definition (D1) (weak dominance)

Let $v, w \in T$. Activity v weakly dominates activity w iff $v_k \geq w_k$ for all $k \in \{1,\ldots,7\}$ and $v_k > w_k$ for at least one $k \in \{1,\ldots,7\}$.

Definition (D2) (strong dominance)

Let $v, w \in T$, $v \neq w$, with $v = g(N)$, $w = g(N')$, $N = \langle I, E; d \rangle$, $N' = \langle I', E'; d' \rangle$, $I \subseteq I'$, $E \subseteq E'$ and $d^i \leq d'^i$ for all $i \in I$. Then activity v strongly dominates activity w iff

$$v_1 \geq w_1,$$
$$-v_k^i \geq -w_k^i \quad \text{for all } i \in I \text{ and all } k \in \{2,\ldots,6\},$$
$$v_7 \geq w_7.$$

Each strongly dominant $v \in T$ is obviously weakly dominant as well; the reverse does not generally hold true. If the time structure of resource utilization is not important, weak dominance will usually be sufficient to eliminate wasteful study letter creations.

Definition (E) (strong and weak efficiency)

An activity $v \in T$ is called strongly (weakly) efficient iff there is no $w \in T$ which weakly (strongly) dominates v.

Obviously, every strongly efficient dynamic activity $v \in T$ is also weakly efficient. It may be assumed that activities v^1 to v^5 (section 3.1) are weakly efficient. The proof of strong efficiency meets resistance because of the usual problem of verification.

We conclude with a discussion of the characteristics of the set T.

(1) Dimensional progression
Because a project can be carried out several times consecutively: $v \in T$ and $\lambda \geq 1$, $\lambda \in \mathbb{N}$, implies $\lambda v \in T$, i.e. T is dimensionally progressive. If, therefore, the creation process is repeated several times, a multiple of output is created by the same multiple of project input and project completion time.

(2) Managerial disposition dominance with respect to time
In so far as the realization of a managerial disposition is not opposed by any dynamic resource restrictions, a project can be carried out parallel in each integer multiple of the output and input quantities in the period required for a

single production process, i.e. let $v \in T$ with $v_7 = -\underline{t}$ and $\lambda \geq 1$, $\lambda \in \mathbb{N}$, then also $\widetilde{v} \in T$ holds if

$$\widetilde{v}_k = \lambda v_k, \quad k = 1,\dots,6, \quad \text{and}$$
$$\widetilde{v}_7 = v_7.$$

Each activity $\widetilde{v}$ of the multiple parallel realization of a project weakly dominates activity λv of the corresponding multiple consecutive realization. Weakly dominated consecutive realizations of a project, or their activities, can also be carried out in the sense of the efficiency definition (E) if parallel production is not possible because of resource restrictions in time, i.e. disposition dominant $\widetilde{v} \in T$ cannot be realized.

(3) No dimensional degression

$\widetilde{v} \in T$ with $\widetilde{v}_k = \lambda v_k, k = 1,\dots,6, \widetilde{v}_7 = v_7$ and $\lambda \neq 1$ implies $\frac{1}{\lambda}\widetilde{v} \notin T$, $0 \leq \frac{1}{\lambda} \leq 1$, because $\frac{1}{\lambda}\widetilde{v}_7 < -\underline{t}$ is unfeasible; i.e. on the transition from multiple parallel realization of a project to a one-off realization, the completion time required must not fall below the minimum project completion time of the one-off realization.

(4) Additivity

Because two projects can be carried out consecutively, or even parallel to one another, $v, w \in T$ implies $v + w \in T$, i.e. T is additive.

Networks, in particular those for multiple parallel realization of a project, may be unfeasible, if the availability of resources over the period of time is insufficient to realize them. Let $\dot{v}_k(t)$ be the input rate of resource k, $k \in \{2,\dots,6\}$, at time t required to realize network $N \in \mathfrak{N}$, $v = g(N)$, and $\dot{\bar{v}}_k(t)$ be the maximum input rate of this resource k at time t, then only those networks can be considered for the production of the project output for which

$$\dot{v}_k(t) \geq \dot{\bar{v}}_k(t), \quad t \in [0,\infty),$$

holds. This situation is illustrated in Fig. 2 for the required input rates $\dot{v}_3^3(t)$ and $\dot{v}_3^4(t)$ of the resource faculty assistant ($k = 3$) in the alternatives 3 and 4 of creating the study letter, whereby the input rates here are entered in positive quantities, in contrast to the conventions of activity analysis. Suppose that the bold marked line shows the maximum input rate $\dot{\bar{v}}_3(t)$ of this resource, then version 4 of creating the study letter is not feasible.

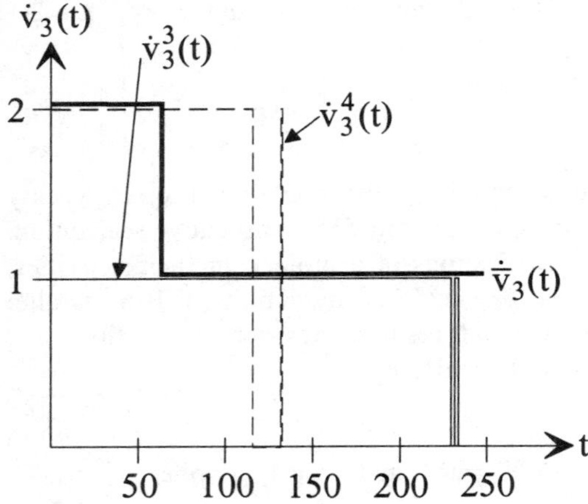

Fig. 2: Unfeasible networks because of restricted input rates

References

Battersby, A. (1977): Network Analysis for Planning and Scheduling, third edition, London-Basingstoke.

Bhatnagar, S. K. (1986): Network Analysis Techniques, New Delhi et al.

Fandel, G. (1991): Theory of Production and Cost, Berlin et al.

Fandel, G. (1995): Wirtschaftlichkeitsaspekte einer Hochschule, Inhalte einer gutachterlichen Stellungnahme über die Fernuniversität, Weinheim.

Fandel, G. (1996): Dynamische Produktionstheorie, in: Kern, W./Schröder, H.-H./ Weber, J. (eds.): Handwörterbuch der Produktionswirtschaft, second edition, Stuttgart, col. 1557-1569.

Kistner, K.-P./Luhmer, A. (1988): Ein dynamisches Modell des Betriebsmitteleinsatzes, in: Zeitschrift für Betriebswirtschaft, pp. 63-83.

Koopmans, T.C. (1951): Analysis of Production as an Efficient Combination of Activities, in: Koopmans, T.C. (ed.): Activity Analysis of Production and Allocation, New York-London, pp. 33-97.

Küpper, H.-U. (1980): Interdependenzen zwischen Produktionstheorie and der Organisation des Produktionsprozesses, Berlin.

May, E. (1992): Dynamische Produktionstheorie auf der Basis der Aktivitätsanalyse, Heidelberg.

Neumann, K./Morlock, M. (1993): Operations Research, München-Wien.

Schwarze, J. (1994): Netzplantechnik, seventh edition, Herne et al.

Shephard, R.W./Al-Ayat, R.A./Leachman, R.C. (1977): Shipbuilding Production Function, in: Albach, H./Helmstädter, E./Henn, R. (eds.): Quantitative Wirtschaftsforschung, Tübingen, pp. 627-654.

Trossmann, E. (1986): Betriebliche Bedarfsplanung auf der Grundlage einer dynamischen Produktionstheorie, in: Zeitschrift für Betriebswirtschaft, pp. 827-847.

Wittmann, W. (1979): Aktivitätsanalytische Ansätze dynamischer Produktionstheorie und ihre Beziehungen zur Planung, in: Mellwig, W. (ed.): Unternehmenstheorie und Unternehmensplanung, Wiesbaden, pp. 273-304.

Summary

Interdependencies between network-based production planning in the case of large-scale projects and activity-analytical aspects of those processes are elaborated by reference to the production of a study letter for teaching purposes. Applying dynamic activity analysis, the networks can be evaluated in respect of their efficiency in consuming resources, and therefore, in turn, from performance and disposition perspectives.

Printing: Weihert-Druck GmbH, Darmstadt
Binding: Buchbinderei Schäffer, Grünstadt